EYES ONLY

EYES ONLY

The Top Secret Correspondence
Between MARSHALL and EISENHOWER
1943-45

Andrew Rawson

SPELLMOUNT

First published 2012 by Spellmount,
an imprint of The History Press
The Mill, Brimscombe Port
Stroud, Gloucestershire, GL5 2QG
www.thehistorypress.co.uk

British Library Cataloguing in Publication Data.
A catalogue record for this book is available from the British Library.

ISBN 978 0 7524 6290 5
Typesetting and origination by The History Press
Printed in the EU for The History Press

CONTENTS

INTRODUCTION

This book is not another history of the European campaign; this is the story of two men and the immensity of their appointments. This first man is General George C. Marshall, Chief of Staff of the US Army, from September 1939 to November 1945. The second is General Dwight D. Eisenhower, Supreme Commander of the Allied Expeditionary Force from December 1943 to December 1945.

The text in these pages is the transcripts of the EYES ONLY cables between Marshall and Eisenhower between January 1944 and July 1945. There are also transcripts of cables issued by General Walter B. Smith, Eisenhower's Chief of Staff before, during and after this period. The cables came at the top of the highest secrecy hierarchy, of EYES ONLY, TOP SECRET and SECRET. They went from Marshall's desk to Eisenhower's desk, or vice versa, and to no one else except their Chiefs of Staff.

This book is not a combined biography of the two great men either. Neither Marshall nor Eisenhower gave commentaries on their work or responsibilities. Instead the cables tell us what they were dealing with on a daily basis, providing primary source material at its best. Usually the discussions are about what might happen in the days and weeks ahead and the decision taken to stop a problem arising or minimize it. The cables tell us what the Pentagon and SHAEF knew about what was happening behind German lines; more often than not it was very little and sometimes mere speculation. Occasionally we get glimpses of just how little the Chief of Staff knew about the conduct of the European campaign, illustrating to what extent Eisenhower was left to get on with the war against Nazi Germany.

While this book is not a complete history of the war in Europe, it does reveal both how the Allies conducted the campaign and the debates that dictated why it was conducted as it was, more than any post-war diary or history. Within these pages are references to some of the most important periods of the war: the six-month build up before D-Day; the 18-month campaign across France, the Low Countries and Germany; and the difficult four-month negotiation period with the Soviets over the future of Europe.

The cables also give us a detailed insight into the day-to-day problems that Marshall and Eisenhower faced. Their in-trays were always full, both with unexpected crises, and issues that had been anticipated well in advance. The German military sometimes seems to be the least of Eisenhower's problems as he tries to find solutions to issues raised by allies, politicians and subordinates. One day he was dealing with correspondence from Roosevelt or Churchill, the next a recalcitrant general.

Time was a precious commodity for both men. Marshall not only had to keep his eye on the war in Europe, but also had to deal with a similar range of problems in the Pacific, overseeing the provision of men, commanders, equipment and supplies in both theaters. On top of all that he had the generals and politicians to deal with in Washington DC. Eisenhower was also a busy man. As well as dealing with his superiors across the Atlantic, he had his three army group commanders and their army commanders to contend with. The rivalry of Montgomery, Bradley and Devers was a continual problem, as was that between Hodges, Patton, Patch and Simpson. Add to that the national differences between the Americans, Canadians, British and French, and it is easy to see why Eisenhower had to be as much a master of diplomacy as of military matters. When the likes of Churchill, de Gaulle and US politicians are added to the equation, it is a wonder that Eisenhower found time to attend to SHEAF's needs.

The Procedure for Sending Cables

Each message had to be dictated, typed and encrypted before it was sent. On receipt it was deciphered and typed out before being delivered straight to the recipient's desk; because 'Eyes Only' meant exactly that; the cables were written at Marshall's desk and read at Eisenhower's desk, and vice versa. Maximum security was used for these highly sensitive transmissions and no one else was allowed to read them without the recipient's permission.

Each cable had the acronym of the sender and recipient at the top; AGWAR for Marshall and either SHEAF MAIN or SHEAF FORWARD for Eisenhower. The way the cables were written made sure that the recipient knew they were of the top level of secrecy. The first line of a cable contained only a vague reference to the contents and the reference number of the cable it was referring to, if appropriate. It was followed by the words EYES ONLY and the surnames of author and the recipient, all underlined. The text followed.

The cable clerk was left in no doubt what they were supposed to do with the document as soon as it had been decoded; a huge stamp was used to make sure that the words EYES ONLY appeared at the top of the page. The recipient could add a distribution and action list once he had read the document. All cables were dated and timed and had a unique reference number, the current number in the sequential numbering systems of all cables sent from the forwarding office. This was done so that the list of EYES ONLY cables would not stand out as having special content and alert the German code breakers.

Transmission and Receipt Locations

At the start of the Second World War the bulk of the War Department offices were housed in the Munitions Building, along Constitution Avenue on the National Mall in Washington DC. It was a temporary First World War era complex and offices had spread out across the city and beyond. Although a new block had been built in the in the Foggy Bottom area in the late 1930s, the War Department was still too cramped and spread over too many buildings to be efficient.

The outbreak of war in Europe in September 1939 meant a new expansion of the US Army and Secretary of War Henry L. Stimson asked President Roosevelt for a new purpose-built structure in May 1941. By July Congress had agreed and allocated the money for what would become the Pentagon, the huge five-sided building we know today in Arlington, on the west bank of the Potomac river. Work was undertaken at a rapid rate over the winter of 1941/42 and by April the first group of offices was opened. The building only took sixteen months to complete.

Across the Atlantic, SHEAF headquarters staff started work under the streets of London in purpose-built air raid shelters in Goodge Street Underground Station. However, Eisenhower and his Chief of Staff, General Walter B. Smith, found working in Central London to be claustrophobic. The number of unwanted visitors, particularly British visitors, to SHEAF's headquarters was another reason for wanting to move out of the city. A temporary headquarters was built in the Teddington End of Bushey Park, near Kingston-on-Thames, ten miles southwest of Central London. It was codenamed WIDEWING. During the run up to D-Day a small command post, codenamed SHARPENER, was established near Southwick, just north of Portsmouth. There Eisenhower was close to his troops and far from prying eyes. His personal office tent and sleeping trailer stood next to a mobile office and telephone switchboard. They were surrounded by trailers filled with maps and teletype machines, including one for the EYES ONLY cables from General Marshall. Tents for aides, guards, cooks and the all-important meteorologists – Group Captain James Stagg, RAF, Donald N. Yates, USAF and Sverre Petterssen, Norwegian Air Force – completed the camp. SHAEF continued to operate from WIDEWING but an advanced headquarters, known as SHAEF Forward, was established on the continent in August. SHAEF was established in the Trianon Palace Hotel in Versailles, France, by the time of the Battle of the Bulge in December 1944, and at the end of April 1945 it moved to Frankfurt. SHAEF came to an end on 14 July when all US armed forces came under US Forces, European Theater (USFET).

Locating the Cables

The road to finding these fascinating primary sources began when I was working on a Masters of Philosophy Degree thesis under Professor Gary Sheffield, with the University of Birmingham's School of Modern and Medieval History between 2007 and 2011.[1] My subject was 'The Divisional Commander in the US Army in World War II' and I was studying the group of 24 general officers who commanded divisions during the Normandy campaign in June and July 1944 as a sample.

A structured investigation of what documentation should be available was put together under my tutor's guidance. Eisenhower changed a number of divisional commanders during the European campaign, but where was the correspondence documenting the reasons for the changes? Although my research began with the start of the generals' careers before the First World War, selection did not really start until 1939. On 1 September 1939, German troops invaded Poland and two days later Great Britain and France declared war on Germany. Coincidently Brigadier-General George C. Marshall was appointed Chief of Staff of the US Army and promoted to full General on the same day in Washington DC. Another key appointment was made in July 1940, when Brigadier-General Lesley J. McNair became Chief of Staff at General Headquarters, US Army.[2] Marshall and McNair together chose the divisional commanders in the US Army during the early months of the war. By the summer of 1940, Nazi Germany occupied most of Europe and President Roosevelt responded by declaring a limited National Emergency starting in October 1940. It sanctioned preparations for defense of the western hemisphere under the plan codenamed RAINBOW I.

RAINBOW I also called for a huge expansion of the army and hence the appointment of many new corps and divisional commanders. In July 1941, McNair drew up a list of names for Marshall, short-listing ten brigadier-generals and fourteen colonels as 'suitable candidates for divisions'.[3] The four senior American commanders on D-Day in June 1944 were on McNair's list: Dwight D. Eisenhower (SHAEF), Omar N. Bradley (First US Army), J. Lawton Collins (VII Corps on Utah Beach) and Leonard T. Gerow (V Corps on Omaha Beach). Continuous outstanding performance during peacetime had been recorded in their 201

1 Birmingham, UK.
2 Temporary Lieutenant-General; McNair's post was renamed Commanding General of Army Ground Forces in March 1942.
3 McNair, 'Memorandum to Marshall, 8 July 1941' (George C. Marshall Research Library, Lexington, VA, Marshall Papers, Pentagon Office Correspondence, Box 76).

Personnel Files as their General Efficiency Rating, a number ranging from the best at around 6.5 to the worst at around 4.5.

Part of the army's increased budget for 1941 was used to fund large scale military maneuvers in Louisiana State, and while they proved useful for testing tactics and doctrines, the majority of incumbent general officers were found to be unsuitable. 'Most of the 42 division, corps and army commanders who took part in the GHQ maneuvers were either relieved or reassigned to new commands in 1942 (including 20 of the 27 participating division commanders).'[4] McNair and Marshall had a lot of work to do.

On 7 December 1941, Japanese planes attacked the naval bases at Pearl Harbor in Hawaii and in the Philippines. The US responded by declaring war on Japan. Four days later Germany declared war on the US as it entered a world war for the second time in its history. US divisions started training in earnest, and command changes were implemented at a rapid rate in the pursuit of efficiency. Most of the 20 divisions destined to fight in Normandy in the summer of 1944 had more than one commander in a short space of time as generals were promoted, reassigned, sacked or retired. In January 1944 Eisenhower was appointed Supreme Commander of the Allied Expeditionary Force, SCAEF. It was now his turn to see how the general officers under his command shaped up. With the help of his subordinate commanders, General Omar N. Bradley, General Courtney H. Hodges and General George S. Patton, assessments of the divisional commanders were made.

While I found some information on the reasons behind the selection of some commanders in the National Archives and Records Administration, College Park, Maryland, the two-stage ordering system – involving searching the microfilmed indexes to locate possible useful documents – was a lengthy process and I was running out of time. Emails to the George C. Marshall Research Library led me to believe there was a microfilmed copy of the documents down in Lexington, Virginia. Opened in 1964 in the grounds of the Virginia Military Institute – where Marshall started his military career, graduating in 1901 – the Foundation houses both the George C. Marshall Research Library and the Marshall Museum. It was there that I struck a rich seam of information.

After searching through the correspondence between Marshall and McNair, I came across the Marshall and Eisenhower cables: Microfilm 184, a single microfilm reel with Eisenhower's Chief of Staff, General Walter Beedle Smith's 1288 pages of cables and indexes. There was a discreet handwritten numbering system given to each cable by Smith, nickname 'Beetle'. He also added the numbers of any relevant cables in his EYES ONLY file and his own private index. It was a simple yet effective way of keeping track of what issues were in Eisenhower's in-tray.

The cables were microfilmed chronologically, and while that system was logical for General Smith, it is not the best way to read them so a different system had to be used. After transcribing all the cables, they were sorted into topics. Quite often there was a question raised and an answer given, usually within 24 hours. Some topics run over several cables as the debate continues. Occasionally, a cable contains two entirely different themes and the author made it absolutely clear when he was switching topic with the words NEW SUBJECT. These entries have been split between the two relevant conversations. The topics were then organized into chronological order, using the date of the original question to organize them. This method allows the reader to follow each discussion from beginning to conclusion without interruption.

4 Gabel, Christopher R., *The US Army GHQ Maneuvers of 1941* (US Army Center of Military History, Washington, DC, 1991) p. 187.

Alterations

The absolute minimum number of alterations has been made to the cables. Spelling and grammatical errors have been corrected, but they were few. The code clerks made very few mistakes and most of those were connected to names, particularly foreign surnames and European place names. Some long sentences have been given the benefit of a comma or semi-colon to allow for easier reading, as the clerks were very sparing with punctuation. Similarly the word 'the' was often omitted, probably because that was the way that cables were dictated, in short snappy phrases, and a few have been added to improve understanding.

In general however, the cables have been left as they were, giving the reader an insight into the language of the day between senior military and political individuals. We see how the likes of Roosevelt, Churchill and Stalin addressed Marshall and Eisenhower and vice versa, and even glimpse occasional snatches of humor. There are also angry exchanges, although never between the two generals, rather they vented their frustration over the shortcomings, failings or attitudes of others.

A Word on Footnotes

The transcripts have been extensively annotated to enhance the reader's understanding of the EYES ONLY cables. Many of the notes simply expand on a discussion, adding detail and statistics. Some explain the circumstances surrounding a sequence of cables, either what brought about the discussion or what was the final outcome.

High ranking personnel were referred to by surname, while lower level officers were referred to in full. Virtually all the names quoted in the text have been identified with their full name and occupation at the time of the cable. Operational codenames are referred to at regular intervals and are written in upper case. While some are well known, many are not, and the codenames are identified, with details of the operation and its outcome.

In many cables we learn about military plans long before any action is due to occur. When appropriate the notes reveal the details of the planning as the discussion unfolds. In this way the reader learns about the twists and turns as a debate intensifies. Sometimes we learn about a plan which is later cancelled or superseded; the pertinent notes explain the reasons for this.

Omissions

While there are over 120,000 words in the Eyes Only cables in this book, another 35,000 have been left out. These have been omitted owing to their content, often referring to simple administrative matters. In the six-month period before D-Day, the cables that have been left out fall into two main categories. Firstly, the debate over the organization of various support services, as a great deal of them were speculative discussions and the ideas never came to fruition. The main services omitted include the Civil Affairs Organization, Signals, Base Sections, Transport, Press Relations and War Crimes. Discussions over appointments and promotions of general officers serving with these supporting services have also been omitted, as well as routine requests relating to appointments of staff officers serving with armies and corps. Once the European campaign got underway, Eisenhower had to submit monthly promotion lists to Marshall, including the details and justification for choosing each officer. While higher level promotions have been included, with the emphasis on well known generals, those of lower level officers, typically colonel to brigadier, have been omitted. Mutual awards between the US and British Armies have also been left out; Montgomery often suggested British awards for American generals and troops serving with 21st Army Group.

Another set of cables omitted are those sent after the 15 August landing on the south coast of France. General Devers sent daily detailed troop movements to SHAEF headquarters, and while the general progress of Operation DRAGOON is given, the details of the advance are not. Similarly, the various travel arrangements of generals and politicians visiting the European Theater and mutual travel arrangements with Montgomery have been left out. A detailed discussion of arrangements for Marshall's stopover in France en route to the January 1945 conference in Malta, codenamed ARGONAUT and CRICKET, is also omitted. During Marshall's occasional visits to Eisenhower, cables from Washington DC and the Pacific were forwarded to SHAEF headquarters for the Chief of Staff's attention. While these cables are important in the story of the war as a whole, they are not relevant to the European Theater. It does beg the question whether a similar collection of the Eyes Only correspondence between Marshall and the Pacific Theatre could be assembled for a similar study.

A prolonged discussion over arrangements for a Japanese regiment to serve on the Italian Front in February 1945 is also omitted. The battalion was made up of soldiers of Japanese origin who had been living in the US at the outbreak of war.

As the war drew to a close, issues relating to demobilizing the Allied armies had to be addressed, and while many of the relevant cables are included, two marginal sets are not. One set details the discussions over the determination of ROGER Day, or R-Day, the set date for determining schedules to return troops to the US or to the Pacific campaign. The issue was relatively minor, and the fact that the date ultimately chosen was the same as Victory in Europe Day, or V-E Day, meant that the discussions were immaterial. The second set of cables omitted relates to arrangements made for bringing the generals home and their placing with Home Commands.

Three main post-war subjects have been omitted. The first concerns the politics relating to the setting of the boundaries of the French Zone of Occupation, as details of map references and lists of districts make tedious reading. The other subjects are the initial plans for Public Relations and Civil Affairs in occupied Germany.

Throughout the cables, comment on what has happened on the ground is rare, and although Marshall asks Eisenhower for weekly debriefings on the progress of the advance through France in the summer of 1944, these soon tail off. Only Devers makes the effort, forwarding details of the spectacular advance through southern France following Operation DRAGOON (previously ANVIL). Marshall had the foresight to leave Eisenhower alone during busy periods such as those around D-Day, Operation MARKET GARDEN in September and the Battle of the Bulge in December. By the time the troops were in action the problems had been discussed, differences had been aired and solutions had been agreed. The two men rarely discuss the progress of a battle; they are too busy considering what comes next.

We do learn how the three army groups discuss plans and report on operations, although not as often as one might think. On the whole, details about military operations rarely appear in the Eyes Only cables although future operations were occasionally considered; Montgomery regularly put his thoughts on the future of the campaign to Eisenhower. Operations were usually planned and orders given well in advance and the paperwork was issued accordingly. Cables were only issued to army group headquarters when last minute changes had to be made; the famous example is Eisenhower's strategic plan issued at the start of the Battle of the Bulge in December 1945.

The Value of Primary Source Material

Many historians have written about the planning and execution of the European campaign in 1944–45, some on the whole campaign, many on selective aspects of it. Some place emphasis on the Marshall and Eisenhower partnership while others focus on the military side of the campaign. While these books give the reader insights into the campaigns and professional relationships, they are inevitably subjective, some more than others. Some historians stick to the facts, while others endeavor to increase the tension or interest in an event with speculation. One example of this is the relationship between Eisenhower and Montgomery, 21st Army Group's British commander. At times it has been fashionable to accentuate their apparent mutual contempt in the interests of a good story. It is true that they came from different backgrounds and had different views on many things, as independently minded generals should have. However, the cables reproduced in this book give us an insight into the true nature of the professional relationship between these two men when they dealt with important strategic matters, without the distortion of a historian's speculation.

Another example is what became known as the 'Knutsford Affair' at the end of April 1944. Patton made outrageous statements in front of a group of people, unaware that a member of the press was in the audience, and there were calls for his dismissal. Historians make different assessments of Patton's behavior and they range from calling him a misunderstood genius to an unstable leader. The week-long trial by cable and the eventual outcome of the affair are reproduced here in the blow-by-blow discussion between Marshall and Eisenhower.

Eisenhower's controversial decision to halt the Allied armies' advance along the river Elbe, leaving Berlin to the Soviet armies, has been argued over by historians for many years. Some state that it was the worst decision he made with hindsight of what happened in the Cold War years in Europe. Only when you read his justification to Marshall and Churchill do you get an insight into the great burden of command placed on SHAEF commander's shoulders. Having read what his reasons were for halting his armies where he did, we, the reader and armchair historian, understand what issues were on his mind. We can never fully understand what it is like to bear the pressures of decisions such as these.

One thing that is clear from these cables is the strong commitment between Marshall and Eisenhower. Mutual support is shown before, during and after the European campaign, even during the most difficult times. The media were repeatedly stirring up issues that the two had to discuss, and more often than not they decided that the best course of action was not to rise to the bait, letting the stories run their course. Over time some of these press speculations, repeated again and again, became cast in historical stone. These cables strip back stories to their origins so we can discover the reaction at the time. Finally, Eisenhower's cable of gratitude on 8 May 1945, the day the official German surrender was signed, illustrates how deeply Marshall's commitment to supporting SHAEF was appreciated.

It is hoped that by studying the messages the reader will gain a remarkable insight into the roles of two great men, General George C. Marshall and General Dwight D. Eisenhower, in the Second World War.

Biographies

General George Catlett Marshall, General of the Army (31 December 1880–16 October 1959)
Marshall grew up in Uniontown, Pennsylvania and enrolled at the Virginia Military Institute, graduating in 1901. He was commissioned as a 2nd Lieutenant in the Infantry in February 1902, serving in the Philippines and Oklahoma before attending the Infantry-Cavalry School at Fort Leavenworth, Kansas. Marshall was promoted to 1st Lieutenant in 1907 and after graduating in 1908 he stayed on as an instructor for two years.

Over the next seven years Marshall served as Inspector-Instructor of the Massachusetts National Guard, with an infantry battalion in Arkansas and Texas and again in the

Philippines. During his stay there he worked with the Field Force organizing it for the defense of Corregidor Island and the Bataan Peninsula, serving with it during a field exercise representing a Japanese landing on Batangas and Lucona.

He was promoted to captain on his return to the US in the summer of 1916, serving in several staff posts before America entered the First World War in April 1917. He joined the General Staff and sailed with 1st Division's first convoy for France; he was promoted to temporary major on his arrival. He served in the Luneville sector, the St Mihiel sector and the Picardy sector over the next twelve months and was promoted to temporary lieutenant-colonel. He was promoted to temporary colonel in August 1918, and assigned to the US Expeditionary Force's General Headquarters and then First Army as he drew up the plans for the St Mihiel offensive. As soon as the battle got underway in September he was tasked with planning and executing the transfer of 500,000 troops and 2700 guns to the Argonne Front. He was appointed First Army's Chief of Operations during the middle of the Meuse-Argonne battle in October. After serving as VIII Corps's Chief of Staff following the Armistice in November 1918, Marshall's last task in Europe was to help plan the advance into Germany at General Headquarters.

Marshall served as General John Pershing's aide-de-camp for the next five years and had been promoted to lieutenant-colonel by the time he took command of a battalion in Tientsin, China. After serving as an instructor at the Army War College, he was assistant commandant of the Infantry School at Fort Benning, Georgia from 1927 to 1932, implementing many changes in how the school was run. He was then promoted to colonel and over the next four years he commanded a battalion and served as senior instructor with the Illinois National Guard. Following his promotion to brigadier-general in July 1936 he commanded 5th Infantry Brigade.

In July 1938 Marshall joined the War Department General Staff, War Plans Division and by October he was Deputy Chief of Staff. After heading the Military Mission to Brazil in the early summer of 1939, he was appointed acting Chief of Staff of the Army in July and promoted to major-general. He became Chief of Staff and full general in September. He would serve as the US Army's Chief of Staff throughout the Second World War and was promoted to the new temporary five-star rank of General of the Army on 17 December 1944; this was made permanent in April 1946. Marshall centralized the professional leadership of the US Army and exercised control over mobilization, staff planning, industrial conversion and personnel requirements. His austere, aloof manner was well known in army circles and his succinct methods were put to good use streamlining administration and tactical organization.

Marshall resigned from the US Army in November 1945; his many decorations included two Distinguished Service Medals and the Silver Star. But his activities were far from over. Marshall acted as President Truman's personal representative to mediate peace between the nationalist and communist Chinese in 1946, and he went on to serve as Secretary of State from January 1947 to January 1949. In April 1948 he was a proponent of the plan for the economic recovery of Europe; the US contributed over $112 billion to the 'Marshall Plan'. He was also Secretary of Defense from September 1950 to September 1951.

Marshall served a term as President of the American Red Cross and as chairman of the American Battle Monuments Commission for ten years. He was awarded a gold medal from Congress and the Nobel Peace Prize in September 1950 for his work.

The great man who Churchill called the 'true architect of victory' of the European Theater in the Second World War died in Washington DC on 16 October 1959. He was buried with full military honors in Arlington Cemetery, Arlington, VA.

General Dwight David Eisenhower (14 October 1890–28 March 1969)
Eisenhower was born in Denison, Texas but his parents moved back to their roots in Abilene, Kansas when he was two. After graduating from high school he worked in the local creamery for two years before deciding to join the armed services. He entered United States Military Academy, West Point, in June 1911 and graduated four years later, having acquired the nickname 'Ike'. He was commissioned as a 2nd Lieutenant in September 1915 and posted to Fort Sam Houston, Texas, where he was promoted to 1st Lieutenant in 1916.

Eisenhower was promoted to captain in May 1917, a month after the US entered the First World War. Rather than head for France, he stayed in the US, serving with infantry units, teaching at army schools and working with army engineers. By the time of the Armistice he was a temporary lieutenant-colonel, and although he was reduced to the permanent rank of major, he commanded several tank battalions over the next three years.

Following a two-year posting in the Panama Canal Zone, Eisenhower attended the Command and General Staff School, Fort Leavenworth, Kansas, graduating first in a class of 245 in June 1926. After a brief period as a battalion commander, he worked for the American Battle Monuments Commission in Washington DC and Paris, France, until September 1929, graduating from the Army War College, Washington DC, in August 1928.

After serving as the Assistant Secretary of War's Executive Officer, he then worked for General Douglas MacArthur, Army Chief of Staff, from 1933 to 1939, first as chief military aide and then as Assistant Military Advisor to the Philippine government. During this period he was promoted to lieutenant-colonel in July 1936. He served on the staff of an infantry regiment and then as regimental executive until he was appointed in quick succession, Chief of Staff for 3rd Division, Chief of Staff for IX Corps and Chief of Staff to Third Army during the Louisiana Maneuvers. During this time he was promoted to brigadier-general.

Following the attack on Pearl Harbor, Eisenhower joined the War Plans Division of the War Department General Staff and was appointed Chief of the War Plans Division in February 1942. In April 1942, Major-General Eisenhower began working for General George C. Marshall as Assistant Chief of Staff of the Operations Division.

In June 1942 Eisenhower was appointed Commanding General, European Theater and appointed Lieutenant-General shortly afterwards. His appointment was renamed Commander-in-Chief, Allied Forces, North Africa, as US troops stepped ashore in Operation TORCH in November 1942. Over the next twelve months his command fought its way across North Africa, invaded Sicily and mainland Italy; he was appointed temporary full general in February 1943 and permanent major-general in August.

In December 1943 Eisenhower was appointed Supreme Commander, Allied Expeditionary Forces. Over the next six months SHAEF planned for the invasion of Nazi-occupied Europe, landing in Normandy on 6 June 1944. For the next six months Eisenhower's command repeatedly pushed back the Wehrmacht to Germany's borders; in December Eisenhower was promoted to General of the Army with five stars. Shortly after the German surrender on 8 May 1945, he was appointed Military Governor of the US Occupied Zone of Germany.

Eisenhower returned to the US in November 1945, replacing Marshall as Chief of Staff, US Army. He served as President of Columbia University, New York City, from June 1948 but in December 1950 he was recalled to active duty. He was named Supreme Allied Commander, North Atlantic Treaty Organization, Europe, and given operational command of both the Treaty Organization in Europe and US Forces, Europe.

Eisenhower retired from active service in May 1952 and a month later announced his candidacy for the Republican Party nomination for President. He was elected President of the United States on 4 November 4 1952, going on to serve two terms from 20 January

1953 to 20 January 1961. His administration experienced difficult times, including the end of the Korean War, the promotion of Atoms for Peace, and the crises in Berlin, Hungary, Lebanon and Suez. At home, issues included civil rights and the growth of the interstate highway system; Alaska and Hawaii also joined the United States.

Eisenhower died on 28 March 1969 and was buried in the Place of Meditation at the Eisenhower Center in Abilene, Kansas. His many decorations included six Distinguished Service Medals and the Legion of Merit; he was also author of *Crusade in Europe* (1949) and *Mandate for Change* (1963).

Walter Bedell 'Beetle' Smith (9 August 1895–5 October 1961)
Smith grew up in Indianapolis, Indiana, and although he left high school without graduating, he attended university. He had to drop out to support his family when his father became ill, and he enlisted as a private in the Indiana National Guard in 1911. Smith was commissioned as an officer on the United States' entry into the war in April 1917 and sailed with 4th Division to France in May 1918. He was wounded during the Aisne-Marne Offensive in July 1918.

Smith returned to work in the Military Intelligence Division of the War Department General Staff and served briefly with 95th Division before dealing with the disposal of supplies during the demobilization period. He joined the 2nd Infantry in March 1919, becoming staff officer 12th Infantry Brigade in 1922. He served in the Bureau of the Budget from 1925 to 1929 and was promoted to captain before he left to serve in the Philippines. On his return in March 1931 he became an instructor at the US Army Infantry School, serving there on and off until September 1939, becoming a major in January of that year. He graduated from the Command and General Staff School at Fort Leavenworth, Kansas, in 1933 and the Army War College in 1937.

Smith was appointed Secretary of the General Staff in 1941 and Secretary to the Combined Chiefs of Staff the following year. During his time in the War Department he prepared records, paperwork and statistics whilst carrying out analysis, liaison and administration; he also often had to brief President Franklin D. Roosevelt on strategic matters. Although Smith was promoted to lieutenant-colonel in May 1941, colonel in August 1941 and brigadier in February 1942, he was disappointed not to be given an operational command.

He became Eisenhower's Chief of Staff at Allied Forces Headquarters (AFHQ) in September 1942 where he used a combination of fine diplomatic skills and brusque demands to get his way. He worked alongside Eisenhower during the North African and Sicilian campaigns and negotiated the Armistice between Italy and the Allied armed forces in Sicily in September. In December 1943, Eisenhower was appointed Supreme Allied Commander for Operation OVERLORD, the invasion of Normandy. A month later Smith was promoted to lieutenant-general and appointed Chief of Staff of Supreme Headquarters Allied Expeditionary Force (SHAEF).

In August 1945 Eisenhower nominated Smith as his successor as commander of US Forces, European Theater (USFET) but the post was given to General Lucius D. Clay. When Eisenhower was appointed Chief of Staff of the United States Army in November 1945, he took Smith as his Assistant Chief of Staff for Operations and Planning. President Harry S. Truman then appointed Smith as the US Ambassador to the Soviet Union at a time when the Cold War was in its infancy. Smith saw the Soviet Union as a totalitarian and secretive state and his views were treated with suspicion. He returned to the US in March 1949 and became commander of First Army; it was his first command since 1918.

Smith was appointed head of a dysfunctional Central Intelligence Agency in 1950, at a time when the US was involved in the Korean War. He successfully reorganized the establishment into three directorates: Administration, Plans, and Intelligence and was promoted to four star general for his efforts in August 1951.

Although Smith retired from the US Army and the CIA in February 1953, he immediately became Under Secretary of State in the new Eisenhower administration. After failing to get British help for the French during their conflict in southeast Asia, he forged a deal with the Soviets to partition Vietnam in May 1954. He retired in October but continued to work in the Eisenhower administration in various posts. He went on to serve as a Member of the National Security Training Commission from 1955 to 1957, on the National War College's board of consultants from 1956 to 1959 and the Office of Defense Mobilization Special Stockpile Advisory Committee from 1957 to 1958. Smith was also a consultant in the Special Projects Office (Disarmament) in the Executive Office of the President from 1955 to 1956, the President's Citizen Advisors on the Mutual Security Program from 1956 to 1957. He then served on the President's Committee on Disarmament in 1958 and was Chairman and member-at-large of the Advisory Council of the President's Committee on Fund Raising from 1958 until his death in August 1961. Smith was buried with full military honors in Arlington National Cemetery, Arlington, Virginia.

I

DECEMBER 1943
AND JANUARY 1944

Establishing SHAEF Headquarters

Smith to Eisenhower   30 December   Ref: Algiers 21147

I have just received your 21147 and have given your message to General Wilson.[1] He will await your return to take over command, and may go on to Cairo to pack during the interim.

Have yet had no time to go into living accommodation. Am sure the house offered by the Ambassador will not be satisfactory to you. He wants you to occupy one floor. I also believe that this Headquarters should get out of London at the earliest possible moment. Aside from the threat of bombing, I do not think we shall ever get shaken down until we get away from Norfolk House[2] as the situation is the same as it was at the beginning of TORCH.[3] I will talk over possible locations with Morgan.[4]

There are two things which you must discuss with utmost urgency while you are in the United States:

First is the Air Command setup covered by my message this morning. We all believe that the appointment of Tedder[5] as Deputy Allied Commander without portfolio and Mallory[6] as Air Commander-in-Chief will make a difficult situation. I personally believe that Tedder should be the real Air Commander and your advisor on air matters, which Mallory now considers himself. I don't think there is a place for both of them.

There is also a question about Tactical Air Forces. These are now organized on a joint basis. Other than Mallory, who is Air Commander-in-Chief, there is no single Commander of the Tactical Air Forces as we had in the Mediterranean.

Both the above consistencies must be corrected and no formal directive should be issued by the Combined Chiefs of Staff until you and Tedder are both here and you make your own recommendations. The present organization of COSSAC Headquarters[7] can be made to conform to the setup you want with the change of a few names and the substitution of a few

---

1 General, later Field Marshal, Sir Henry Maitland Wilson, GCB, GBE, DSO (1881–1964), nicknamed 'Jumbo'. On 8 January 1944 Wilson succeeded Eisenhower as Supreme Allied Commander in the Mediterranean at Allied Forces Headquarters (AFHQ), taking strategic control over the Italian campaign.
2 Norfolk House, at 31 St James's Square, London.
3 The invasion of French North Africa by American and British troops, which began on 8 November 1942.
4 Lieutenant-General Sir Frederick E. Morgan KCB (1894–1967) Chief of Staff to the Supreme Allied Commander (Designate) Morgan had directed planning of Operation OVERLORD since March 1943 and became Deputy Chief of Staff to Major-General Walter Bedell Smith, covering Intelligence and Operations when Eisenhower took command.
5 Air Chief Marshal Arthur William Tedder, GCB (1890–1967), Deputy Supreme Commander of SHAEF.
6 Air Chief Marshal Sir Trafford Leigh-Mallory KCB, DSO & Bar (1892–1944) was appointed Commander in Chief of the Allied Expeditionary Air Force in August 1943, making him air commander for the invasion of Normandy.
7 Chief of Staff, Supreme Allied Commander Headquarters; General Morgan from March 1943 and General Walter Bedell Smith (1895–1961), nicknamed 'Beetle', under General Eisenhower.

individuals. However, the organization is very top heavy. I talked with the Deputy C.I.G.S.[8] this morning on personnel and made some progress. Will see General Brooke[9] this evening and Ismay[10] tomorrow. Devers[11] returns to Algiers with me and I will put him into the picture as rapidly as possible.

Suggest you leave the written memorandum authorizing Wilson and Devers to command to be delivered to me on my arrival, to be used if necessary.

Smith to Eisenhower   *30 December*   *Ref: 6792*

I have just had a talk with Wigglesworth[12] and a preview of the command set-up proposed here. The thing which disturbs me the most is the proposed air command, which either leaves Tedder without any direct air function, with Mallory the Commander and principal advisor of the C-in-C, or, as an alternative, if you decide to make Tedder your air advisor, would leave Mallory without any function.[13]

I am also concerned about the plans here for the establishment of two Tactical Air Forces. Wigglesworth and I are convinced this is most unsound at the moment. Apparently this proposal is incorporated in a British Chiefs of Staff paper which has been, or is about to be, sent to the Combined Chiefs of Staff for approval and the issuance of a directive to the Allied C-in-C. Strongly urge that you send a message to General Marshall requesting that no action be taken by the Combined Chiefs of Staff on further command directives until you and Tedder are here and can be in the picture, and until you have had a chance to submit your recommendations.

Smith to Eisenhower   *31 December*   *Ref: 6824*

If C-in-C has already left, Gilmer forward to Galey in Washington.[14] I find that the matter of air command of which I spoke has already been covered by Combined Chiefs of Staff directive issued some time ago. There is a difficult command situation from the air point of view, and I am meeting with Spaatz[15] and Eaker[16] tomorrow after which I will send you a long message to Washington.

I think accommodation provided will please you thoroughly. Very nice house in London, with all the facilities you like, including lots of fire-places. Either telegraph cottage or another one, very close for the country. Everything else in the way of accommodation

8 Lieutenant-General Ronald M. Weeks, 1st Baron Weeks KCB, CBE, DSO, MC, TD (1890–1960), Deputy Chief of the Imperial General Staff.
9 Field Marshal The Rt. Hon. Sir Alan Francis Brooke, 1st Viscount Alanbrooke, KG, GCB, OM, GCVO, DSO & Bar (1883–1963), Chief of the Imperial General Staff (CIGS).
10 General Hastings L. Ismay, 1st Baron Ismay, KG, GCB, CH, DSO, PC (1887–1965), nick name 'Pug', Deputy Secretary (Military) to the War Cabinet and Additional Secretary (Military) to the Cabinet as Churchill's chief military assistant.
11 General Jacob L. Devers (1887–1979), nicknamed 'Jake', had just been appointed Commanding General North African Theater of Operations, US Army and Deputy Supreme Allied Commander, Mediterranean Theater, serving under General Sir Henry Maitland Wilson.
12 Air Marshal Sir (Horace Ernest) Philip Wigglesworth KBE, CB, DSC (1896–1975), previously Deputy Air Commander-in-Chief at Mediterranean Air Command and to be appointed Deputy Chief of Staff (Air) at SHAEF.
13 Although Leigh-Mallory put together the air plan for Operation OVERLORD, Tedder would take control of many aspects, an arrangement Eisenhower approved of because he and Tedder had worked closely together during previous campaigns.
14 Colonel Dan Gilmer, Secretary, General Staff, SHAEF to his opposite number in Washington.
15 Lieutenant-General Carl Andrew Spaatz (1891–1974), nicknamed 'Tooey', appointed commander US Strategic Air Forces in Europe in January 1944.
16 General Ira C. Eaker (1896–1987), Commander-in-Chief of the Mediterranean Allied Air Forces, controlling the Twelfth and Fifteenth Air Forces and the British Desert and Balkan Air Forces.

is taken care of perfectly by Jimmy Gault's[17] arrangements. Telegraph cottage much improved since your occupancy, particularly from a heating stand point.

Have just had a long talk with C.I.G.S. Will probably get Gale,[18] but not Strong[19] except for a short time, to get things going in G-2. Other personnel requested will be available.

Making tentative arrangements for a very early move of this Headquarters to Aldershot. C.I.G.S. has been most helpful and only question now is of communications. Gault will immediately survey living accommodation in that area, and he thinks prospects are good.

General Wilson's plans are now to go on to Cairo returning to Algiers shortly before your return. Spaatz's plane will be available. Will not have to use the two documents I suggested.

Handing Over Command of the Mediterranean

Eisenhower to Smith   *6 January 1944*   *Ref: 6490*

Your telegram announcing arrival received. This morning I saw a telegram from AGENT[20] to CARGO[21] asking that Allied Command in the Mediterranean be transferred as of the 8th. I recommended to CARGO that he not only accept this, but to inform AGENT that you and I had foreseen this possibility and that I had left with you a written note authorizing General Wilson to take Command when he considered it necessary. In view of this development and the need for my going to the new station at the earliest possible date, I believe it would be best for me to go there directly from here. In this event Devers should also assume command of the American Theater on the date you and he may agree. Unless you find this plan completely unworkable I will tentatively plan to carry it out. However, I would like you to inform both Commanders that it would be my intention to come back to FREEDOM[22] purely as a visitor within a week or ten days after I reach my new station merely to say goodbye to the many officers to whom I am indebted for fine service. I would count on staying there one day only.

I am leaving this city for a few days but essential messages can reach me. Please consult Colonel Lee[23] as to possibility of moving all my personal belongings and personal assistants and domestics without awaiting my return. Ask him also to convey my warmest regards to all my personal family, including special American contingent.

Please take up the following with Tedder.

I anticipate that there will be some trouble in securing necessary approval for integration of all Air Forces that will be essential to success of OVERLORD. I suspect that use of these Air Forces for the necessary preparatory phase will be particularly resisted. To support our position it is essential that a complete outline plan for use of all available aircraft during this phase be ready as quickly as possible. I therefore believe that Tedder should proceed to the new station at once and consult with Spaatz and others in order to have the plan ready at the earliest possible date. In your reply please indicate how soon Tedder believes he can depart.

---

17 Colonel James Gault, Eisenhower's British military assistant.
18 Lieutenant-General Sir Humfrey M. Gale, KBE, CB, CVO, MC (1890–1971), Chief Administration Officer Supreme Headquarter Allied Expeditionary Force.
19 Major-General George V. Strong (1880–1946), Assistant Chief of Staff, G-2 Intelligence, US Army.
20 Codename for Churchill.
21 Codename for Roosevelt.
22 Code name for Allied Forces Headquarters in Algiers, Algeria, Eisenhower's combined operational command in North Africa and the Mediterranean before he was appointed commander of Supreme Headquarters Allied Expeditionary Force, SHAEF.
23 Colonel Ernest R. Lee, nicknamed 'Tex'.

Eisenhower's Departure for the United Kingdom

Eisenhower to Smith   13 January 1944   *Ref: 7079*

Under present schedule I leave here Thursday evening and arrive in Prestwick, via the Azores, on Saturday afternoon. I will go from Prestwick to London by train and arrive there Sunday morning. If Colonel Lee is still in your Theater please give him the essentials of the schedule. This information has already been sent to London and Colonel Gault. My arrival is to be kept secret.

I have taken up here the various matters raised by Montgomery[24] and feel that the final decision may <u>not</u> be taken until I can arrive in London. I am almost reluctant to consider giving up ANVIL[25] and still feel that through some expedient we can increase OVERLORD lift. There are certain weighty reasons other than strictly tactical that must be considered. Among these is denial to French Forces of a significant part in the French Invasion. Another is the fact that this Operation was definitely agreed upon at Tehran[26] It is my belief that all the Chiefs of Staff will oppose <u>us</u> if we are forced eventually into the decision to abandon ANVIL[27]. On the other hand I think we can slightly diminish the Armored Landing Craft assigned that Operation in favor of OVERLORD.

I hope that the deal with respect to Morgan and Whiteley[28] goes through as you suggested. I am also hopeful that you will <u>not</u> be delayed longer than the 20th.

Army and Corps Commanders in the Mediterranean

Marshall to Eisenhower   17 January   *Ref: R-8213*

After consultation with Alexander,[29] Devers reports that Clark[30] should retain command of the Fifth Army in Italy and not assume command of the Seventh Army for ANVIL as you planned. Middleton[31] has been put in charge of ANVIL planning temporarily by Devers. Devers asks that Hodges,[32] Simpson[33] or any other of my choice be assigned immediately to the Seventh Army for ANVIL. ANVIL certainly requires an army commander with battle experience against the Germans. There are only three that appear to meet this requirement.

---

24 Field Marshal Bernard Law Montgomery, 1st Viscount Montgomery of Alamein, KG, GCB, DSO, PC, (1887–1976) commander of 21st Army Group.

25 The original name for the planned Allied landing in southern France, it would later be called Operation DRAGOON. There is an apochryphal story that the final name was chosen by Winston Churchill, who was opposed to the plan and had been 'dragooned'.

26 The Tehran Conference (codenamed EUREKA) was the meeting of Stalin, Roosevelt and Churchill between 28 November and 1 December 1943, where the final strategy for the war was planned.

27 During its planning stages, the invasion of southern France was known as ANVIL, to complement SLEDGEHAMMER, the code name for the invasion of Normandy. Subsequently, SLEDGEHAMMER was renamed OVERLORD and ANVIL was renamed DRAGOON.

28 General Sir John F. M. Whiteley, GBE, KCB, MC, (1896–1970) nicknamed 'Jock', initially became Assistant Chief of Staff, Intelligence (G-2) at SHAEF before becoming deputy to the Assistant Chief of Staff, Operations (G-3), Major-General Harold Bull in May 1944.

29 General Harold R.L.G. Alexander, 1st Earl Alexander of Tunis, KG, PC (UK), GCB, OM, GCMG, CSI, DSO, MC, CD, PC (Can) (1891–1969), commander of 15th Army Group which was about to start a four-month campaign to break the Gustav Line.

30 Lieutenant-General Mark W. Clark (1896–1984), commander of Fifth US Army which attacked Monte Cassino for the first time on 17 January.

31 Major-General Troy H. Middleton (1889–1976), the commander of 45th Infantry Division had been suffering with a painful knee, requiring his relief from combat.

32 Lieutenant-General Courtney H. Hodges (1887–1966), commander of Third US Army and about to be transferred to command First US Army.

33 General William H. Simpson (1888–1980), nicknamed 'Texas Bill', commander of Fourth US Army which was renamed Eighth US Army. He would command Ninth US Army in Europe after August 1944.

Bradley[34] of course, is not available. It rests between Clark and Patton.[35] With Bradley, Hodges and Patton now set up for the U.K., there will be an extra Lieutenant General there until the Army Group Commander is designated. What do you think of Patton retaining command of Seventh Army and carrying out ANVIL?

I had thought that Clark would continue in command of Fifth Army until the Rome area was reached. Lucas[36] would then replace him. Thereafter as soon as U.S. Divisions largely disappeared from Fifth Army line up, ~~Clark~~ Lucas would be replaced, probably by a Britisher, although maybe a French officer if such divisions are to compose the bulk of Fifth Army.

Devers also asked that an additional Corps Commander be sent to the Mediterranean to be used as relief for present Corps Commanders who are beginning to show the strain of extended combat service, in order to give them a rest, but not with the view necessarily, to their permanent relief. Give me your views on the advisability of replacing Woodruff,[37] Crittenberger[38] or Walker[39] or possibly Cook[40] who goes in April, by Collins,[41] and sending whoever is thus replaced to the Mediterranean for Devers to use as a reserve commander. Also, for the extra Corps commander, let me know what you think of using Truscott.[42]

Marshall to Eisenhower   *18 January*   *Ref: 9*
Reference my R-8213 regarding Devers and ANVIL: In fourth paragraph, fourth line, the name Clark should have been Lucas, reading "Lucas would be replaced, etc."
Since radioing you in this matter Devers has communicated his desire to make no changes – Clark to command ANVIL, Lucas to command Fifth Army and Truscott to command Corps.

Eisenhower to Marshall   *18 January*   *Ref: 109737*
My own understanding of the previously planned changes in U.S. Army command in the Mediterranean Theater agrees with yours. That is, Clark was to remain in command of the Fifth Army until completion of SHINGLE[43] and would then be replaced by Lucas. Lucas would remain in command of the Fifth Army until the British finally took over, since I believe that after a channel of entry into France is opened up from the south, all the available American and French divisions would be absorbed in that venture. However, if both Alexander and Devers believe that General Clark should remain in command of the Fifth Army, then I am of the opinion that Patton would be the best man to plan and lead

34 General Omar N. Bradley (1893–1981), commander of First US Army Group, including First Army, and commander of Twelfth Army Group after August 1944.
35 General George S. Patton Jr. (1885–1945), nicknamed 'Blood and Guts', had been relieved as commander of Seventh US Army in Sicily after slapping a soldier on 3 August 1943. He would be appointed head of the fictional First US Army Group (FUSAG) in southeast England, as part of the deception plan to make the Germans focus on the Pas-de-Calais. He would command Third US Army in Europe.
36 General John P. Lucas (1890–1949), nicknamed 'Old Luke', commander of VI Corps in Italy. He would be relieved a month later following a poor performance in command of the Anzio Beachhead.
37 Major-General Roscoe B. Woodruff (1891–1975).
38 Major-General Willis D. Crittenberger (1890–1980), commander of III Armored Corps in the US.
39 Major-General Fred L. Walker (1887–1969), commander of the 36th Infantry Division.
40 Major-General Richard G. Cook (1889–1963), nicknamed 'Doc' or 'Gib', commander of XIII Corps in the US who would become Patton's deputy at Third Army headquarters in August 1944.
41 Major-General J. Lawton Collins (1896–1963), nicknamed 'Lightning Joe' and commander of the 25th Infantry Division in the Pacific, chosen to command VII Corps in Normandy.
42 General Lucian K. Truscott Jr. (1895–1965), 3rd Infantry Division commander in the Anzio beachhead.
43 The amphibious landing at Anzio in Italy, designed to outflank the Gustav Line. The landings started on 22 January but did not go as planned and for a time it looked as if the beachhead would be eliminated. It took until May before the break out towards Rome occurred.

the ANVIL affair.[44] This might prove especially advantageous if we are finally compelled to reduce ANVIL initially to the status of a threat rather than to mount it as a large scale offensive operation. Patton's reputation as an assault commander, which is respected by the enemy, would serve to increase the value of the threat.[45]

To tell you one possible drawback to this plan, I must venture into the realm of conjecture. It is my impression that Devers and Patton are not, repeat not, genial. You see I am being perfectly frank with you have because I have nothing but impression on which to make the above statement. I think, however, that both of them are sufficiently good soldiers that possible personal antagonism should not, repeat not, interfere with either one doing his full duty as a soldier. On the favorable side of the picture and in addition to the consideration of Patton's prestige, there is the factor that Patton is already on the ground, is well acquainted with and liked by the French, and is also well acquainted with such personnel of the Seventh Army staff as still remains with him.

Moreover, leaving Patton in the Mediterranean will allow Hodges to come here with his own Third Army staff with which he is, of course, thoroughly acquainted. I personally believe therefore that Patton should stay in the Mediterranean and Hodges should come here. Any decision you make will be acceptable to me. In this connection one of these two army commanders should proceed here soon and begin the necessary organization of an American army. You are quite right in your belief that there is no necessity at this moment to have three lieutenant-generals here but on the other hand two are required.[46]

With respect to corps commanders, it would appear that retaining Clark in command of the Fifth Army would prohibit the immediate promotion in the Mediterranean of Truscott to corps command, since Devers wants one who is fresh. Truscott has been in the front line probably more than any other officer in the whole Mediterranean. I definitely desire both Collins and Truscott as corps commanders and I should like to have them here at the earliest possible date. I will make available for transfer to the Mediterranean any one or two corps commanders that Devers may select, except for Gerow,[47] who according to Bradley has done so much of the preliminary planning for the assault that he could not be allowed to go without prejudice to this operation.[48]

I have become convinced that the infantry assault in OVERLORD must be broadened and because of geographical considerations two American corps will be involved.[49] I would have Gerow and Truscott lead this assault, and consequently should like to have Truscott here as quickly as possible. His three months of planning will give him a respite from the battle line while his experience and outstanding qualities of battle leadership will make him of inestimable value. A few days ago I sent an informal inquiry to Devers concerning his willingness to

---

44 Clark would stay in the Mediterranean with Fifth Army while Patton would move to the UK to eventually command Third Army in France. Lucas would be relieved from VI Corps after the Anzio beachhead failed to destabilize the German positions south of Rome. Churchill angrily stated 'I had hoped we were hurling a wildcat into the shore, but all we got was a stranded whale.'
45 The Germans followed Patton's movements whenever possible, believing that he would command the next attack against mainland Europe. Eisenhower would use this fixation on Patton to his own advantage.
46 Hodges would start as Bradley's deputy at First Army while Patton commanded the fictitious First US Army Group (FUSAG). After 12th Army Group was formed at the end of July 1944, Hodges would command First US Army and Patton would command Third Army.
47 Major-General Leonard T. Gerow (1888–1972), nicknamed 'Gee'.
48 Collins would command VII Corps on Utah Beach and Gerow would command V Corps on Omaha Beach in Normandy.
49 Both Eisenhower and Montgomery wanted to increase the original COSSAC plan for the landings from three divisions to five. By landing on Utah Beach on the east side of the Cotentin Peninsula, Cherbourg could be taken quicker. The extra beach would also allow First US Army to straddle the river Vire, rather than have to cross it.

let Truscott come up here and while I have not received an answer to that message I am telling you my desires very frankly since the question is raised by your telegram.[50]

The arrival here of both Collins and Truscott and the sending to Devers of only one officer of his selection such as Woodruff, Crittenberger or Walker, would leave me with one surplus corps commander. I will be glad to have you name the additional man to be replaced.

To sum up all the above I feel immediate need for both Truscott and Collins and for an army commander. To obtain Truscott and Collins I will make available to Devers, or for other assignment by the War Department, an equal number of officers either from officers already here or yet to come.

Eisenhower to Marshall   *19 January*   *Ref: W-9745*

Yesterday I sent you a long telegram based on your R-8213. This morning I have received your number 9 which says that Devers has changed his mind. I must say it is a great disappointment to me. However, Devers still apparently wants an additional Corps Commander and since I am getting Collins I would be perfectly willing to let Crittenberger go to Africa.[51]

I think you might still consider the advantage of sending Truscott here in exchange for one of our Corps Commanders, which move would not only give him a rest from the battle line but would enable us to use his particular experience to the best advantage.

Marshall to Eisenhower   *20 January*   *Ref: R-8316*

General Patton is now without an assignment in the Mediterranean Theater and Devers desires orders issued for him. Do you want him sent to the U.K. now?

I considered ordering him home for a short time prior to his going to England. However, in view of the publicity given his case, his presence here, if not kept secret, might result in reopening the entire matter with vituperative discussions[52] and speculations as to his future. You realize how difficult it would be to keep his presence secret.[53]

In accordance with your wishes as stated here, Hodges is being held in the U.S. until you call for him.

Third Army Headquarters is moving to UK. I have submitted names of Crittenberger, Woodruff, Reinhardt,[54] Haislip[55] and Walker to Devers for indication of his preference for extra Corps Commander. 3rd Division is set up for SHINGLE and decision must be delayed on Truscott.[56]

Eisenhower to Marshall   *20 January*   *Ref: W-9777*

I agree with you that Patton should not go to the United States. Although he would have been a good man for ANVIL, if he is not to be used in that capacity, he should be ordered here for duty since I need an additional Army Commander. One disadvantage to this arrangement is that Hodges will be separated from his Third Army Staff and will be presumably without a definite assignment for the next several months.

50 Truscott would stay in Italy and replace Lucas in command on VI Corps in the Anzio beachhead.
51 Crittenberger would go to Italy and replace General Lucas at IV Corps in March 1944, taking command of the Anzio beachhead.
52 Malicious discussions.
53 Both the American Press and German intelligence were anxious to follow Patton's movements. The press were always hoping for a good story; the Germans believed he would lead the attack on mainland Europe.
54 Major-General Emil F. Reinhardt (1888–1969) would eventually command 69th Infantry Division in Europe.
55 Major-General Wade H. Haislip, nicknamed 'Ham' (1889–1971), commander of XV Corps throughout the European campaign.
56 The 3rd Infantry Division was about to land on the beaches of Anzio.

I will call for Hodges well in advance of the beginning of the operation so that he may accompany Bradley throughout and be fully ready when the time comes to employ American Army Group headquarters, to take command either of First Army or the First Army Group.[57]

First Thoughts on OVERLORD

Eisenhower to Marshall   *22 January*   *Ref: W-9856*

Yesterday I had a long conference with the Prime Minister, who seems fully recovered. He emphasized his anxiety to support to the limit all our activities, stating several times that the cross-channel effort represented the crisis of the European war from the viewpoint of the U.K. and the U.S. He said he was prepared to scrape the bottom of the barrel in every respect in order to increase the effectiveness of the attack, remarking that the calculations of planners who have been compelled to work within the confines of the estimated availability of resources must not be permitted to limit our strength where we can do anything better through intensification of effort or through sacrifice at other places. There is a very deep conviction here, in all circles, that we are approaching a tremendous crisis with stakes incalculable. Every man with whom I have so far dealt is definitely sober and serious, but confident of the outcome if all of us do our very best. Practically all the principal commanders and staff officers are on the ground and conferences are steadily clearing away some of our perplexing problems.

After detailed examination of the tactical plan I clearly understand Montgomery's original objection to the narrowness of the assault. Beaches are too few and too restricted to depend upon them as avenues through which all our original build-up would have to flow.[58] We must broaden out to gain quick initial success, secure more beaches for build-up and particularly to get a force at once into the Cherbourg peninsula behind the defensive barrier separating that feature from the mainland. In this way there would be a reasonable hope of gaining the port in short order. We must have this.[59]

Altogether we need five divisions assault loaded. This means additional assets in several lines but chiefly naval, with special emphasis on landing craft.[60] The staff is preparing a detailed message to the Combined Chiefs of Staff, which will be ready for dispatch very soon.

Naturally we should do everything to preserve a strong ANVIL, with an assaulting strength of at least two divisions. I fervently hope that we can do so and still get here the minimum strength necessary to have reasonable prospects of success, even if we have to wait until the end of May, although this will cost us a month of good campaigning weather.[61] These are preliminary conclusions.

---

57 Hodges acted as First Army's deputy, dealing with training in the UK prior to the invasion while Bradley attended planning conferences. During the Normandy campaign, Hodges acted as Bradley's 'eyes and ears', monitoring the progress of divisions when they went into battle for the first time, advising commanders and correcting their mistakes before reporting back.

58 Montgomery and Smith were briefed on 3 January; Montgomery objected to the narrowness of the assault. It would have resulted in confusion as armies and corps shared beaches during the days that followed the landings. A wider front would make it harder for the Germans to decide where to counterattack. The invasion frontage was expanded from 25 to 40 miles, using five beaches with one division landing on each beach.

59 The addition of Utah Beach would make it easier to establish a foothold on the west bank of the river Vire and then capture Cherbourg port. At this stage no one had much confidence in the artificial harbours, codenamed 'Mulberries', being prepared.

60 Montgomery had already criticized COSSAC's planning figures for the capacity of available landing craft.

61 To get the number of landing craft for OVERLORD, half of the ANVIL landing craft had to return the UK. The date had to be postponed from 1 May to 1 June to get another month's production while assault divisions had to reduce the number of vehicles they took ashore.

Proposing the Best Commanders in Army Ground Forces

Marshall to Eisenhower   26 *January*   *Reference 30*

I want you to feel great freedom in making such readjustments as may appear desirable to you in the matter of Division and Corps Commanders. We have over here some admirable men, particularly in the Division Command category. You have at least one of two regarding whom I have doubts. I am ready to effect transfers if you so desire. The following are the experienced Corps Commanders in the U.S. not obligated for Africa or the Pacific:[62]

1. <u>Alvan C. Gillem, Jr.</u> (1)   3. W. H. H. Morris [ticked]
2. J. W. Anderson   4. John Millikin

In addition the following are new Corps Commanders with very little experience:

1. F. W. Milburn   3. H. Terrell
2. J. B. Anderson   4. L. A. Craig

All of the foregoing are listed approximately in the order of efficiency by General McNair...[63]

Eisenhower to Marshall   28 *January*   *Ref: W-10158*

Thank you very much for your Number 30 which lists available corps and divisional commanders. General Bradley has already indicated to me one division commander of whom he is quite doubtful and I regard it as certain that I will be proposing to you changes within a short time.[64]

I just had news that Collins is on the way here, but because of the present developments in Italy I doubt that I can count on Truscott. This is a great disappointment to me because he has served with me almost continuously for three years.[65]

I have not yet heard as to which of several corps commanders Devers will want. Frankly I hope he picks Crittenberger.

[Eisenhower's undated handwritten notes on changing Corps Commanders]

Ratings:	General Bradley	General Patton
Truscott	1	1
J. L. Collins	2	4
Gillem	3	5
Middleton	4	3
Keyes	5	2

62 Marshall had given Eisenhower a list of excellent experienced and inexperienced general officers suitable for corps command. They were listed in order of merit as scored by their General Efficiency Ratings, an average of the past five years performance in various posts as scored by their commanding officers.
63 Marshall also gave Eisenhower a list of 12 armored and 34 infantry division commanders. He gave him the freedom to relieve any division commanders in his invasion force in exchange for one still training their own division in the US. Again they are listed in order of merit.
64 Major-General Charles H. Gerhardt (1895–1976), nicknamed 'Jumping Charlie' commanding 29th Infantry Division, part of which was due to go ashore on Omaha Beach on D-Day. Gerhardt proved to be satisfactory and commanded the 29th until the end of the European campaign.
65 By now it was clear that the first attempt to capture Monte Cassino had failed; it would take another 111 days and three more battles before the monastery was taken. Truscott was VI Corps' deputy commander and soon to be the commander when General John Lucas was relieved.

We would replace Woodruff by Truscott, Crittenberger by Collins, Gillem or Middleton.
[Eisenhower and Bradley's wishes]
Bradley wants <u>Truscott</u> for one of the armored Corps instead of Woodruff. He does <u>not</u> want
Crittenberger. Would rather have Collins or Gillem. He wants Gerow, Truscott and Collins.
[Bradley's personal perferences]

Taking the Blame

Eisenhower to Marshall   *28 January*   *Ref: W-10156*

Accurately informed as to the situation what I must do, with respect to the U.S. Chiefs of
Staff. Upon my return here from an inspection yesterday, I find that there was a little bit of
hurt feeling concerning procedure used by joint planners in obtaining information involving
British resources. Due to distance and to differing customs these little incidents are bound
occasionally to occur. I want to make a personal request of you, as a matter of urgency, to
help me minimize any bad effect of these and to prevent knowledge of them getting into
circulation, because of the danger of hurting this whole effort. If any such cases arise in the
future and come to your attention please make it appear, whenever possible, that the mistake was made by me, since I am always in a position to go and make a personal explanation
or apology, even when I and my headquarters may have had nothing to do with the case.
The particular instance of yesterday has already been forgotten. Admiral Cunningham,[66]
who we all admire, was the individual who was upset but Smith saw him personally last
evening and everything is serene. The incident, however, leads me to seek in advance your
cooperation in being instantly ready to apply salve instead of an irritant onto fancied hurts
that may arise out of individual personality or conviction, or of mere lack of understanding
on the part of some person.[67]

   Such things as the above are one of the consequences of the location of these headquarters. I am already in process of moving out to WIDEWING,[68] which will help some.
My intention was to begin the immediate building of a headquarters on the coast but the
existing communication nets are vast, and the moving of this headquarters would entail so
much expense in signal equipment and troops, that I am sadly forced to agree that my main
headquarters must remain at WIDEWING until it can cross the Channel. I will follow my
usual custom and establish my advance headquarters on the coast, probably at Portsmouth,
where I will normally remain once the operation begins until I can get overseas.[69] I am forwarding to you a signal corps dissertation on this subject which you might like to glance
over and then give to Handy[70] for his archives.

---

66 The Rt. Hon. Sir Andrew B. Cunningham, 1st Viscount Cunningham of Hyndhope KT, GCB, OM, DSO and
two Bars (1883–1963), nicknamed 'ABC', First Sea Lord of the Admiralty and Chief of the Naval Staff, was
responsible for the overall strategic direction of the Royal Navy.
67 Eisenhower knew that small problems can quickly become big problems, especially when decisions are
being discussed on opposite sides of the Atlantic by officers from different cultures and military backgrounds.
This was his way of attending to problems quickly in the interests of planning for OVERLORD.
68 SHAEF's headquarters staff had used shelters in Goodge Street Underground Station on the Northern
Line but Eisenhower did not like working in Central London. WIDEWING was the codename for his headquarters at Camp Griffiss in the Teddington End of Bushey Park, near Kingston-on-Thames, ten miles southwest of
Central London.
69 A small command post, codenamed SHARPENER, was established near Southwick, just north of
Portsmouth. Eisenhower's personal office tent and sleeping trailer stood next to a mobile office and telephone
switchboard; trailers filled with maps and teletype machines were close by. The camp also had tents for senior
aides, meteorologists, guards and cooks.
70 General Thomas T. Handy (1892–1982), Assistant Chief of Staff, G-3 Operations, working for Marshall,
taking over from Eisenhower, and Deputy Chief of Staff after October 1944, again working for Marshall.

The upshot of all this is that my headquarters will be closer under the noses of the London authorities than I desire but I must accept this penalty, and you may be sure that I will be forever on the job to prevent difficulties arising because of this. In particular, the U.S. Joint Chiefs of Staff can be certain that I will under no circumstances take advantage of this accident of geography in order to keep officials on this side of the water better acquainted with any problems and more.

Coordination and Supply of French Resistance Groups

Marshall to Eisenhower   *25 January*   *Ref: 28*

At a recent conversation with the President apropos[71] of your telegram relating to the need for getting ahead with Civil Administration Planning for France, question of what we were doing on Combined Staff level for coordination and supply of resistance groups in France came up. He made it clear that if there was any hesitation in your mind or anyone else's as to propriety of dealing with Committee resistance representatives, it could be disregarded. There was no reason from the point of view of National Policy why your staff could not go ahead with definite plans.

I understand that planning and considerable operating have already been carried out in England, but largely through British sources and on less than the Combined Staff level which might now be advisable, since concrete Combined Operations are in view.

There has been considerable criticism in the press emanating from Algiers to the effect that French have not been consulted in connection with the formulation of resistance plans. There have, of course, also been criticisms of lack of supplies.

This is simply to let you know informally that the President assumed that you would feel entirely free to take whatever steps you felt desirable to make this resistance as helpful to you as possible, including dealing with any suitable representatives of the Committee in this regard. I believe that on this basis you could, so far as the President is concerned, discuss at once all matters of resistance with them leaving out for the time being, and as long as you deem desirable, all information as to time and place of landing.[72]

Eisenhower to Marshall   *28 January*   *Ref: B-64*

For your information we have had in the past, and are now continuing, contact with and assisting the French resistance groups through the French Committee of Action, working with S.O.E./S.O., which is under my general supervision and direction.[73]

It is noted that advice will be received shortly from the Combined Chiefs of Staff as to matters of civil administration.

---

71 Regarding.

72 There were two resistance groups in France at this time. The Francs-Tireurs partisans, FTP, the military branch of the French Communist Party agreed to merge with the Forces Françaises de l'Intérieur, FFI, in February 1944. On 23 June 1944, SHAEF placed 200,000 resistance fighters under the command of General Marie P. Koenig (1898–1970) at the request of the French Committee of National Liberation. Koenig was already commanding the Free French who participated in the invasion. FFI resistance fighters used their own weapons, wore civilian clothing and wore an armband with the letters 'FFI'; many were ex-soldiers. They collected intelligence, carried out acts of sabotage and would seize key points ahead of the Allied advance.

73 Special Operations Executive, Special Operations, British.

First Assessment of the Landing Craft Situation[74]

Eisenhower to Marshall   28 January   *Ref: B-56*

I had a great deal of trouble and embarrassment in assembling the data to reply to the Joint Chiefs of Staff message, because it was felt here that the entire matter was on a Combined Chiefs of Staff level and that much of the information was already in the hands of the Combined Staff Planners. As an example, and for your private information, Admiral Cunningham refused to give an answer to paragraph (b) unless I worded it as in our B-55 which is the explanation of the peculiar phraseology. Please do not, repeat not, mention this to anyone but do what you can to preserve the amenities and stay in Combined Chiefs of Staff channels when indicated. I know exactly how our people feel about this landing craft matter, but I find people here are becoming rather touchy as the tension increases.

Smith to Handy   29 January   *Ref: B-70*

I have been going into the matter personally with the following results.

1. We have hitherto worked on the line that LCTs completed after 1 March could not, repeat not, be assembled and trained in time to take part in OVERLORD on 1 May.
2. On this premise our availability figure on 1 May was as stated in B-55, namely 636, of which 468 were British and 168 were U.S.
3. Admiralty have now completed a reassessment of the situation and by reliance on expected increase production, by accepting LCTs completed up to 15 March as available for service on 1 May, this availability figure has now been raised to 695 of which 168 as before are U.S. craft.
4. On 1 May it is anticipated there will also be in the U.K. the following LCTs:
   a. Craft in use for training naval crews for new production LCTs, which will come forward during buildup; 18.
   b. Production from 15 March to 1 April; 60.
   c. Production from 1 April to 13 April; 57.
5. The reassessment by Admiralty also shows that if the date of OVERLORD is postponed until 1 June the availability figure on that date would be 782 of which 168 would be U.S. craft as above. There will also be the 18 training craft as in paragraph 4 plus the production figure from 15 April to 31 May, namely 65 LCTs. Please note that this information cancels our reply in B-55 to paragraph D of your W-29.
6. Admiralty have signaled to B.A.D. Washington[75] revised figures correcting Appendix B to Annex 5 of Combined Chiefs of Staff; 428 for LCTs.
7. It is hoped that the foregoing, which gives new figures and supersedes all previous information on LCT availability, will clear up all earlier misunderstanding. It certainly gives a better picture and is probably the very most we can expect.
8. I would add that if any further LCTs come forward for service as a result of improved construction rates, or for another reason, they will be allocated to OVERLORD. We are definitely assured of this.
9. As regards the serviceability factor of 85% for LCTs mentioned by General Eisenhower in his message to you, please note that this is based on all past experience with British

---

74 This was the first series of cables over what would be an increasingly intense discussion over obtaining the required number of landing craft, particularly now that the width of the invasion force had been increased to five divisions.
75 An unknown department.

forces and has been confirmed in recent exercises.[76] If sufficient time and facilities could be made available to lay up LCTs for a period before OVERLORD this figure would be bettered for the assault phase. But it must be remembered that this would be paid for later in the buildup, since LCTs which would have been coming forward after repair to replace casualties would not, repeat not, then be available.[77] Consequently, I believe it is better and safer to work on a factor of 85% serviceability for the overall picture.

Exchanging Corps Commanders with Devers

Eisenhower to Marshall   29 January   *No Reference*
I am a bit puzzled as to why Devers has not stated the name of the Corps Commander he requires. His query is now more than a week old and I am quite ready to send a man along as quickly as he will name him. The reason I want to do it quickly is that I want Collins to get into the saddle as soon as he arrives.

Eisenhower to Devers   1 February   *Ref: M-68*
In accordance with a request of yours received from General Marshall about ten days ago, I reported that any corps commander here except Gerow was available for service in your Theater. Will you please inform the Chief of Staff immediately as to the name of the corps commander you select because the reassignments can no, repeat no, longer be delayed.

Eisenhower to Marshall   3 February   *Ref: W-10496*
I have just received from Devers a radiogram stating that he no longer desires a Corps Commander from among those now on duty here. Since Collins has already arrived and will take immediate command of a Corps, this gives me one surplus Corps Commander and the consensus of opinion here is that Crittenberger is the one that should be displaced. At this moment I do <u>not</u> see any really suitable local assignment for Crittenberger but I suspect that his return to the United States may create a problem for you, since I assume all your Corps Command positions are filled. Do you desire that I carry him in some capacity for the present or should I send him home?[78]

---

76 Or a 15 per cent breakdown factor, making landing craft unavailable for the second wave.
77 The planners intended to keep all their landing craft working in the run up to OVERLORD and those scheduled to be serviced around D-Day would be used to replace losses.
78 This is another example of Devers holding onto experienced staff in Italy, staff which Eisenhower wanted. Crittenberger would be promoted to command VI Corps shortly afterwards when General Lucas was relieved.

2

FEBRUARY 1944

First Thoughts on OVERLORD and ANVIL

Eisenhower to Marshall   *6 February*   *Ref: W-10678*

I have just returned from an inspection of two of our divisions and find them in good spirits and engaged in really efficient training. I understand that there is some difference of opinion between the U.S. and the British Chiefs of Staff as to the overall picture for the European spring campaign. I am particularly anxious to have your personal views on the problems we have presented because I feel that as long as you and I are in complete coordination as to purpose, that you in Washington and I here can do a great deal towards achieving the best overall results.

As you know from my former messages, I honestly believe that a five division assault is the minimum that gives us a really favorable chance for success. I have earnestly hoped that this could be achieved by 31 May without sacrificing a strong ANVIL.[1] One extra month of landing craft production in the United Kingdom and the United States, including L.S.T.s,[2] should help a lot. I think that late experience in Italy tends to confirm the necessity for having the OVERLORD landing force sufficiently strong so that it can achieve quick success, particularly in securing ports. If we have to start small and wait for a build up, we are running bigger risks than we should.[3]

Moreover, I believe that late developments in Italy create the possibility that the necessary forces there cannot be disentangled in time to put on a strong ANVIL. This is a factor that must be considered. Some compensation would arise from the fact that as long as the enemy fights in Italy as earnestly and as bitterly as he is doing now, the action there will in some degree compensate for the absence of an ANVIL.[4]

Most of our organization problems are being solved and we are definitely making progress, but the overall decisions involving OVERLORD and ANVIL must be quickly crystallized and given to us so that we may proceed definitely with our work.

Count up all the divisions that will be in the Mediterranean, including two newly arrived U.S. divisions, consider the requirements in Italy in view of the mountain masses north of Rome, and then consider what influence on your problem a sizable number of divisions heavily engaged or advancing rapidly in southern France, will have on OVERLORD.[5]

---

1 Extra landing craft could be obtained by postponing OVERLORD from 1 May to 1 June. The number of vehicles each division could take ashore also had to be cut to 2500.
2 Landing Ship Tank, which could carry eighteen 30 ton tanks or 22 × 25 ton tanks or 33 × 3-ton trucks and had berths for 217 men.
3 Eisenhower is referring to the Anzio beachhead, which was in difficulties, and possibly the initial landing on the Italian mainland at Salerno in September 1943.
4 The combined aim of the Italian campaign and Operation ANVIL was to engage as many German divisions in the Mediterranean as possible, stopping them from moving north to counter Operation OVERLORD.
5 In other words would increased pressure in Italy or an invasion of southern France engage more German divisions.

I will use my influence here to agree with your desires. I merely wish to be certain that localitis[6] is not developing and that the pressures on you have not warped your judgment.

Marshall to Eisenhower   *6 February*   *Ref: 78*

Judging from the discussion and differences of opinion at the present time, the British and American Chiefs of Staff seem to have completely reversed themselves and we have become Mediterraneanites[7], and they heavily pro-OVERLORD. The following are personal views:

OVERLORD of course is paramount and it must be launched on a reasonably secure basis, of which you are the best judge. Our difficulties in reaching a decision have been complicated by a battle of numbers, that is, a failure to reach a common ground as to what would be the actual facilities. As to this, the British and American planners here yesterday afternoon agreed that there is sufficient lift to stage at least a seven division OVERLORD and at the same time a two division ANVIL on the basis of May 31st.[8] This is in apparent disagreement with the British planners in London, or with Montgomery, I don't know which.

As to ANVIL my personal feeling is this: Do you <u>personally</u> consider that of the combined landing craft thought to be available, so much must go to OVERLORD that only a one division lift will remain for ANVIL?[9] If you consider this absolutely imperative then it should be done that way. However, the effect will be that approximately eight or nine less divisions will be heavily engaged with the enemy, divisions which will be available in the Mediterranean. Can you afford to lose this pressure, considering an additional factor, that we are almost certain to get an uprising in Southern France to a far greater degree than in the North?[10]

As to the British preferences to the Italian situation I would say this: If we find ourselves in Italy in early April still unable to establish our lines north of Rome, then ANVIL would of necessity be practically abandoned, because we would have a good and sufficient fight on our hands for a considerable number of troops and the use for at least a one divisional lift for end runs.[11] However, if we have established ourselves north of Rome by that time, early April, there will not be a place for all the divisions available in the Mediterranean, unless it is believed that an advance into the Po valley is the profitable enterprise. With this I do not agree, because it would inevitably require heavy amphibious lift in order to get the lines through the mountains and would involve innumerable delays.[12]

Initial Landing Craft Estimates

Eisenhower to Marshall   *8 February*   *Ref: W-10786*

Thank you for your No. 78. You have placed your finger on the point that, to me, appears critical in the Mediterranean aspect of our spring campaign, which is that we must strive in every way to promote a battle there that engages efficiently <u>all</u> combat forces we can make available. This is the point I have stressed in local conversations. The great advantage of a

---

6 Being biased towards local operations.
7 In support of Operation ANVIL and increasing the pressure in Italy.
8 Launching OVERLORD on 31st May and ANVIL a few weeks later.
9 ANVIL would have to be cancelled if landing craft were withdrawn from the Mediterranean and one of Eisenhower's last tasks while Commander in Chief of the Mediterranean Theater was to draft a plan for ANVIL to coincide with OVERLORD as a two pronged attack against German-held France. Montgomery wanted to abandon ANVIL, reducing it to an intelligence threat rather than an actual landing. Smith and planners in England agreed, believing that the two landings were too remote from each other.
10 Marshall is weighing up how to deploy as many divisions as possible in the scenario, to keep more German divisions in the Mediterranean and away from Normandy.
11 Further landings along the Italian coast to outflank the German defensive lines.
12 General Mark Clark's Fifth Army was stuck at Monte Cassino and Anzio remained a small beachhead until mid-May.

successful ANVIL is that it would open up a certain channel through which all our forces could be engaged, and would have an earlier effect upon the enemy situation in France than would a continuation of the Italian campaign, even on an intensive basis. As you pointed out, however, if we cannot achieve our aims in Italy we are committed to that battle and probably with everything we have than there.[13]

The time element does not permit us to wait too long to make certain of what is going to happen in Italy, and we must soon make our estimate of what will occur and plan accordingly.

To disabuse[14] your mind about my own personal approach this problem, I must go back a little bit into history. The first time I heard any description of the OVERLORD plan, was long before I knew I would have anything to do with it. This was subsequent to the experience we had gained in the Sicilian operation.[15] A brief outline of the plan was given to me by Major General Chambers,[16] then visiting Algiers. After listening to him I told him that I believed there had been some misinterpretation of our experience in Pantellaria and in Sicily,[17] and that the attack was being made on too narrow a front and with insufficient land forces.

About the end of December, when I knew I was going to the United States for a short visit, I had General Montgomery come to see me and General Smith and told him to go to England to study the plan in detail. I told him to seek for an intensification of efforts to increase the troop load in OVERLORD, which I told him in my opinion, was necessary, but emphasizing also my desire to retain ANVIL on at least a two-division basis. I pointed out that in Sicily, where we attacked with six divisions, we had some bad moments at Gela,[18] and that if we could have landed more motor equipment, including armor, in the first assault on the Eastern coast, that in my estimation we would have overrun the island much more rapidly than we did.

While I was in Washington I received the first analysis of OVERLORD made by Montgomery and Smith.[19] That estimate agreed with my own views, except that their immediate answer was to abandon ANVIL but adhere to the target date of the 1st of May. I felt so strongly that ANVIL should be preserved, while we were achieving the necessary strength for OVERLORD, that I replied we would accept a date of 31st of May in order to get an additional month's production of every kind of landing craft from both countries. As a matter of fact, I think the 31st of May date is in some respects a better one than the first day of the month, because of the added time given to our Air Forces, upon which we are depending so heavily for success.

It was not until I had formed my own conclusions on these matters and had submitted a long telegram to the Combined Chiefs of Staff, that I learned that the British Chiefs of Staff more or less went along with my own views, except that I believe some of them have never attached the same importance to ANVIL as I have.[20]

---

13 If troops could land on the southern coast of France and advance quickly north, the new beachhead would divert German divisions from Normandy.

14 To free from misconception.

15 Before July 1943; the COSSAC directive for amphibious operations from the UK was issued in April 1943.

16 Brigadier-General William E. Chambers was an American staff officer working on COSSAC invasion planning.

17 Pantellaria is a small island off the south coast of Sicily. Its capture was codenamed Operation CORKSCREW and it was used as a vital base for Allied aircraft during the invasion of Sicily, codenamed Operation HUSKY.

18 Seventh US Army landed in the Gulf of Gela area of Sicily.

19 The first week in January.

20 Montgomery wanted to abandon ANVIL and concentrate on increasing the commitment to OVERLORD.

In the various campaigns of this war, I have occasionally had to modify slightly my own conceptions of a campaign, in order to achieve a unity of purpose and effort. I think this is inescapable in Allied operations but I assure you that I have never yet failed to give you my own clear personal convictions about every project and plan in prospect. So far as I am aware, no one here has tried to urge me to present any particular view, nor do I believe that I am particularly affected by localitis. I merely recognize that OVERLORD, which has been supported earnestly for more than two years by the U.S. Chiefs of Staff, represents for the United States and the United Kingdom a crisis in the European war. Real success should do much to hasten the end of this conflict but a reverse will have opposite repercussions, from which we would recover with the utmost difficulty.

To give you a brief picture of what I believe to be the necessary:

• It is my personal conviction that we must assault in the first wave with five divisions heavily reinforced with armor.

• The assault must be preceded by two months of intensive air preparation.

• We will drop at least one full Airborne division and one, and possibly even two, additional R.C.T.s[21] at dawn on D-Day. We have the necessary resources for this.

• We want to reinforce divisions on the second tide of the day. These must be in landing craft but will be loaded so as to economize on craft.

• At the same time we must have the strongest possible support from the Mediterranean, so planned as to utilize the great bulk of the forces we have there.

• From D-Day to D plus 60 this thing is going to absorb everything the United Nations can possibly pour into it. Thereafter it should assume the form of an operation for which the main requirements will be land forces, cargo shipping and tactical air strength.

Handy to Smith   *8 February*   *Ref: R-9085*

Eisenhower will have had General Marshall's message before this and no repetition is necessary. Sorry the connection was so bad. The figures I gave you this afternoon were as follows:

OVERLORD as of 15 May:

AGC-LSH,[22] 1 U.S., 3 British, 4 total
Relief Headquarters ships, 2 U.S. APA[23] and 1 U.S. AKA[24] are fitted as relief Headquarters ships
APA- LSI (L),[25] 7 U.S., 17 British, 24 total (Note: Includes 1 British LSI (L) now in Southeast Asia and 2 British LSI (L) in trooping which can be made available for either OVERLORD or ANVIL. An executive order as to their allocation will be required)

---

21 Regimental Combat Team; a US infantry regiment and its combat support and logistics troops.
22 Amphibious General Communications Vessel.
23 Attack Transport Ships would take troops close to the beach and then transfer troops to smaller landing craft.
24 Attack Cargo Ship which carried 14 LCVP, 8 LCM across the Channel.
25 Landing Ship, Infantry, British term for the Attack Transport Ship.

XAP,[26] 3 U.S., 3 total   AKA, 6 U.S., 6 total
LSI (M),[27] 3 British, 3 total   LSI (S), 6 British, 6 total
LSI (H), 21 British, 21 total   LSG,[28] 2 British, 2 total
LSD,[29] 2 British, 2 total   LST,[30] 142 U.S., 49 British, 191 total
LCT,[31] 190 U.S., 616 British, 806 total   LCI (L),[32] 94 U.S., 60 British, 154 total

Our planners estimate that the shipping listed above would carry 170,000 personnel and 20,200 vehicles. The figures were based on QUADRANT[33] serviceability factors and your loading data for each type of craft. The figures assume that three British LSI (L) will be assigned to OVERLORD and include the additional American assault shipping and craft which has been made available.

The combined planners figure that, in addition to the above, the following would be available for ANVIL as of 1 or 15 May:

AGS-LSH, 1 U.S., 2 British, 3 total
Special Headquarters ships, 2 U.S. (the USS Biscayne and Duane. These are specially fitted as smaller headquarters ships), 2 total.

LSI (L), 9 British, 9 total   XAP, 3 U.S., 3 total
LSI (M) 1 British, 1 total   LSI (H) 2 British (fitted as a Brigade Headquarters ship) 2 total
LSI (S) 1 British, 1 total   LSG, 1 British, 1 total
LSD, 1 British, 1 total   LST, 48 US, 29 British, 77 total
LCT, 60 US, 70 British, 130 total   LCI (L) 62 US, 70 British 132 total

The figures given above for OVERLORD and ANVIL have been agreed to by the combined planners. The combined planners agree that there is lift for at least seven divisions in personnel and eight in motor transport for OVERLORD, still leaving a two division lift for ANVIL.

The above represents all the assault shipping and landing craft that the planners figure can be made available for a late May OVERLORD. As to your question about LSTs, the above figures do not count the April production. The LSTs are built on inland waterways. They must be moved to New Orleans, crewed, brought to Hampton Roads[34] or New York to join convoys, and then proceed to the U.K. From the time an LST arrives in New Orleans until it is in U.K. has been at least six weeks.

Will you please give us a list of the assault shipping and landing craft which you figure will be available and what you estimate they will lift. If we have this data, we at least can determine the differences and run down the discrepancies.

The combined planners have not been able to get an entirely satisfactory solution to the M.T. ships[35] you asked for. It looks as though they will have to come from one of the

---

26 Merchant cargo ship.
27 Landing Ship, Infantry, suffix L for Large and 1800 troops, M for Medium and S for Small and 800 troops, H for Hand-hoisting.
28 Landing Ship, Gantry, which carried 15 Landing Craft Medium, or LCMs, carrying tanks.
29 Landing Ship, Dock, which also carried LCMs.
30 Landing Ship, Tank, which carried 18 × 30 ton tanks or 22 × 25 ton tanks or 33 × 3-ton trucks.
31 Landing Craft, Tank, for landing tanks on beaches.
32 Landing Craft, Infantry (Large) could carry 210 soldiers.
33 The QUADRANT conference which approved COSSAC's OVERLORD plan in August 1943.
34 The US Navy and US Coastguard shipyards in southeast Virginia.
35 Similar to LSTs.

following sources: Your build-up in U.K. (BOLERO[36] and SICKLE[37]), Mediterranean-Indian Ocean maintenance, Russian protocol, U.K. imports, or Pacific requirements. The matter is being examined by the combined Transportation Committee as a matter of urgency.

Out of your stated requirement of 197 squadrons,[38] the combined planners agree that there is still an apparent shortage of seven fighter squadrons.

| *Marshall to Eisenhower* | *9 February* | *Ref: 93* |

It is desired that you deliver the following message to the British Chiefs of Staff from the U.S. Chiefs of Staff:

Begin: As a result of an exchange of communications between General Marshall and General Eisenhower and several telephone conversations between General Handy and General Smith, a mutual understanding appears to have been reached as to the facilities available for OVERLORD and ANVIL. The U.S. Chiefs of Staff now propose that the issue be finally decided in the conference between General Eisenhower, as a Representative of the U.S. Chiefs of Staff, and the British Chiefs of Staff. End.[39]

General Hull and Admiral Cooke, who have all the facts regarding landing craft, are proceeding to London immediately to be available to you in a purely advisory capacity in this matter. You will be informed when they leave and expected time of arrival.[40]

| *Eisenhower to Marshall* | *11 February* | *Ref: B-142* |

(Note to Code Clerk: Upon deciphering this message deliver it immediately in a double sealed envelope to the Secretary General staff and no one else; for General Marshall's eyes only).

For your personal information I have gone into all the implications of OVERLORD plan versus RANKIN plan in connection with possible British and American spheres of activity on the continent.[41]

It is impossible to divorce RANKIN planning from OVERLORD planning, since the most likely contingency is that OVERLORD will develop into a phase of RANKIN. Nevertheless, if the decision is made on higher political levels to switch British and American areas of responsibility, I am certain that there will be no, repeat no, trouble in transferring British and American troops when the situation stabilizes sufficiently to take the necessary logistical moves. You may consider it desirable to inform the President accordingly.

---

36 The movement of one million US troops to Britain was planned by General Henry H. Arnold (1886–1950), USAF; the word BOLERO was substituted for Great Britain in correspondence.
37 The movement to and build up in of 69 US Air Force groups in Great Britain.
38 Originally 192, revised to 197 by Handy on 8 February.
39 While Eisenhower agreed that ANVIL was important, he was concerned about its feasibility because he was close to the situation.
40 Major-General John E. Hull (1895–1975), Marshall's representative, and Rear Admiral Charles M. Cooke, Jr. (1886–1970) principal planning officer for Admiral King, Commander in Chief of the US Fleet and Chief of Naval Operations.
41 COSSAC also prepared Operation RANKIN in case of a sudden change in Germany's position. (A) was the 'substantial weakening of the strength and morale of the German armed forces' to the extent that a successful assault could be made by Anglo-American forces before OVERLORD, (B) was the German withdrawal from occupied countries, and (C) was the German unconditional surrender and cessation of organized resistance.

A New Commander for the 101st Airborne Division

Eisenhower to Marshall   9 February   *Ref: B-126*

General William C. Lee's[42] recent heart attack will make it impossible for him to return to command his airborne division. My present thought is to take Brigadier General Max Taylor[43] from the 82nd Airborne Division to replace Lee, make one of the regimental commanders second in command of the 82nd Division, and give Raff[44], who, as you will remember, did so well as a commander during the Tunisian campaign, an airborne regiment. It occurs to me that you might prefer to send an airborne division commander from the States as replacement for Lee, considering the promotions involved in my solution, and if so why would prefer Swing, Miley or Chapman in the order named.[45] If not, I'm sure Taylor will make a good division commander, and he has the advantage of combat experience.

Marshall to Eisenhower   9 February   *Ref: 92*

If you prefer Taylor to Miley or Chapman, assign him accordingly. Swing must go to the Pacific with his Division. I think Raff an excellent assignment, but I should have thought he would be a good Brigadier.

General Patton Requests his Engineer

Eisenhower to Marshall   12 February   *Ref: W-11026*

In the various requests I have made upon General Devers for officers with troop commands in Italy, I have accepted his refusals without question. However, in the case of Brigadier General Garrison H. Davison,[46] Engineer of the Seventh Army, I should like to make an appeal to you.

   This officer has been with General Patton since the landing at Casablanca and is not only widely experienced in the technical requirements of engineers on the battlefield, but has become a mainspring in his staff organization. In view of the fact that practically all of the U.S. battle experienced officers on this side of the Atlantic are now in the Mediterranean Theater, I strongly feel that our senior commanders are clearly entitled to a few individuals in this category.[47]

   General Patton has personally requested me to make this appeal to you, and I completely concur in his need for an engineer officer of Davidson's caliber and experience.

Marshall to Eisenhower   20 February   *Ref: 148*

In the matter of Davidson, Devers states that he is the only key officer left on the Seventh Army staff, that he has released to Patton practically all his (Patton's) former key officers, that Davidson is needed to carry on the planning and organize staff, and that he cannot be released now. In view of Devers strong statement I do not feel justified in summarily taking Davidson away from him.

---

42 Major-General William C. Lee (1895–1948), known as 'Bill', was often referred to as the 'Father of the US Airborne'. General Taylor instructed his paratroopers to shout 'Bill Lee' when they jumped on D-Day.
43 Major-General Maxwell D. Taylor (1901–1987), known as 'Max' was appointed commander of the 101st.
44 Colonel Edson D. Raff (1907–2003), nicknamed 'Little Caesar', would command 507th Parachute Infantry Regiment after D-Day; they would become known as 'Raff's Ruffians'.
45 Major-General Joseph M. Swing (1894–1984) and the 11th Airborne were deployed to the Pacific in June 1944; Major-General William M. Miley (1897–1997), nicknamed 'Bud', and 17th Airborne Division deployed to mainland Europe in December 1944; Major-General Eldridge Chapman (1895–1954), nicknamed 'Gerry' and 13th Airborne Division deployed to mainland Europe early in 1944.
46 Brigadier-General Garrison H. Davidson (1904–1992).
47 One of several claims made by Eisenhower that he was being denied experienced officers he knew from the Mediterranean campaign.

Compromising the Shipping Plan[48]

Eisenhower to Marshall   *14 February*   *Ref: W–11152*

This morning Admiral Cooke and General Hall met with me and my Naval commander,[49] together with members of our respective staffs. It appeared to me that all concerned tackled the job of adjusting differences in conceptions and calculations in a spirit of common understanding as to the tremendous issues involved in the campaign and in mutual determination to reach the best possible solution.

I am quite certain that all matters of landing craft and personnel and cargo shipping are going to be adjusted with reasonable satisfaction, except so far as LSTs are concerned. We are working towards the end of meeting essential requirements of OVERLORD and still preserving the two division lift in the Mediterranean in order that strong supporting operations can be undertaken there. However, we found that even counting on a possible increment of ten additional LSTs from the U.S. and ten additional from a higher serviceability figure in the U.K., we would still have an unacceptable situation with regard to LSTs because of the great effect on the vehicular build up. It was the tentative opinion that conditions of the tide, currents, winds and enemy action will combine to make doubtful the efficiency of the ordinary MT ship in landing vehicles during the build-up stage, until after we have secured and have placed sizeable ports operation. Yet these vehicles are absolutely essential to use if our forces are to be mobile and able to capture the ports we need.[50]

Unless the Naval conferences which are now proceeding can devise some way of overcoming our difficulty, our only course is to turn to the Mediterranean for additional increments of LSTs, of which there will be remaining only 77 in the area after current commitments are met. Although unloading from MT ships should not present as great a difficulty in the Mediterranean as on the exposed Channel Coast, I am convinced that a further reduction of Mediterranean LSTs in the number of 20 to 30 would bring a response that ANVIL would be impossible.

Admiral Cook has also advised me that our naval supporting fire is too weak. This question, as well as that of additional escorts in the Channel, has not yet been fully discussed.[51]

We have not reached the final conclusions and already the great value of sending Cooke and Hull here has become apparent. I am fully prepared to accept many of their recommendations, and the purpose of this telegram is merely to keep you informed as to our progress and to let you know that from our early conferences the LST appears to be the one great question in the landing craft problem to which no really satisfactory answer now seems apparent.

Eisenhower to Marshall   *19 February*   *Ref: W-11500*

I met this morning with the British Chiefs of Staff and presented my conclusions. The gist of the plans I presented was the acceptance of a number of expedients in the assault and build-up, in an effort to preserve the strength in the Mediterranean for the two-division ANVIL.

Expedients included increasing personnel loads, trading AKAs to the Mediterranean for a number of LSTs and LCI(L)s, counting on increased serviceability factors and the like.

---

48 Conferences at Norfolk House (SHAEF headquarters) over the next few days came up with a compromised shipping plan.

49 Possibly Admiral Cunningham, First Sea Lord of the Admiralty and Chief of the Naval Staff.

50 Landing Ship Tank as opposed to Mechanical Transports; they were needed to deliver large numbers of tanks and other vehicles to the beachhead and the argument is that LSTs perform better in heavy seas.

51 This is direct fire at targets close to the beaches during the landing, required until the ground troops have advanced far enough inland to allow artillery to be deployed ashore.

Admittedly, this has occasioned a certain loss of flexibility in our tactical plan and the acceptance of additional risks and doubtful factors that are undesirable. But when we began the
development of the plan we felt that the preservation of an ability in the Mediterranean to
do ANVIL was of great importance to us. [52]

Developments of the past week in Italy have been leading me personally to the conclusion
that ANVIL will probably not be possible because of the tactical situation in the area. [53] It
begins to appear to me that all the troops available will have to be used for the Italian operations; yet our whole sacrifice here in favor of preparation for ANVIL would go for nothing if
the operation cannot be carried out in any event.

Planning for these operations both here and in the Mediterranean must be quickly established on the firmest possible basis. The minimum requirements which I submitted this
morning to the British Chiefs of Staff, which will undoubtedly go to you at once, should not
be considered acceptable except on the basis of at least a two division ANVIL.

For this purpose, I told the British Chiefs of Staff today that I consider it of the utmost
urgency that the Combined Chiefs of Staff quickly decide whether the prospects in the
Mediterranean can really offer any reasonable chance of executing ANVIL. Immediately
upon any decision by the Combined Chiefs of Staff that ANVIL cannot be executed on a
full two division assault scale, then we should promptly be authorized to count on taking
from the Mediterranean everything that we need over the pre-SEXTANT estimates for that
Theater, so that the added strength here and the continuous fighting in Italy many compensate for the absence of ANVIL. [54]

Smith to Handy   *21 February*   *Ref: B-176*

General Eisenhower has read the transcript of our conversation and confirms my interpretation of his views with respect to ANVIL. However, he emphasizes again the fact that if a
decision is made not to, repeat not to, undertake ANVIL, then we should be assured of immediate call on the additional shipping and craft which can be used to reinforce OVERLORD. As
you know, the allocation proposed by General Eisenhower to keep ANVIL alive has entailed
a sacrifice, particularly in flexibility. If ANVIL can not, repeat not, be mounted, which seems
most likely now in view of the trend of the battle in Italy, then we will have lost a diversion-
ary effect of an attack from the south and must strengthen our own assault accordingly. It
seems to us that the final decision on ANVIL could be made sometime during March and it
certainly should be made not, repeat not, later than April 1st, if we are to have any benefit
from landing craft from the Mediterranean.

New subject: Cooke did not, repeat not, give us much encouragement on ten additional
LSTs from American production, about which we talked on the phone last week. We understand that time to provide these LSTs may set back the training of future crews to a later
date than is planned at present by our Navy, but know you will understand that even the
seven or eight additional LSTs will make an enormous difference to us now we have reduced

---

52 Eisenhower is prepared to make changes to the OVERLORD planning to make sure that ANVIL goes
ahead. However, he is concerned that the compromises will be for nothing, and will jeopardize the Normandy
battle, if the landing in southern France does not go ahead.
53 Fifth Army's second attempt to make progress at Cassino, Operation AVENGER, began on 17 February
after the monastery area had been bombed; it ended in failure a day later.
54 The Combined Chiefs of Staff conferences in November and December 1943 were codenamed SEXTANT.
Eisenhower wanted a quick decision so that there was time to move landing craft to the UK if ANVIL was
abandoned.

the flexibility of our operation to an irreducible minimum. Anything you can do to assist in obtaining these additional LSTs will be sincerely appreciated.

Combined Chiefs of Staff to Eisenhower 21 February   *Ref: 151*
Reference your proposal to British Chiefs of Staff on February 19th and their COS(W-1156) to United States Chiefs of Staff, urging complete abandonment of ANVIL:

You were delegated to represent United States Chiefs of Staff in conference with British Chiefs of Staff on the question of OVERLORD – ANVIL. At the present moment we have no clear cut statement of the basis of your agreement or disagreement with them, and the situation is therefore seriously complicated. Please seek an immediate conference and reach agreement or carefully stated disagreement, and the Joint Chiefs of Staff will support your decision, subject of course to the approval of the President.

Admiral Leahy[55] to Eisenhower   21 February   *Ref: 154*
At conference Joint Chiefs of Staff just had with the President this date, the memorandum of the United States Chiefs of Staff furnished you for information in 153 was read to him, and the President directed that the following be sent to you as being additional to the prime military considerations: "call attention that we are committed to a Third Power and I do not feel we have any right to abandon this commitment for ANVIL without taking the matter up with that Third Power".[56]

Combined Chiefs of Staff to Eisenhower 21 February   *Ref: 133*
United States Chiefs of Staff furnish herewith for your information, the text of a memorandum that they have this date submitted to the representatives of the British Chiefs of Staff.

United States Chiefs of Staff have considered the message of the British Chiefs of Staff, COS W-1156, and General Eisenhower's proposal, COS W-1157. We agree that the present state of uncertainty regarding ANVIL should be terminated. We disagree that ANVIL should be canceled. On the contrary, in view of the fact resources can be made available for the two division lift in the ANVIL assault, it is our opinion that the decision should be made to plan to mount ANVIL with a two division lift, but that all combat ground forces in the Mediterranean should be considered available to further the occupation and security of the Rome area.[57]

United States and French units being rehabilitated should be re-equipped and trained for ANVIL as required. It should be possible to do this without interfering with the war in Italy. Consideration should be given to the use of French units in the ANVIL assault, some of which are now receiving amphibious training in North Africa.

The foregoing views of the United States Chiefs of Staff, if agreed to, would be accepted by the Combined Chiefs of Staff, with the understanding that if the campaign in Italy has not developed favorably for the Allies by April 1, the situation will be reviewed with a view to a new decision as to the furtherance of the campaign in the Mediterranean, which may require the deferment of ANVIL.[58]

We agree with General Eisenhower's recommendations in paragraph 6 of COS W-1157, that six United States AKA's be reallocated from OVERLORD to ANVIL and that 20 British

55 Fleet Admiral William D. Leahy (1875–1959), President Roosevelt's Chief of Staff.
56 A commitment to ANVIL had been made by Roosevelt, Churchill and Stalin at the Tehran conference; Roosevelt is concerned about the implications of abandoning ANVIL without consulting Moscow.
57 The Combined Chiefs of Staff agree with Eisenhower that ANVIL must go ahead.
58 Setting 1 April as the review date over the Italian campaign, allows time to transfer resources to the UK to join OVERLORD.

LSTs and 21 British LCI(L)'s be reallocated from ANVIL to OVERLORD in order to meet OVERLORD requirements, and still retain sufficient craft for a two-division lift for ANVIL.

We noted that in paragraph 7 of COS W-1157, Supreme Commander, Allied Expeditionary Force, reports that there will still be a shortage of 15 LSTs' for OVERLORD, which must be provided from increasing the loading, increased serviceability, United States production, and increased serviceability of LCT's, whose vehicle lift can be substituted for LST's. The United States will provide seven LST's at the expense of LST training, but these seven LST's will not arrive in the United Kingdom until about the middle of May.

In accordance with General Eisenhower's request in paragraph 8 of COS W-1157, we recommend that Combined Chiefs of Staff confirm the allocation of 64 MT ships from combined sources and three LSI(L)'s and two LST's from British sources.

The necessity for, and provision of, additional escort groups should be considered in conjunction with the overall Naval support requirements of the Naval staff of the United Kingdom and the United States.

We recommend that the attached message be sent to General Eisenhower (enclosure and a copy be sent to General Wilson for information). [59]

Eisenhower to Marshall   *22 February*   *Ref: W-11674*
I think your 153 represents the best decision that can be made under current circumstances. While prospects for ANVIL, in the hoped for strength of a two division assault and a total strength of at least ten divisions, seems to me to have deteriorated in the past ten days, I still believe we should preserve for some time sufficient flexibility as to insure, as far as we can, against a possible stagnation in the Mediterranean situation at the time of OVERLORD, with only a portion of our troops there engaged against the enemy. I am strengthened in the belief that we should retain more flexibility, because of the fact that if a review in the latter part of March should indicate that ANVIL is not feasible, we could still reinforce our means of buildup in OVERLORD from the equipment in the Mediterranean. We must not lose the initiative in the Mediterranean at the very time when we need it most. However, the orders to the Mediterranean Theater should positively state that ANVIL planning is not to interfere with the current battle. These orders should be most emphatic.

We are having a meeting with the British Chiefs of Staff this morning, so as to settle this matter. In my opinion it should be reviewed again in sufficient time so that if it becomes apparent that there is no hope for ANVIL, as now conceived, the movement of equipment, additional to that already agreed that could start by April 1st.

In this connection, and reference the message from the President contained in your number 154, I suggest that the Third Power should be informed that ANVIL is of course contingent upon the necessary degree of early success in the present Italian campaign, but that in any event alterations in the Mediterranean Theater will be conducted on such a basis as to employ the bulk of our troops offensively. If this notification were given now, we would have in advance the necessary flexibility in decision when the time comes.

With respect to possibility of doing anything concrete towards ANVIL in the Mediterranean while the present battle is going on, we must face facts as they are. The present battle demands every available resource. While two experienced American divisions

---

59 The compromise was to make alterations to OVERLORD planning and keep planning for ANVIL. The review would give time to move shipping from the Mediterranean to the English Channel if the Italian campaign did not allow for ANVIL to go ahead. It was a compromise reached only after the President reminded the Combined Chiefs of Staff that he had made a commitment to the landing in southern France to Stalin and would have to refer its cancellation to Moscow.

are now out, or coming out of the line for a period of rehabilitation, the prospects grow stronger that they will have to re-enter the same battle within a few weeks. However, in the meantime they are getting ready to fight again and if the situation should suddenly turn in our favor, and they should not be needed again in Italy, their additional training for ANVIL could be quickly accomplished. What we must have definitely in sight eventually, is a total strength of some ten to twelve divisions to push into South France after the opening is made. If incessant battling in Italy should continue to absorb the great bulk of the total United Nations resources there, then, as you mentioned in a letter to me, the situation automatically resolves itself.[60]

Smith to Devers, Hull and Cooke   *24 February*   *Ref: M-128*
There follows two messages from the British Chiefs of Staff to the Joint Staff Mission, Washington, dated February 23.

[MESSAGE 1]
Following from Chiefs of Staff COS W-4168, referenced JSM 1528 and 1529, the following conclusions were agreed this morning at meetings held between British Chiefs of Staff and General Eisenhower, representing the U.S. Chiefs of Staff:

The campaign in Italy must, until further orders, have overriding priority over all existing and future operations in the Mediterranean, and will have first call on all resources, land, sea and air, in that Theater.

Subject to the above, the Allied Commander-in-Chief, Mediterranean Commander, should prepare alternative plans and make such preparations as can be undertaken without prejudice to operations in Italy, for amphibious operations in the Mediterranean, with the objective of contributing to OVERLORD by containing and engaging the maximum number of enemy forces. The first of these alternatives should be ANVIL on approximately the scale and date of originally contemplated, i.e. a two division assault building up to about ten divisions, to be launched shortly after OVERLORD. Full considerations will be given to the maximum use of French Forces.[61]

The Allied Commander-in-Chief, Mediterranean Theater, should, for the present, base these plans on the assumption that the assault shipping and landing craft at present allocated to him will be at his disposal with the following exceptions:

a) 20 LSTs, to consist of as many British LSTs as possible, the balance being U.S., and 21 British LCI(L)s are reallocated from ANVIL to OVERLORD and will sail for United Kingdom on or about April 1st, after having been refitted;

b) 6 U.S. AKAs are reallocated from OVERLORD to ANVIL.[62]

The arrangements set out in paragraphs 2 and 3 above will be reviewed on 20th March, in the light of the situation then existing in Italy. Unless, as a result of this review, it is then

60 The second attempt to capture Cassino, breaking through the Gustav Line and opening the road north to Rome, started on 17 February and ended in failure the following day. It would be another four weeks before Fifth US Army would be ready to attack again, during which time the Anzio beachhead remained in a precarious position.
61 In summary, continue to commit fully to the Italian campaign, to keep German forces engaged there, and land on the south coast of France with two divisions, building up to ten divisions.
62 The exchange of AKAs for LSTs and LCI(L)s.

decided that ANVIL, on the scale and date quoted in paragraph 2 above, is practicable, six landing craft (over and above a one division ship-to-shore lift) as can profitably be employed in OVERLORD, will forthwith be withdrawn from Mediterranean. The Allied C-in-C, Mediterranean, will then revise plans prepared under paragraph 2 above on the basis of the assault lift remaining in the Mediterranean.[63]

If conclusions to paragraph 1 to paragraph 4 above are approved by the President and Prime Minister, they will be transmitted forthwith to Generals Eisenhower and Wilson.

[MESSAGE 2]
Following from Chiefs of Staff COS W-1168 (2); agreed that the Minister of War Transport, in consultation with W.S.A., should be invited to provide 64 additional M.T. ships required for OVERLORD.

1) Took note with satisfaction that the U.S. would provide seven additional LSTs for OVERLORD and expressed the hope that these craft would not, repeat not, arrive in the United Kingdom later than mid May.

2) Took note that the British would make available the following additional resources for OVERLORD: one LSH, three LSI(L)s, one LSI(H), two LSDs.

Obtaining Experienced Corps Commanders

Marshall to Eisenhower   *17 February*   *Ref: 124*
Detailed reports of the 7th Division operation against Kwajalein Island in the Marshalls[64] indicate that General Corlett's[65] training of the division, cooperation with the Navy (Turner incidentally),[66] plan of battle, landing, artillery support, tanks and infantry action, organization of beaches for supply, continuity of methodical effort and even details on burial of the dead, etc., approached perfection. He has been designated to command a Training Corps in Hawaii; if you care to use him as a Corps Commander he will be flown to you immediately.

Eisenhower to Marshall   *19 February*   *Ref: W-11493*
Have consulted my Army Commanders and we are certain that we desire Corlett for assignment as Corps Commander. Due to advanced state in planning it is probable that he would not have command of an Assault Corps but would take over one scheduled for later entry into action. However, he would be available here for consultation with all Division and Corps Commanders in planning, so that his experience would be available to all. Since both Army Commanders are out of the city, I cannot say for certain which of the presently assigned Corps Commanders Corlett will replace. From preliminary conversations I suspect it will be Reinhardt. I personally think that Corlett's early arrival here will be of great advantage to us. Thank you.

---

63 The Italian situation would be reviewed on 20 March and if ANVIL has to be cancelled, the landing craft can be transferred to the UK ready for OVERLORD.
64 An eight day battle starting on 31 January 1944, illustrating that General Marshall was looking for anyone with any combat experience, no matter how limited. General Corlett had earlier commanded the Kiska Task Force which invaded a deserted Kiska Island in the Aleutian Chain in August 1943.
65 Major-General Charles H. Corlett (1889–1971), nicknamed 'Cowboy Pete', took command of XIX Corps which landed on Omaha Beach on 10 June.
66 Admiral Richmond K. Turner (1885–1961), nicknamed 'Terrible', commander of various Amphibious Forces during the Pacific campaign.

Marshall to Eisenhower 20 February *Ref: 148*
Corlett is being brought back by air and will be sent to you as soon as possible.

Eisenhower to Marshall 21 February *Ref: W-11601*
General Bradley and I have just had a conference, in which we agreed that in the absence of fully tested battle commanders we must take as the three Corps Commanders of this Army the very best prospects we can find.[67]

We have concluded that Woodruff[68] should be relieved, although we are not in the position of citing any specific failure on his part. It is merely that our own observations of him and his methods have failed to inspire in us the confidence that we believe we would feel with Corlett commanding that Corps.

Consequently, we expect to put Corlett in command of this Corps in Bradley's Army, but I should like to be authorized, if possible, to inform Woodruff upon his relief here that he will get command of the Corps from which Corlett is now being relieved. I believe this would be only justice to the man, and obviously he has done a good job in training troops at home or he would not have been made a Corps Commander.

Will you please direct the personnel division to expedite Corlett's passage in every possible way.

Eisenhower to Marshall 24 February *Ref: W-11774*
In further acknowledgment of your willingness to give me experienced Corps Commanders, request either Middleton (if in good health) or Fred Walker in exchange for Reinhardt, now commanding VIII Corps. Am counting on receiving Charles Corlett in exchange for Roscoe Woodruff, to whom I trust you will give the Corps Command set up for Corlett.

Marshall to Eisenhower 24 February *Ref: 171*
Corlett arrived on west coast yesterday. He is to have five or six days with his family and then will proceed to the United Kingdom by air.

We have gone into the question of Woodruff's reassignment. General McNair does not want him as a Corps Commander but he is willing to use him eventually as a division commander, although at the present time he has no vacancies for him. I have asked Devers if he desired Woodruff, giving him the circumstances connected with his relief. Devers has replied that he cannot use him now.

It is apparent from the above that you cannot give Woodruff the assurance you would like to. If you do not want to use him in another capacity you should return him to the United States and advise me of the action you have taken.

Marshall to Eisenhower 25 February *Ref: 175*
Reference your W-11774 regarding replacement of Reinhardt with Walker.

The fighting at Cassino did not indicate that Walker had aggressive qualities, such as you will require in a Corps Commander. Furthermore, I would hesitate to take away from Clark in the present difficult situation in Italy a Division Commander who appears to be acceptable to him.[69]

---

67 General Gerow had no combat experience but he had been involved with planning the invasion since July 1943; he had also been Eisenhower's close friend for many years.
68 General Woodruff eventually commanded 24th Infantry Division in the Pacific.
69 Walker would be relieved in June 1944 following a difficult crossing of the Rapido river in Italy in January 1944.

The doctors state that Middleton's arthritic knee would give him trouble if he submits it to severe usage for prolonged periods of cramped position. I telephoned Middleton this morning in the Tennessee area, where he is in command of a Corps in maneuvers, and he tells me that since his long jeep rides and steep climbing in Italy his knee has given him practically no trouble, that it had not given him for years past. He feels competent for duties of the OVERLORD type. I told him that the serious matter was in sending a Corps Commander who might later have to be relieved.[70]

McNarney had talked to General Maietta at Walter Reed regarding Middleton and the general medical feeling is, and McNarney's honest opinion having talked to Middleton some time ago, is that Middleton could go through the training phase, the landing and at least a portion of the fighting phase in OVERLORD; that later the strain of service might require relief. Of course he might be put out as a casualty for other reasons during the same period. I have gone over all Corps Command possibilities and Middleton seems so much more able of those available that I believe it better to take him with the possible later physical complications. Radio me your desires.

Eisenhower to Marshall   *26 February*   *Ref: W-11884*
I agree with your conclusions in the matter of Fred Walker. I also think it wise to get Middleton over here. I am struggling my best to get a high degree of combat experience represented in this Force and I am quite ready to take a chance on Middleton's arthritis.[71]

This means of course I will have another surplus Corps Commander, namely Reinhardt. I dislike exceedingly to pass any problem of this type on you since these men, who were previously selected by others as Corps Commanders, are being relieved merely because we here believe someone else is better suited to do their job and not because of demonstrated inefficiency, I feel that there is no other way out.

However, I am making a complete survey throughout both armies and the Theater to determine whether it would be possible for us to use either Woodruff or Reinhardt to good advantage in any capacity. I will give you the final telegram on the matter in a day or so. In the meantime, I request for you make arrangements to send Middleton.

Marshall to Eisenhower   *28 February*   *Ref: 188*
Middleton is being sent to you immediately. You will be notified when he leaves. McNair can use Reinhardt as a Corps Commander and would like to have him.

As stated in my 171, 24 February, he will use Woodruff as a Division Commander but not as a Corps Commander. It is not necessary that you make a great effort to find a job for them. If you want one or both, keep them; otherwise order them home and we will take care of the problem of reassignment here.

Marshall to Eisenhower   *1 March*   *Ref: 205*
Understand Lucas was replaced in command of VI Corps because according to Devers "he looked old and completely tired out. All were agreed that he had done everything that could have been done with the means available." He was appointed Deputy Commander of the Fifth Army, but this I think was a face saving device.

---

70 Middleton had combat experience in Sicily and Italy but had been relieved following troubles with a knee. He was treated in a Naples hospital before being sent back to the Walter Reed Hospital in Washington DC.
71 On being told of Middleton's medical condition, Bradley is quoted as saying 'I would rather have a man with arthritis in the knee rather than one with arthritis in the head,' while Eisenhower told Marshall, 'I don't give a damn about his knees, I want his head and heart and I will take him into battle on a litter if we have to.'

McNair wants him for Corps Command here in the States. However, before disposing of his case I would like to know if you might desire his services in his old capacity as your 'Eyes and Ears' man or as a spare experienced Corps Commander. Be perfectly frank in your answer since I am only making this query because I thought there was a possibility you might wish to have his experience available.[72]

Eisenhower to Marshall   *3 March*   *Ref: W-12217*
Woodruff and Reinhardt will be relieved upon the arrival of Corlett and Middleton respectively. Both will be sent back to the United States.

With respect to Lucas, my opinion is that we have now lined up about as efficient a group of Corps Commanders for our first two Armies as we can secure, and I do not desire to make further changes unless something unforeseen should occur. Moreover, my requirements in an 'Eyes and Ears' man are different from what they were back in the Mediterranean and my present concern is in the back areas and such problems as economy in manpower, motor transport and in general all round discipline and efficiency in the support of combat troops by the S.O.S.[73]

Lee and I have brought Hughes[74] up here to be an 'Eyes and Ears' man for a very considerable period so I do not need Lucas. However, we would very much like to see him, so as to pump him on additional lessons coming out of the recent Italian fighting. I would be appreciative if you would order him home via the United Kingdom and to remain here until I release him, which would be a period of a week to ten days.[75]

Marshall to Eisenhower   *4 March*   *No Reference*
Devers has been told to send Lucas home by way of England for consultation with you, as requested in your W-12217 of the 3rd of March. The time of Lucas' relief will be up to Devers. Lucas is to command a corps here on his return.

General Hodges as a Deputy for Bradley

Eisenhower to Marshall   *21 February*   *Ref: W-11600*
Because of Bradley's necessary presence in London for planning purposes, we could use General Hodges[76] very advantageously, for the moment, as a Deputy for Bradley. Assuming that Hodges' rank has now been established on the proper basis, I would like for you to send him as soon as convenient, because he can do very useful work here, pending the time that he gets a command of his own.

---

72 While Lucas had been relieved from his command and would not be given another command in Europe or the Mediterranean, Marshall and McNair still thought enough of him to give him equally high command, and then higher, in the US.
73 Services of Supply, General John C. H. Lee's (1887–1958, nickname Courthouse), logistics command.
74 Major-General Everett S. Hughes (1885–1957), previously Commanding General Communications Zone US North African Theater of Operations and recently appointed Special Assistant to Supreme Allied Commander.
75 Lucas returned to the US in March and was appointed Deputy Commanding General of Fourth Army in Texas, later becoming Commanding General.
76 General Hodges handed Third Army over to General Patton and became General Bradley's assistant commander with First Army. He would deal with training before the invasion and act as Bradley's eyes and ears after it. He became commander of First Army following the formation of 12th Army Group under General Bradley.

Marshall to Eisenhower   *21 February*   *Ref: 156*

Hodges' rank has not yet been adjusted. His nomination has not passed through the White House. However, we see no reason why you could not use him as you propose in your W-11600, 21 February. Let me know if you want him to come right away.

Eisenhower to Marshall   *22 February*   *Ref: W-11664*

We can use Hodges immediately. It is my understanding that we will carry him nominally as Commanding General Third Army until rank has been adjusted, even though his actual duties will <u>not</u> be in connection with Third Army.

3

MARCH 1944

The Relief of the Deputy Air Commander

Eisenhower to Marshall   3 March   *Ref W-12257*

Major General Butler[1] of the Army Air Forces is now serving as Deputy to my principal Air Commander. I am not aware of this officer's past record and accomplishments in the Army Air Forces but he is <u>not</u> suitable for his present assignment. He must be replaced at once by someone of the caliber of Norstad[2] or Vandenberg[3] but in the grade of Major General.

I will make Butler available for other assignment immediately upon arrival of his relief. While the entire American portion of the staff serving under Butler must be strengthened, the matter of his personal replacement has become critical.

I have consulted with Spaatz on this problem over a number of weeks and we have exhausted the possibilities both here and in the Mediterranean in order to get a man of satisfactory character and rank. While several men such as Major Generals Anderson,[4] Cannon[5] and Kepner[6] would be good, their present tasks are such that an immediate transfer is impossible.

I earnestly request that you inform General Arnold[7] of the urgency of this matter. Spaatz suggests that I ask whether Arnold could make Giles[8] available. If a Brigadier should be selected, I request he be promoted before arriving here.

Marshall to Eisenhower   4 March   *Ref: 227*

Butler will be relieved as requested. Full information desired as to whether or not this officer failed to perform his duties assigned due to clash of personalities between Butler and Mallory or due to general inefficiency. In order for me to take appropriate action I want you to state this case fully.

Giles cannot be spared at this time. I recommend Brigadier General Hoyt S. Vandenberg as Butler's replacement. Should Vandenberg be selected, an effort will be made to have his

---

1 Major-General William O. Butler (1895–1962) commander of Army Air Forces.
2 General Lauris Norstad (1907–1988) Director of Operations of the Mediterranean Allied Air Forces based in Italy.
3 General Hoyt S. Vandenberg (1899–1954), KCB, was transferred to the European Theater in March 1944 and in April 1944 designated Deputy Air Commander in Chief of the Allied Expeditionary Forces and Commander of its American Air Component.
4 Major-General Frederick Anderson (1905–1969), General Spaatz's deputy commander of operations at US Strategic Air Forces in Europe.
5 General John K. Cannon (1892–1955) commander of commanding general of both the Twelfth Air Force and the Mediterranean Allied Tactical Air Force in the Mediterranean Allied Air Forces.
6 General William E. Kepner (1893–1982), commander of 8th Fighter Command in the European Theater at this time.
7 General Henry H. Arnold (1886–1950), nicknamed 'Hap', Commander in Chief of the US Army Air Forces.
8 General Barney McK. Giles (1892–1984), deputy commander of the US Army Air Forces.

promotion approved prior to his arrival. Contact Spaatz and Eaker with the view of having Butler reassigned to duty in the European Theater of Operations or the Mediterranean Theater of Operations, provided relief is due primarily to personality clash and not inefficiency.

Eisenhower to Marshall   6 March   *Ref: B-225*
The difficulty with General Butler is that he is completely negative. There have been no, repeat no, clashes of personality. It is merely that Butler has failed to build up the American side of this particular staff and has seemingly nothing constructive to offer to either the Americans or the British. The importance of the American contingent of this staff is obvious and it must be headed by a strong, able type, whose word and opinions will carry some weight. Butler's trouble may be that he is simply completely unsuited to this particular kind of work and, through diffidence and uncertainty, is not able to act effectively.

General Eaker recently informed General Spaatz that he would like to have General Butler take the job formerly held by Royce[9] in Cairo. This would release Giles to take over a combat wing. Since this request would indicate that Eaker considers Butler a suitable administrative type, I suggest that it be approved.

I believe Vandenberg could take over the job of deputy in Leigh Mallory's headquarters very well but because I must have there an American of rank and prestige, it is extremely important that he be made a major general before coming here. On the other hand, the need for him is urgent, especially to get the American side of the air staff properly built up. I request therefore that action be taken as soon as possible.

Marshall to Eisenhower   7 March   *Ref: 238*
William O. Butler, Major General, will be relieved from your command in the immediate future. Brigadier General Vandenberg will be made available. Action under way to secure his promotion to Major General at earliest date practicable.

Staff Changes

Marshall to Eisenhower   10 March   *Ref: B236*
To provide Third Army with a first class chief of staff, I am detaching General Gaffey[10] from the 2nd Armored Division and assigning him to headquarters Third Army. I do not, repeat not, believe it is wise to recommend the promotion of Brigadier General Rose at this time although he is an excellent type of officer, and I prefer to take a good armored division commander from the States.[11] I request that you send here by air transportation with number one priority any of the following and in the priority named: Major Generals Paul Newgarden, John W. Leonard, Vernon E. Pritchard, E. H. Brooks.[12] Request immediate reply.

---

9 Major-General Ralph Royce (1890–1965), Deputy Commander of the Ninth Air Force to Lieutenant-General Lewis H. Brereton (1890–1967) and later Major-General Hoyt Vandenberg.

10 General Gaffey had been Patton's Chief of Staff at II Corp headquarters during the Tunisian campaign before commanding 2nd Armored Division in Tunisia and Sicily. While Patton was had excellent command skills and leadership qualities he needed a good staff officer to run his headquarters for him.

11 General Maurice Rose (1890–1945) was promoted to command 3rd Armored Division in August 1944.

12 Paul W. Newgarden (1892–1944), commander of 10th Armored Division was killed in a plane crash on 14 July 1944; John W. Leonard (1890–1974), nicknamed 'Peewee', commanded 9th Armored Division throughout the European campaign; Vernon E. Pritchard (1892–1949) commanded 1st Armored Division from July 1944 to the end of the Italian campaign; Edward H. Brooks (1893–1978), nicknamed 'Standing Eddie', took command of the 2nd Armored Division.

Marshall to Eisenhower 8 *March 1944*
Brooks will be sent to you immediately by number one air priority.

Assessment of the OVERLORD Situation
Eisenhower to Marshall 10 *March* *Ref: B-252*
General preparation and training here are proceeding satisfactory. I am too rigidly tied down to headquarters, which has moved just outside London, so that it is difficult for me to make the troop visits which I earnestly desire to make and which I believe essential. This morning it appears to me that the air problems are at last in good order and will be presented officially to the Chiefs of Staff quickly. All Air Forces here will be under Tedder's supervision as my agent and this prospect is particularly pleasing to Spaatz.

I am concerned about the landing craft situation which is keeping everybody, down to and including regimental combat teams, in a partial state of uncertainty. If the matter does not clear up within a couple of days I shall send Smith on a hurried trip home although, I badly need him at this juncture.

Please tell General Arnold that in spite of the glowing prospects he has painted for his particular type of airborne operations, the ground situation we are facing is one that will yield only to stern fighting. The fact is that against a German defense, fingers do not stab out rapidly and join up in the heart of enemy held territory unless there is present, solid tactical power and overwhelming strength. Recently a Russian general casually remarked that when they wanted to make a real drive, they preferred to get a superiority at the critical spot of about four to one. So I think that Arnold might restudy his analogy with the Anzio beachhead by simply realizing that that the beachhead is not, repeat not, a separate operation, but had the same purpose as would have had a very strong airborne operation.[13]

In spite of the fact that we have been we have been pouring into Anzio from 3,000 to 5,000 tons a day and have increased the strength to some 150,000 men, that force has not succeeded in joining up with the main body. Moreover, it must be apparent that without direct access to the sea, the troops we have put into Anzio could have not survived. Yet in that region there is inconsequential air resistance and only a total of some nineteen enemy divisions in the whole of Italy. At the very best we are going to have here lively air opposition and a strong and well organized ground resistance. His idea must be applied after the beachhead forces gain the power to put on a sustained offensive.

Thanks for Support for OVERLORD
Marshall via Eisenhower to Prime Minister 15 *March* *Ref No. 298*
Your personal through Dill[14] is much appreciated. I am greatly reassured to have this indication of your personal interest and strong leadership in all that pertains to OVERLORD. Our anxiety here to insure that whatever operations are undertaken in the Mediterranean they will be calculated to hold in the Theater, from Southern France to the Balkans, the largest number of German Divisions during the first month of OVERLORD.
Copy sent to the Prime Minister.

---

13 This is the first mention of airborne operations on D-Day, and Eisenhower is scathing about comparing previous airborne operations in Italy with the resistance he expects to encounter in Normandy.
14 Field Marshal Sir John G. Dill, GCB, CMG, DSO (1881–1944), Chief of the British Joint Staff Mission and then as Senior British Representative on the Combined Chiefs of Staff.

News from the Italian Front

Marshall to Eisenhower   *16 March*   *Ref No. 314*

The news from the Italian Front indicates that there is no probability of a decisive tactical change in the situation, from that which existed at the time you met with the British Chiefs of Staff, to represent the United States Chiefs of Staff in the OVERLORD – ANVIL matter. The operation at Cassino which started yesterday may bring about within a reasonably short time the amalgamation of the beachhead with the main line, but there is nothing to indicate a sufficient break in the German resistance to permit a further advance on Rome during March.[15]

Our concern here is over the possibility, if not the probability, that the Germans, in taking desperate measures which they will certainly do to crush OVERLORD, will endeavor to hold up our troops in Italy and recall from Southern France, from Italy, and from the Balkans, and by withdrawal on the Russian Front to the Riga Line, obtain from that Army, a large reserve of divisions available for the operations in Western France. Both Dill and I have had this fear and it was accentuated by General Hull's conversations with General Alexander in Italy, the latter stating, in reply to Hull's query, that six or eight divisions could materially delay his, Alexander's, advance to the Pisa – Rimini Line. Alexander now has 21 divisions in Italy and is proceeding with movements to increase this number to 28. The Germans have 24 divisions in Italy of which 19 are in the south.

So it would appear that if Alexander can be materially delayed, the Germans, in a series of planned withdrawals to, and maybe through, the Apennines, could free 10 to 15 divisions for France, not to mention those from Southern France and elsewhere that I previously mentioned. In connection with Alexander's statement, Dill's people worked up an estimate in which they conclude that 19 German divisions would be required to hold us in check in Italy.

We know from MAGIC[16] that the Germans are fearful of a landing in the Northern Adriatic or on the coast of Southern France. However, if they become aware of the fact that the facilities of such a landing are not available, they could rearrange their forces to your great disadvantage.

We must of course connect up the Anzio Beachhead with the main front of the Army in Italy. Under present conditions, however, I see no great purpose to be achieved in Italy aside from maintaining pressure on the enemy, to prevent the transfer of his forces to your front.

Eisenhower to Marshall   *18 March*   *Ref: B-296*

Thank you very much for your 314. You have of course expressed the possibility in the Mediterranean that gives much concern to me and my staff. Early in the coming week I will give you a rather detailed account of my personal views, together with dates, etc. Last evening General Smith talked to Handy, and I think that he presented my personal convictions on this matter rather accurately. Two major facts that influence my thinking are, first that we accepted a loading plan here that is not, repeat not, satisfactory in the absence of an ANVIL; and second, that no matter what we do, we must retain within the Mediterranean the greatest possible lift that can be spared from here, in order that if the enemy attempts delaying action and the reduction of strength in that Theater, Wilson can stage operations which with surely hold down a number of divisions. I spend all my

---

15 The third battle for Cassino started on 15 March and although some progress was made, the monastery and heights were not taken.
16 The US used the codename MAGIC for decryptions of Japanese cables made on the PURPLE cipher machine. This could have come from one of the reviews made by the Japanese Ambassador to Germany.

time thinking of these very serious matters and will try to send you a full exposition on Monday. As always my deep appreciation is due to you for your constant readiness to support our actions.[17]

Landing Craft Requirements

Marshall to Eisenhower   *16 March*   *Ref No. 314*

During the month since Cooke and Hull visited London, your examination and detailed development of plans should have made clear whether or not you have a critical shortage in landing ships and craft. Estimates here would indicate that all presently allocated LST's should close in to the United Kingdom, under the present plans, prior to the 30th of April except perhaps seven from the United States production which may not arrive until about May 15th.

We are about to open discussions with the British Chiefs of Staff concerning ANVIL and they have requested Wilson to let them have his estimate of the Mediterranean situation on March 18th. The basis for the final decision appears no better than a month ago. The only clear-cut decision would be to cancel the ANVIL operation.

I should greatly appreciate your personal views concerning this whole situation, including your present appraisal of the landing craft situation and the latest dates that you can accept craft for use in OVERLORD.

It is my intention, with which Arnold agrees, that we will support your desire regarding the ANVIL decision, whatever it may be. So the foregoing statement of my views is not to be accepted by you as a pressure from me to have matters arranged, other than the way you would wish to see them set up.

Eisenhower to Marshall   *20 March*   *Ref: B-311*

The staff is preparing messages to the Combined Chiefs of Staff, bearing on the subjects of our requirements. The purpose of this message is to give you my purely personal conclusions.

I firmly believe that ANVIL as we originally visualized it is no longer a possibility, either from the standpoint of the time in which to make all the necessary preparations, or in probable availability of fresh and effective troops at the appointed date. The serious sacrifices we have made here in our loading plans, in our great desire to insure an ANVIL, must therefore be made good in so far as they can be, consistent with leaving in the Mediterranean the necessary craft to mount a definite threat and to maintain the offensive. This Mediterranean minimum, I think is the ship to shore lift for one division. The bulk of all other serviceable landing craft presently allocated to the Mediterranean must come here, so that we may have the greatest possible chance of success.

We badly need a bit of margin and more flexibility. To show you how much we have limited ourselves in favor of a possible ANVIL, our present loading schedule uses up all our LSTs, repeat LSTs, on the first three tides. Since the LST turnaround is three days, we will have no, repeat no, LSTs reaching the beaches after the morning of D+1 (Dog plus one) until the morning of D+4 (Dog plus four).[18] Any such situation was acceptable to me only as long as I felt reasonably sure of a strong and simultaneous ANVIL. Under present circumstances

17 Eisenhower's focus in on keeping the maximum number of German divisions away from northern France. While he had no control over what the Germans do on the Eastern Front, he could influence the combination of maximum pressure in Italy and maximum threat against the south of France.
18 The LSTs delivered tanks and vehicles direct to the beach and were key vessels until the artificial harbors were ready.

we must reinforce our resources in this regard. Our needs in LCI(L), repeat LCI(L), is equally pressing.[19]

Present abandonment of former ANVIL must not, repeat not, lessen our intention of operating offensively in the Mediterranean, initially in Italy and extending from there towards France as rapidly as we can. We must constantly look forward to maximum possibilities in this regard, even if ambitious amphibious operations must be delayed. By threat, feint and actual operations we must make the enemy keep big forces in that region.

Getting More Naval Fire Support

Marshall to Eisenhower   19 March   *Ref: 340*

Smith asked Handy to approach Cooke, in an effort to obtain more naval fire support for your assault, battleships especially.[20]

Cooke states that all United States battleships except one have been directed to the Mediterranean and that there is some difficulty about suitable ammunition for the one remaining. Furthermore, Cooke feels that it is not advisable for us to send these ships to you when there are sufficient British battleships available. He states that he did all the missionary work he possibly could do while he was in London, that he agrees fully with you that naval fire support is insufficient, but that he now feels that the only way in which this additional support can be obtained is for you, as the Supreme Commander, to ask for it from the British.[21] Cooke's idea is that this is not strictly a naval matter, but it is both Army and Navy, and that you, as the responsible Commander, should state the fire support you consider you need, based on the requirements of the ground forces, and then it is up to the naval authorities to provide as much of it as they can.

The foregoing outlines what our naval people believe is the practicable approach to this problem. I concur with their view and suggest that, if you are unable to get any help in this way, you present the matter to the Combined Chiefs of Staff.

Eisenhower to Marshall   20 March   *Ref: B-311*

I want every bit of naval gun support that the naval commander believes can be deployed among the minefields that stud the coastline. More mine sweeping strength is mandatory and the more we get of it, the more gun fire we can bring to bear.

Eisenhower to Marshall   20 March   *Ref: B-307*

Smith's request to Handy was not, repeat not, exactly understood. The facts are as follows: Admiral Ramsey[22] is, repeat is, asking for more naval fire support. I believe his request will be for one battleship, eight or more cruisers, and some additional destroyers. My understanding is that the British will be unable, repeat unable, to furnish these ships and that our request, which is being submitted as visualized in your No. 340, will be transmitted to

---

19 The LCIs would deliver infantry direct to the beach until the temporary harbors were ready.
20 The first study of what ships would be required to neutralize the shore defenses was made in January 1944 but the conclusions far exceeded the number of ships available; over 20 battleships or cruisers would be needed to silence the coastal batteries and another 20 cruisers or 100 destroyers to keep the shore troops pinned down. A February study of the Tarawa operation in the Pacific proved that the troops defending the beach were a bigger danger to the assault force than the coastal batteries.
21 In February Admiral Ramsay assigned only one battleship, one monitor, seven cruisers and sixteen destroyers to the Western Naval Task Force.
22 Admiral Sir Bertram Home Ramsay KCB, KBE, MVO (1883–1945), Naval Commander in Chief of the Allied Naval Expeditionary Force.

the Combined Chiefs of Staff, with a recommendation by the British Chiefs of Staff that U.S. Navy vessels will be provided. [23]

What Smith asked Handy was that if the decision is made to send U.S. naval vessels, the U.S. Navy will substitute three of four battleships for a corresponding number of cruisers. This is based on our feeling, entirely as laymen, that we would like more battleship fire, although both Admiral Ramsay and the First Sea Lord disagree with the idea that more battleships are needed, and believe that cruiser fire is even more effective under the circumstances. [24]

I know that Cooke and some of Admiral Stark's [25] staff feel as I do, but they have no, repeat no, official connection with OVERLORD. I am not, repeat not, prepared on the technical question of cruisers versus battleships to take issue with my own naval commander and with the British Admiralty, who are responsible for providing the gunfire support for OVERLORD, particularly since it appears that if the additional vessels which are being asked for are provided, this support will be adequate in so far as concerns the actual number of ships and guns employed. However, like some of our own naval officers, my personal feeling is that the presence of a few more battleships would be very comforting. [26]

We did not, repeat not, know at the time that Smith's suggestion was made, that all U.S. battleships had been directed to the Mediterranean, and the possibility of substituting battleships, which we thought were operating in this area, for a similar number of cruisers seemed a good idea. Admiral Ramsey has indicated his willingness to accept this substitution. Since it seems that ANVIL as previously conceived is no longer, the assignment of these ships to the Mediterranean would be worth further consideration.

Eisenhower to Marshall   26 April   *Ref: S-50791*
The Prime Minister held another conference yesterday on naval gunfire support, and at this meeting it developed that the NELSON, which is scheduled to return to the United States for refit about the 1st May, will be made available for OVERLORD, if she can be given a later date for refitting in our ship yards.

The addition of another battleship means much to us, as you can well imagine. Will you please ask Admiral King to use his good offices to produce an affirmative reply when the British Naval request for a deferred reconditioning date for the NELSON is made through normal channels. [27]

Control of the Air Forces for OVERLORD

Eisenhower to Marshall   21 March   *Ref: B-316*
I have just seen an exchange of telegrams between the British Chiefs of Staff and the United States Chiefs of Staff concerning the words "supervision" and "command", as applied to my control of Air Forces allotted for the support of OVERLORD.

---

23 Ramsay requested that US warships were assigned and by May, three US battleships, two cruisers and 34 destroyers had been assigned to Admiral Kirk's command; a few British ships were detached at the same time.
24 The Tarawa report noted that naval bombardment could neutralize open emplacements but not concrete covered structures; he noted that 'The heaviest casualties were caused by the failure to neutralize strong points and dug-outs during the period immediately before and after the touch-down of the assault.' Cruisers were the most effective ships for these tasks.
25 Admiral Harold R. Stark (1880–1972), nicknamed 'Betty', Commander of US Naval Forces in Europe and Twelfth Fleet commander, directed the naval build up and training in the UK before D-Day.
26 While cruisers might have been more effective for neutralizing beach defenses, the sight and sound of battleships shelling inland targets were good morale boosters for the assault troops waiting to go ashore.
27 HMS *Nelson* was being refitted but she did support the Normandy landings until she was damaged by two mines on 18 June.

It is true that in my original draft I used the word "supervision" in describing the responsibilities that would devolve upon me in the handling of Air Forces. At that time my main concern was to secure agreements in the development of the overall air plan, the method for passing of responsibility on operational control and the certainty that authority for coordination of all this effort lay in the hands of the Supreme Commander, which, I intend shall be exercised through Air Chief Marshal Tedder.[28]

The question of exact terms and phraseology did not arise at that time, but it was clearly understood that authority for operational control of forces definitely allocated to OVERLORD, whether they were engaged on close in targets or in deep penetrations for the destruction of the German Air Force, should reside with me. The general reservations agreed upon were that the coastal command as such, would have to remain under its present system of command; that the Combined Chiefs of Staff could at any time assign additional or emergency tasks to me to be executed by the Air Forces; and finally, that if the safety of Great Britain itself were at any time in danger, the British Chiefs of Staff should have the unquestioned authority to meet the situation with their own troops of all kinds. I am somewhat astonished that in view of all these arrangements, there should have been any reluctance on the part of the British Chiefs of Staff to accept the word "command", because I readily understood and agreed to the obvious reservations and my object is to carry out a general outline plan for air operations agreed upon between the Chief of the Air Staff and myself.[29]

As long as any question has arisen on this point, I personally much prefer some word that leaves no doubt as to the right of the Supreme Commander to control these Air Forces under the conditions stated. In all our conversations this point seemed so well and clearly understood, that it never occurred to me to question the complete intent to make me clearly and definitely responsible for operational control of these forces, until such time as OVERLORD was well established on the Continent and the directive would be reviewed by the Combined Chiefs of Staff.

A Serious Security Breach

Bissell[30] to Eisenhower *17 March* *Ref No. 325*

1. Package received post office, Chicago, 16 March showing address from G-4 Administrative Division, 119 Norfolk House, to G-4 Administrative Division, 10 West Division Street, Chicago, Illinois. Address in Chicago is an apartment house in German neighborhood. Package is torn single envelope and, while it did not reach address, it is unknown how many persons may have examined it in transit. Package in bad order and contents exposed. Cover showing APO 887, stamp of 24 February and British cancellation stamp of 23 February.

2. Apparently Y Day, code words OVERLORD and ANVIL, and American order of battle have been compromised.

3. [List of contents]

---

28 Air Chief Marshall Trafford Leigh-Mallory had been appointed Commander-in-chief of the Allied Expeditionary Air Forces in August 1943 and drew up the air plan for OVERLORD. Tedder had been commander of Allied Air Forces in the Mediterranean but when he was appointed Eisenhower's Deputy he made a point of wresting control of D-Day air planning from Leigh-Mallory.
29 It appears that while the British Chiefs of Staff accepted SHAEF's plans for supervision and control of the air forces deployed over Normandy, they would not accept the word 'command'.
30 General Clayton Lawrence Bissell (1896–1973) was serving with the Office of the Assistant Chief of Staff for Intelligence on the War Department General Staff.

4. Has your attention been brought to this?

5. At this end, check is being made of persons living in Chicago address, possible cable traffic to and from that address, and mail handling of package since arrival in United States. Best clue to violator is analysis of handwriting, and recommend you obtain special handwriting specimens of persons in G-4 Division before such persons know they are suspected, if possible. Specimens should be in pencil since address was so written. If you desire, will return by officer courier documents and envelope in which received or if you prefer, send handwriting specimens here for comparison.

Eisenhower to Bissell   *18 March*   *Ref: B-292*
Investigation of report contained in your 325 requires immediate examination of all papers, documents etc, and their wrappings and/or envelopes. Request the above evidence be dispatched by office courier via Top Priority air passage. Further, request progress reports by cable of your investigation. No, repeat no, previous information concerning this matter received by this headquarters and we are most concerned.

Bissell to Eisenhower   *18 March*   *Ref: 330*
Papers leaving today by air, by hand Lieutenant Colonel Willis A. Perry, C.A.C., of WDGSI.[31]

Eisenhower to Marshall   *22 March*   *Ref: 350004*
Consideration of serious danger to OVERLORD security arising from report contained in your 325 demands full information as to extent of compromise of classified documents in question.

Your evaluation of this point requested, since under certain circumstances it may be necessary to abandon code words OVERLORD and ANVIL, except for cover purposes, and change date of Y Day. We assume mail cover has been put on Chicago address? Request reply be expedited. Your 347 requests intensified inquiry on W.A.C. sergeant.

Bissell to Eisenhower   *24 March*   *Ref: W-13763*
At least twelve unauthorized civilians are known to have had access to contents of package in this country. Five of these are known to have been aware of contents. Condition of package was such that other unknown persons may have had access and it is entirely possible that not all of original documents in package have been recovered. Impossible at this late date to trace the exact handling and packaging after arrival in this country, therefore, it is believed the documents recovered must be considered compromised.

Eisenhower to Marshall   *24 March*   *Ref: S-50009*
Technical Sergeant Richard Emil Tymm, 722232, G-4 Division this headquarters, whose home address was 10 West Division Street, has admitted that envelope in question is addressed in his handwriting but does not remember mailing documents.[32] Tymm's sister, Mrs. Agnos Stevens lives at West Division Street address. Father, John Tymm lives at 1362 Evergreen Street, Chicago. Soldier formally had apartment at 3656 North Magnolia Avenue, Chicago. Request immediate action as follows:

---

31 CAC War Department, General Staff, Intelligence.
32 It was soon established that Tymm was of German extraction, heightening suspicions about his motives.

1. Place mail cover on all the above addresses.
2. Complete search of premises indicated above.
3. Thorough interrogation of soldier's relatives and follow up on leads furnished by them.
4. Exhaustive investigation of subject's background.

Information contained in your W-12715 not sufficient to base decision regarding extent of compromise of Y-Day and code words OVERLORD and ANVIL. Request detailed comments. Tymm now in custody of Army Medical Authorities here.

Bissell to Eisenhower   *24 March*   *Ref: W-13764*
All civilians connected with Tymm are being adequately investigated by the Federal Bureau of Investigation. Interrogation and background investigation of these persons is not appropriate at this stage, as this would destroy possible opportunity to secure further information, which might lead to publicity. Request complete record of your interrogation of Tymm be forwarded immediately. Action taken here to prevent any publicity, and suggest similar action your place.

Eisenhower to Marshall   *25 March*   *Ref: S-50033*
Additional lead in case of Technical Sergeant Tymm as follows: Fiancée Mary Tymm (no relation) resides 838 North Hermitage Avenue, Chicago 22. Request fiancée be interrogated and residence searched.

Eisenhower to Bissell   *29 March*   *Ref: S-50081*
Decision regarding action to be taken as a result compromise of documents, now awaiting your reply to following questions:

1. What is known concerning loyalty and integrity of the twelve persons who had access to documents?
2. Is it now too late to seal above persons?
3. If not too late, can persons be sealed immediately?

Court martial of Tymm being held in abeyance, pending receipt of your report regarding investigation of his relatives and connections. Record of our interrogation of Tymm en route to you by air courier. No publicity will be given case until conclusion of trial period.

Bissell to Eisenhower   *29 March*   *Ref: W-15776*
Nothing derogatory yet discovered about twelve persons known to have had access to documents. Not known what others may have had access or whether all documents recovered. All persons known to have had access have been warned and are under observation but discretion cannot be guaranteed.
    Have you developed motive, accomplices or espionage connections at that end? Desire no publicity at any time, without complete prior coordination with War Department. Air courier has not yet arrived.

Widely to Bissell   *31 March*   *Ref: S-50116*
Summary of developments to date, in case of Technical Sergeant Richard Emil Tymm, are furnished below for your information and guidance in connection with current investigation your end. Observation and interrogation of Tymm have so far failed to reveal motive or

accomplices for espionage connections. Soldier and his superiors' state he was extremely overworked at the time documents left this headquarters. Examination of documents reveals they were intended to go from G-4 Division in Norfolk House to another section of G-4 Division located in another building in London.[33]

Based upon facts as adduced so far, and pending the outcome of your investigation, we believe soldier guilty of extreme negligence caused by mental strain. Scotland Yard detectives assigned to M.I.5. concur in this belief. Regarding possible implications of compromise of information contained in documents, it is the belief of this headquarters that if this, or similar data, has been conveyed to enemy other than in its original documentary form or photostats thereof, it would probably be cancelled off against the voluminous information fed him by his many unreliable agents and by cover and deception methods.

Judge Advocate withholding court martial of Tymm, pending receipt of your report of investigation. Has investigation proceeded to point where possibility of espionage can be determined? If determined here that deposition of key witnesses in United States will not meet requirements of trial, will it be possible to fly such persons to this headquarters? No publicity will be given this case without coordinating with the War Department.

Whiteley to Bissell   *1 April*   *Ref: 17210*
Thus far no indications of espionage connections, but final determination withheld pending completion of certain investigations and receipt record of your interrogation, reported en route by air courier. Estimate two weeks to complete inquiries in progress. Investigation of BYRD negative. When and if desired, key witnesses can be sent.

The OVERLORD–ANVIL–Italy Problem[34]

Marshall to Eisenhower   *25 March*   *Ref: W-14078*
In the discussion yesterday, regarding the proposed directive covering OVERLORD – ANVIL – Italy, we proposed that once the beachhead and the Fifth Army front joined, the major concern in the Mediterranean is to prepare for a later ANVIL, July 10 as the target date, and that Rome would not be considered a primary effort to the disadvantage of the proposed ANVIL. Dill indicated the British would view this with concern, because of the political importance of Rome.

Our view is that the chances of the Germans holding and fighting on a broad front are greater south of Rome than north of Rome.[35] Also Wilson's appreciation of what he could do in joining up the beachhead by 15 May, and taking Rome by 15 June, reflects so pessimistic a view that it weighed heavily in our consideration of the importance of making Rome an immediate objective.[36]

What we are afraid of is the Germans instituting an economical delaying action up to the Pisa – Rimini line, reasonably secure in the knowledge that we are not set for operations elsewhere in the Mediterranean.[37]

We have recommended to the British Chiefs of Staff that to meet your requirements for OVERLORD, there be transferred from the Mediterranean to the United Kingdom 26 LST,

---

33 It transpired during the interrogation that Tymm had probably been thinking of home as he addressed parcels and had accidently written his sister's address on one.
34 With 1 April looming it was time to reassess the Italian campaign as time was running out to transfer shipping from the Mediterranean to the English Channel if ANVIL was cancelled.
35 Holding the Gustav Line south of Rome rather than the Gothic Line north of Rome.
36 Rome would not be taken until 4 June.
37 The Pisa–Rimini Line north of Rome was known as the Gothic Line.

40 LCI(L), 1 LSH (Bulolo), 1 LSE and 1 LSD. All of these craft, except 12 LST, to arrive by 30 April, the remaining 12 LST to arrive by 15 May. We have also recommended the transfer of three United States fighter groups and seven British Spitfire squadrons.

In all of this, I understand that our proposal for a 10 July ANVIL involves diverting to the Mediterranean landing craft due to leave for Pacific in late May and June, in order to provide at least a two division lift for ANVIL. We will not make this diversion, which means a serious delay in the Pacific, with the possibility of losing our momentum, unless some sizable operation of the nature of ANVIL is on the books. The importance of Rome in comparison in this other factor appears to us to weigh light in the balance.[38]

Suggest you keep in content with British Chiefs of Staff, rather than wait until they have again come to a conclusion regarding our proposal of yesterday.

Eisenhower to Marshall   *27 March*   Ref: S-50051

I can not, repeat not, tell you how much I appreciate your W-14078. We have already contacted the British Chiefs of Staff and will hold a conference tomorrow afternoon. I must say that the purpose you intend is in exact accord with my own ideas, particularly as to the relative importance of objectives in the Mediterranean.

One detail in which my own headquarters may have a suggestion to make to you, is concerning the three long-range fighter groups that you have recommended be transferred here. The operations of the Fifteenth Air Force deep into hostile territory are so important to the direct support of OVERLORD, in the attack of fighter factories and transportation centers, that I believe it would be better to retain these three groups in the Mediterranean. General Eaker has been here for conferences and has shown in detail how his fighter groups are being employed. On the other hand, I think the seven British Spitfire squadrons should come as quickly as possible.

Eisenhower to Marshall   *27 March*   Ref: S-50068

I have just finished a long conference with the British Chiefs of Staff on the general subject of your W-14078 to me. The Prime Minister was not, repeat not, present and his views were not, repeat not, known to the conference, but the following is given to you as representing the conclusions expressed by the British Chiefs of Staff.

There was positive agreement that no, repeat no, particular geographical location, including Rome, had in itself any significance from the military viewpoint, in comparison with the mission of the Allied Commander-in-Chief in the Mediterranean which, as already given him, is to carry on operations of maximum support to OVERLORD.

It was agreed that current operations should urgently seek the union of the main front and the beachhead.

There was also a general agreement that no matter what might be the military situation in the Mediterranean about early July, that an amphibiously mounted assault by two divisions, with a substantial follow-up, will be essential to the achievement of our objectives in the area, primarily, the effective support of OVERLORD.[39]

It was also agreed that, depending upon the enemy intentions and actions, we would be faced, at that time, with two possible situations differing sharply in character. Either case will require a strong amphibious operation of the kind described in your telegram. The first

---

38 The invasion of Saipan in the Philippine Sea with 128,000 US Army and Marine troops was planned for mid June 1944. Once the island had been taken airfields could be built and mainland Japan could be bombed.
39 At this point the British Chiefs of Staff supported ANVIL.

of these situations would be the one described in your third paragraph: "what we are afraid of is the Germans instituting an economical delaying action up to the Pisa – Rimini line". In this event, the conclusion was expressed that the strongest possible attack against Southern France would be clearly indicated as necessary. The second situation would be one in which the enemy continued throughout the spring and early summer to reinforce his Italian front and continued to wage an all-out campaign to retain his present positions, which would require employment of the great bulk of all our disposable forces in the Mediterranean.[40] If this type of situation should eventuate, the British Chiefs of Staff believe that the Combined Chiefs of Staff would have to select at some date near the actual operation, the exact place and strength of the operation, depending, among other things, upon the possibilities for supporting it both by air and for normal follow up and maintenance.

So far as I can see the only thing that prevents the British Chiefs of Staff, from a strictly military point of view, from answering your telegram by a simple yes, is the fear that there might be a situation existing in the Mediterranean around early July which would indicate some other place than generally proposed for ANVIL, as the best for launching the projected operation, but they fully agree that a sizeable amphibious operation will be essential.

I read to the conference that portion of your telegram which says "we will not, repeat not, make this diversion, which means a serious delay in the Pacific with the possibility of losing our momentum, unless some sizeable operation of the nature of ANVIL is on the books." I used this sentence to show them that, in my opinion, you were concerned in launching the strongest and most ambitious amphibious operation that the military situation would then permit, so as to introduce an additional threat against the European mainland and so as to accomplish the greatest possible support for OVERLORD. I expressed the view that no matter where the Combined Chiefs of Staff might later decide this attack should best be made, the development of the Corsican airfields would be necessary.[41] Consequently, it seems to me that all of the planning and preparation can go ahead at full speed, and still conform to any decision, as to exact location, the Combined Chiefs of Staff might make at the critical moment.

It was clear that the British Chiefs of Staff were most grateful for the earnest, and even sacrificial efforts, that the American Chiefs of Staff are making in order to support the great venture of OVERLORD. So far as I can see, they were merely fearful that a present complete freezing of ideas as to where, and in what ultimate strength, an amphibious attack on the scale of two assault divisions with strong supporting formations should be launched, might later cause much embarrassment. I reminded them that there should be at that time, about eight French divisions in Africa and that if necessary we could permit this French force to make the assault with nothing more than air, sea and maintenance support from others.

I was given to understand that a formal reply would be sent to you as quickly as possible.

A French Journalist Stirs Things Up

Eisenhower to Marshall   27 March   *Ref: S-50060*

For the second or third time, I have noticed stories apparently originated by a man named Pertinax[42] in the United States, to the effect that I have either directly, or indirectly,

---

40 The Germans did indeed hold onto the Gustav line and Cassino until mid May, before falling back north of Rome.

41 Squadrons based in Corsica could support either the Italian campaign or the beachhead in southern France; or both.

42 Pertinax was the pseudonym of the French journalist André Géraud (1882–1974) who was living in exile in New York.

criticized proposed instructions of the President involving dealings with the French. While I know that so far as you are concerned I do not, repeat not, have to deny any such absurd allegation, I still think it most unfortunate that any newspaper can be allowed to insinuate that commanders in the field are tacitly insubordinate. It is probable that nothing at all can be done about such things, but after working for two solid years as hard as I know how for the development of the spirit of unification and complete team play, it is disappointing to think that any single individual in the whole United States could be led to believe that I would myself be guilty of even a whisper of insubordination.

Whenever I might consider that any proposed instructions from higher authority are based upon misconception of fact, I would naturally feel free to present my case to you or to the Combined Chiefs of Staff in the proper manner, but if I or any of my staff were guilty of direct or indirect criticism of the kind indicated in the stories, I would personally relieve the offender from duty and would expect to have the same fate dealt out to me.[43]

Marshall to Eisenhower   *29 March*   *Ref: W-15703*
Pertinax is a French newspaper columnist who has been here since the German invasion. His writings here have very limited distribution and clientele. Neither War Department nor President is under the slightest misapprehension as to your position and attitude, nor has the general reading public taken any particular note of the Pertinax writings. I think it best to disregard this matter, though I appreciate your expression of concern. Your message to me has been sent to the President.

General Giraud Wants to Move to London[44]

C.I.G.S. to Wilson and Eisenhower   *30 March*   *Ref: 82442 MO5*
Colonel Poniatowski, General Giraud's staff officer who is now in London, has enquired whether a visit to London by Giraud at present juncture would be advisable from a military point of view.

Discussion of future operations would be extremely awkward, on account of security difficulties which precluded any communication being made to the French which might prejudice OVERLORD, but some kind of communication will doubtless have to be made to Giraud in view of conversations you have already had with him.

Poniatowski has been advised to inform Giraud, that in due course when plans are firm you will make communication to him as the recognized agent of the Combined Chiefs of Staff, and that it would be best for Giraud to await this communication before deciding whether he wishes to come to London.

It will be necessary when the time comes for the terms of the communication to be agreed with Eisenhower.

C.I.G.S. to Wilson   *31 March*   *Ref: 82764 CIGS*
Please cancel 82442 MO5, 30 March. The whole question of communicating information to French on future operations is still under discussion. In the meantime, you should tell Giraud nothing about future operations without further instructions.

---

43 It appears that Eisenhower is furious that the press can print unsubstantiated allegations about him and his subordinates.
44 General Henri H. Giraud (1879–1949). Giraud and de Gaulle were co-presidents of the Comité Français de la Libération Nationale and Free French Forces until Giraud lost his appointment in November 1943. He was also commander-in-chief of the French forces until the Allies discovered that he was maintaining his own intelligence network and he was forced to resign.

Devers to Eisenhower   *3 April*   *Ref: F-27004*

Giraud is becoming very restive. He feels that he is being pushed aside.[45] He is anxious to communicate to you things he thinks you should know. Part of this, Rooks sent in a letter to Smith. Believe if a firm date could be set when he can come to England and also a firm date when the French division is desired in U.K., this will revive his low spirits at the moment. Do not believe you would have to give him anything else in the form of information.

Eisenhower to Devers   *4 April*   *Ref: S-50163*

Thanks for your message on Giraud. I know how he feels but the fact is that there is no, repeat no, way he can be invited to come to England except through the British Chiefs of Staff, who know his desire but do not, repeat not, feel that the present is an appropriate time since there are several unsettled questions of importance which he is sure to wish to discuss. The move of the French division is a certainty and the only question that remains is the transportation of its equipment. I am sure that he will have a firm date very shortly.

Devers to Eisenhower   *4 April*   *Ref: F-27704*

Today the French Committee passed a decree without consultation with General Giraud, which practically takes from him his command and power. He is deeply hurt and although I talked to him for an hour tonight, he positively states he will resign late tomorrow, the 5th. He agreed to hold a cable to you until that time, in which he will request that you support him in securing from the British Government permission to retire and reside in London until he can enter France.

Will keep you informed of events.

---

45 Pushed aside by General Charles A. J. M. de Gaulle.

4

APRIL 1944

Preparing for ANVIL

Eisenhower to Marshall   3 April   Ref: S-50156

At a conference this noon with AGENT,[1] I saw a draft of the telegram the British Chiefs of Staff are sending to you at once. They agreed to include in the directive to Wilson a paragraph specifically directing the preparation for ANVIL with target date as you suggest, with the plan subject to change only by the direction of the Combined Chiefs of Staff.

I am hopeful that with ANVIL definitely slated as to time, Admiral King[2] may find it possible to send us some naval vessels from that area to strengthen our gunfire support, with the idea that they would be back in the Mediterranean in time to support ANVIL.[3]

Eisenhower to Marshall   12 April   Ref: S-50310

On April 3 I saw a telegram from the British Chiefs of Staff to the U.S. Chiefs of Staff on the subject of mounting ANVIL. Having heard nothing further on this subject I assumed that that telegram, which was couched in the form of a proposed directive to Wilson, had become the basis of a general agreement and that we could count on additional lift of 26 LSTs and 40 LCI(L)'s becoming available in the Mediterranean. Only today I learned that since that time this matter had been the subject of further radio correspondence, and that the views of the two Chief of Staff groups were so divergent that the U.S. Chiefs of Staff have decided to send this equipment on to the Pacific. I earnestly hope that this decision is not, repeat not, irrevocable and that by further exploration of the subject the British Chiefs of Staff may find it possible to accept the American viewpoint.

I thoroughly agree with you, that it would always be possible to divert from a planned and prepared ANVIL to support an operation on the Italian mainland, while a reverse movement of this nature would not be practicable.

I also agree that unless firm decisions and actual preparations are immediately undertaken it will not be possible to mount ANVIL in July.

If the reluctance of the British Chiefs of Staff to give Wilson a firm directive is based upon a fear that his necessary operations in joining the bridgehead with the main front might be prejudiced[4], what would you think of committing the ANVIL assault to the French divisions still in Africa? The ground command for ANVIL could be given to a good French general who would be under the complete control of Wilson, because of his dependence upon the Allies for air, naval and maintenance support. This plan would, I believe, be seized

---

1 Prime Minister Churchill.
2 Admiral Ernest J. King (1878–1956), Commander in Chief, US Fleet and Chief of Naval Operations.
3 Vessels would have to sail from the Mediterranean to work in the English Channel and then return once the Normandy beachhead had been secured.
4 Joining the Anzio beachhead after breaking through the Gustav Line.

upon by the French and would certainly offer a minimum of interference with the fierce battling that must ensue before the two Italian fronts are joined up. This battling may leave American divisions temporarily incapable of further offensive action.

In any event I hope that efforts will continue, in order to bring the views of the British Chiefs of Staff sufficiently in line with your own, so that the additional lift that is going to be so badly needed in the European Theater this summer can be agreed upon by the Chiefs of Staff. It is obvious that the next few months in the European Theater will be critical and momentous ones, and we very badly need the strength both here and in the Mediterranean to exert our full force against the Germans during that period.

I realize how great a sacrifice the U.S. Chiefs of Staff were offering to make by providing these landing craft. I clearly understand that it is not in my province to attempt to intervene in Chief of Staff discussions but the issues at stake are so great, that I felt I should submit to you personally my earnest conviction that no stone should be unturned, in order to achieve an understanding that will allow us to have this additional strength.[5]

I go north this evening but will be back Saturday morning.

Marshall to Eisenhower   13 April   *Ref: W-22575*
Giving reference as your S-50310 of April 12th, the following transactions between the British and United States Chiefs of Staff will supply the necessary information covering your discussion.

The United States Chiefs of Staff at a formal meeting presented the following proposition, but under the instructions from the British Chiefs of Staff, Sir John Dill felt compelled to decline acceptance.

CCS 465/19, 8 April 1944, memorandum by the United States Chiefs of Staff:

1. We have considered the comments of the British Chiefs of Staff contained in CCS 465/18 in respect to the directive to General Wilson.

2. As we see it, the fundamental difference between our views, lies in the conception as to which course of action will place us in the best position to render the maximum aid to OVERLORD, no matter which of their capabilities the Germans attempt to exercise in Italy, and in particular, as to our course of action in Italy after the beachhead is joined.

3. We do not agree on the relative importance of ANVIL as compared to continued offensive operations in Italy. We believe the sound decision is to mount ANVIL while maintaining strong pressure on the German forces in Italy. Our course of action should not "turn on whether the Germans decide to fight it out in Southern Italy after the beachhead is joined or whether they will then withdraw forces and retire". After having seized the initiative in the Mediterranean, we should not accept a plan which permits the Germans to determine our course of action. Because of its vital effect on overall strategy, the Italian situation calls for the most vigorous action by commanders on the ground. The Combined Chiefs of Staff should emphasize most forcefully to the Allied Commander-in-Chief, Mediterranean,[6] the necessity for such action, even though not all the desirable means can be provided, nor the time allowed to carry out ideal arrangements. The

---

5 Eisenhower was anxious that Operation ANVIL went ahead to draw away German reserves from the Normandy battle. He was also short of landing craft and sending so many to the Pacific would hinder his plans for Operation OVERLORD.
6 General Wilson.

requirements listed by the Allied Commander-in-Chief, Mediterranean, for the maintenance of the Allied action in Italy, in our opinion, are based too largely on perfection of
arrangements. We cannot permit this to slow down the drive of the overall strategy for
the conduct of the war. The large number of armored divisions, separate brigades, etc.
available, in addition to our overwhelming superiority in the air and on the sea, should
make it possible to overcome the deficiencies he indicated. The German adaptation of
troops of every character to the execution of a determined purpose might well be our
model.[7]

4. We agree with the British Chiefs of Staff in recognizing that all our plans must be subject
    to change as the situation develops. However, we are convinced that giving priority to
    further operations in Italy at the expense of ANVIL, after the beachhead and main line
    are joined, would leave us impotent to cope with a German withdrawal from Italy. If, on
    the other hand, we have meanwhile placed ourselves in a position to mount an amphibi-
    ous operation on the scale of ANVIL, we present a constant threat which the Germans
    cannot ignore.[8]

5. We note that the British Chiefs of Staff are apprehensive of the creation of a virtual stale-
    mate just at the most critical time for OVERLORD. We are not convinced that this would
    follow as a result of the timely preparation of those formations required for ANVIL. But
    if it should appear that such a situation would ensue, we would still be in a position to
    reinforce our effort in Italy, either by land or by strong amphibious attack.[9]

6. The United States Chiefs of Staff agree that we must create a situation which will permit
    an option as to our Mediterranean operations in support of OVERLORD. To do this, we
    feel that we should be prepared, after joining the beachhead, either to launch ANVIL or
    to proceed with all-out offensive operations in Italy. This, we conclude, can only be done
    by:
    1st. Giving highest priority to operations to join the beachhead and main line, mean-
    while making such preparation for ANVIL as the practicable consonance therewith;
    2nd. After joining the beachhead, giving the highest priority to preparations for ANVIL,
    meanwhile conducting operations in Italy with all the forces not required for ANVIL.

7. We therefore recommend that the directive to Allied Commander-in-Chief Mediterranean
    be revised as indicated in the attached appendix. Furthermore, we feel it essential that
    the revised directive be issued at once.

APPENDIX
Draft directive to Allied Commander-in-Chief, Mediterranean
OBJECT
1. To give the greatest possible assistance to OVERLORD.

---

7 A scathing assessment of the conduct of the Italian campaign. Marshall is intimating that if Allied
divisions were as effective and flexible as their German counterparts, then the campaign would be taking on a
different course.
8 The US Chiefs of Staff are concerned that the Germans can control the Italian campaign and withdrawal
along Peninsula to new prepared positions at will, allowing divisions to be move north to counter OVERLORD.
A similar withdrawal and redeployment of divisions could not be carried out in southern France.
9 Even if ANVIL preparations were pushed ahead, it would not be too difficult to make a shift the amphibious attack to the Italian if necessary.

METHOD

2. (a) Launch as early as practicable a coordinated, sustained all-out offensive to join the beachhead with the main line in Italy. Thereafter maintain pressure to contain the maximum number of German formations in Central Italy, through such offensive action as is practicable with prejudice to preparations for ANVIL.

(b) Develop a positive amphibious threat against the Mediterranean coast of France and employ air forces, as if in preparation for an amphibious assault, in order to delay the movement of German forces in the Mediterranean towards OVERLORD. This thrust should be fully developed by OVERLORD D-5 and fully maintained for as long as possible after D-Day. The process of building up the threat should not start before D-31.

(c) Prepare plans for ANVIL on at least a two divisional assault basis, to be launched at the earliest practicable date. Target date 10 July.

(d) ANVIL is the most ambitious operation which can be undertaken in the Mediterranean, and plans for this will be pressed forward vigorously and wholeheartedly, together with all preparations which do not prejudice the operations to join the beachhead with the main line. The undertaking of these preparations for ANVIL will in no way preclude a change of plan by the Combined Chiefs of Staff should an undeniably better course of action be presented by changing circumstances.

COMMAND AND CONTROL

3. You will continue to exercise operational control over your forces after the ANVIL landing until Supreme Commander, Allied Expeditionary Force can assume this responsibility.

4. Instructions in respect to coordination with SCAEF of operational, administrative, civil affairs and SOE/SO matters will be transmitted to you by him. As a result, the United States Chiefs of Staff presented another paper acquiescing to the British view, which amounts to the cancellation of ANVIL and their unwillingness to divert the landing craft from scheduled operations in the Pacific on the basis proposed by the British.

Prime Minister Churchill gives Eisenhower his Thoughts

Churchill via Marshall to Eisenhower   13 April   *Ref: W-22575*

Yesterday there came to me direct from the Prime Minister the following:

1. Although the fighting at the bridgehead[10] and on the Cassino front has brought many disappointments you will, I trust, recognize that at least eight extra divisions have been brought into Italy, down to the south of Rome and heavily mauled there. If at Tehran we had been told that the ANVIL, there suggested, would detach eight divisions from the German front against OVERLORD we should have rejoiced. BONIFACE[11] shows that Hitler has been saying that his defeats in South Russia are due to the treacherous Badoglio[12] collapse of Italy which has involved 35 German divisions. At any rate, I believe that our action in Italy has played a large part in rendering possible the immensely important advances made in South Russia, which as further benefit are convulsing the satellites.[13]

---

10 The Anzio beachhead.
11 British intelligence's original name for ULTRA, the signals intelligence gathered by the Government Code and Cipher School at Bletchley Park.
12 Pietro Badoglio (1871–1956), Prime Minister after Benito Mussolini's arrest; he declared war on Germany on 13 October 1943 and was replaced in June 1944.
13 Romania, Bulgaria and Hungary.

2. I have not hitherto intervened in the intricate and lengthy correspondence which has been proceeding between the United States and British Chiefs of Staff about ANVIL. Seven German divisions, with two in reserve equals nine, have been already assigned to the defense of the Riviera front.[14] I do not believe an advance up the Rhône Valley is practicable in any period which will influence our main operations this summer.[15] On the contrary I am sure the German general in the West[16] will concentrate on winning his battle there and will fight merely delaying actions in Southern France. Were we to succeed in landing by some variant of ANVIL it would be better to move westwards towards Bordeaux than northwards up the Rhône Valley.[17] In either case a two division assault supported by eight follow-up divisions, mostly French, would be good as far as it went, but could not go far enough in time to sway the main battle. The fact however, that nine enemy divisions have been assigned to the Riviera defence and that 25 are now in Italy, of which 18 are south of Rome, a total of 34 divisions, acquits the Mediterranean armies of not playing their part.[18]

3. I gather from the correspondence between the two staffs that we are now all agreed upon the priority for joining the main army with the bridgehead early.[19] Naturally we are all grieved that the opening date of this battle is postponed till 14th May.[20] General Alexander has arrived home and has convinced us that an all-out sustained major offensive cannot be launched earlier. Moreover, the timing of this great battle in the south will accord harmoniously with the date of OVERLORD. All available forces, British, American and Allied, will be in heavy action on both fronts simultaneously.

4. At the moment my own position is as follows. We should above all defeat the German Army south of Rome and join our own armies. Nothing should be grudged for this. We cannot tell how either the Allies or the enemy will emerge from the battle until the battle has been fought. It may well be that the enemy will be thrown into disorder and that great opportunities of exploitation may be open. Or we may be checked, and the enemy may continue to hold his positions south of Rome against us with his existing forces. On the other hand he may seek to withdraw some of his divisions to the main battle in France. It seems to me that we must have plans and preparations to take advantage of the above possibilities.[21]

5. Regarding ANVIL, hereinafter called ANVIL Z, I believe that whatever happens on the mainland of Italy, the enemy forces now detached to the Riviera can, in the meanwhile, be fastened there by feints and threats. One thing that alarms me, however, is lest[22] our

---

14 Southern France.
15 The attack direct north from the planned landing area in southern France the and advance up the Rhône would divide the German front in two and threaten to cut off all forces west of the river.
16 Field Marshal Gerd von Rundstedt (1875–1953).
17 In doing so, advancing to the west coast of France and opening a new port for troops being shipped across the Atlantic.
18 It has been argued, both at the time and by historians, that the Italian campaign did little to influence the eventual campaign in northern France. Churchill makes it clear that Fifth US Army and Eighth British Army were keeping a significant number of German divisions tied down in Italy.
19 Advancing north from Cassino to Anzio.
20 The fourth battle for Cassino actually started on 11 May and the monastery was captured a week later.
21 Following the fall of Cassino, the Germans withdrew from the Gustav Line to the Gothic Line north of Rome.
22 In case.

directive to General Wilson should make him fall between two stools. This would mean that we should be denied the exploitation of any victory gained south of Rome (and victories are wonderful things), or the power to pin down German divisions in Italy and yet on the other hand not be able to make a major operation out of ANVIL Z.

6. Taking paragraph 6 of CCS 465/19, I agree with the first proposition but do not think the second proposition can be judged until we see the result of the battle. For instance I would not now rule out either a vigorous pursuit northward of the beaten enemy, or an amphibious cat's claw higher up to detain him or cut him off.[23] I should have thought we could contrive plans and preparations to render possible either this, or ANVIL Z, in one form or another. After all, the power to put men into ships is one thing and question where to disembark them is another.

7. I am sorry that we are not to have the additional landing craft you thought of deducting from the Pacific effort. We should all like to see them in the Mediterranean. But if you judge there is too much vagueness and option to justify their employment there, so must it be. The consequences will be to reduce all amphibious possibilities to a one division scale.

8. Finally, I repeat that if we can keep 34 German divisions in the Western Mediterranean Theater the forces there will have made an immense contribution to OVERLORD. I have hardened very much upon OVERLORD and am further fortified by the evident confidence of Eisenhower, Brooke[24] and Montgomery.

9. When you have reflected on the above, I ask you to consider the following formula:

(1) The prime duty of all the forces in the Mediterranean is to pin down as many German divisions as possible away from OVERLORD.
(2) Secondly, to achieve the above we must give the highest priority to operations to join the ANZIO bridgehead and the main front, meanwhile, making such preparations for ANVIL as are practicable in consonance[25] therewith.
(3) Thirdly, after joining the bridgehead we must survey the situation arising from the results of the battle in Italy, as well as the first results of OVERLORD and the dispositions of the enemy.
(4) Fourthly, we must then decide whether to go all out for ANVIL or exploit the results of victory in Italy. It must be recognized that this option will not exist unless the LSTs from the Pacific are assigned now to the Mediterranean.
(5) Every good wish to you, King and Arnold.[26] How I wish we were all together, but I trust we shall be reassembled before the supreme struggle begins.

You can draw your own conclusions.

---

23 The amphibious landing at Anzio had looked like cat's claw striking behind the Gustav Line on an operations map. Churchill was considering another Anzio style operation around the Gothic Line.
24 General Sir Alan Brooke (1883–1963), Chief of the Imperial General Staff and chairman of the Chiefs of Staff Committee.
25 In agreement.
26 Admiral King, Commander in Chief, US Fleet and Chief of Naval Operations, and General Henry H. Arnold, Commander in Chief of the US Air Forces.

Marshall to Churchill   *14 April*   *Ref: W-22810*

Please deliver the following message from General Marshall to the Prime Minister.

I have been delaying answer to your OZ-1895 until the receipt of the proposed directive from your Chiefs of Staff. I now learn from Dill that in all probability no directive will be proposed until an answer from me has been made to your personal message.

We appear to be agreed in principle, but quite evidently not as to method. If we are to have any option as to what we can do when the time comes, preparations for ANVIL must be made now, even though they may be at the partial expense of future operations in Italy after the beachhead has been joined to the main line. Unless this has been done, in our view there will be no option, whereas if preparations for an ANVIL are made, Wilson will have an amphibious force available to carry out another, and perhaps a less difficult, amphibious operation than ANVIL, should the circumstances at the time make the latter appear inexpedient.[27]

Furthermore, the urgency of our need for these landing craft in the Pacific at this particular period is very great. We have established a momentum in that Theater and possess a decisive superiority in naval and aircraft and also an adequate force of ground troops. It is an exceedingly serious matter to hamstring this force, as it were, through the lack of landing craft to implement its operation. This would result in the loss of the acquired momentum which means so much towards shortening the period of the war in the Pacific. This sacrifice in the Pacific can be justified only with the assurance that we are to have an operation in the effectiveness of which we have complete faith.[28]

Marshall to Churchill   *19 April*   *Ref: W-24751*

To get on with operations in the Mediterranean on a firm basis without further delay, the United States Chiefs of Staff are agreeing to the Directive for General Wilson proposed by the British Chiefs of Staff. We must now throw everything we have in the Mediterranean into the battle in Italy, in order to reduce the German capability to move forces to oppose OVERLORD.

Since Eisenhower's assault is not to be supported by a landing in southern France, every possible deceptive effort – air, sea and ground – in the Mediterranean will have to be utilized to hold the German divisions in Southern France during the critical days of OVERLORD. Wilson, with the means available, should be able to take prompt advantage to the utmost of the command of the sea and the tremendous air force in his Theater.[29]

Regarding LST's for later Pacific operations, our best estimates at this time indicated that there should be sufficient LST's for the various operations required to defeat Japan, but the definite allocation will have to be made on the basis of approved plans. The necessity of offsetting the delays in naval and other ship construction created by the accelerated LST program is the reason for willingness here to continue at the rate of peak production.

Report on Air Operations

Eisenhower to Marshall   *12 April*   *Ref: S-50299*

As you will note from the reports of air operations, we are seizing every opportunity to force

---

27 Marshall wants planning and preparations for ANVIL to go ahead because the amphibious operation could be switched to northwest Italian coast if a better opportunity to support OVERLORD presented itself.
28 Marshall also had to consider the campaign in Pacific Theater and after the capture of the Gilbert and Marshall Islands, preparations were underway for an invasion of Saipan in June.
29 ANVIL had been reduced to a deception plan, the landing craft sent to the Pacific and all Mediterranean efforts had to be focused on breaking the Gustav Line and linking up with the Anzio beachhead.

the Luftwaffe to fight. When our penetrations go very deep we have to pay a good price but Spaatz's crowd is taking a big toll of the enemy, and once we get a really good operation against about three or four important targets east of Berlin we won't have to go that far for a long time. For the past two weeks all air operations have been under my general direction and although it takes a little time to get new operational lines completely sorted out where there have been so many independent voices and authorities, everything in that particular field is working satisfactorily.[30]

The three great questions to which final answers cannot possibly be given until after the event, involve the minefields in the channel, the batteries on the coast, and the artificial harbors. You may be confident that every possible precaution is being taken to minimize our risks and I am personally sanguine.[31]

The wisdom of bombing certain of the thickly populated transportation centers is a matter that we are discussing constantly with political authorities but all the questions that arise are being settled on a perfectly reasonable basis and everyone is ready to do anything to further the prospects of success.[32]

Eisenhower Justifies his Organization

Eisenhower to Marshall   *25 April*   *Ref: S-50706*

Quoting a memorandum from Admiral King, I have studied this matter of proper organization for this particular Theater incessantly for almost two years. A plan somewhat along the lines suggested by Admiral King was in the process of development in North Africa, when the ANFA conference[33] decided that in that Theater there would be three Commanders-in-Chief, one each for the air, ground and navy. A study of the matter indicated that no, repeat no, matter what character was issued by the Superior Allied Headquarters, each of these three Commanders-in-Chief was certain to have a very complete operational and logistic staff of its own, and the efforts became one of integrating without duplicating.

Our problem is a broader one than the unification under one command of the army, navy and air components of one nation; it requires the unification of these elements of two major countries. Each of these Commanders-in-Chiefs rightly regards himself as my principle and direct advisor in matters pertaining to his own element, and the only difference between this Theater and the African one, is that as our frontages expand, I should have two principle ground commanders instead of only one.[34] These commanders and their staffs are in fact, components of these headquarters and are geared directly with my organization. Moreover, in the two important phrases of planning and intelligence, the staff of my headquarters is a combined one in every sense of the word, with approximately equal British and American air and naval representation.

I have studied Admiral Nimitz's staff, on the basis of information brought to me by

---

30 The Combined Bomber Offensive had been targeting defensive structures along the coast, OKWs lines of communications, in particular transportation centers to isolate the Normandy area, and industries related to building fighter planes. Ninth AAF dropped 33,000 tons of bombs on French railway targets during April alone. Oil targets started to be added in May.

31 Optimistic.

32 The constant dilemma was how to assess the advantages of damaging a vital railway target against the chance of causing French civilian casualties.

33 The January 1943 conference, codenamed SYMBOL, between Churchill, Roosevelt and de Gaulle, held at the Anfa Hotel in Casablanca, Morocco; Stalin did not attend due to the heavy fighting in Stalingrad.

34 Eisenhower's problem was that his frontage for the sixty days following D-Day would be too small for two ground commanders. As it expanded it had to be divided. Bradley would be the American representative as commander of 12th Army Group and Montgomery would be the British and Commonwealth representative as commander of 21st Army Group.

visiting American officers, and I am quite convinced that with a problem such as his, I would organize exactly as he has.[35] I am most emphatically in sympathy with Admiral King's feeling that staff representation of the American Navy should be proportionate to the operational contributions American Naval units are making, and I believe that this additional American representation should be on Admiral Ramsey's staff. Such an increase would probably result in additional representation of the American Navy on my own planning and intelligence staffs, because Admiral Ramsey would have a larger number of American officers and could give me more individuals.

On paper there may appear to be a shortage of naval and air offices on the Supreme Staff. It must be remembered, however, that a vast proportion of the special jobs involving civil affairs, communications, all types of engineering and similar activities, are filled by people selected from civil life, who are normally commissioned in the Army rather than in the other services.

Beyond this, because my three Commanders-in-Chief meet frequently with me, accompanied by senior staff members, and that constant interlocking staff work is performed by the appropriate sections of the several staffs, I believe that our organization is best suited to the peculiar requirements of our conditions and of our Theater.

General Girard Wants a New Posting

Marshall to Eisenhower   *25 April*   *Ref: W-27196*
The State Department has been advised by Murphy[36] that General Giraud has expressed hope that:

1. He be detailed by the Supreme Allied commander, Mediterranean Theater, to proceed to Italy where he could be available for consultation as tactical adviser, or:
2. He be detailed to London in a similar capacity, or:
3. He be invited to Washington where he might be useful has a technical adviser to the Combined Chiefs of Staff.

The State Department has indicated to the President that if General Giraud[37] decided to leave North Africa, it is the Department's view that it would be best for him to go to England. The President has asked me for recommendation as to the advisability of assigning General Giraud to duty on your staff in an advisory capacity. I have told the President that General Giraud's presence in England in this capacity might create difficult or embarrassing situations during the coming operations. However, I informed the President that I was asking you for your comments, which I would forward on receipt. I do not want to have General Giraud imposed on you if this might embarrass you in any way.

Eisenhower to Marshall   *26 April*   *Ref: S-50779*
It would be very embarrassing indeed if General Giraud came to England in any official capacity, particularly at the present time. As you know, General Koenig has been sent here as commander of the French forces in the United Kingdom, and as head of the French Military

---

35 Fleet Admiral Chester W. Nimitz, GCB, USN (1885–1966), Commander in Chief of the US Pacific Fleet and Commander in Chief of Pacific Ocean Areas for US and Allied air, land, and sea forces. The Pacific Theater was dominated by combined naval, amphibious and air operations, needing greater representation from the Navy and Air Force than Eisenhower did.
36 Robert D. Murphy (1894–1978), President Roosevelt's eyes and ears in the French North African colonies.
37 Sometime Commander-in-Chief of the French forces in North Africa.

Mission. Initially at least, his attitude has been all that could be desired. We opened conversations with him last week strictly on a military basis, and he was thoroughly cooperative.

Obviously, Giraud would not, repeat not, be willing to place himself under Koenig's orders, and would expect to be assigned directly to this Headquarters. For security reasons it is impossible at this time to acquaint any French officer with the details of a military plans, let alone bring him onto this staff. This fact is fully appreciated by General Koenig, but I doubt if Giraud would appreciate it. Furthermore, if he were so assigned, the immediate result would be to create suspicion in the French Mission, and to resurrect here the personal hostilities and factional disputes which existed in Algiers. I am convinced that it would then become impossible for us to work with the French Military Mission.

There is no, repeat no, question that Giraud has lost much of his former standing with the French Army. His failure to take any action to protect French officers from arrest or persecution by the more extreme elements of the Algiers Government has cost him the confidence of the majority of French officers.

I strongly urge that if he comes to England, it be in the status of a private citizen and not, repeat not, in any official capacity. For your private information, I am quite certain that the British Government will be most reluctant to agree to his coming here officially, as it is fully alive to the difficult situation that would be precipitated, both with Koenig and with the French committee. On the other hand, because of our obligations to Giraud, there is very little question that he would be received willingly in a private capacity.

Patton's Career on the Line

Marshall to Eisenhower   26 April   *Ref: W-28238*
Newspapers today carried glaring reports of General Patton's statements, reference Britain and America's rule of the world. We were just about to get confirmation of the permanent ranks. This I fear has killed them all.[38]

Smith to Marshall   27 April   *Ref: S-50822*
I have just read W-28238 over the phone to General Eisenhower who is observing a maneuver. He will reply to your message when he returns here tomorrow.

For your personal information, after much argument by myself and the Public Relations officers, General Eisenhower agreed very reluctantly to release General Patton's presence here. His reluctance was due to his belief that some incident like the present one, would occur as soon as Patton could be quoted in the press. We argued that if Patton's name was not released, it will provide ammunition for some unscrupulous columnist to write that General Eisenhower and the War Department were keeping Patton's presence here concealed because of an unwillingness to let the American people know that he was to exercise a command in the invasion forces. As usual General Eisenhower was right.[39]

Incidentally, the British press carried nothing that I have seen regarding any statement of the nature that Britain and America would rule the world. Coverage here was limited to rather innocuous quotes of the 'Blood and Guts' type.

---

38 There are many varied accounts of what became known as the 'Knutsford Affair'. This is the day by day correspondence between General Marshall and General Eisenhower during the eight days when General Patton's career was on the line.
39 It appears that it is not what Patton said that was the problem but the fact that he was reported in the press. This left Eisenhower with no option but to reveal Patton's presence in the UK and in doing so jeopardize SHAEF's attempt to deceive the Germans into believing that he was still in the Mediterranean. Eisenhower and the press were, not for the first or the last time, at loggerheads.

Eisenhower to Marshall   *29 April*   *Ref: S-50908*

Your W-28234 was communicated to me by General Smith while I was absent on an exercise, and it was my first intimation that Patton had broken out again. Apparently he is unable to use reasonably good sense in all those matters where senior commanders must appreciate the effect of the own actions upon public opinion, and this raises doubts as to the wisdom of retaining him in High Command, despite his demonstrated capacity in battle leadership. In this case the only excuse he gave to Smith, who has talked to him, is that he spoke to about 60 people at a private gathering and did not, repeat not, know that any representative of the press was present. His actual words according to my reports were "Since it seems to be the destiny of America, Britain and Russia, to rule the world, the better we know each other, the better off we will be."[40]

While his exact remarks on this occasion where incorrectly reported and somewhat misinterpreted in the press, I have grown so weary of the trouble he constantly causes you and the War Department, to say nothing of myself, that I am seriously contemplating the most drastic action. I am deferring final action until I hear further from you. Specifically I should like to know whether you still feel, after the lapse of several days, that his latest statements have caused such serious reaction at home as to prevent the War Department securing Congressional approval of any of its recommendations. Regardless of the answer to the above question, do you consider that his retention in High Command will tend to destroy or diminish public and governmental confidence in the War Department? If the answer to either of the above is in the affirmative, then I am convinced that stern disciplinary action must be taken so as to restore the situation. I request that you give me a reply as soon as convenient and I will then make a final recommendation.

Marshall to Eisenhower   *29 April*   *Ref: W-29722*

Reference your S-50908 regarding Patton: His remarks as quoted have created a stir throughout the United States. I quote excerpts from an editorial this morning in the Washington Post:

> "General Patton has progressed from simple assault on individuals to collective assault on entire nationalities. As Congressman Mundt[41] observed, he has now 'succeeded in slapping the face of every one of the United Nations except Great Britain'. The General insists that he excepted the Soviet Union too. But the distinction does not seem to us to be vital".

The editorial then refers to his remarks on welcoming the Germans and Italians into hell and also his reference to the 'English ladies' and 'American dames' with this comment:

> "... this was intended no doubt as gallantry and perhaps as a rough sort of military humor. The truth is, however, that it is neither gracious nor amusing. We do not mean to be prissy about the matter but we think that Lieutenant-Generals, even temporary ones, ought to talk with rather more dignity than this. When they do not, they run the danger of losing the respect of the men they command and the confidence of the public they serve. We think that this has happened to General Patton. Whatever his merits as a

---

40 There are several versions of what Patton said. This is the wording that Marshall and Eisenhower were given.
41 Karl E. Mundt (1900–1974), Republican Congressman for South Dakota.

strategist or tactician, he has revealed glaring defects as a leader of men. It is more than fortunate that these have become apparent before the Senate takes action to pass upon his recommended promotion in rank from Colonel to Major General. All thought of such promotion should now be abandoned. That the War Department recommended it is one more evidence of the tendency of, on the part of members of the military, to set up a clique or club. His brother officers must have had some awareness of General Patton's lack of balance, etc, etc. We confess to some perplexity as to the entire practice of permanent promotions in the midst of war. Why cannot all of these wait until the war is over and we can judge the records of our military men with some perspective? General Patton's case affords an object lesson."

Like you, I have been considering the matter on a purely business basis. Its effect on you and the troops, and on the confidence of the public in the War Department and in you, is opposed to the unmistakable fact that Patton is the only available Army Commander for his present assignment who has had actual experience in fighting Rommel and in extensive landing operations followed by a rapid campaign of exploitation. Whether or not we can forgo the latter advantage because of the unfavorable effects referred to, I leave entirely to your decision. You carry the burden of responsibility as to the success of OVERLORD. If you feel that the operation can be carried out with the same assurance of success with Hodges in command, for example, instead of Patton, all well and good. If you doubt it, then between us we can bear the burden of the present unfortunate reaction. I fear the harm has already been fatal to the confirmation of the permanent list.[42]

McNarney[43] to Eisenhower　　　　　*2 May*　　　　　*Ref: W-30496*
Your S-50965, April 30, arrived after General Marshall had departed on inspection tour. I am attempting to get in touch with him and until you hear from me again take no further action in the Patton case.

Marshall to Eisenhower　　　　　*2 May*　　　　　*Ref: W-30586*
Reference your S-50965 and my number W-29722 regarding Patton, the decision is exclusively yours. My view, and it is merely that, is that you should not weaken your hand for OVERLORD. If you think that Patton's removal does weaken your prospect, you should continue with him in command. In any event, I do not want you at this time to be burdened with the responsibility of reducing in his rank. Send him home if you see fit, and in grade, or hold him there as surplus if you so desire, or, as I have indicated above, continue him in command if that promises best for OVERLORD. I fear the quotation from one editorial may have resulted in over-emphasis in your mind of the necessity for drastic action to meet difficult resulting situation here at home. Incidentally, the numerous editorials, while caustic regarding his indiscretion, lack of poise or dignity, suitable to his position, have not demanded his release from command.[44]

Do not consider the War Department position in the matter. Consider only OVERLORD and your own heavy burden of responsibility for its success. Everything else is of minor importance.

---

42 Patton's permanent rank had been colonel since 1938 but his temporary rank had been lieutenant-general since March 1943. His promotion to temporary general was delayed until March 1945.
43 Lieutenant-General Joseph T. McNarney (1893–1972), Deputy Chief of Staff of the Army.
44 While the press liked to quote Patton and comment on what he said, they did not demand his dismissal, making the decision over his future easier.

Eisenhower to Marshall   3 May   *Ref: S-51128*

There is no question that the relief of Patton would lose to us his experience as commander of an Army in battle and his demonstrated ability in getting the utmost out of soldiers in offensive operations. Because your telegram leaves the decision exclusively in my hands, to be decided solely upon my convictions as to the effect upon OVERLORD, I have decided to retain him in command. A complete record of the entire case, including the measures I have taken to insure that no further incidents of this character will occur, will be forwarded in due course to the War Department.[45]

Eisenhower to Patton   3 May   *Ref: S-51129*

Because the War Department has directed that exclusive responsibility for decision in your case is left in my hands, I am once more taking the responsibility of retaining you in command in spite of damaging repercussions resulting from a personal indiscretion. I do this solely because of my faith in you as a battle leader and from no other motives.

In order that there may be placed on file a record of my disapproval of your recent action, and of the explicit instructions I have given you regarding your public utterances and actions, I shall place the letter I recently wrote to you on this subject in the official files.

No further action will be taken in this case and I expect you to plunge into the task of preparing your army with undiminished vigor, at the same time that you exercise extreme care to see that while you are developing the moral and fighting spirit, you will not be guilty of another discretion which can cause any further embarrassment to your superiors or yourself.

Please acknowledge receipt of this telegram.

---

45 In summary Marshall left the decision to Eisenhower and Patton kept his command because he was too valuable to lose. However, Patton was left in no doubt that only his excellent combat experience in the Mediterranean had saved him. His promotion prospects had also been put on hold.

5

MAY 1944

A Serious Security Violation

Eisenhower to Marshall   *3 May*   *Ref: E-26153*

In the public dining room of Claridges Hotel[1] on 18 April, in the presence and hearing of persons who neither knew, nor were entitled to know, operational plans, Major General Henry J. F. Miller, Air Corps,[2] made statements regarding future operations that constitute such a critically serious violation of security as to make it imperative that exemplary action be taken here, both for punitive reasons and as a deterrent.[3] Judge Advocate[4] considers that the evidence, while clear, is not of a character to warrant punishment by a court martial more severe that can be given administratively. Request you give me the authority of the President to demote him at once to his permanent Regular Army rank of colonel and return him to United States. Such action is supported by conclusions of Inspector General[5] and is concurred in by Spaatz.

Eisenhower to Marshall   *4 May*   *Ref: W-31941*

Authority is granted to reduce Major General Henry J. F. Miller, Army Air Corps, to his permanent Army rank and return him to the United States without delay by direction of the President. Forward complete report to Inspector General on the case.[6]

The President's Congratulations

Marshall to Eisenhower   *5 May*   *Ref: W-32154*

The President has not yet made a definite decision as to the advisability of making an announcement reference your S-50861 dated 28 April. However, if it should appear desirable to make such an announcement, he has informed me that it would be as follows:

> "A landing on the coast of France has been made in full force by a combined American-British Army under the command of General Eisenhower. Speaking for America, I

---

1 Brook Street, Mayfair, London.

2 Miller was commander of Air Material Command European Theater of Operations; he retired in May 1944.

3 While telling guests about how difficult it was to get crucial supplies, Miller was quoted as saying: "On my honor the invasion will come before June 15." An alternative version has Miller complaining to a nurse that some important items would not reach the UK until 15 June, well after the invasion.

4 The Judge Advocate was the US Army's legal advisor, dealing with all aspects of law and served as prosecutor during courts-martials.

5 The Inspector General was principally charged with making sure that units were ready for combat, acting as a third party inspector. However, in this case he was charged with his secondary role, the investigation of non-criminal allegations.

6 Eisenhower ordered an immediate investigation and then reduced Miller to his permanent rank of Lieutenant Colonel and gave him 24 hours to leave the UK.

send heartfelt wishes for good fortune to each and every one of our heroic soldiers and sailors, and we do not forget our British and Canadian comrades who are fighting shoulder to shoulder with us, or our Russian allies on the Eastern Front. All of us together working in unison, will bring final defeat to the Nazi destroyers of world peace, together with their duped satellites."

The President is going to discuss this matter with me next week. In the meantime, I would like any comment you have to make on the above announcement.

Marshall to Eisenhower   *10 May*   *Ref: W-34552*
Reference announcement by the President, see W-32154, May 4, 1944. The President has returned to Washington and will probably want to discuss this matter at once. Could you expedite your comments?

Eisenhower to Marshall   *11 May*   *Ref: S-51648*
I have the following comments, reference your W-32154. Based on military considerations alone, I believe that neither the President, nor the Prime Minister, should make statements directly to the people of Europe before the success of the landing is assured.[7] Statements by both on D-Day for the American and British press will undoubtedly have to be made, however, the statement should be limited to good wishes and encouragement to the Allied troops, and should further the cover plan. They should particularly avoid emphasizing the NEPTUNE area, and they should be in harmony with the initial communiqué.

At a later date when the success of the landing is assured, and it is designed to call for the active rather than the passive assistance of the unorganized people of Europe, broadcasts by the President and the Prime Minister will have great effect in strengthening my hand.[8]

I have discussed all the above with the Prime Minister, who is an agreement. The important consideration is the difficulty of controlling unorganized, and to a certain extent, the organized European resistance, and the grave danger that it may all flare up prematurely, resulting in terribly repressive measures by the Germans, before we are in a position to interfere in any way.

For your information, I propose to ask de Gaulle and the heads of the exiled governments to instruct their people on D-Day that our initial landing in our part of Europe is only the beginning of liberation, and that their people are to carry out the instructions which have already been issued to organized resistance groups and the instructions which have been issued through, and by the authority of the Supreme Commander, to unorganized

---

7 Eisenhower wrote his own letter of good wishes and copies were circulated to all soldiers, seamen and airmen. It began 'You are about to embark upon the Great Crusade, toward which we have striven these many months. The eyes of the world are upon you. The hopes and prayers of liberty-loving people everywhere march with you. In company with our brave Allies and brothers-in-arms on other Fronts, you will bring about the destruction of the German war machine, the elimination of Nazi tyranny over the oppressed peoples of Europe, and security for ourselves in a free world ...'

8 Roosevelt turned his speech into a prayer titled 'Let Our Hearts be Stout' and read it over the radio after he was notified that the invasion had begun. It began 'My Fellow Americans: Last night, when I spoke with you about the fall of Rome, I knew at that moment that troops of the US and our Allies were crossing the Channel in another and greater operation. It has come to pass with success thus far. And so, in this poignant hour, I ask you to join with me in prayer: Almighty God: Our sons, pride of our nation, this day have set upon a mighty endeavor, a struggle to preserve our Republic, our religion, and our civilization, and to set free a suffering humanity. Lead them straight and true; give strength to their arms, stoutness to their hearts, steadfastness in their faith...'

elements.[9] These instructions will be that covert acts and passive resistance are to be continued, but that overt acts should be reserved until I give the signal, at a time when the state of military operations justifies the risks taken by the civil population.[10]

Dealing with the French Committee

President to Eisenhower via Marshall   13 May   *Ref: W-36054*
I have today sent the following quoted message to Prime Minister Churchill:

> "Your 674: I have no objections whatever to your inviting de Gaulle and others of the French Committee to discuss your [garbled] on military or political matters; however, you must consider, in the interest of security, keeping de Gaulle in the United Kingdom until the OVERLORD landing has been made.
>
> "It is my understanding that General Eisenhower now has full authority to discuss with the Committee all matters on a military level. I do not desire that Eisenhower shall become involved with the Committee on a political level, and I am unable at this time to recognize any government of France until the French people have an opportunity for a free choice of government."[11]

I hope my previous directive was wholly clear to you. I know you will understand that any matters relating to the future Government of France are a political and not a military matter.

The American position has always been firm on this point.

We must be certain that the words "Free Determination", which date back to the Atlantic Charter, shall be preserved in substance and in spirit. Therefore, no existing group outside of France can be given the kind of domination over the French people in France, which would dominate the free expression of choice.

The French Committee denies that it has any such intention, but so many instances have occurred in the last two years that I am unable to accept that declaration wholeheartedly.

That is why you, as Supreme Commander, must assume this additional task.

We must always remember that the French population is quite naturally shell-shocked, just as any other people would be after such sufferings at the hands of German occupation. It will take some time for them quietly and normally to think through the matters pertaining to their political future. We, as the liberators of France, have no right to color their views or give any group the sole right to impose one side of the case on them.

I know that you will understand my desire that self-determination for them shall be our true aim.

---

9 Charles de Gaulle was scheduled to speak to the French people after Eisenhower. He refused to read out the text written by Eisenhower because it made no mention of himself or the French Committee for National Liberation; de Gaulle insisted on reading his own text when he arrived in London on 4 June and a bitter showdown with Churchill followed. As the airborne divisions headed for France on the night of 5/6 June, de Gaulle's ambassador, Pierre Vienot, shuttled between the two men; de Gaulle's decision to withdraw 100 (some say 200) French liaison officers from the invasion force only increased the tension. Eventually, de Gaulle made his own stirring speech to the French people but he still held back the liaison officers as a bargaining chip.
10 Eisenhower also drafted a message in case the invasion failed: 'Our landings in the Cherbourg area have failed to gain a satisfactory foothold and I have withdrawn the troops. My decision to attack at this time and place was based on the best information available. The troops, the air and the navy did all that bravery could do. If any blame or fault attaches to the attempt it is mine alone.'
11 Marshall sent a paraphrased copy of this message to Eisenhower on the same day, cable number W-36189.

Smith to Marshall   *14 May*   *Ref: S-51841*
(Code Clerk AGWAR: When this message is decoded deliver the strip literally directly to the
Secretary of the War Department General Staff on duty and to no, repeat no, one else.)

Message begins. Reference your W-36189, we had already received a message direct from the
President quoting his reply to the Prime Minister. This, General Eisenhower has not, repeat
not, yet seen, as he is away on an inspection trip. In this message to General Eisenhower,
after repeating his reply to the Prime Minister, the President added the following quote:

>"I hope my previous directive was wholly clear to you.
>   I know you will understand that any matters relating to the future government of
>France are a political and not a military matter. The American position has always been
>firm on this point. We must be certain that the words 'Free Determination', which date
>back to the Atlantic Charter, shall be preserved in substance and in spirit. Therefore, no
>existing group outside of France can be given the kind of domination over the French
>people in France, which would dominate the free expression of a choice. The French
>Committee denies that it has had any such intention, but so many instances have
>occurred in the last two years that I am unable to accept their declarations wholeheart-
>edly. That is why you as Supreme Commander must assume this additional task.
>   "We must always remember that the French population is quite naturally shell-
>shocked, just as any other people would be after such suffering at the hands of German
>occupation. It will take some time for them quietly and normally to think through the
>matters pertaining to their political future. We, as the liberators of France, have no,
>repeat no, right to color their views or give any group the sole right to impose one side of
>a case upon them. I know that you will understand my desire that self determination for
>them while be our true aim." End of President's message.

During the past two days the following has taken place. Yesterday, as a result of our direct
request, the Prime Minister authorized General Koenig[12] to send one message in French
cipher to Algiers in an effort to explain to the F.C.N.L.[13] the necessity for the suspension of
French cipher communications and re-establish some basis for future military discussions.
As an indication of the strength of French feeling, Koenig refused to submit this perfectly
innocuous message to any Englishman for censorship, but was willing that it be censored by
an American. I censored it personally. No, repeat no, reply has yet been received.
    Last night, after receiving the President's message above referred to, the Prime Minister
called me and read it to me. He said that he intended to invite de Gaulle here, but would now
do so only on condition that de Gaulle remained here until after D-Day, and during his stay
would not communicate with Algiers. I am certain that any such invitation would be indig-
nantly refused and advised against it. As far as I know, the invitation will not be extended at
this time but will, repeat will, be the extended for some date near, but after D-Day.
    With regard to the entire matter of dealing with the French, General Eisenhower of course

12 Kœnig served as the Free French delegate to the Allied headquarters under Eisenhower but was given
command of the Free French troops which would participate in the Normandy invasion. He also served as a
military advisor to de Gaulle. He was given command of the French Forces of the Interior, unifying French
Resistance groups under de Gaulle's control in June 1944.
13 French Committee of National Liberation, formed by Generals Charles de Gaulle and Henri Giraud
on 3 June 1943, coming under de Gaulle's leadership on 9 November. It challenged the legitimacy of the
Vichy Government and unified all French forces against the Nazis and their collaborators; it evolved into the
Provisional French Government under de Gaulle.

is in complete agreement with the President's statement that questions relating to the future Government of France are political and not military. His attitude with respect to the French Committee has been to deal with it on a military basis and to use it, and its representatives, in planning matters of civil administration, in order to assist the military operation. So far we have dealt only with the Committee as the sole organized body of Frenchmen available.

General Eisenhower is alive to the fact that the use of the Committee will tend to enhance its political prestige but we have felt that the military advantage to be gained from the Committee's assistance justifies dealing with it on a military basis, bearing in mind the importance of keeping such a political advantage to a minimum. Our association with the Committee would have the single purpose of helping military operations. Any attempt by the Committee to use that association to entrench itself as the government of France would of course be repudiated, nor would our dealing with the Committee prevent us from dealing also with any other non-Vichy group of Frenchmen which could be of use to us in fighting Germans.

Perhaps we are too close to the practical aspects of the problem to understand clearly the position of our government. We have had the text of the President's formula in dealing with France and the text of the alternative British formula, but as you know we have not, repeat not received any formal directive. Consequently, we have been working within the framework of the American text as represented by the Secretary of State's public statement on foreign policy of April 11. We have only just learned that Mr. Hull's[14] remarks regarding relations with the French do not, repeat not, represent the President's views.

I am sure that nothing would suit General Eisenhower better than to have his responsibility rigidly confined to matters of purely military concern, but no one, repeat no one, who has dealt with a foreign government at close range as we have, can fail to realize that when a military commander is operating on foreign soil there is no clear-cut line of demarcation between military and civil or political questions.

Finally, there is one more difficult condition, and a delicate one, which affects us in the absence of a formal directive from the Combined Chiefs of Staff. When General Eisenhower, as Supreme Allied Commander, received a unilateral directive on such vital matters as those covered in the President's telegram, he is placed in a very difficult position. In order, faithfully and effectively, to carry out the mission which has been assigned to him, he must constantly be aware of his responsibilities to both governments and he is scrupulous in the discharge of those responsibilities. In dealing with matters of high governmental policy as affecting the two governments which he represents, he cannot, repeat not, act as an American Theater commander, since these matters are inseparable from his role as Supreme Allied Commander. The Prime Minister always says, as he told me again last night, that he stands with the President on all questions dealing with the French. This statement, of course, can be taken for what it is worth, but it must always be remembered that the one ministry which the Prime Minister does not, repeat not, control is the Foreign Office.[15]

The time is so short and the implications of the problem are so great that I think this lengthy message was justified to explain, from our viewpoint, the great importance of

---

14 Cordell Hull (1871–1955), the longest-serving American Secretary of State, serving in President Roosevelt's administration from March 1933 to November 1944.

15 While support for de Gaulle and the underground resistance was growing, Roosevelt was determined to undermine his plans to become head of a new provisional government of France. The Americans were determined to install a military government of occupation until the whole of France had been liberated and the French people were in a position to elect a democratic government. Roosevelt had even refused to have discussions with de Gaulle. Churchill, meanwhile, was caught in the middle, on the one hand furious with de Gaulle for causing trouble and on the other acknowledging that he was the one French leader who had always stood against Hitler.

obtaining for the Supreme Commander, if possible, a clear cut combined directive on our relationship with the French.

Marshall to Eisenhower and Smith   *15 May*   *Ref: W-36713*
We have not received the text of the alternative British formula which you referred to in S-51841, 14 May 1944. Will you please transmit the text of the British formula to us?

Smith to Marshall   *16 May*   *Ref: S-51907*
Proposed American and British texts of directive to Supreme Commander have only been shown to me informally and confidentially. However, the only major difference is that the American text provides that General Eisenhower may, repeat may, deal with the French Committee for National Liberation or with any other non, repeat non, Vichy group of Frenchmen, whereas British text indicates that dealings will be exclusively with French Committee for National Liberation.

Eisenhower to Marshall   *16 May*   *Ref: S-51959*
I have received from the President a personal message dated 13 May on the French situation. Have also read General Smith's personal message to you dated 14 May, commenting on the message from the President. General Smith's radio presents some of the problems in French collaboration and represents in general the views of this headquarters.

Today I have a message from the Prime Minister saying that he now considers it advisable to defer asking General de Gaulle to come to London until D-Day. In this way, no question of security will be involved and we would still have time to work out some of our more difficult problems with de Gaulle, because it will be a considerable period before questions of civil government become acute.[16]

I request that you have the following delivered to the President, as my reply to his message:

> "You may be quite certain that my dealings with the French Committee will be confined to military matters and unrelated civil administration, and will be conducted on a military level. I understand your anxiety in this matter, and I assure you that I will carefully avoid anything that could be interpreted as an effort to influence the character of the future government of France. However, I think I should tell you that so far as I am able to determine from information given to me through agents and through escaped prisoners of war, there exists in France today only two major groups, which one is the Vichy gang, and the other seems to be almost idolatrous in its worship of de Gaulle. This may merely be an indication of the 'shellshock' to which you refer, but its effect will be a practical one when we have succeeded in liberating areas that will fall outside the strictly military zone and should therefore be turned over to local self government. It is possible that we then shall find a universal desire to adhere to the De Gaullist group. I fully share your apprehension as to the intentions of some members of the French Committee concerning the future, but I am merely presenting to you the picture that may develop inside France itself.

---

16 Although de Gaulle had stayed in North Africa and had been kept out of D-Day planning, Roosevelt and Churchill recognized that he had to be present when the invasion began ready to make his speech to the French people. He was delayed until 4 June, only 48 hours before the troops landed on the Normandy beaches.

I will not, repeat not, of course, express any such opinions to the French Committee, nor will I concede them any exclusive right to deal with me in the handling of French liberated territories. Actually, I cannot foresee any development which would call for early establishment of civil control over large sections of France. I will keep you informed of all developments.

Because this is an Allied command, I hope that your desires on this subject, of which I am already aware, can eventually come to me as a joint directive of the two governments. This would help me."

Signed Eisenhower.

The French Resistance in Southern France

Wilson to Eisenhower   13 May   *Ref: F-45271*
Native resistance groups in South France are the subject.

Points to control the uprising by having our agents direct attacks against enemy communications and vital installations.

If the rising should occur, the participants will be compromised and will have to take to the mountains to avoid reprisals by the Germans. After D-Day I propose to land selected French officers and non-commissioned officers and French speaking O.S.S.[17] personnel to organize and lead native groups against the enemy and his communications. At the same time, I shall make an all out effort to supply and equip these native groups.

Prior to D-Day, I propose to land American and British saboteurs to operate against the Nice – Marseilles railway lines and communications in the Rhône Valley and Carcassone Gap.[18]

If, however, it is your firm policy to dampen down popular uprisings outside of NEPTUNE area, as discussed with me, I shall, of course do everything within my power to implement the policy.

Grateful for an early expression of your views and desires.

Eisenhower to Wilson   15 May   *Ref: S-51900*
Resistance in France considered to take two forms:

1. Organized resistance groups, whether under S.O.E./S.O. or French control.[19]
2. General civilian resistance.

It is our firm policy to restrict general civilian resistance to such covert action as may be possible without inviting mass reprisals. Their overt action to be delayed until it can be related to tactical operations. Your assistance in implementing this policy would be appreciated.[20]

Organized resistance groups throughout France will put into effect their prearranged

---

17 The Office of Strategic Services was the US intelligence agency formed to coordinate espionage activities behind enemy lines for the US Armed Forces during the Second World War. It was the predecessor of the Central Intelligence Agency (CIA).

18 To interfere with troop movements from the south of France to the Normandy area.

19 The UK formed the Special Operations Executive (SOE) to conduct warfare against the Axis powers by means other than direct military engagement.

20 Eisenhower was concerned that general acts of sabotage immediately after D-Day would only give limited help to the Allied effort and would invite German reprisals. Instead he wanted acts of sabotage to be coordinated with the overall campaign to reap the maximum benefits.

D-Day plans on receipt of action messages from B.B.C., to be issued by Special Force Headquarters, London.[21] Their action is designed to:

1. Delay enemy forces moving by rail,
2. Delay enemy forces moving by road,
3   Sabotage enemy telecommunications,
4. Carry out general guerilla tasks.

Action to reinforce resistance groups forms, subject of a coordinating directive which will be cabled you about 17th May (this directive will exclude rail line priorities initially).

For your information can we consider top priority rail route is that running Montauban – Brive[22] northwards. Would appreciate anything you could do to delay enemy movement on this railway between D+1 and D+3.

As regards your proposals to land U.S. and British saboteurs pre D-Day, and French post D-Day. Consider that there is no security objection to landing JEDBURGH's[23] (which contain one Frenchman in each team) pre D-Day, where such action would support vendetta, and provided their instructions give them no opportunity to draw inference that no actual attack is coming in from the south in the immediate future.

The Danger of Bombing the French Railways

Marshall to Smith   16 May   *Ref: W-37216*

Saint-Didier[24] brought up the question of the bombing of railway installations, costing the lives of French citizens. I will take this up later with General Eisenhower.[25] Meanwhile I pass on this seemingly practical request of Bethouart[26] through Saint-Didier: That General Eisenhower request Koenig to provide him with a chart of the vital rail installations in France, with the French recommendations as to the points most critical for the operation of the railroads.[27] As I see it superficially at the moment, this involves no disclosure of secrecy as to the character of OVERLORD, as we already engaged in a general bombing throughout Northern and Northwestern France.

---

21 The first message, consisting of the first three lines of Paul Verlaine's poem, 'Chanson d'Autome', alerted resistance groups to prepare their sabotage plans. The second message, consisting of the next three lines of the poem, let the groups know it was D–1 and time to go into action. Although German intelligence knew that the poem related to resistance activities against rail targets, having tortured the information out of a captured SOE operative, they did not realize it was related to D-Day.
22 Montauban north of Toulouse and Brive-la-Gaillarde, south of Limoges.
23 Operation JEDBURGH represented the first cooperation between SOE and the Special Operations branch of OSS. Each three-man team had a commander, an executive officer, and a non-commissioned radio operator; one of the officers was French while the others were either British or American. JEDBURGH teams parachuted in by night to meet the local Resistance or Maquis group. They provided leadership, expertise and advice; they could also arrange airdrops of arms and ammunition. The first team in, codenamed 'Hugh', parachuted into central France the night before D-Day, and on 9 June Eisenhower handed over command of the JEDBURGH teams to the French. 93 JEDBURGH teams were deployed between June and December 1944.
24 General Auguste-Marie Brossin de Saint-Didier (1888–1971), Head French Military Mission, Washington.
25 Spaatz had wanted to concentrate on oil targets but Eisenhower insisted on focusing on stopping German troops reaching the beachhead. The British War Cabinet was initially opposed due to the possibility of a high number of civilian casualties, estimated at 160,000.
26 General Marie É.A. Béthouart (1889–1982), Chief of Staff of the French Committee for National Defense from April 1944 until August 1944, then commander of the I French Corps.
27 On 14 April Eisenhower had taken over direction of the strategic air forces in support of OVERLORD and three days later issued his directive for the transportation bombing campaign. Churchill did not want to attack targets where 100 or more civilians would be killed but by 18 April the War Cabinet had cleared all rail targets except two in the Paris area.

Marshall to Eisenhower　　　　　　　*16 May*　　　　　　　Ref: W-37353

This is further to my W-37216, with reference to Saint-Didier's request concerning the bombing of railway installations. I have discussed this with the United States Chiefs of Staff. We assume that you have probably already availed yourself of all the information which the French can furnish you. However, we feel that a request from you to General Koenig for information, such as that suggested by Bethouart through Saint-Didier, would assure the French that we are doing our very best to keep civilian casualties to a minimum. The Chiefs of Staff agree I should send you this personal message.

Suggest that, if you consider this practicable, you request Koenig to provide you with a chart of the vital rail installations in France and the French recommendations as to the points most critical for the operation of the railroads. Koenig should be willing to furnish this advice without asking for any commitments or information in return.

Smith to Marshall　　　　　　　*17 May*　　　　　　　Ref: S-51984

At the moment, since we are giving no, repeat no, information whatever on OVERLORD to the French, it would be impossible to have French officers in, or directly assigned to, this headquarters, where the whole atmosphere is charged with OVERLORD.[28]

In my first conference with General Koenig, I arranged that he and his senior air man should consult with Tedder on bombing, particularly railway targets and those involving probable loss of life among French citizens. Algiers does not, repeat not, know of this because of the stop on communications, but their representative in Washington should be so informed. Actually this amounts to a gesture on both sides, as Koenig realizes that we have definitely more information on the subject than is available to him, since the foremost European and French railway experts studied and assisted in the formation of the railway plan, and nothing has been done so far because our conversations with the French mission have practically ceased for the moment.

As you probably know, the problem of reconciling the French to civilian losses has occupied the Prime Minister and the British Cabinet. A minor Cabinet crisis was precipitated by the railway bombing plan, which was fought through with the greatest difficulty after almost two weeks of nightly debates and rather bitter arguments. I am sure that this vital program would not, repeat not, have been carried through without the firm support of the British Chiefs of Staff, who were completely convinced of its necessity. However, as a result of these conferences and because of Cabinet feeling, a number of targets which threatened the greatest loss of French life were eliminated. To my surprise, Koenig takes a much more cold blooded view than we do. His remark was "this is war, and it must be expected that people will be killed. We would take twice the anticipated loss to be rid of the Germans." I have had to remind him on occasions that the French civil population may not, repeat not, take such a complacent view. Fortunately, and to our great relief, the civilian casualties have been very much less than our most conservative estimates.[29]

Please consider the above is an interim applied to your W-37353 as General Eisenhower left last night to visit the fleet and divisions in Northern Ireland.

---

28 Churchill also vetoed this plan to bring in French railway experts.

29 SHAEF and 21st Army Group intelligence believed that the attacks had hardly affected the French rail network; they were wrong. The rail network was already under pressure due to damage sustained during the German Blitzkrieg of 1940 followed by poor management under the Nazis, prolonged underfunding and sabotage. The start of heavy bombing raids in April finished off the network and rail traffic fell by 60 per cent. By 26 May all bridges over the Seine north of Paris had been demolished. More attacks followed and by D-Day 2700 sorties had been flown against rail targets, damaging over 1400 locomotives and many more passenger and freight cars.

Last Minute Problems with Ports, Ammunition and Fuel

Eisenhower to Marshall   23 May   *Ref: S-52375*

I have been holding conferences with shipping people and others, including the Prime Minister, over a critical port situation that has developed here. Briefly the bare background is as follows: Berths in ports in the U.K. and internal transport are stretched to limit. Southern ports are, of course, no longer available for imports.[30]

BOLERO cargoes were agreed at certain numbers monthly, but in the earlier months these numbers were not reached because cargoes were not available. Arrivals this month will be 40 in excess of agreed number for May and the excess for June arrival as now planned is thirteen. Some of these ships contain materials urgently required for the operation and the only possible chance of making room for discharge of those which are vital to us, is to hold up U.K. import cargoes.

The British import program has already been cut into materially, but in present circumstances further reduction is necessary to meet minimum OVERLORD requirements. This involves considerable dislocation, but the Prime Minister has authorized temporary reduction in U.K. imports of up to 500,000 tons, which is equivalent to about 250,000 tons BOLERO cargoes, provided it is agreed at highest level that shipping assistance will be made for making good this 500,000 tons later in year, as the planned import total for the year is the absolute minimum. I promised the Prime Minister to ask you to request the President to give the desired assurance in this regard.

General Lee is communicating this evening with Somervell regarding many of related details.

Everyone here has plunged into this problem with the greatest goodwill and I cannot see where anyone is to blame. We simply have developed one of those bottlenecks, incident to big operations and the only chance of breaking it is to cut further into the current import program. I will be exceedingly grateful for your help in the matter.

Eisenhower to Marshall   26 May   *Ref: E-29855*

Exhaustive surveys by Army Group, First Army, and Theater Staffs have established minimum estimates for ammunition expenditures on the Continent.[31] All these plans were discussed thoroughly with General Lutes,[32] who was in complete agreement that the measures proposed assured adequate ammunition supply here.

It now develops that because of certain changes to which I am not personally aware, the War Department has disapproved the recommendations of this Theater. I request that you ask General Somerville[33] to resurvey this problem from the very highest level, in order to assure us that at a later date, we may avoid the rising of an acute emergency to meet, which will occasion certain changing of the schedules, as well as many other difficulties. If complete adherence to the Theater Program is impossible because of limitations on which War Department has no immediate control, adequate measures should be taken to meet our program insofar as possible.[34]

---

30 The southern ports, were filling up with ships and landing craft, waiting to be loaded with assault troops.
31 Each unit, infantry, armored or artillery, had to carry an amount of ammunition suitable for its operations, either offensive or defensive or just holding a sector; they also had to maintain a minimum reserve. Ammunition had to be transported to the UK and then across the English Channel before it could be sorted out. It then had to be split into dumps and transported forward by road for distribution amongst the front line units.
32 General Leroy Lutes (1890–1980) Director of Plans and Operations, Army Service Forces.
33 General Brehon B. Somervell (1892–1955) Commander in Chief Army Services Forces.
34 Artillery ammunition was the main problem due to the quantity required and the weight of ordnance. Ground commanders would have to revise their plans if their minimum estimates were cut.

This question extends also to the entire program of recommended out-loading from PEMBARK.[35] It is related to the question concerning which I sent you a recent urgent cable, which is present capacity and necessity for changes in loadings, so as to occasion the minimum of re-handling and reloading.

The Theater Staff is immediately sending to the War Department a more detailed explanation of the whole project, together with references to previous correspondence and cables on the same subject.[36]

Marshall to Eisenhower   *31 May*   *Ref: W-44062*
The British Chiefs of Staff have requested an increase in the assignment of 100/130 aviation fuel[37] from U.S. June production to four million barrels for the United Kingdom. United States Chiefs of Staff do not agree with this increase for the following reasons.

First, and of great importance, in making assignments from June production, all other area requirements were reduced to a minimum, and hence any additional assignment could only come at the expense of high altitude and replacement crew training in the U.S.[38] You of course recognize the gravity of a failure to meet your requirements for fully trained crews for the next several months.

Second, the assignment of aviation fuel from June production will not improve your present position, as shipments will not reach the U.K. until August when your consumption should have passed its peak.

Third, your present assignment from June production of 3,064,000 barrels, plus British controlled production, plus some reduction due to FRANTIC[39] and decreased training in the United Kingdom, should give adequate stockage to meet your operational requirements through August. The United States Chiefs have agreed that, should emergency conditions cause you to greatly exceed your estimated peak consumption, aviation fuel can, and will be, delivered in the U.K., at the expense of other consumers within 30 days of the origination of the request.

Your concern over this important matter is appreciated and the gasoline situation has been gone into carefully. We want you to feel free to use all your air in any way you require to insure success and to assure you that, should a critical situation develop, prompt action will be taken to meet the emergency.

Will an Unfortunate Error Give Away D-Day?

Marshall to Eisenhower   *30 May*   *Ref: W-43551*
We are concerned over the receipt by State Department here of a message from the British Foreign Office, regarding a proposal by British and American ambassadors to call on Spanish authorities on D minus 5, relative to the evacuation of Allied casualties and the entry of food supplies through Barcelona. This ROYAL FLUSH plan[40] apparently presents a serious hazard regarding the disclosure of D-Day which, as yet nobody in the State Department is

---

35 PEMBARK, codename of the New York overseas supply depot.
36 Only ten days before D-Day, SHAEF and the War Department were in disagreement over the amount of ammunition required for a successful offensive. Ammunition shortages were a constant a problem during the campaign as front line divisions demanded more than the estimates made. One of the greatest difficulties was getting sufficient quantities across to Normandy in poor weather conditions.
37 The standard high octane fuel for aviation piston engines.
38 Reducing training to conserve fuel stocks.
39 Bombing raids against German targets opposite the Russian front.
40 A series of diplomatic deceptions to suggest that Sweden, Spain and Turkey might be contemplating joining the Allies, or allowing them to use air bases and similar benefits.

aware of. Mr. Matthews[41] has drafted for Mr. Hull a message for our Ambassador in Madrid, as follows:

> In accordance with forthcoming military operations on the Continent and in accordance with the desires of the United States Chiefs of Staff, you are directed to concert with your British colleague and then to make an immediate approach to the Spanish government in strict confidence to request that certain facilities be granted by the Spanish authorities. You should urgently ask that the Spanish Government authorize the extension of facilities for the evacuation of Allied casualties and the entry of food supplies for France through Barcelona. You will endeavor to impress upon the Spanish Government the importance which is attached to this request. Without waiting for the Spanish Government's decision, you should either through our consulate in Barcelona, or an officer detail from your mission, make local inquiries at Barcelona as to the availability of the dock labor, berthing arrangements in the port and billeting facilities. Your British colleague is being instructed to institute similar enquiries. You should report urgently the Spanish reaction to our request and mark the telegrams on the subject 'SURF', followed by "Most Secret for the Secretary only."

What is your reaction to this procedure and particularly to the disclosure of the date to the State Department officials?

Smith to Marshall   *31 May*   *Ref: S-52912*
I regard it as extremely unfortunate that the request of the State Department should have indicated the time relationship between the proposed action and D-Day. Under the circumstances it appears certain that a number of individuals in the State Department would automatically become aware of the exact incidence of D-Day, if the ambassadors should be instructed to make their presentation on exactly D-Day minus five. The original instructions given to the British ambassador were to make his presentation on June 1 but his orders have now been revoked pending further instructions. In any event, the proposed representations by the ambassadors to the Spanish government remain an important part of our plans and I suggest that without relating the matter in any way to D-Day, the ambassadors merely be instructed to make their representation on June 3rd.

Marshall to Eisenhower   *31 May*   *Ref: W-44282*
We have requested State Department to dispatch without delay to the American Ambassador in Madrid the message quoted to you in your W-43551 dated 30 May, reference your S-52912, 31 May. The dispatch to the American ambassador has been modified to instruct him to concert with the British Ambassador for briefing, and to take his cue as to timing of action from British Ambassador. This is in accord with suggestion made in telegram for Foreign Office dated 29 May and avoids breach of security here. It is recommended that you inform Foreign Office of action taken here and request Foreign Office to send appropriate instructions to British ambassador in Madrid.

---

41 Herbert Matthews (1900–1977), US State Department.

6

JUNE 1944

Planning Bombing Raids to Help the Russians

Deane[1] to Marshall, Arnold and Spaatz   *1 June*   *Ref: 184*

General Spaatz indicated in reference cable,[2] that for the first FRANTIC missions[3] it was desired to attack targets at Galatz, Mielec and Riga, with alternative targets as the marshalling yards of five different localities. These proposals were submitted to the Red Army General Staff for approval and were finally disapproved by them on May 30. I had a long argument on the subject which was previously reported to General Arnold.[4]

Early this morning I was again called by the Red Army General Staff for a discussion of the subject of targets. They were concerned that our operations might interfere with some of the plans for their ground and air operations. This seemed to be particularly true in the area south and east of Riga. They wanted to know if we would be willing to change our plans, if they informed us that our operations would interfere with their plans; also would we be willing to attack targets on their request in order to help them in their plans.

Finally, they wanted the clear interpretation of our conception of the temporary bomb line established in the Balkans. They have looked on this line as being extremely rigid. I emphasized that the bomb line was temporary until adequate liaison could be established, but that even while the line existed we would be perfectly willing to have them operate west of it, provided we were informed of their intentions and did not have plans to operate in the same area at the same time.

General Slavin[5] indicated that the General Staff was reconsidering their disapproval of our original request, and I rather expect that they will withdraw the objections to our hitting the targets at Galatz, Mielec, and at Riga. In the future, I think it would be well if we would simply inform them of our plans as far in advance as possible without asking for specific approval, always being ready with alternative objectives if they ask us not to attack a certain target for specific reasons.

General Slavin asked me to express these views in a letter to him. I have therefore written him the letter and present a paraphrase of it as follows, with the request for you either to confirm the views I have expressed therein, or instruct me as to how you wish the letter to be amended:

---

1 Major-General John R. Deane (1919–), Head of the US Military Mission to Moscow.
2 Spaatz 13113.
3 Secret bombing missions between June and September 1944 carried out by US Air Force planes deep into Nazi held territory. Bombers and fighters flew to Soviet airbases and then used them to attack targets behind the Eastern front. Heavy equipment was transported by sea to Archangel, north of Leningrad. They were of limited success because of the lack of Soviet air defenses around the airbases and a lack of trust between the Allies.
4 General Henry H. Arnold, commander of the US Air Forces.
5 Major-General Nikolai V. Slavin (1903–1958), Head of Directorate for Liaison with the Allies, General Staff, later Assistant to the Chief of Staff, Red Army.

"May I inform you in confirmation of our conversation of last night, that the United States Chiefs of Staff earnestly desire to utilize U.S. aircraft to assist the advance of the Soviet Army to the fullest possible extent, consistent with carrying out the American part of the combined bomber offensive.

The U.S. Chiefs of Staff also wish to avoid any action which will interfere with the operational plans of the Red Army. For this reason, we shall inform you of all targets which we propose to attack when operating from Russian bases or when operating too and from Russian bases, as soon as they have been decided upon. Should you indicate in sufficient time that an American air attack on one of our proposed objectives will interfere with the operations of either the Soviet Army or the Soviet Air force, I am certain that out attack will be shifted to another objective until your objections are withdrawn.

I have always felt that the temporary bomb line now established in Romania is not necessarily restrictive to both sides. May I therefore suggest that we try to arrange a Soviet – British – American agreement, to establish closer liaison in Moscow in connection with Balkan air operations? Colonel Gormly[6] in Poltava has been sent to the USSR to serve as a liaison officer from the Anglo – American Mediterranean Air forces. If the Soviet Army General Staff could select someone to meet with him daily, I believe it would be possible to do away with the temporary bomb line and effect coordination exclusively through liaison. We now have adequate communications between Moscow and Caserta for this purpose.

Because these matters are of such importance, I request that you do not take the views that I have expressed in this letter as commitments until I have had an opportunity to obtain confirmation from the U.S. Chiefs of Staff. I shall cable them today requesting such confirmation."

Watching the Weather Forecasts[7]

Eisenhower to Marshall   1 June   *Ref: S-52957*
Weather forecasts, while still indefinite are generally favorable. I will keep you informed on this point. Everyone is in good heart and barring unsuitable meteorological conditions we will do the trick as scheduled.

Eisenhower to Marshall   3 June   *Ref: S-53110*
Weather prospects, so far as sea conditions are concerned, are rather favorable. From air viewpoint, the forecasts are not yet firm but we have almost an even chance of having pretty fair conditions. In any event I should say that only marked deterioration beyond that now expected would disarrange our plans.[8]

Good News from Italy

Wilson to Smith   4 June   *Ref: F-54720*
Hope to send you the following message later today: "The Allies are in Rome." Am sending you this advanced information so that you can lay on such broadcasts as you may wish.[9]

---

6 Colonel Gormly.
7 The weather across the English Channel during the first week of June was not what the Allies had expected. It ranged from poor to variable and Eisenhower had to keep a daily watch on the reports made by James M. Stagg's meteorological team.
8 Although the weather on 3 June was good, there was bad weather moving in from Nova Scotia and Stagg advised that there would be a 36-hour window of better weather starting on 6 June. Eisenhower had to make the difficult decision to postpone OVERLORD for 24 hours. D-Day would be 6 June.
9 After four months and four offensives, the Gustav Line was finally broken in May. Rather than pushing inland from Anzio, General Clark ordered his troops north towards Rome. The Germans declared it an open city and Allied troops entered on 4 June.

Stalin sends Good Wishes

Premier Stalin to Prime Minister   6 June   *No Referencee*

I have received your communication about the success of the beginning of the OVERLORD operation.

> "The summer offensive of the Soviet forces, organized in accordance with the agreement of the Tehran conference, will begin towards the middle of June on one of the important sectors of the front. The general offensive of the Soviet forces will develop by stages by means of the successive bringing of armies into offensive operation. At the end of June and during July, offensive operations will become a general offensive of the Soviet forces.[10]
>
> I shall not fail to inform you in due course of the progress of the offensive operations."

First Message about the Normandy Landings

Eisenhower to Marshall   6 June   *Ref: 90016*

Local time is now eight in the morning. I have as yet no information concerning the actual landings, nor of our progress through beach obstacles. Communiqué will not be issued until we have word that leading ground troops are actually ashore.[11]

All preliminary reports are satisfactory. Airborne formations apparently landed in good order with losses out of approximately 1,250 airplanes participating, about thirty.[12] Preliminary bombings by air went off as scheduled. Navy reports sweeping some mines, but so far as is known, channels are clear and operation proceeding as planned. In the early morning hours, reaction from shore batteries was sufficiently light that some other naval spotting planes have returned awaiting call.

The weather yesterday, which was original date selected, was impossible all along the target coast. Today conditions are vastly improved both by sea and air and we have the prospect of at least reasonably favorable weather for the next several days.

Yesterday, I visited British troops about to embark and last night saw the great portion of a United States Airborne division just prior to its take off. Enthusiasm, toughness and obvious fitness of every single man were high and the light of battle was in their eyes.

I will keep you informed.

Report from the Normandy Beachhead

Marshall to President and Secretary of War   14 June   *Ref: S-53824*

Conditions on the beachhead are generally favorable with but minor difficulties or delays. The Germans appear unable to muster a sizeable counter-attack for some days to come. Interruption of communications by air forces appears to have been effected. Operations of French resistance groups now appear to be growing in importance and effect.

The role of all troops, and particularly higher commanders, is high. Replacements of men and materials are being promptly executed through the U.S. beachhead. I was much impressed by the calm competence of First Army Commander Bradley, and by the aggressive

---

10 Operation BAGRATION began on 22 June and by 19 August the Soviets had cleared the western areas of the Soviet Union and entered Poland and Romania, destroying most of Army Group Center.

11 Troops started landing at 06:30am and 160,000 troops were ashore on the five beaches, Utah, Omaha, Juno, Gold and Sword, by the end of the day. Although advances inland were less than planned, the Allies had a firm foothold on the Normandy coast; only on Omaha Beach was the success of the landing in doubt.

12 Planes started to drop the 24,000 airborne troops behind enemy lines just after midnight but many units were scattered across wide areas, and it took all day before units were under command. The dispersion of paratroopers caused as many problems for the Germans as the Allies, because they were not sure where the real threats were.

attitude of his corps commanders[13]. Our new divisions, as well as those which have been battle tested, are doing splendidly and the airborne divisions have been magnificent.

The organization of the breaches was on a remarkable scale of efficiency under Generals Hoge[14] at OMAHA and Wharton[15] on UTAH.

The creation of the artificial harbor off OMAHA Beach proceeds with rapidity, I think exceeding expectations.[16] It is a tremendous affair and bears a very important relationship to the success to our expansion and drive into France.

Eisenhower and his staff are cool and confident, carrying out an affair of incredible magnitude and complication with a superlative efficiency. I thing we have these Huns on the top of the toboggan slide, and the full crash of the Russian offensive should put the skids under them. There will be hard fighting and the enemy will seize every opportunity for a skillful counterstroke, but I think he faces a grim prospect.

Releases and estimates from General Eisenhower's headquarters have been, and should, continue to be conservative in tone. The foregoing is my personal and confidential estimate.[17]

Difficult Dealings with de Gaulle

Marshall, Kings and Arnold to McNarney for the President   14 June   *Ref: S-53809*

About 5:30 London time this evening, General Eisenhower's headquarters was notified that the British War Cabinet wished General de Gaulle to visit the OVERLORD beachhead tomorrow morning. That they were making arrangements with the British Admiralty for de Gaulle to be transported on the French cruiser Conbattant. In the absence of General Eisenhower, General Smith informed Mr. Peake,[18] British Political Officer at Supreme Headquarters, that in view of the expressed desire and action of the British Cabinet, General Eisenhower would interpose no objection to the visit, but that the visit must be confined to the British beachhead and to General Montgomery, with arrangements all being made by the British Ministry through their Admiralty and General Montgomery; that de Gaulle must not make any broadcast for public statement while he is in France and that the P.M. was to inform the President of the visit.[19]

General de Gaulle had previously requested General Eisenhower's permission to visit the beachhead and had been informed that his request should be made through the British Ministry, and that General Eisenhower would interpose no objection if the Prime Minister desired the visit to be made, since he was the guest of the British Government.

13 General J. Lawton Collins with VII Corps inland of Utah Beach and General Leonard T. Gerow with V Corps inland of Omaha Beach.
14 Brigadier-General William M. Hoge (1894–1979), commander of Provisional Engineer Special Brigade Group on Omaha Beach.
15 Brigadier-General James E. Wharton (1894–1944), commander of 1st Engineer Special Brigade on Utah Beach. Wharton was killed in action by a sniper on 12 August, the day he took command of 28th Infantry Division.
16 The Mulberry Harbor.
17 This was the first complete assessment of the beachheads received by President Roosevelt in the White House and Secretary of State Herny L. Stimson (1867–1950), and it was an encouraging one.
18 Charles B.P. Peake had been appointed COSSAC's political advisor in September 1943. Early in 1944 he was appointed Political Officer to make suggestions on French civil affairs and help to find a French political authority for SHAEF to deal with.
19 A furious Churchill was pressurized into allowing de Gaulle to visit France on 14 June and during his short stay in the Bayeux area his popularity was clear to all. The memorial to de Gaulle's visit is at Courseulles-sur-Mer, in the center of Juno Beach.

Today and at dinner with de Gaulle this evening, Mr. Eden[20] is endeavoring to develop a working agreement with the French that might be acceptable to the United States and the British.

Presumably de Gaulle's visit to France tomorrow will evoke demonstrations favorable to him there and later in the press.

The situation at the moment in the OVERLORD operation is critical and growing increasingly complicated. de Gaulle has refused to permit over 100 French specially trained liaison officers to report to the beachhead, which leaves a serious deficiency in the adequacy of arrangements made by military commanders who are beset by the burdens of a furious battle.[21] General Bradley yesterday, without knowledge of circumstances, expressed his serious concern over the dilemma in which he finds himself. Furthermore, it now appears that de Gaulle's people are labeling the prepared currency as counterfeit, etc.

The issue from the point of view purely of military operations is that General Eisenhower finds himself as an Allied commander without specific directive, and with the two governments he serves in effect in disagreement. The Prime Minister's support of your position is understood, but in this matter he dominates neither the Cabinet nor the Foreign Office. The situation is serious and its effect on military operations unhappy at best, and may be dangerous in view of possible reactions of the French underground and resistance groups, who have generally expressed their allegiance to de Gaulle. de Gaulle now enjoys a strong tactical position which he will undoubtedly exploit to the limit.[22]

After the result of Eden's efforts of today and de Gaulle's trip to the beachhead are known, we will discuss the matter with Ambassador Winant[23] and Ambassador Phillips[24] and give you our further views of the effect of the situation on conduct of operations.

Phillips to the State Department   *16 June*   *No Reference*

General Eisenhower has seen the reference to himself made by de Gaulle and reported by Murphy,[25] and contained in your telegram to the Embassy in London dated June 13th. General Marshall suggests that you should know that General Eisenhower deeply resents de Gaulle's statements concerning his (Eisenhower's) attitude which are, of course, completely without foundation. General Eisenhower is maintaining scrupulously the attitude indicated by the policies of the President and the State Department.[26]

---

20 (Robert) Anthony Eden, MP, 1st Earl of Avon, KG, MC, PC (1897–1977), a member of the executive committee of the Political Warfare Executive working for the British Foreign Office and leader of the British House of Commons.

21 Some sources put the number at 200. The liaison officers were due to go ashore on D-Day but de Gaulle held them back as a bargaining tool until he was allowed ashore. The liaison officers would have worked as translators for the Allied troops, particularly with the G-2 intelligence staffs, questioning French citizens and partisans about the whereabouts of German troop concentrations, installations and fortifications. Without them, troops often had to advance blindly into German-held territory.

22 The US incorrectly suspected that de Gaulle was a puppet of the British government. While De Gaulle was hindering Allied operations by refusing to allow the liaison officers to join the battle, it was recognized that his visit to France would be significant as the leader of the Free French. To prevent him from doing so would undermine French morale and make it difficult to work with the partisans.

23 Ambassador John Gilbert Winant, OM, (1889–1947), US ambassador to Great Britain.

24 Ambassador William Phillips, appointed the Secretary of State's representative to SHAEF's Chief of Staff Walter B. Smith in September 1943. Early in 1944 he was appointed Political Advisor and worked alongside Charles Peake.

25 Robert Murphy, the American emissary to Vichy France and later Eisenhower's political advisor.

26 de Gaulle's comments probably stem from Eisenhower's refusal to allow him access to the American sector.

Eisenhower to Marshall   *18 June*   *Ref: S-54099*

The following is a tentative estimate of the French situation after conversations with Lovett.[27] de Gaulle left on the evening of 16th to return to Algiers. Before his departure arrangements were made for conversations to begin on Monday, 19 June between Vienot[28] and four assistants representing the F.C.N.L., and five British representatives headed by the J.A.G., War Office[29], including Foreign Office and Treasury. These negotiations are to produce an agreement for the civil administration of France, and it is understood that if the British and French come to a satisfactory understanding, both will bend their best efforts to obtain the concurrence of the United States.[30]

The French will want to begin discussions on the basis of their memorandum to Murphy and MacMillan of September 7. The British will decline to negotiate on this basis as the memorandum is modeled on agreements reached in 1914–1918 with a recognized French government.[31] I am informed that the British will insist on negotiating with the Committee as such and not, repeat not, as the provisional government of France. They will submit a draft with suitable modifications along the lines of the civil affairs agreement with Belgium.

I believe that the British are prepared to go as far as in their opinion the position of the President will permit. It is thought that they are fully aware that the President will not, repeat not, accord recognition as a provisional government and will not, repeat not, consent to the F.C.N.L. being the issuing authority for currency. I am not, repeat not, sure what their reaction will be to the Committee's certain insistence that no, repeat no, other French group is to be concerned with civil administration in France. Arrangements have been made which it is believed will permit us to keep you currently informed of the progress of these negotiations.

At the time of his visit to Normandy, de Gaulle was well received and with some enthusiasm. However, there are indications that he was somewhat disappointed in the warmth of his reception. Before leaving London he had a conversation with Eden, which is reported to have been the most satisfactory talk anyone has had with him for a long time. It is reported that he stated that he would not, repeat not, insist on recognition as the situation required a practical solution. It is also reported that with reference to the special issue of currency, he said only that the matter must be settled speedily.

It is hoped that Monday or Tuesday we shall be able to send you a copy of the British draft agreement. I shall also submit a memorandum answering as best we can in detail before questions put by Lovett.

Holmes to McCloy[32]   *23 June*   *Ref: S-54430*

Events have progressed so far that it would only be possible to reorient the negotiations along the lines of your W-53476 on the very highest level. The British Government is committed to negotiate directly with the French and have been so engaged since Monday. Although the British delegation is headed by Sir Henry MacGeagh and includes Kirby,[33] it also includes

---

27 Possibly Robert A. Lovett, Assistant Secretary for Air to Secretary of War Henry L. Stimson.
28 Diplomat Monsieur Pierre Vienot was left behind to discuss civil affairs problems with British representatives.
29 Judge Adjutant General, War Office.
30 This correspondence relates to the negotiations over the interim government for France replacing the Vichy government, which had been in place since the Fall of France in 1940.
31 The French government continued to function throughout the First World War.
32 John J. McCloy (1895–1989), Assistant Secretary of War and a key figure in setting US military priorities. President of the World Bank 1947–1949 and US High Commissioner in Germany 1949–1952.
33 Sir Henry D.F. MacGeagh, KBE, TD, KC, British Judge Advocate General.

Ward of the Reconstruction Department, Mack of the French Department and Malkin, legal adviser; all three of the Foreign Office.[34] The negotiations are really under the personal control of the Eden. Bovenschen[35] has extremely limited influence on them, and it would be profitless to discuss these matters with him. However, with Smith's concurrence I have informally conveyed the views expressed in your telegram to Charles Peake, British Political officer of SHAEF, who confirmed also informally my estimates of Bovenschen's position in the matter and also that any change in the present method of approach was highly unlikely and could be accomplished only at the highest level. I am told by both Peake and Winant that the U.S. was notified of the British Government's intention to undertake these negotiations.

I had been promised a copy of the original draft which the British offered to the French but I was told yesterday that Eden had objected, saying as soon as anything approaching a final form is reached, he himself will communicate it to the U.S. Government. Through a confidential source I have been able to see a copy of this draft which is modeled on the agreement with Belgium; the delegate as approved in the ordinance of the French National Committee of March 1944, substantially replacing the Military Mission provided in the Belgian agreement. It is specified that the agreement shall be in the form of an exchange of notes between the British Government and the French National Committee not the Provisional Government of France. It provides the same general authority of the Supreme Allied Commander, as in the case of Belgium, and stipulates that the F.N.C.L. will conduct civil administration until such time as a Provisional Government is formed. Financial questions are not mentioned, except to state that a separate financial agreement will be made. It is understood that this is being discussed between the French and British treasury officials.

Although I have no details I am assured that the discussions thus far have gone forward in a friendly and satisfactory manner. Good British sources continue to emphasize the changed and reasonable attitude of de Gaulle, particularly in his conversation with Eden just prior to departure for Algiers. Eden then said that he noted that de Gaulle had not asked for recognition of the Committee as the Provisional Government and he assumed that this was not the main issue. To this de Gaulle assented.

Eden took de Gaulle to task for the tone of the Algiers Press, with regard to the U.S. and British Governments, and de Gaulle promised to obtain an improvement. de Gaulle said that he was in doubt about the timing of his visit to the United States but Eden encouraged him to make the visit in accordance with the invitation.[36]

It should be borne in mind that relations with the French have almost become a major domestic political issue here. The Prime Minister is under great pressure from the Cabinet led by the Foreign Office, and from Parliament, as well as the press, for outright recognition of the Committee as the Provisional Government of France. He succeeded in postponing debate on the subject in the Commons but will probably not be able to do so for any extended period of time.

Request that for reasons of security you send messages on this subject Eyes Only.[37]

---

34 J.G. Ward, W.H.B. Mack and Sir William Malkin of the Foreign Office.
35 Permanent Under Secretary for War, Sir Frederick C. Bovenschen, KCB, KBE (1884–1977).
36 On hearing the news, Roosevelt invited de Gaulle to Washington in July 1944 and received him with the same respect as a head of state.
37 de Gaulle appointed his own men to set up local administrations in liberated areas, usurping the American plan for a military government of occupation. The FNCL would seize power and form a Provisional Government of the French Republic following the liberation of Paris.

Bad Weather in Normandy

Eisenhower to Marshall	*20 June*	*Ref: S-54240*

Situation with respect to build up has had a serious, but we hope temporary, setback.[38] With good weather predicted, imports and heavy tows for Mulberries were in the Channel yesterday when heavy weather arose and caused a large percentage of loss.[39] Landing by small craft practically ceased and damage to small craft sharply exceeded repair rate. Conditions are still bad. All this re-emphasizes need for quick capture of Cherbourg, for which heavy naval support will be required. New conditions also nullify our earlier estimates on possibility of releasing landing craft. Detailed reports and new estimates will go forward to the Combined Chiefs of Staff as quickly as possible, but in the meantime I wanted you too to be conversant with the situation in this regard which has changed materially since you left here several days ago. The slowness in arrival of VIII Corps (British) has again postponed attacking the eastern sector.[40] Now expect it Thursday morning. On the bright side of the picture is our rapid advance on Cherbourg. If we can capture it in a few days without serious damage it will alter the whole picture in a short time.[41]

Eisenhower to Marshall	*21 June*	*Ref: S-54306*

This is the third day that un-loadings have practically ceased because of bad weather. Yesterday and today the weather has been so bad that sailings have had to stop from United Kingdom ports. The Mulberries, while not, repeat not, finished, have been lifesavers, and the Gooseberries have been indispensable.[42]

I think that when Admiral King sent his message concerning the withdrawal of American naval forces, he was calculating on the unloading rate we had experienced up until the time he left here and was counting upon an earlier ANVIL than General Wilson reports as possible. In any event, the bad weather has further aggravated our former bad position in the LCT category and will force us to use LSTs freely as quickly as we can resume shipments. Otherwise we will be completely stymied.[43]

We are now an estimated five days behind in buildup. The vehicle position is bad. The staff is preparing a complete analysis of our situation which will be submitted to the Combined Chiefs of Staff quickly, but in advance I may say that we feel we can spare everything after Cherbourg is captured, except for some destroyers and LSTs. I am sure that Admiral King knows how anxious I am to stage an ANVIL at an early date and, therefore, how earnestly I want to get into position here so as to release U.S. naval units. However, I should like the U.S. Chiefs of Staff to know that our situation is not, repeat, not as good as we have reason to expect it would be, and our former calculations will have to be materially revised.[44]

---

38 Since Marshall had visited the beachhead the weather had taken a turn for the worse, severely hampering the supply situation in Normandy. The weak links in the supply chain were the landing craft ferrying supplies from ships to the shore.

39 Mulberry A on Omaha Beach had only been open for ten days when it was badly damaged on 19 June. 21 out of 31 caissons were damaged beyond repair and the salvageable caissons were used to repair Mulberry B at Arromanches.

40 VIII British Corps's first attack would be Operation EPSOM, 26–30 June, but it failed to outflank and seize the city of Caen.

41 Cherbourg would not be captured until 2 July and the port would not be operational until late August.

42 Around ten block ships, codenamed 'Corn Cobs' were scuttled on each of the five beaches, creating sheltered waters, codenamed 'Gooseberries'. The Gooseberries at Omaha Beach and Arromanches were turned into harbors, codenamed 'Mulberries'.

43 The smaller LCTs could not be used in the bad weather while the larger LSTs were more seaworthy.

44 Admiral King had planned to move shipping to the Mediterranean, ready for Operation ANVIL.

Bad weather on the coast has also permitted the enemy to bring up reinforcements and likewise interfered with our attacks on NOBALL targets.[45] I hope that Cherbourg will fall quickly, following which I intend to strive with airborne, and possibly a complete corps, into the Brittany Peninsula very rapidly, because I believe the Brittany Peninsula is now very lightly held. This will protect our right flank and rear in the advance towards the Seine and will reduce the E-Boat and submarine threat from our right flank.[46]

In the meantime, I am quite sure that Admiral King will understand the necessity for us holding on to U.S. naval strength for the moment and that we will strive in every way to release it, so that ANVIL can be properly and speedily prepared. Once before in this war Admiral King stepped into a breach to save the situation for us. I am counting on him to see the stark necessity of doing so again.

Further Arguments over ANVIL

Eisenhower to Marshall   *20 June*   *Ref: S-54239*

Wilson's number B-12995 dated 19 June, of which you have a copy, seems to discount the fact that the Combined Chiefs of Staff have long ago decided to make Western Europe the base from which to conduct decisive operations against Germany. To authorize any departure from this sound decision seems to me ill advised and potentially dangerous. In my opinion, to contemplate wandering off overland via Trieste to Ljubljana[47] is to indulge in conjecture to an unwarrantable degree at the present time. Certainly it involves dispersion of our effort and resources. Even granted successful achievement of this objective by autumn, I am unable, repeat unable, to see how the overriding necessity for exploiting the early success of OVERLORD is thereby assisted. The fundamental factor of the situation is stated in paragraph two of this telegram, namely, the necessity for seizing ports quickly in France, through which the weight of our forces can be poured. We must concentrate our forces to the greatest possible degree and put them into battle in the decisive theater. To do so they must all land in France and work towards the common center. AFHQ apparently fails to appreciate that the achievement of a successful bridgehead in France does not, repeat not, of itself imply success in Operation OVERLORD as a whole. In spite of any local successes achieved in Northern France, Operation OVERLORD will be in urgent need of any assistance possible from elsewhere for some time to come.

In my view, this is the moment of definite coordinating action to be taken by the Combined Chiefs of Staff in relation to the whole campaign in Western Europe. I think that Wilson should be directed to undertake Operation ANVIL at the earliest possible date.

I am unable, repeat unable, to see the force of Wilson's insistence that he can not, repeat not, execute ANVIL until 15th August, nearly 60 days from now. This operation has been under active consideration since last year. We are now contemplating stripping ourselves here of resources to aid its early execution. Recently a serious situation due to bad weather, with slowing up of buildup and with excessive losses in landing craft, has arisen in this regard. Reports are going forward to the Combined Chiefs of Staff as quickly as possible.

---

45 NOBALL targets were V1 rocket launching sites, bivouac areas, field headquarters, supply points in support of field operations, troop concentrations and and weapon marshalling. These targets were mobile tactical targets as opposed to strategic fixed targets around industrial complexes.

46 Eisenhower hoped to seize Cherbourg and the Brittany ports, thereby denying their use to the German Navy while allowing his own shipping to use them to offload supplies, relieving the pressure on the vulnerable beach harbours

47 From northeast Italy into Yugoslavia; Ljubljana is now the capital of Slovenia.

As I have emphasized to Wilson, in my view, time is the vital factor, and the overriding consideration must be for him to launch an operation in France, and nowhere else, which holds out a reasonable prospect of success at the earliest possible date. To speculate on possible adventures in South Central Europe in the coming autumn, to my mind, has no, repeat no, reference to current operations in this Theater. As a matter of fact, we know that in spite of our brilliant successes in Italy, the enemy has been moving sizeable formations out of South France into the OVERLORD area. Both the enemy and ourselves now consider OVERLORD the vital operation. It is imperative that we obtain and maintain superiority over him, and this must be done in France as quickly as we can. We need big ports.[48]

Marshall to Eisenhower   *22 June*   Ref: W-54372

I am in accord with your views on Wilson's message and on operations in the Mediterranean in support of OVERLORD. You were called on by the Combined Chiefs of Staff to submit a similar report of your views to them. I assume that you are doing this but Wilson possesses the vantage of having gotten his report in first. There should be no delay in getting a firm decision on ANVIL, if we are to provide the necessary additional resources in time to make it possible to launch the operation at an earlier date than 15 August. I realize you intend to make available the available resources from OVERLORD at the earliest possible date.

We appreciate your problems resulting from the bad weather in the channel. The Navy considers that amphibious resources should leave by 1 July if we are to meet an August 1 ANVIL date. The Navy further considers that the dispatch of 24 LST's out of some 200 cannot seriously affect your present operations, while it may make a very great deal of difference in the timing of ANVIL.

The United States Chiefs of Staff are now considering recommending to the Combined Chiefs of Staff that General Wilson be immediately directed to launch ANVIL at the earliest possible date, and in any case not later than 15 August current.[49]

Marshall to Eisenhower   *22 June*   Ref: W-54341

Upon arrival in Washington, I find following radio from Devers dated June 20:

"I learned after you departed, that MacMillan[50] this morning left hurriedly for London expressly to influence the Prime Minister to back the advance into the valley of the Po and thence northeast, through the Ljubljana Gap and thence into Germany. I thought this important enough for you to know, since the decision is Eisenhower's."[51]

Eisenhower to Marshall   *23 June*   Ref: S-54429

General Wilson's representatives have been conferring with the staff here, and as a result I have today transmitted my recommendations to the Combined Chiefs of Staff. Reference your W-54372. These are:

---

48 Eisenhower is making it clear that the Normandy beachhead is far from secure because in many places his frontline is only a few miles from the coast, and will be until the Cotentin Peninsula and Cherbourg port have been taken. He is adamant that there has to be a second landing in southern France to divert German attention away from Normandy. The bad weather means that he is concerned about releasing naval resources too early.

49 While Marshall agrees with Eisenhower on ANVIL, he has set dates and figures to work with.

50 Maurice Harold Macmillan, 1st Earl of Stockton, OM, PC (1894–1986), Minister Resident in the Mediterranean 1942–1945 and Prime Minister of Great Britain 1957–1963.

51 Macmillan must have found out Wilson's wishes and wanted to get them to the Prime Minister so that he could enter the ANVIL debate.

1. That ANVIL be launched, preferably by August 15th and no later than August 30th, either on the scale desired by General Wilson or with less acceptable resources.

2. If this is impossible, that all French divisions, plus one or two American divisions previously allocated to ANVIL, be made available for OVERLORD as soon as shipping and port capacity permit their transportation and maintenance.

Marshall to Eisenhower   *28 June*   *Ref: SHAEF 108/28*

For your information, the reply of the British Chiefs of Staff to our proposed course of action contained in our number 55794, 24 June, is briefed as follows:

> "Mediterranean Allied forces can assist OVERLORD best by finishing the destruction of the enemy they are now opposing, and by continuing to fight the maximum strength of the enemy reinforcements resisting the advance. General Wilson states that withdrawal of resources from General Alexander must begin on 28 June if a target date of 15 August is to be met.[52] The withdrawal now of forces from Italy to achieve this target date is unacceptable to the British Chiefs of Staff. The target date of the end of August would still prejudice operations in Italy. Withdrawal of forces for ANVIL would hamstring General Alexander so that any further activity would be very modest. The adequacy of their resources for both ANVIL and Italy is gravely doubted.
>
> In view of paragraph 5d of SCAF 53, the British Chiefs of Staff seriously doubt the wisdom of General Eisenhower releasing landing craft for ANVIL.
>
> The governing factor may prove to be port capacity in the OVERLORD area. By the end of September, General Eisenhower ought to be in possession of ports and small harbors capable of rapid deployment. Provided General Eisenhower can retain all landing craft and assault shipping, port capacity in the OVERLORD area should permit concentration of all available forces, including those from the Mediterranean.
>
> Maximum benefits should be reaped from Maquis[53] in the Rhône Valley and General Alexander may be able to extend a hand in their direction using French divisions left to him. The threat of an amphibious assault should be emphasized in order to contain the German divisions.
>
> The Germans must divert more divisions to defend Italy than to oppose an attack in the Rhône Valley, which would be too late to threaten this summer.
>
> The British Chiefs of Staff recommend a directive which gives priority to OVERLORD, provides that General Eisenhower retain all landing craft he needs for amphibious assaults and the development of the coastline as he captures it. SCAEF should have first call on all divisions from all quarters. General Wilson should direct General Alexander to continue his offensive in Italy and should threaten an assault on Southern France, while preparing to send General Eisenhower one or more U.S. divisions and/or French divisions which SCAEF can receive and which we have ships to transport. This ends the British proposal."[54]

The U.S. Chiefs of Staff had dispatched a reply this afternoon which is briefed as follows:

---

52 Target date for landing on the coast of southern France.
53 The mainly rural guerrilla bands of the French Resistance.
54 The British Chiefs of Staff have turned Eisenhower's supply problem against him, using it to suggest canceling ANVIL to concentrate on Normandy and Italy while only threatening an assault in southern France.

"The British proposal to abandon ANVIL and commit everything to Italy is unacceptable. Enemy forces in Italy are so badly whipped that they cannot fight in France for some time, except for four divisions whose retention in Italy by the enemy is almost mandatory, if reasonably aggressive action is continued by General Alexander with means available, while still mounting ANVIL.[55] The U.S. Chiefs of Staff do not consider the arguments that General Alexander will not have sufficient forces to be either logical, or in keeping with the existing situation. The initial withdrawals for ANVIL are three U.S. and two French divisions. The two new U.S. divisions will be available shortly in Italy. With regard to the grave doubt as to the air resources, the U.S. Chiefs of Staff consider this comment proposes a condition of war-making on the Allied side, which is a most serious reflection on the fighting ability of our ground forces. This view on the air situation is not acceptable to the U.S. Chiefs. 5,500 Allied operational planes are at present opposed by 300 enemy planes in Italy. Although outnumbering the enemy in the air over the NEPTUNE beachhead about ten to one, we grant him the power of delivering a counterattack and are now concerned over his concentration for this attack on the bridgehead. Applying to the enemy the rule proposed for our own forces in Italy and ANVIL, no German attack against a bridgehead would be a possibility.

General Eisenhower states that, in agreement with his Commanders-in-Chief, he wants ANVIL and can spare the craft. He has the responsibility for the success of OVERLORD. We think his judgment should be accepted.[56]

While the Italian campaign has profited us, its success has been partly due to the ill-advised determination of Hitler to fight south of Rome.[57] When and if the German General Staff takes over, we are confronted with a possible negligible result from our large Mediterranean forces.[58]

It is deplorable the British and U.S. disagree when time is pressing. The British statements concerning Italy are not sound or in keeping with the early end of the war. The U.S. desires to put as many U.S. divisions in France as soon as possible. Progress by Alexander in Italy does not contribute to this. General Wilson wants a decision by 27 June. There is no reason for discussing further except to delay a decision which must be made. The wording of the directive proposed in the U.S. Chiefs' original paper gives sufficient latitude, both as to forces and date. The U.S. Chiefs 'ask' that it be sent to SACMED[59] at once."

Eisenhower to Marshall   *29 June*   *Ref: S-5760*

It is my belief that the Prime Minister and his Chiefs of Staff are honestly convinced that greater results in support of OVERLORD would be achieved by a drive towards Trieste[60] rather than to mount ANVIL. They are aware, of course, of the definite purpose of the United States Chiefs of Staff to mount an ANVIL and I have been even more emphatic in

---

55 At this time German troops were falling back north to the Gothic Line, their last line of prepared defence in Italy running between Pisa and Rimini.

56 The US Chiefs of Staff did not believe that the ground situation or the air situation was as bad as General Alexander was making out. Their comparison of the air situation in Normandy and Italy allows them to turn the argument against the British Chiefs of Staff. They supported Eisenhower's assessment of the Normandy situation and the need for ANVIL.

57 This refers to the five-month battle around Cassino and Anzio.

58 This statement is intriguing because on 20 July there was an attempt to assassinate Hitler in the Wolf's Lair. The attempt had been supported by many members of the German General Staff, so what prompted the US Chiefs of Staff to make this statement a month before the attempt?

59 General Sir Maitland Wilson. Wilson's title became Supreme Commander, Mediterranean Theatre of Operations.

60 At the northeast end of the Adriatic Sea, and the gateway to the Istrian Peninsula.

my support of this operation than have your telegrams on the subject. I have the further impression that, although the British Chiefs of Staff may make one more effort to convince you of the value of the Trieste move, they will not, repeat not, permit an impasse to arise, and will, consequently, agree to ANVIL. In this event, I believe that they will propose a stronger operation than previously conceived, by including in it a number of the experienced British divisions now in the Mediterranean, with the further recommendation that Alexander take over responsibility for ANVIL as the principal offensive operation in that Theater. I feel that their idea would be to keep intact the tactical ground and air staff that has been functioning so well in Italy. They would then frankly recognize the Italian area as a secondary one and turn over the troops there to General Clark[61] or other qualified officer.

All the above is fact, tinged with conjecture, but does represent the impressions gained by me and by General Smith in separate conversations with the Prime Minister.

I would personally be quite happy to see General Alexander in command of the operation. I consider him a most able soldier with particular qualifications in commanding ground forces of several nationalities. Moreover, I would like to see the plans in the Mediterranean drawn on the basis of making ANVIL just as strong as possible, even up to something like sixteen or more divisions. Since, in the long run, France is going to be more the business of Great Britain than ourselves, I would be delighted to see more British divisions in that country. Another consideration is the fact that with Alexander in command, there will be no, repeat no, holding back in the Mediterranean of any resources that can make the operation a success. If this proposal should be made and accepted, I suggest that a reminder be included that when ANVIL proceeds sufficiently far, so that I believe I can exercise direction over it, the whole force is to become part of the Allied Expeditionary Force.

If there should develop some unforeseen, rapidity with respect to our own advance here, allowing us to gain additional ports to the southward of Cherbourg quickly, we could always then divert any divisions scheduled for later phases of ANVIL buildup directly into this area.

The main factor now is a necessity for speed in decision.

All the above is for your confidential information and is merely to appraise you in person of what I believe to be the situation here, and of my own reactions.

Weather here continues to be abominable.

Marshall to Eisenhower	*30 June*	*Ref: SHAEF 66/30*

For your information, this message gives further developments:

Yesterday, the 28th, the President sent to the Prime Minister a message stating he concurred completely in the stand of the United States Chiefs, and that General Wilson's proposal to use all our Mediterranean forces to fight on into Northern Italy and beyond was unacceptable to him. Nothing could be worse than the deadlock in the Combined Chiefs of Staff and this must be prevented by the President and Prime Minister who should support SCAEF.[62] SCAEF wants ANVIL and wants action, preferably before 30th August. ANVIL, as quickly as possible, is the only operation by which Wilson can give OVERLORD material and immediate support. This ends the President's message which apparently crossed the one from the Prime Minister briefed below in this cable.

The substance of the British Chiefs reply to our memorandum contained in your W-57012, 27 June, to you is briefed below:

---

61 General Mark W. Clark, commander of Fifth US Army in Italy.
62 General Eisenhower, Supreme Commander, Allied Expeditionary Force.

"The British Chiefs regret that the United States Chiefs find their proposals unacceptable and share their anxiety for a quick decision. They think patient discussion is necessary to avoid a false step. BONIFACE of 28 June from G-22175 vindicates British estimate of enemy reaction to campaign in Italy. Alexander's offensive has already drawn four O.K.W. divisions.[63] General Wilson estimates that a full strength advance would draw at least ten divisions. ANVIL cannot be managed without decreasing possibility of destroying Kesselring's Army,[64] which we now have.

With regard to air power, British Chiefs are still convinced there are not sufficient air resources to do both ANVIL and destruction of Germans in Italy and believe this view is shared by Commanders on the spot. The possibility of German Generals taking over from Hitler should not influence strategy at this time.[65] The foundation of our strategy should be the continued use of maximum forces whenever the enemy can be induced to fight. History will not forgive commitment of substantial forces to an operation which will not mature for three critical months and may pay small dividends for three more. British Chiefs see no prospect that they can advise His Majesty's Government contrary to the stand that they have adopted today."

This ends message from British Chiefs to which United States Chiefs have made no reply. On 28 June the Prime Minister sent the President a message, the substance of which is briefed below:

"The Prime Minister considers the following points dominant. Overall strategic concept should be to engage the enemy on largest scale, with greatest violence and continuity. Ports must be acquired for the direct and quick entry into Europe of the 30 or more United States divisions now in the United States. In choosing places to attack, regard must be given first to the tactical relation to main effort, and secondly to the strain produced on the central power of Germany, the O.K.W. Optimum is to combine both. Political situations, such as submission of Nazi satellites and revolt of peoples are important. No more LST's available than necessary for two major ventures. We should examine choices in light of preceding points."[66]

"OVERLORD is priority, but 40 plus divisions by the end of August will not establish mastery in Western France. Number of divisions for SCAEF should be limited only by ships and ports in Western France. In addition to the ports envisaged we should consider Port-en-Bessin, Courseulles and other small ports.[67] Landing craft increases discharge at these. Hence movement of large numbers of craft to any diversion elsewhere is a mistake. They should re-examine all facilities for reception of forces along French Atlantic coast in light of our new experience. Havre and St Nazaire are more important to OVERLORD than ports in the Mediterranean."[68]

---

63 Interception of German cables reporting their thoughts on developments in the Italian campaign. Four OKW reserve divisions have been sent to shore up the Italian front.
64 Generalfeldmarschall Albert Kesselring (1885–1960), commander of all German forces in Italy, combining the roles of Commander-in-Chief South, and Army Group C.
65 This is a second reference to the possibility of the German High Command taking over from Hitler.
66 Churchill summarizes the need to take more ports so that the full weight of the US Army can be deployed to Europe as quickly as possible; if they are not then there will be a stalemate soon.
67 Two small ports on the Normandy coast.
68 Havre on the north coast of France and St Nazaire on the west coast. Time spent moving landing craft from one beachhead to another was time lost in landing troops and supplies.

"We should not only increase the buildup but should also relate the types of troops to fighting prospects. Here the Prime Minister refers to an attached tabulation containing his idea of the actual and planned buildup of the United States forces in the United Kingdom for May to August inclusive. 553,000 United States soldiers are arriving during these four months but only seven divisions. Counting fighting troops of 20,000 a division, this leaves 378,000 servicing troops. Perhaps by severe readjustment, a higher priority could be given to four or five more divisions.[69] Due to the fact that May and June casualties have been much below estimates, we should be justified in sending two additional divisions rather than 50,000 replacements. There are three French divisions available from North Africa and four which might be withdrawn from Italy if ports, shipping and support troops could be found. General Eisenhower foresaw this in SCAF 53, paragraph 7b."

The Prime Minister examines an operation landing at Cette,[70] directed on Bordeaux, and concludes that this heavy-footed method of approach would not take Bordeaux before December and would not influence the war in 1944. This operation does not compare with a coup-de-main which might take Bordeaux and give the bridgehead for French and United States troops.[71]

We are left with the bleak and sterile Toulon – Marseilles operation. This gives 130 more miles to Bordeaux than from Cette and the landing cannot begin until 30 August, even if LST's can be spared by 10 July.

The capture of Toulon – Marseilles by 30 August and the landing of ten divisions by 30 September might have the objective of a march on Lyon 160 miles away.[72] This would put all the French and some American divisions into the battle and give close contact with the Marquis, who have a moderate guerrilla [force] in the mountains. This project has great hazards. The Prime Minister then goes on to say that all the enemy on the Riviera could be brought against us, plus forces moved by the O.K.W through the Alps.[73] The country is formidable, superior forces would confront us throughout withdrawal of any of the enemy from OVERLORD, and the enemy could easily escape. Bordeaux, Cette, Marseilles; none of these, even with great success, would directly influence the battle in 1944.

Before we embark on either of the two forms of ANVIL, we must count the cost. General Wilson, General Alexander in his private and personal to the Prime Minister, and General Smuts,[74] also in his private and personal to the Prime Minister, put before us the proposition of an attack eastward across and around the Adriatic. This movement is equally unrelated tactically to OVERLORD as are the variants of ANVIL. There is a grave question whether we should ruin all hopes of Allied victory in Italy and condemn ourselves to a passive role in the Theater. The Prime Minister would greatly regret seeing General Alexander deprived of much of his offensive strength for the sake of a march up the Rhône, which the Combined Chiefs of Staff have described as unprofitable.[75]

The message concluded by proposing reinforcement to NEPTUNE, doing justice to the opportunities of the Mediterranean commanders, confining ourselves to diversions and

---

69 A ratio of two service soldiers to every combat soldier.
70 Actually Sète, between Narbonne and Montpellier in the Languedoc–Roussillon area of southern France, and an advance northwest towards Bordeaux.
71 Either an amphibious or airborne attack to take the Bordeaux garrison by surprise and the docks intact.
72 An advance north from Marseilles and Toulon.
73 From Italy into France.
74 Field Marshal Jan Smuts, OM, CH, ED, KC, FRS, PC (1870–1950) served on the Imperial War Cabinet.
75 An advance from the Marseilles area, north through the center of France.

threats in the Gulf of Lions,[76] leaving Eisenhower his landing craft, increasing port capacities of OVERLORD and a resolution not to risk one campaign to win the other. Both can be won. Thus ends the Prime Minister's message.

The United States Chiefs prepared for the President a reply to the Prime Minister which it is understood has been dispatched. The substance is brief below:

While agreeing with the Prime Minister's overall strategic concept, the President is convinced that it must be based on the main effort, with closely coordinated supporting efforts aimed at Germany's heart. OVERLORD, victories in Italy, and early assault of Southern France, combined with Russia's efforts, will most surely realize Germany's unconditional surrender. This was all envisaged at Tehran and the President appears mindful of the agreement with Stalin on the attack on Southern France and his views favoring this assault and classifying all other Mediterranean operations as unimportant.

Political considerations are important factors but the primary job is to strike at Germany's heart.

The OVERLORD build up is Eisenhower's job. We send him the United States soldiers he asks for. If he wants more divisions, they will be ready. Until we run out of forces in the United States, or cannot give Eisenhower what he wants, the President opposes the waste of switching troops from the Mediterranean to OVERLORD. The use of ships and ports to shift forces from one battle area to another will give us fewer forces in combat areas.

The President's interest is in beating the Germans on Eisenhower's front and getting into Germany, rather than limiting this battle to put on a second major effort in Italy. We have sufficient forces in Italy without the ANVIL resources to chase Kesselring, and at the very least contain his forces. That the Germans will pay ten more divisions to keep us out of Northern Italy is inconceivable.

Wilson says we can now take five divisions from Italy for ANVIL. The other 21 in Italy, plus numerous brigades, will give adequate ground superiority. Our air power gives overwhelming air support during critical moments of either operation.

Agreed that Bordeaux or Cette are out of the picture. On Istria,[77] Alexander and Smuts disregard the vital considerations of our ground strategy believed to be necessary to end the war quickly, and the time factor connected with the campaign into the Balkans. Difficulties in the latter exceed those pictured by the Prime Minister for the Rhône Valley. It is doubtful that six divisions could be put into the fight below the Ljubljana Gap within a decisive period.[78] Meanwhile, we would struggle to get into France the 35 United States divisions now in the United States, plus Corps, Army and Service troops. President cannot agree to the use of American troops in the Balkans, or in assaulting Istria, and does not see the French accepting such use of their forces.

The Toulon area has suitable beaches and communications, and the Rhône Corridor is better than the Ljubljana Gap, and certainly a lot better than the mountains over which we have been fighting in Italy. Eisenhower's statement that he thinks ANVIL is important, and will furnish the means without undue detriment to NEPTUNE, impresses the President, as does Wilson's statement he can do the job if told to do it now.

Since we agreed at Tehran to do ANVIL, the President cannot abandon this operation without consulting Stalin. If we can't agree to direct Wilson by 1 July to do the job

---

76 The bay stretching from Marseilles to Spanish border.
77 The peninsula of Istria is at the north end of the Adriatic Sea in what was Italy, then Yugoslavia and is now shared between Slovenia and Croatia.
78 Advance through the Ljubljana Gap towards Vienna.

as quickly as we can, we must send a message to Stalin at once. If we abandon ANVIL, we must discuss the use of French forces with them since this decision might keep them out of battle in France. President urges the directive proposed by United States Chiefs be issued. It is evident that dragging out this argument will kill off ANVIL as an operation of major aid to Neptune.[79]

Eisenhower to Marshall   *1 July*   *Ref: S-54849*
I have been informally advised that the Prime Minister will probably telegraph the President today, agreeing to ANVIL. This information has not, repeat not, been verified and is extremely confidential. Assuming that we have gained this one fundamental point, I hope that Wilson will merely be given a clear cut directive to attack as quickly as possible, and as strongly as possible with whatever command arrangement and composition of forces he and his advisers may decide upon. In other words, I am hopeful that no details of execution will become the subject of further negotiation. What we need is speed in order to get a port through which the maximum number of American divisions can come to France.[80]

Best Wishes for Montgomery's New Attack

Eisenhower to Montgomery   *26 June*   *Ref: S-54520*
I learnt that your attack on the east flank started this morning;[81] all the luck in the world to you and Dempsey.[82] Please do not hesitate to make the maximum demands for any air assistance that can possibly be useful to you. Whenever there is any legitimate opportunity we must blast the enemy with everything we have.

I am hopeful that Bradley can quickly clean up the Cherbourg mess and turn around to attack southward while you have got the enemy by the throat on the east. I am sure that Bradley understands the necessity of hitting harder and incessantly. Again good luck.

---

79 Stalin was expecting an amphibious assault on the southern coast of France, and a last minute change of plan to advance into Istria to meet his armies as far east as possible would have made him suspicious. At the same time French troops were anxious to get involved in the liberation of France and would not have been happy to be sent to a different front.

80 Finally after six months of wrangling, and at the last moment, the British Chiefs of Staff are about to grant their agreement to ANVIL. Final preparations had to start immediately because D-Day was only six weeks away.

81 Operation EPSOM between 26 and 30 June 1944 was an attempt to outflank and capture the city of Caen. Although Second Army did not take the city, it did pull all available German reserves to its front.

82 General (knighted three days later by King George VI) Miles C. Dempsey, GBE, KCB, DSO, MC (1896–1969), commander of British Second Army.

7

JULY 1944

Extending the Cover and Deception Plan

Eisenhower to Marshall   *6 July*   *Ref: S-55125*

OVERLORD Cover and Deception plan (FORTITUDE)[1] has proved remarkably effective. Reliable intelligence indicates that the enemy is preparing for decisive Allied effort by First US Army Group in Pas de Calais area under the command of Patton.

Since under existing plans the enemy will unquestionably soon learn of the presence in the lodgment area of First US Army Group, and Patton with his Third Army, it has been necessary to devise a new and plausible plan for continuing the cover threat. The new cover plan involves retention of First Army Group nominally in the United Kingdom, re-designation of First Army Group in France under Bradley's command as Twelfth Army Group, down-grading Patton from his fictitious status as Commander of First Army Group to actual Command Third Army, and naming a suitable well known commander of high reputation as the commander of the proposed fictitious First Army Group, comprising assumed United States and British Divisions in the United Kingdom. The designation of 'Twelfth Army Group' has been selected for Bradley's Army Group to obviate confusion in mail and other communications resulting if a number identical with one of the Armies in this Theater were to be selected.[2]

All arrangements to implement the new cover plan can be made here except that a suitable National Commander for the First Army Group is not available in this area. Desire therefore to suggest for your consideration that some well known officer such as McNair[3], DeWitt[4], or another of corresponding reputation be ordered to this Theater without delay. He would be required here for a considerable period, probably at least three months, the exact period being determined by the length of time the new cover plan remains effective. During his stay the Officer would be usefully employed, and he would have unusual opportunities for observation.

The names I have given you are suggested because they have been fairly well advertised throughout the world. While I thought of using Simpson[5] for this purpose, I feel that his

---

1 Operation FORTITUDE NORTH was a threat to Norway while FORTITUDE SOUTH was a threat to the Calais area; they were part of a wide deception plan, Operation BODYGUARD. Under Operation QUICKSILVER the Germans believed that the Allies had the genuine 21st Army Group under Montgomery and a fictitious 1st US Army Group, or FUSAG, under General George Patton poised ready to cross the Pas-de-Calais.
2 Hence Bradley's 12th Army Group and Montgomery's 21st Army Group.
3 General Lesley J. McNair (1883–1944), Commanding General, Army Ground Forces; details of his death are discussed later.
4 General John L. DeWitt (1880–1962), Commandant of the Army and Navy Staff College in Washington DC.
5 General William H. Simpson, Ninth US Army commander.

name will not be of sufficient significance to the enemy. If you find it impossible to comply, I will have to start immediately to build up Simpson as well as I can.

I would be most grateful for a radio reply as time is pressing and I cannot overemphasize the great importance of maintaining as long as humanely possible the Allied threat to the Pas de Calais area, which has already paid enormous dividends and, with care, will continue to do so.

Marshall to Eisenhower   *7 July*   Ref: W-61630
McNair is out of town and returns tomorrow, Saturday night, so I have no opportunity to determine his views, In view of McNair's prominent and well known position here, he appears to be the logical man for this position. I propose to put General Lear[6] in command of Army Ground Forces during McNair's absence. The fact that Lear has taken over the Ground Forces and McNair has left the country will assist, I believe, materially in your deception plan. I will inform you further as soon as McNair returns and his wishes on the matter are known.

You are authorized to make the necessary changes in designations of Army Groups to fit your plans.

A Corps Commander falls Ill

Eisenhower to Bradley   *6 July*   Ref: S-55099
Walker reporting to you in accordance with our understanding.[7] In the event it develops that you will need an additional corps commander for a period of several weeks, it will be agreeable to me if you desire to give the job to Eddy[8] and put Stroh[9] in Eddy's place. Even in this case we would not, repeat not, evacuate Corlett[10] but would keep him after recovery as a spare corps commander. Please keep me advised.

A New Airborne Commander

Eisenhower to Arnold   *13 July*   Ref: FWD-12387
I agree with you that Vandenberg[11] has the necessary qualifications for an airborne command; however, there are questions of personality involved in this command which are difficult and delicate. The airborne commander must be superimposed over Major General Ridgway, who is quite senior and who has commanded in combat with great distinction, and over General Browning,[12] the British airborne commander, who has long and varied experience both in the air and on the ground. Cannon,[13] because of his seniority and extensive combat experience, could have been placed in this command without much difficulty. Vandenberg, though able, lacks Cannon's prestige. Furthermore, because of the rank of

---

6 General Benjamin Lear (1879–1966) was serving on the Secretary of War's Personnel Board. His nicknamed was 'Yoo Hoo'.
7 General Walton H. Walker (1889–1950), nicknamed 'Johnny' or 'Bulldog', was commander of XX Corps. He was called forward to act as the 'Eyes and Ears' man for XIX Corps headquarters, visiting front line units while the sick Corlett remained at corps headquarters.
8 General Manton S. Eddy (1892–1962), nicknamed 'Matt' ,commander of 9th Infantry Division.
9 General Donald A. Stroh (1892–1953), assistant commander of 8th Infantry Division.
10 General Charles H. Corlett (1889–1971), nicknamed 'Cowboy Pete', commander of XIX Corps.
11 General Hoyt S. Vandenberg (1899–1954), (USAAF/USAF), Deputy Air Commander-in-Chief of the Allied Expeditionary Force and commander of the American Air Component.
12 Lieutenant-General Sir Frederick A. M. Browning GCVO, KBE, CB, DSO (1896–1965), nicknamed 'Boy', commander of I British Airborne Corps.
13 General John K. Cannon (1892–1955), commander of the Twelfth Air Force and the Mediterranean Allied Tactical Air Force, Italy.

his subordinates, it will undoubtedly be necessary to promote the airborne commander to Lieutenant General. Is Vandenberg the air officer whom you would select to advancement to this high rank? Will you please also clear this with General Marshall and let me have yours and his personal reactions as a matter of urgency. Accumulating evidence confirms the necessity of this airborne command under strong and capable leadership.

Eisenhower to Marshall   *13 July*   *Ref: FWD-12388*
I have just sent General Arnold a message on the airborne command and the selection of its commander which he will show you.

In connection with this assignment and because of the rank and personalities involved, it has been suggested that Brett[14] might be a better choice than a younger and more junior air officer. I realize the importance of his present command and simply mention his name in the thought that you might have this possibility in the back of your mind when General Arnold brings up the matter for discussion.

Marshall to Eisenhower   *14 July*   *Ref: W-64817*
With reference to your FWD-12388, July 13, regarding Brett. He is available if you want him. The Air Corps questioned his lack of experience in this particular assignment and took note of his difficulties in Australia. Arnold feels Brett and Emmons[15] are the only two men immediately available to meet your requirements as to rank and he does not favor Emmons.

I have ordered Brett to report immediately to the War Department so that he will be here probably tomorrow, and if you still desire his assignment we will give him a hurried build-up here and send him on to you.

Eisenhower to Marshall   *15 July*   *Ref S-55586*
I have personally explored opinion here as to suitability of Brett. Reference your W-64817

I must withdraw our suggestion in this case since I am convinced he will not, repeat not, fit the bill. The same applies to Emmons. I am forced to return to the consideration of Vandenberg, who has every qualification except rank and, for the present, a publicized name. Could you get Vandenberg made a lieutenant general for me without too great embarrassment? He is 45 years old and everyone here is convinced he can do the job superbly. While I agree as a policy we should require people to make good on specific jobs before giving them promotion that normally goes with it, in this particular case the rank is more than normally essential in the first instance.

If you believe you can do this please notify me, as I will start Vandenberg at once on the ground work of the task and complete the organization of his command as soon as his promotion comes through.

Marshall to Eisenhower   *15 July*   *Ref: W-65637*
Having named Vandenberg initially, Arnold feels his selection would be sound. However, I am unwilling to promote him to Lieutenant General. We think that serious consideration

---

14 Lieutenant-General Lewis H. Brereton (1890–1967) commander of the Ninth Air Force, the US component of the Allied Expeditionary Air Force.
15 General Delos C. Emmons (1889–1965), commander of the Hawaiian Department just after Pearl Harbor, commanding general of the Western Defense Command after June 1943 and recently appointed commander of the Alaskan Department at Fort Richardson.

should be given to assigning the airborne task to Brereton[16] – Vandenberg to Ninth Air Force, vice Brereton – Royce[17] to A.E.A.F.,[18] vice Vandenberg. Let me have a reaction to this.

Eisenhower to Marshall   *17 July*   *Ref: S-55659*

I have adopted the suggestion in your W-65637 and will assign Brereton to this important job.

Spaatz and I had already come to the conclusion that this is what we might have to do. As you know, I believe that if we could once get airborne operations organized on a maximum scale, and operating under bold conceptions, there may be presented to us opportunities for strokes that would immeasurably shorten the war. In preliminary discussions with Brereton we believe that a critical member of his team will be an extremely able and experienced chief of staff from the ground forces. This man need not, repeat not, necessarily be experienced in airborne operations but he must have been close to tactical operations in Europe. There are two men in the Mediterranean that could fill the bill admirably. They are respectively Major-General Gruenther[19] and Major-General Lemnitzer,[20] with our preference in the order given. I realize that Clark[21] may find it most difficult to give up his chief of staff, but I am hopeful that he can do so, because he has had a growing concern for many months. The combination of Brereton and Gruenther would be one from which we could expect the maximum development in this important line.

I request that you determine the willingness of Clark to let us have Gruenther and, in the event this is reported as impossible, to find out whether we could have Lemnitzer.

We are anxious to get going rapidly.

Marshall to Eisenhower   *25 July*   *Ref: W-70115*

Brigadier General Floyd Parks,[22] the proposed Chief of Staff for Brereton leaves by air today for England. He has been briefed so far as possible regarding all details of airborne operations including equipment, corps artillery improvisations, etc.

Air Support for Operation GOODWOOD

Eisenhower to Montgomery   *13 July*   *No Reference*

We are enthusiastic on your plan. I think that Coningham[23] has already given you the assurance you desire concerning air. All senior airmen are in full accord because this operation will be a brilliant stroke which will knock loose our present shackles. Every plane available will be ready for such a purpose.

I earnestly hope that even if conditions are such as to prevent the perfection of air support be so desirable, you will still find ways and means of carrying out your plan. In any

---

16 Brereton was appointed commander of the Combined Airborne Headquarters, reporting directly to SHAEF. He recommended the organization was called the First Allied Airborne Army.

17 General Ralph Royce (1890–1965), deputy commander of the Ninth Air Force.

18 Allied Expeditionary Air Force commanded by Air Chief Marshal Sir Trafford Leigh-Mallory.

19 General Alfred M. Gruenther (1899–1983), Fifth Army's Chief of Staff.

20 General Lyman L. Lemnitzer (1899–1988), had been on Eisenhower's staff since the summer of 1942, forming plans for the invasions of North Africa and Sicily.

21 General Mark W. Clark.

22 General Floyd L. Parks (1896–1959), US Army Ground Forces Chief of Staff and then First Allied Airborne Army Chief of Staff.

23 Air Marshal Sir Arthur Coningham KCB, KBE, DSO, MC, DFC, AFC, RAF (1895–1948), nicknamed 'Mary' (a corrupted form of 'Maori', because he was Australian and served in the New Zealand Expeditionary Force in the First World War).

case, except in the most adverse conditions, a very considerable portion of the air can always operate effectively.[24]

We are so pepped up concerning the promise of this plan that either Tedder or myself or both will be glad to visit you if we can help in any way.

Please make reply direct to Air Chief Marshal Tedder, SHAEF Main, since my whereabouts for the next 24 hours will be uncertain.

Placing a Failed Commander with an Old Friend

Eisenhower to Devers   *14 July*   *Ref: S-55541*
The following is for consideration by you and Clark.

Major-General William C. McMahon[25] has just been relieved from combat after his division had been in action four days. In my opinion this division was well trained by McMahon before going into action, but due to certain rather unusual conditions and to inexperience through-out the division, a considerable confusion resulted which was at least partially traceable to him and which necessitated his relief. I think McMahon still has real usefulness either in command or in a staff position, but I think it would be difficult for him to function successfully in this Theater at this time. I know that Clark has a great personal admiration for this officer.

The purpose of this message is to find out whether you and Clark might desire the officer either in his present grade or in that of Colonel. I will hold him for a couple of days awaiting your reply before I take any further action.

Devers to Eisenhower   *19 July*   *Ref: B-14217*
In a staff position I can use Major General William C. McMahon as Brigadier-General. Please advise me of action taken by you. Should this assignment be desired, request that he be reduced to Colonel and recommended for promotion to Brigadier-General on next list.[26]

Eisenhower to Marshall   *19 July*   *Ref: FWD-12416*
Major General William C. McMahon has been relieved from the battle line by his Corps Commander, fully concurred in by Bradley, for failure to lead his division actively. His division had been in action only four days, but both the Corps and Army commander felt that his test had been sufficiently conclusive to demonstrate that he is not, repeat not, a good division commander in spite of acknowledged qualifications along other lines. Knowing Clark's high regard for this officer I communicated circumstances to Devers, asking him whether he or Clark would like to request transfer of McMahon in present or lower grade to Mediterranean. I have received following reply: "Request McMahon be reduced to colonel and recommended for promotion to brigadier general on next list since I can use him in staff position as brigadier general."

I recommend that you give me the authority of the President to reduce McMahon, together with authority to transfer him to the Mediterranean. I will promote him to colonel

---

24 Operation GOODWOOD, Second British Army's planned attack east of Caen, was due to start on 18 July. The RAF dropped 4800 tons of bombs and USAF dropped over 500 tons on the German front line prior to H-Hour and then the USAF dropped a further 1340 tons on artillery positions. Fighter bombers simultaneously attacked targets. VIII Corps advanced seven miles and made the Germans send reinforcements to the area rather than move them west to confront First US Army.
25 Major-General William C. McMahon (1895–1990) only commanded 8th Infantry Division for four days in action before he was relieved.
26 General Clark employed McMahon as Deputy Chief of Staff for Personnel, G-1, Fifth Army and later Fifteenth Army Group in Italy. The two had been roommates at the US Military Academy, West Point, in the class of 1917 and had been friends ever since.

immediately upon his reduction and in the meantime, request you notify Devers whether or not you will place him on list for promotion to brigadier. I know he has many fine qualifications, and in my opinion it was tension and over anxiety that caused his poor performance as a division commander.[27]

Preparations and Strategy for ANVIL

Marshall to Devers   16 July 1944   *Ref: W.I. 66124*

After considering all factors, I agree that we should set up an Army Group[28] for ANVIL and am glad that General Wilson wants you to command it. Eisenhower agrees with this. While details of the formation of an Army Group are up to Wilson and you, its task indicates it should probably be primarily an American headquarters, with a carefully chosen French representation. Logistical support will remain primarily an American responsibility. Eisenhower favors the Army Group idea, so as to keep control over all civil affairs matters as well as troop and supply priorities and major tactical decisions. All of these matters will require increasing coordination with Eisenhower as the ANVIL operation progresses.

You should do your best to keep the headquarters small. Probably most of the personnel required can be found in your Theater. We will do our best to give you such top personnel as required. Time is short and you will need to press the formation of your new headquarters. I believe that your Theater is now functioning so that you will not be burdened with a great amount of administrative routine. You should, however, take any necessary additional steps to ensure that you can give your time and energy to commanding the troops fighting under you, while still carrying your responsibility as the American Theater Commander.

The decision as to the additional American divisions for ANVIL, beyond the three in the assault, must await developments. We must push into OVERLORD everything which can be accepted and used. If we can move additional divisions, and Eisenhower agrees to their use in the Mediterranean, I hope that they can go directly into ANVIL through ports you have opened. Developments in Italy must determine the timing and way in which we move U.S. forces from there to ANVIL. If the forces in Italy bog down on their Pisa – Rimini Line, we should not long delay putting Fifth Army divisions into the fight in southern France.[29] I hope that Alexander will quickly get into the Po Valley. Then the Fifth Army, or portions of thereof, could be moved into France, possibly some of it moving overland. This, however, must be a Combined Chiefs of Staff decision.[30]

The important thing is that we push ANVIL to the utmost as the main effort in the Mediterranean. The large forces we will still have in Italy should enable us to maintain strong and unrelenting pressure on the enemy. While satisfying OVERLORD, we will do our utmost to satisfy Wilson in the two battles he has to fight in southern France and in Italy.

There should be no waiting for a perfection of arrangements or for the optimum in supplies and equipment. I believe we are approaching the point in Europe where carefully planned bold and rapid action in the application of our forces may reap successes which will shorten the war.

---

27 Eisenhower recognizes that while McMahon is not suited to commanding a division in combat, he has many useful abilities and uses his networking knowledge to make use of them by transferring him to Clark.
28 It would be the Sixth Army Group commanded by Lieutenant-General Jacob L. Devers. It consisted of Seventh US Army commanded by Lieutenant-General Alexander Patch and French First Army (before 25 September 1944 French Army B) commanded by Général Jean de Lattre de Tassigny (1889–1952).
29 After the capture of Rome on 4 June, the Allies advanced north to the Gothic Line, taking Florence. This was the final defensive line running from north of Pisa on the west coast to south of Rimini on the east coast. The Polish II Corps were just about to clear the port of Ancona so that ships could deliver supplies close to the front line.
30 Fifth US Army remained in Italy.

Slessor[31] *to Tedder at SHAEF*   *23 July*   *Ref: JCS 275*

1. From the discussions which Forbes and Alms[32] have had here and with S.P.O.C. Algiers,[33] it seems that it might be extremely useful to have a small number of Dakotas based in the LEGHORN area[34] to land in supplies to the Massif Central about D-Day. Landing is suggested rather than dropping not because of parachute shortage but because stores needed include 3-inch mortar ammunition, which is not suitable for dropping.

2. Apart from question of availability of aircraft, this is by no means a firm commitment yet because we are not certain about landing grounds. Would be grateful if you would personally consider whether Hollinghurst[35] could make, say six plus two Dakotas and suitable crews available temporarily if project did materialize. Forbes thought it might be possible for Holly to do this, and he will no doubt discuss further when he returns.

Good Wishes for Operation COBRA, the Normandy Breakout

Eisenhower via Montgomery to Bradley 25 July   *Ref: FWD-12438*

Please pass the following to Bradley together with any special message you may wish to send him:

"Dear Brad: My high hopes and best wishes ride with you in your attack today, which is the largest ground assault yet staged in this war by American troops exclusively. Speaking as the responsible American rather than the Allied commander, I assure you that the eyes of our whole country will be following your progress and I take full personal responsibility for answering to them for the necessary price of victory. But a break-through at this juncture will minimize the total cost.[36]

General Montgomery's plan calls for a vigorous and continuing offensive by the other armies in the line, thus allowing you to pursue every advantage with an ardor verging on recklessness and with all your troops, without fear of major counter offensive from the forces the enemy now has on this front. All these attacks are mutually supporting and if Second Army should secure a breakthrough simultaneously with yours, the results will be incalculable. Good luck to every one of you. Ike"[37]

The Future of Army Command

Marshall to Eisenhower   *25 July*   *Ref: W-70115*

Since the withdrawal of the French divisions from the active front in Italy, the French Corps

---

31 Marshal of the Royal Air Force Sir John (Jack) C. Slessor GCB, DSO, MC (1897–1979), deputy to Lieutenant-General Ira Eaker (1896–1987), the Commander-in-Chief Mediterranean Allied Air Forces.
32 Forbes and Alms, unknown officers.
33 Special Project Operations Center, Algiers.
34 Livorno, a city in Tuscany, northwest Italy.
35 Acting Air Vice Marshal Sir Leslie N. Hollinghurst GBE, KCB, DFC (1895–1971), commander of No. 38 Group, formed to transport airborne troops.
36 3000 US aircraft carpet-bombed a narrow section of the front shortly before H-Hour, causing over 100 casualties among the US ground troops but many more German. VII and XIX Corps advanced over fifteen miles to the southwest of St Lô over the next four days, breaking out of the bocage and into good tank country. It was the beginning of the end of German resistance in northwest France.
37 It appears that at best Montgomery was hoping to breakthrough southeast of Caen and at worst draw as many German armored divisions to his sector, weakening the sector facing First US Army. He succeeded in doing the second; when COBRA was launched, First Army only faced 1½ Panzer divisions while Second Army faced 6½ Panzer divisions.

sector has been passed to the Eighth Army[38] which leaves Clark's Fifth Army with only a Corps front. It may be at that some period later it could be arranged to have the present Fifth Army front turned over as a reinforced Army Corps to the British Eighth Army. This will release Clark and a very highly developed Army staff. On the other hand, it may be that Clark's commitments will carry him up the coast and into France by that route. I merely mention this entirely undecided phase of the matter, in order that you may know that there is a possibility that Clark and his staff might later be available to you if you wanted them.

The Fifteenth Army headquarters, of course, will be sent to you without a commander.[39] And the same applies to the XXI Corps,[40] unless you desire Craig[41] who is our most aggressive prospect. Incidentally, why would it not be a good thing to order Craig over to you have to be available for either a Corps or Division command in the event that you need either one? He could be getting some practical experience as a Deputy Commander.

Eisenhower to Marshall   *26 July*   *Ref: FWD-12466*
I will be very glad indeed to have Craig over here as soon as he can be spared, and thank you for the suggestion. He will, as you say, get practical experience as a Deputy Commander, and will be available to pinch hit in case of emergency. I will answer this message in more detail later.

A 'Friendly Fire' Incident Compromises the Normandy Cover Plan
Marshall to Eisenhower   *25 July*   *Ref: W-70115*
Should you desire to give[42] McNair an Army command we will be glad to release him here for this opportunity. I do not imagine there would be any possibility of obtaining Truscott before the middle of September at the earliest, as he has the critical Corps command for the landing in ANVIL.

Eisenhower to Marshall   *25 July*   *Ref: FWB-12450*
Bradley just telephoned me that McNair was killed this morning while observing the beginning of the attack by one of the frontline companies.[43] This has serious implications in connection with the cover plan,[44] so request that no announcement of any kind be made until we reorient the plan, which we expect to do within 24 hours. Bradley recommended and I approved burial in France, as for other casualties.[45]

Marshall to Eisenhower and Smith   *26 July*   *Ref: W-70705*
Announcement will not be made and I expect to notify nobody, including next of kin, until we hear from you again. This means, however, that it will be necessary to give me the

---

38 British Eighth Army, commanded by Lieutenant-General Oliver Leese KCB, CBE DSO (1894–1978), at this time.

39 Fifteenth Army was activated in August and moved to the UK in October; it transferred to the Continent in December.

40 XXI Corps joined Seventh US Army in January 1945 under Major-General Frank W. Milburn's (1892–1962) command.

41 Major-General Louis A. Craig (1891–1984) was appointed to command 9th Infantry Division following General Eddy's promotion in August 1944.

42 General Lesley McNair.

43 McNair was observing the opening attack of Operation COBRA from a front line foxhole. His son, Colonel Douglas McNair, chief of staff of the 77th Infantry Division, was killed by a sniper two weeks later on Guam.

44 Operation QUICKSILVER, part of Operation FORTITUDE SOUTH, which was to convince the Germans that First US Army Group, FUSAG, was poised to attack the Pas-de-Calais.

45 General McNair's grave is in the Normandy American Cemetery and Memorial overlooking Omaha Beach; his headstone is the same design as the rest, from general down to private.

quickest possible signal upon reorientation of the plan. It also means that I must charge you with ensuring that there is no leakage of news, whether through press, radio, letter, commercial cable, travelers or any other means. Burial plans approved.

Eisenhower to Marshall   *26 July*   Ref: FWD-12466

As continuation of the threat to the Pas de Calais area depended to a considerable extent on the reputation of McNair, and particularly as his appointment as Commanding General First U. S. Army Group has already been passed to the enemy, it would then be desirable to sign another general officer from the United States with a reputation comparable to McNair's to replace him as First U. S. Army Group commander.[46]

I appreciate that it may not, repeat not, be possible to make a suitable replacement available in time to be effective. Consequently, Simpson is being designated, for cover purposes, acting commander of the First U. S. Army Group. It will take about two days to pass this information to the proper destination through secret channels, and it would be desirable to do this some little time before the public announcement of McNair's death is made. However, I know that you will be in a difficult position until this is done particularly since, although we are taking every human precaution, there is always the possibility of a leak. Therefore, we are expediting action, and believe that it will be entirely satisfactory for the War Department to release on the morning of 29 July an announcement that General McNair was killed in action while observing operations in France. Suggest that you do this about 9:00 a.m. your time and we will hold a similar announcement until 3.00 p.m. our time 29 July. Thus the War Department announcement and our own will reach the public about the same time.

Marshall to Eisenhower   *27 July*   Ref: W-71287

We are in a particularly vulnerable position. We have not told next of kin because this action would certainly produce a leak here. Meanwhile, we feel there is a constant danger from your side through written or cable communications, and through individuals returning to the United States. It would seem that delaying announcement until information on successor reaches the enemy would probably result in the news reaching here for the first time from enemy sources. Further, since General McNair's appointment has already been passed to the enemy, we do not understand the advantages of holding up the announcement until the enemy knows who the successor is. The release would not include the designation of the command involved.

We feel there is a strong possibility that the release by the enemy, or through a patent leak here, would result in more damage than an official release, since the War Department would be totally unable to explain the reason for the delay. On the other hand, an official release would not arouse any suspicion on the enemy's part that the information they have received was purposely passed to them. However, you must by the judge in the matter.

If you concur it is proposed that a simultaneous release be made at 13:00 Eastern War Time, Thursday, July 27. It will be necessary for lawyers to tell next of kin one hour earlier. Please expedite reply.

Eisenhower to Marshall   *27 July*   Ref: S-56306

Have personally talked to my top security man and we concur in procedure stated in your

---

46 False radio signals reported units massing in southeast England, while double agents working under the Double Cross System passed false information to German intelligence.

W-71287. My announcement will be made at seven this evening, which will be simultaneous with your release at 13:00 hours Eastern War Time today. My announcement will be as follows;

"The Supreme Commander regrets to announce that Lieutenant General McNair, United States Army, has been killed in Normandy by enemy action."

In notifying next of kin, will you be kind enough to present my personal and sincere sympathy. I will later write to Mrs. McNair a personal letter.

Marshall to Eisenhower   *1 August*   *Ref: W-73959*
Reference death of McNair: His pilot and aide, who were present at his death, returned to Washington and not having received any instructions, informed at least four or five individuals of the facts. We are endeavoring to suppress the story here in line with your desire to avoid an air-ground antagonism, but this will be futile unless more care is taken on your side. It would be advisable to give correct facts at home if leak is to be anticipated.

Eisenhower to Marshall   *3 August*   *Ref: S-56676*
When we sent you our FWD-12450 reporting McNair's death and our S-56316 reporting the accidental bombing of some our own troops by the Eighth Air Force,[47] it had not been definitely reported to me that McNair was killed by one of our own bombs. I told you of this possibility in my personal letter of July 26th. Later investigation has developed that there is no doubt that this was the case and I regret that we failed to inform you of this properly.
I consider it absolutely futile and harmful to try to conceal this bitter truth. I recommend that the War Department make a statement to the effect that I have reported that General McNair was killed while observing an attack with a front line company, apparently by one of our own bombs that unfortunately fell short while hundreds of big bombers were bombarding the forward elements of the enemy. My own public relations officer will release a similar statement this evening, at 3 o'clock P.M., Washington War Time.

I realize that this statement may tend to increase the intensity of any incipient air-ground argument. However, both General Smith and myself, as well as other ground and air officers, have given the press a complete background to the incident. I am certain that so far as air and ground troops in this Theater are concerned, the general reaction has been that while the affair is deeply regretted, it must spur us on to perfection of technique and must not operate to create a rift between the air and ground forces.[48] The following sentences are from a letter I have just received from Bradley: "This operation could not have been a success it has been without such close cooperation of the air. In the first place the bombardment which we gave them last Tuesday was apparently highly successful, even though we did suffer many casualties ourselves."[49]

---

47 Eighth US Air Force.
48 Bradley wanted the bombers to approach from the east, out of the sun and parallel to the Saint-Lô–Periers road, an impossible task because of time and space constraints as well as the high chance of errors. Instead most planes approached from the north, perpendicular to the front line.
49 600 fighter bombers attacked strong points and artillery positions followed by 1800 heavy bombers and then a larger number of medium bombers. They attacked an area 5.5km wide by 2km deep. 111 American soldiers were killed and another 300 wounded.

De Witt to take McNair's Place

Eisenhower to Marshall   29 July   Ref: FWD-12483

We will want DeWitt. Details as to time of departure and content of press announcement will be given later after cover people have completed their plans.

Eisenhower to Marshall   1 August   Ref: FWD-12534

In order to maintain our cover plan at its maximum strength we feel that De Witt should be sent here as soon as you can conveniently spare him. The press release should state that De Witt is being sent to the European Theater to replace McNair. No statement as to the date of his departure from the United States, arrival in the United Kingdom or the nature of his assignment should be made.

Marshall to Eisenhower   4 August   Ref: W-75056

General DeWitt will leave Saturday. Estimated time of arrival will be furnished you later. General DeWitt requests that Lieutenant Colonel T. M. McGrail, Infantry, formerly his Aide and now understood to be on staff duty in your Theater, be assigned to him and meet him at Prestwick.

Press release will be made here when notification has been received of DeWitt's arrival in the United Kingdom, or on departure as you elect. Subject to your concurrence in wording release will read: "Lieutenant General DeWitt has been ordered to the European Theater to replace Lieutenant General McNair."

Eisenhower to Marshall   5 August   Ref: FWD-12610

We are assigning Lieutenant Colonel McGrail as De Witt's aide and he will meet him at Prestwick.

Concur in the wording of the press release regarding De Witt's assignment. For security reasons this announcement should not be released until De Witt has arrived in the United Kingdom.

The Press Invent Stories about the Russian Army

Eisenhower to McNarney   27 July   Ref: S-56332

I am forwarding to you today in a report from my Public Relations Officer on the subject of the query submitted to you by the State Department, as to statements made here concerning Russian citizens in the German army. The gist of the report follows.[50] No, repeat no, representative of mine has ever made any statement on this subject. The statement alleged to have been made by a representative of this headquarters in substantially the same as stories printed by A.P. and U.P. correspondents in Normandy. There were passed by the censors because obviously security is not involved, and it would be practically impossible and most undesirable to apply censorship to such matters. The Public Relations Division holds daily press conferences but on the date in question there was no mention made of Russia or of Russian soldiers.[51]

This headquarters does not issue statements bearing upon matters outside its own jurisdiction and you are perfectly safe in informing the State Department that no representative

---

50 The report is not in the Eyes Only file.
51 In summary, reporters had probably learnt through unsolicited sources that Russian citizens had been captured while serving in the German Army. While true, it would have caused embarrassment and difficulties between the Allies, and consequently undermined the Alliance if the US Army were seen to be reporting the facts to the press.

of mine has attempted to express an opinion, or to give details of information concerning the alleged presence of Russians in the German Army.[52]

Responding to Criticism of Montgomery

Eisenhower to Surles[53]   30 July   *Ref: FWD-12498*

In a few recent articles from the United States, I am told there has been some sharp criticism of Montgomery. I realize that every writer is entitled to express his own opinions but the articles in question apparently ignore the fact that I am not only inescapably responsible for strategic and general missions in this Theater, but they seem to also ignore the fact that it is my responsibility to determine the efficiency of my various subordinates and make appropriate reports to the Combined Chiefs of Staff if I become dissatisfied.[54]

My only concern in these articles is that criticism directed against any one of my principal subordinates, and therefore by inference approving of my actions and efforts, is certain to disturb the spirit of teamwork that I have so laboriously worked for during the past two years. Will you please emphasize in your off the record and background conferences, my definite responsibility for strategy and major activity and point out that when criticism is believed to be necessary it should be directed toward me equally, at least with any of my principal subordinates.

Please tell the Secretary that I finally hope to establish myself on the continent within five or six days and remain there.

A Request for Regular Updates

Marshall to Eisenhower   31 July   *Ref: W-3221*

The Washington representatives of the British Chiefs of Staff have expressed a lack of knowledge concerning your plans and your estimate of the situation. They have suggested that periodic appreciations, similar to those which have been furnished by Wilson, would be helpful.[55]

It is true until your 12493 arrived Saturday, we had not received recently any information on your thoughts concerning the situation and your probable cause of action. For instance, we received no information of Bradley's present offensive except an unexplained reference in a radio from Mr. Stimson referring to COBRA, whatever that was.[56]

Will you give your thought to sending periodic messages concerning your intentions, plans, and your ideas on the progress of the campaign? Any information you do not wish to send to the Combined Chiefs of Staff can be sent to me personally. If you feel able to send such messages, it would place us in a better position to deal with enquiries and size up the situation.[57]

---

52 Russians were enlisted to serve in supplementary services and they were called Hiwis, an abbreviation of *Hilfswilliger*, a willing helper. Some were used in combat but their willingness to fight varied according to the pressure they were put under by German troops.

53 Major-General Alexander D. Surles (1886–1947), director of the Department of War's Bureau of Public Relations.

54 The relationship between Eisenhower and Montgomery has always been described as a difficult one. This cable illustrates how Eisenhower wishes to distance himself from criticism in the press and focus on the professional relationship and mutual respect of the two generals.

55 Wilson reported on progress in the Mediterranean Theater.

56 This cable illustrates how little Washington knew about the detail of SHAEF's operations in Normandy. COBRA was the codename for First US Army's attack on 25 July.

57 This makes it clear that Marshall and Eisenhower used the Eyes Only cables to air private thoughts, make suggestions and hold discussions without involving the Combined Chiefs of Staff.

Let me have your frank reaction to on this matter so that, if indicated, I can make some statement to the local Combined Chiefs of Staff organization.

[Handwritten note] G-3 [General Bull] please see me about this at your convenience.

[Handwritten note] General Bull discussed this personally with Chief of Staff at 16:00 hours, 1 August.

Eisenhower to Marshall   *3 August*   *Ref: S-56667*

I am sorry that I have not kept you more fully abreast of future plans, as I did in North Africa. My excuse is that in my anxiety to push events the matter had merely slipped my mind. Hereafter I will have the staff draw up a suitable weekly appreciation for the Combined Chiefs of Staff. My current and personal appreciation follows:

I omit any detailed review of the developments up to the present because I assume that the Chiefs of Staff are aware of the major factors that have been involved. However, I should like to make it clear that when we found in the early days of the operation that the enemy was rushing the major portion of his mobile forces into the Caen area, I personally approved Montgomery's policy of taking up a firm defensive and containing action in that region, while we secured Cherbourg in the west and then turned United States forces southward to roll up the enemy forces.[58]

From the beginning, Montgomery, Bradley and I have agreed that we should attempt to maneuver and attack, as to pin down and destroy substantial portions of the enemy in our immediate front, so as to have a later freedom of action. The alternative would be merely a pushing back with consequent necessity for slowly battling our way forward towards necessary geographical objectives.[59] One of these is the Brittany Peninsula, which we must have quickly. The other is more elbow room in the east. Storms at sea and bad flying weather slowed up our projected schedule, but in general that policy has been faithfully pursued ever since.

The first purpose of the attack at Caen was to get the bottleneck of the Orne crossing behind us rather than in front of us, and to take advantage of any break that might occur in the German line to exploit rapidly to the southward into good tank country. A complete breakthrough was not accomplished but the first portion of the objective was secured at the same time that we were carrying on offensive operations in the west.[60]

Bradley's offensive was set up to drive rapidly toward the Avranches area and to secure an open flank if we possibly could, so as to be free to operate both into the Brittany Peninsula and to roll up the German line.[61] Supporting this attack the Second Army was to act aggressively throughout its front and to be ready to seize any favorable opportunity that might develop for a major offensive. As Bradley's attack gained some ground it appeared that this opportunity had occurred in the region of Caumont and Second Army's attack was rapidly mounted to take advantage of that opportunity.

---

58 Organized resistance ended in Cherbourg on 26 June and the city was finally cleared on 1 July. First US Army began its attacks south through the bocage towards the road running between St Lô, Périers and Lessay the following day. It wasn't until 20 July that the road was cut and on 25 July the new 12th Army Group launched Operation COBRA, southwest of St Lô.

59 In summary, the strategy was to draw in German reserves and destroy them while Allied numbers increased to a point where SHAEF could break out of Normandy.

60 2nd British Army Operations, EPSOM, WINDSOR, CHARNWOOD, ATLANTIC and GOODWOOD around Caen.

61 Avranches on the west coast of France; by advancing down the coast, 12th Army Group would have a safe flank and be able to capture ports at the same time.

At this moment the enemy is bringing up such reinforcements as he can gather from within France to bolster up his lines and to establish a defensive position that will prevent us breaking into the open. We are attacking viciously in an effort to accomplish our purpose before the enemy can be successful in establishing new and strong lines.

Future prospects must therefore be gauged by the varying degrees of success that we may achieve in the battle now raging. The first and most favorable prospect is that both our major attacks will enjoy a great degree of success. Should the Second Army succeed in getting a firm hold of Vire, while Bradley makes good his seizure of the Avranches area, and then both forces operate towards the portion of the enemy now heavily engaged between those attacks, we should not only gain a real tactical victory but should destroy so many of his troops west of the Vire that we will have created practically an open flank. In this event would consider it unnecessary to detach any large forces for the conquest of Brittany and would devote the great bulk of the forces to the task of completing the destruction of the German Army, at least that portion west of the Orne, and exploiting beyond that as far as we possibly could.[62]

If a lesser degree of success attends our current attacks, we may expect the enemy to establish in some strength a defensive line stretching from Caen to Avranches, possibly south of Vire. At that point the enemy would be extended but on the other hand, our troops would probably be quite tired. We could expect that if the enemy succeeds in doing this he will have done it by stripping to some extent the area south of Caen, where he has shown the greatest anxiety to prevent any advance. If he does this, Montgomery will immediately thrust forward again in that region.[63]

The task of gaining Brittany will then require another major thrust by Bradley on his right flank and the rapid conquest of Brittany may require more troops than under the more favorable contingency discussed above. In this event, our immediate effort along the general front would be somewhat ambitious and would be limited to finding favorable opportunity for attack.[64]

You will note that in both these conceptions the rapid occupation of Brittany is placed as a primary task, the difference being that in one case we believe it would be rather easily done and in the other we would have to fight through the defensive line and commit more forces to the job.[65]

Finally, if the enemy should succeed in blocking our land advance on the line Avranches – Caen (which I do not for a moment believe he can do), then we would set up a special operation called SWORDHILT to capture Brittany. It would be a combined amphibious – airborne operation, striking somewhat to the east of Brest, on the north coast. The garrison of the peninsula has been much reduced and an operation of this kind would have real chance of success. You will note this is the final alternative and I do not believe I will have to mount it.[66]

It is my hope that once we have secured the Brittany Peninsula, we will find that our total

---

62 This is the scenario hoped for, which turned into the Battle for the Falaise Gap.

63 This is Eisenhower's Plan B. If the Germans stop 12th Army Group they would have done so by weakening the front facing 21st Army Group.

64 The Brittany Peninsula would become a problem as the chance to trap German Seventh Army around Falaise increased. 12th Army Group would have to leave a token force behind to cover the peninsular, while the bulk of First and Third Armies headed east.

65 Brittany was targeted because of its naval and U-Boat bases at Lorient, St Nazaire and Brest. Although the peninsular was taken easily, the ports held on. Nantes was taken on 6 August, St Malo two weeks later and Brest on 18 September after a ferocious battle; all the facilities had been badly damaged. Lorient and St Nazaire were surrounded to prevent further casualties and did not surrender until the end of the war.

66 This is Eisenhower's Plan C, an amphibious and airborne landing on the Brittany Peninsula to outflank the German positions around Avranches.

capacity for receiving and maintaining additional divisions has been increased, and that we can absorb all that can be brought in to us. If this should prove to be the case, then anything extra that can be brought to Europe would come in here rather than through the gateway in the Mediterranean. The next step would be aggressive action towards the northeast to destroy the bulk of the German mobile forces, all generally located along our present front and stretching up to include the Pas de Calais.[67]

In any event, and regardless of the completeness of victory in the current battle, this command will continue to maintain the offensive to the absolute limit of its power. On this point all my commanders are in complete agreement with me. I personally believe that if we could be fortunate to have a period of ten days to two weeks of really good weather, we can secure a most significant success. Even without such weather, I believe we are in good shape to reach the geographical objectives both in the east and west that we must maintain, and that in the meantime, we may do far more than this.

It is apparent that for the moment the enemy continues to regard his extreme eastern flank as his most sensitive one. This is unquestionably due to the fact that he still fears an invasion to the north of the Seine and feels that he must therefore block the direct and open approach toward Paris, or toward the region of the Pas de Calais.[68]

Personally, I am very hopeful as to the immediate results, and believe that within the next two or three days we will so manhandle the western flank of the enemy's forces that we will secure for ourselves freedom of action through destruction of a portion of the forces facing us.

---

67 Eisenhower would have expected the Germans to make a fighting withdrawal across northeast France. However, Hitler's insistence on holding ground and counterattacking was drawing German Seventh Army into a trap.

68 Operation FORTITUDE, the deception plan to make the Germans believe that the Allies were going to make an amphibious landing in the Pas-de-Calais was still working. It meant that large numbers of German troops were being held along the north coast of France and in front of Montgomery, weakening their position in front of Bradley.

8

AUGUST 1944

Command Issues in the 90th Infantry Division

Eisenhower to Marshall   2 August   *Ref: E-41105*

General Landrum, as you know, was given command of the 90th Division late in June.[1] The division was then in combat and has been in continuously since that time. Landrum has had no real opportunity to reorganize and retrain the division. Middleton feels that this division, in view of the past performances, requires new and enthusiastic leadership. Bradley concurs in the recommendation, and is convinced that Landrum is not the proper type to bring the 90th Division out of its present low state of battle efficiency. He feels that it requires a commander of more color and one who has not been associated with any of the unpleasant experiences of this division.

Bradley further feels that Landrum is not responsible for the condition of this division at the present time, and in view of his successful experience at Attu, he recommends that Landrum be returned to the United States to assume command of a division coming over here later, or such other assignment as may be available for an officer with his qualifications.[2]

I concur in Bradley's recommendation, and request your permission to return Landrum to the United States in his present grade. This recommendation differs from formers ones under somewhat similar conditions, but in this case I am willing to take Landrum back with a division that he has had a hand in preparing for combat.

Eisenhower to Marshall   2 August   *Ref: E-41104*

Relieved as Assistant Division Commander, 90th Infantry Division, is Brigadier General Samuel T. Williams,[3] for unsatisfactory performance in combat. Division, Corps and Army commanders' reports indicate that while General Williams is energetic and personally very brave, his performance has been such that he cannot be considered suitable for assignment as an Assistant Division Commander.

Unless General Williams is especially desired by some branch or division of the War Department in his present grade, I request that you give me the authority of the President to reduce him to his permanent grade of Lieutenant-Colonel. I will immediately appoint him to the grade of Colonel, and can absorb him in this Theater. The report of the circumstances in connection with his relief will be forwarded to War Department promptly.

---

1 General Eugene L. Landrum (1891–1967) took over from General MacKelvie on 14 June after 90th Division had only been in action for four days. He had been General Collins' assistant commander at VII Corps headquarters.
2 Landrum did return to the US and was given command of 71st Division.
3 Brigadier-General Samuel T. Williams (1896–1984), nicknamed 'Hanging Sam'.

Eisenhower to Marshall   4 August   *Ref: E-41508*
General Williams requests that in lieu of remaining here after recommended action in my
cable, he be permitted to return to the United States for assignment under command of
General Terrell, where he feels that he can give good service. It may be that under General
Terrell's, or another command, Williams may find himself and for that reason, if agreeable
to you, I recommend his return.[4]

Eisenhower to Marshall   19 August   *Ref: CPA-90233*
You will be glad to note that the 90th Division has been transformed into a very effective unit
and is now reported by General Patton as one of his best organizations. This is unquestionably due to the outstanding leadership qualities of Brigadier General McLain, a National
Guardsmen formerly with the 45th and later with the 9th Division.[5] I intend to include him
on a special list of recommendations for promotion that I will submit to you soon to fill vacancies caused by casualties in battle either through reduction, death or physical disability.

Eisenhower to Marshall   24 September   *Ref: FWD-15607*
I note that on the list of divisional commanders slated to come to this Theater is the name
of Major General Landrum. I have just received the efficiency reports on Landrum, prepared
by General Middleton, who is noted for his soundness of judgment and spirit of fairness.
Middleton's report, concurred in by Bradley, is so low than I am forced to request you to
remove Landrum from the list of division commanders to come over here. Specifically, he
is rated 'satisfactory' only in all qualifications except in physical endurance, which is 'very
satisfactory'. Under remarks, Middleton says "inclined to be too cautious when employing
troops in combat. Has too much of the cautious defensive attitude".

I regret that the serious nature of these unfavorable opinions was not completely known
to me when I returned Landrum to the United States. At that time, I was given to understand
that while he would probably make a very good division commander, the job of rehabilitating the 90th Division, which had gotten off to a very bad start, was too much for him.
Consequently, in view of what McNair told me of Landrum's outstanding performers at
Attu, I departed from my usual custom of asking authority for the reduction of a general
officer returned from this Theater because of dissatisfaction with the services. I hope you do
not feel in this instance that I have let you down.

Middleton states that Landrum is fit for "training troops or replacement center of staff
duty".[6]

A Promotion for Bradley?

Eisenhower to Marshall   3 August   *Ref: S-56678*
If you still have a vacancy on the list of regular Major Generals would you consider promoting Bradley from permanent Brigadier General to Major General? Yesterday Bradley assumed
command of the Army Group[7] and as soon as our operations widen out sufficiently to estab-

---

4 General Henry Terrell (1890–1971) had commanded 90th Division until his promotion to XXII Corps in
January 1944. Williams had been his assistant commander and believing that he had been hard done by,
wished to serve under his old commander.
5 General Raymond S. McLain (1890–1954) had seen action in Sicily and Italy with 45th Division and in
Normandy with 30th Division. He would go on to become the only National Guardsman to command a corps
in combat in Europe after November, after only three months as a division commander.
6 Middleton as VIII Corps commander had observed Landrum's performance in July. Landrum was immediately transferred to command an Infantry Advance Replacement Training Center.
7 12th Army Group.

lish clear cut zones of occupation for both British and Americans, he will operate directly under me and independently of 21 Army Group. I am confident you will agree he has richly earned some definite recognition and I know that between promoting him on the temporary list, or the permanent list, Bradley himself would prefer the latter.[8] It is rather well accepted in this particular Theater that since the American Army does not have the Field Marshal grade, our four star rank[9] is equivalent to the highest rank of the British Army and our three star officer is generally regarded as equivalent to the four star rank in the British Army.

While I am submitting this proposition in order to get your reaction I would be highly pleased and gratified to see you promote Bradley at this time on the regular list.

Eisenhower to Marshall   *16 August*   *Ref: CPA-90225*
Your W-80880 just received. I am glad that the committee has approved Patton and I cannot believe he has made any statements whatsoever in view of my orders to him. However I will repeat these orders, including your message, and will use censorship also.[10]

Did you receive my recommendation reference Bradley?

Marshall to Eisenhower   *16 August*   *Ref: W-81638*
I agree with you and more as to Bradley's ability, recent performance and future potential, but in view of many factors complicating such nominations I am not yet ready to propose his. I plan to do so, but a different timing is indicated. You are free to tell Bradley of what you recommend and what I eventually intend to do.

Eisenhower to Marshall   *17 August*   *Ref: CPA-90228*
Thank you for your message reference Bradley. Your statement will be equally as effective as the actual promotion.[11]

Operation DRAGOON

Eisenhower to Marshall   *5 August*   *Ref: FWD-12617*
I learn that the Prime Minister has sent a message to the President relating to DRAGOON.[12] I will not, repeat not, under any conditions agree at this moment to a cancellation of DRAGOON. While we have always believed that if there were immediately available in this region sufficient port capacity and communications facilities to support unlimited forces, then all possible strength should be brought here directly. The fact is that usable ports and communications in the necessary quantity and quality do not, repeat not, exist at this moment.[13] Moreover, we cannot foresee the speed of the Brittany campaign and, therefore any prediction as to the time that we can use existing or manufactured ports in that region, and the communications leading from them, is largely guess work.

I do believe, and have so stated in the past, that provided our establishment of ports and communications here is very rapid, it may later prove advisable to shift into this area some of

---

8 Bradley was a permanent brigadier-general and temporary lieutenant-general at this stage. Officers were usually appointed to temporary posts for the duration of the war to fill posts in the expanding army.
9 Stars were rank insignia on helmets and shoulder tabs: one star for brigadier-general, two for major-general, three for lieutenant-general and four for full general.
10 There are no other comments about Patton's behavior so Eisenhower's reprimand must have worked.
11 Bradley's promotion to full general (four stars) did not occur until March 1945.
12 This is the first time that ANVIL is referred to as DRAGOON; the amphibious landing on the south coast of France, was only ten days away, 15 August.
13 Cherbourg had been in Allied hands for five weeks but the docks were still being repaired, while Brest would remain in German hands until 19 September.

the formations now intended for later buildup of ANVIL. However, all of these things depend upon future developments and it is my considered opinion that at this moment there is nothing that justifies a recasting of plans in the Mediterranean, but rather that DRAGOON should be pushed energetically and speedily. I firmly believe that as quickly as the initial crust is broken through, the operations in that area, coupled with the Marquis, will have a great effect.

It is possible that the Prime Minister may have misconstrued or misunderstood my stated opinion on these matters, but I have never wavered for a moment from the convictions above expressed.

Opening Cherbourg and Brest

Eisenhower to Handy   *7 August*   *Ref: FWD-12655*
Please have following message delivered immediately personally from me to Admiral King.

"I have just seen copy of your message detaching Admiral Wilkes[14] and assigning Admiral Struble[15] to this Theater. I request as a matter of urgency that you permit Wilkes to remain here until the arrival of Struble. The important task at Cherbourg is well under way, and should not, repeat not, be interrupted at this critical juncture by a change in command. It will be of inestimable value to retain Wilkes on his present job for the next ten days or two weeks.

I am anxious to centralize all American naval affairs on this Continent in the hands of one man. Under present plans this man is Admiral Hall.[16] Under him are two distinct tasks of the greatest importance to the U.S. Forces. These tasks are the rehabilitation and functioning of the U.S. bases on the Cherbourg peninsula as one task and the same responsibility on the Brest peninsula as the other. Our plans are, therefore, for Admiral Hall to have general charge on the Continent with one of his principal subordinates handling the Cherbourg Peninsula and the other the Brest Peninsula.

The plan will make Admiral Hall the single American officer operationally responsible to the Naval Commander-in-Chief while, as before, we will be administratively responsible to COMMAVEU.[17]

I have consulted Admiral Bieri[18] on this project and he agrees completely on the above request and plan.

I will be deeply appreciative of your approval of my request."

Ammunition Shortages

Eisenhower to Somervall[19]   *8 August*   *Ref: FWD-12707*
In reviewing the current ammunition supply situation, I find that tactical commanders' plans call for expenditure of 155mm howitzer and 81mm mortar light ammunition over the period of the next 30 days at rates which can not, repeat not, be supported from present stocks and

---

14 Vice Admiral John E. Wilkes (1895–1957) was commander of all ports in northern Europe, covering Normandy before covering southern France in August.
15 Rear Admiral Arthur D. Struble (1894–1983), Chief of Staff to Rear Admiral Kirk, who was responsible for US Navy participation in the Normandy invasion.
16 Rear Admiral John L. Hall, Jr (1891–1978) commanded the difficult amphibious assault on Omaha Beach on D-Day.
17 Admiral Stark's title as Commander of Naval Forces in Europe (COMMAVEU).
18 Rear Admiral Bernhard H. Bieri, USN (1889–1971) served on the staff of the Commander-in-Chief of the US Fleet.
19 General Brehon B. Somervell (1892–1955), commander of the Army Service Forces, the logistical arm of the US Army.

War Department releases and still leave adequate reserves in the Theater.[20] In order to permit firing at the rate of 48 rounds per gun per day for 155mm howitzer and nineteen rounds per mortar per day for 81mm light, and still have available the equivalent of seven units of fire in reserve at the end of the next thirty days, we must receive in the Theater prior to 1 September in round numbers, 270,000 rounds of 155mm howitzer all types, and 250,000 rounds of 81mm light ammunition.[21]

I consider it imperative that tactical commanders' requirements for next 30 days be met in full, and request your personal assistance in arranging for the quickest possible shipment of these quantities, as well as unshipped balances of July releases which amount to about 390,000 rounds of 155mm howitzer ammunition.[22] I am having implications on the current tactical situation studied carefully, as they may result in a substantial lowering of requirements for September shipment, but present situation is important enough to bring it to your personal attention. The above is based on exhaustive studies of our inventories and previous messages.[23]

A Change in Plan to Trap German Seventh Army[24]

Eisenhower to Marshall   *7 August*   *Ref: FWD-12674*

Following is the first of the weekly appreciations referred to in our cable S-5667 dated 2 August.

The enemy's efforts to seal off the lodgment area have been defeated. So many of his forces west of the Vire have been destroyed that practically an open flank has been created and the conquest of Brittany is well under way.

Our broad strategy is to swing the right flank of the Allied armies toward Paris, hold the Paris-Orleans gap and to force the enemy back on the Seine, over which river all the bridges have been destroyed between Paris and the sea. We have three main objectives:

a) To secure the Brittany ports quickly, and maintain right flank protection.
b) To destroy as much of the enemy's Seventh Army strength as possible this side of the Seine.
c) To destroy his forces between the Seine and Somme and secure the Seine ports.

Sub paragraph b) of this plan begins with an immediate attack southward by the Canadian Army, with all other available forces taking up the attack quickly in a general advance toward the east and north. Plans are being made for a strong airborne and air landing force to be used to facilitate the advance and assist in the destruction of the enemy.

---

20 Eisenhower had complained to Marshall on 26 May (cable E-29855) that SHAEF's minimum estimates for ammunition expenditures had been cut by the War Department.

21 The amount of ammunition required to keep the minimum reserves and the logistics involved moving it all from the armaments factories to the frontline is difficult to comprehend.

22 The next 30 days would be when the Allies advanced rapidly across France, the logistics problem would eventually bring the advance to a halt near the German border.

23 By this stage there were over one million troops in Normandy. Ammunition problems had started with the bad weather limiting shipping in the English Channel and damaging the temporary Mulberry harbors. The wrecked state of the Cherbourg port and the delay in taking the Brittany ports only added to the difficulties.

24 This cable describes the original intentions for 12th Army Group but they would quickly change when it was clear that the German counterattack at Mortain would give Third Army the opportunity to swing around the German Seventh Army's south flank, paving the way for what would become known as the Battle of the Falaise Pocket.

Eisenhower to Marshall   9 August   *Ref: S-57189*

At the beginning of the week I established my Advance Headquarters in France, but have returned to England for one day to inspect two divisions. Upon arrival here, I found the War Department telegram relating to speeding up the arrival of divisions. The Staff is preparing a calculated answer but I want to assure you that in principle I thoroughly approve of the idea to such an extent that in my opinion, even if our calculations make it appear that we may have to unload one or more of these divisions in England, we should still bring them.

Under my urgent directions all possible strength in France is being turned to the destruction of the forces now facing us. I am not willing to detach from the main army at this juncture, additional forces merely in order to save a week or so in the time of capturing the Brest Peninsula ports. I firmly believe we have a great opportunity for a victory which, if fairly complete, will allow us complete freedom of action in France and will have incalculable results. For this, I need every unit here and we are hurrying forward into the battle every unit as rapidly as it can arrive at the beach.[25]

Patton, Bradley and Montgomery are all imbued with this necessity and alive to the opportunity. Patton has the marching wing, which will turn in rather sharply to the northeast from the general vicinity of Le Mans and just to the west thereof, marching toward Alençon and Falaise. The enemy's bitter resistance and counterattacks in the area between Mortain[26] and south of Caen make it appear that we have a good chance to encircle and destroy a lot of these forces. You can well imagine how badly I want additional troops and the second that the issue of this battle is determined, I will turn into Brittany forces to accomplish the quick downfall of those ports.

Everyone is in good heart.

Yesterday the Eighth Air Force in supporting the British attacks south of Caen again dropped some bombs in friendly territory. It appears in this instance the accident came about through enemy action. Specifically, his heavy Ack-Ack[27] knocked out about thirteen of our bombers and at least in one instance one of these fell into one of our own ammunition dumps and caused a very considerable upset. However, all of us believe that the day bomber is still useful in rather close support, depending merely upon our degree of training for this sort of work and upon suitable conditions.

I will return to my command post in France within a day or so.

Eisenhower to Marshall   17 August   *Ref: CPA-90228*

This is a personal and confidential report to you.

Due to the extraordinary defensive measures taken by the enemy north of Falaise and which have taken so long to puncture, it is possible that our total bag of prisoners will not be so great as I first anticipated. However, my personal opinion is that he still has a very large portion of his combat elements west of the gap. In any event, the beating up of his formations along our whole front has been such that, with the cleaning up of the pocket and a resumption of our advance east and northeastward, the opposition will be greatly weakened.[28]

---

25 The Battle of the Falaise Pocket was only days away. Eisenhower wanted to destroy German Seventh Army and he was prepared to delay the attacks on the Brittany ports to achieve it.
26 Operation LÜTTICH was the unsuccessful German counterattack made by XLVII Panzerkorps against the American positions near Mortain between 7 and 13 August.
27 Anti-aircraft fire, from the phonetic code for the letter A.
28 By 22 August the pocket had been closed and while around 12,000 men were killed in the sector and around 45,000 were taken prisoner, up to 50,000 escaped. German Seventh Army had lost most of its armor and transport, leaving approximately 500 tanks and assault guns behind; many more vehicles were lost west of the Seine.

The enemy is now assembling a formation on the Paris–Orleans front, probably for counterattack. Bradley is now in position to make a strong thrust to provide more troops to help clear up the Brittany Peninsula, which we must now do without delay. My decision of some days ago to devote only minimum forces to Brittany while we swept around to complete a major tactical victory, limited us to the use of the bottleneck near Avranches for supplying all forces enveloping the enemy's left and those thrusting eastward, as well as those operations in the Brittany Peninsula. These latter troops have received small quantities by L.S.T. landings on the coast, but we must now gain better anchorages and ports.[29]

Plans for an Airborne Operation

Tedder to Eisenhower and Smith   *16 August*   *Ref: S-57739*

Proposed airborne operations reference: In view of rapid development of situation in Western France, I strongly urge that possibilities be examined of making real strategic use of the airborne force.[30] In my view use of this force west of Seine is now unjustifiable. I also consider that the use of any large airborne force to cover the crossing of the Seine is also unjustifiable in view of the lack of defenses and enemy's known weakness.

It appears probable that in another week the enemy forces in Pas de Calais area will be negligible. I suggest we urgently consider employing the bulk of all of our available airborne force to seize Boulogne and Calais.[31] The supply of forces established there would be of most simplicity. Even allowing for damage to ports, sea supply and reinforcement should become possible after very short delay.[32] Possession of a base in this area would greatly assist operations east and north of Seine. Occupation of the area from which the flying bombs and rockets[33] are dispatched might well be the final blow to German High Command, which is obviously staking so much on his hopes for these weapons.[34]

Eisenhower to Marshall   *17 August*   *Ref: CPA-90228*

Improvement of communications, particularly on our right flank, is absolutely essential. We have already had to divert Troop Carrier Command to the supply of Bradley's right wing.[35] This is, of course, one of the advantages that possession of the Troop Carrier Command gives us. We will probably have to land about 2,000 tons a day for Bradley for the next few days.[36]

---

29 Around 40,000 troops held Brest and while VIII Corps' attack started on 23 August, the German commander did not surrender it until 19 September, after making sure the port facilities had been destroyed.
30 1st British Airborne Division had yet to be deployed, while 6th British Airborne, 82nd American and 101st Airborne Divisions had rested and refitted after the Normandy battle.
31 The capture of these two ports would greatly assist the logistics problem developing across France, as 12th and 21st Army Groups depended on fleets of lorries to keep them supplied.
32 Supply planes could fly across the English Channel while ships and landing craft could deliver supplies over the beaches until the ports were opened.
33 There were large numbers of V-1 launching sites across the Pas-de-Calais and they were all pointing towards London. The morale boost for the people of south east England if they were captured would be enormous.
34 When it was clear that First Allied Airborne Army would not be employed west of the Seine, the Deputy Supreme Commander and the SHAEF deputy G-3 proposed using it to take Boulogne or Calais or north of the Somme between the Oise and Abbeville, and north of the Aisne in the neighborhood of Soissons. General Brereton's plans for an operation to capture Boulogne were abandoned at the end of August when it became clear that 21st Army Group would bypass or capture the city before the operation could be launched.
35 IX Troop Carrier Command had three troop carrier wings, 14 troop carrier groups and one pathfinder group. At its height it had approximately 1350 operational aircraft and 2000 gliders.
36 Hundreds of lorries known the 'Red Ball Express' had to carry supplies forward. However, as the advance continued the number of lorries and the amount of fuel required to travel longer distances became restrictive.

This brings me to the question of the next airborne operation, which I hope to make a big one. The first possibility is one that I will carry out only if necessary, which is to help us across the Seine. This move would not be a particularly decisive one in itself, and I hope that the beating we give the forces now on our front is such that we can dash across the Seine without the aid of airborne troops.[37] If this should prove to be the case, a fine operation will be to place a large airborne force in the Pas de Calais area. In such a position it would be perfectly located to help destroy the German forces still remaining on our front, and could operate in tactical coordination with the troops that had forced the crossings of the Seine. In that area also air supply would be a very simple operation. Seizure of the area would of course practically eliminate present flying bomb activity and I am convinced it would have the most tremendous moral effect, favorable for ourselves and adverse for the enemy. Moreover, if we got this whole coast cleared up, normal supply for the British forces would be facilitated.[38]

Marshall to Eisenhower   *17 August*   *Ref: W-82265*

The plans outlined appeal to me as sound. I was very glad to be advised of your plans against the Pas de Calais with the airborne forces. I had felt that the vicinity of Rouen was the first point indicated, but that in view of the movement of German divisions from the Pas de Calais towards the Seine[39] and the gradual evacuation of the Falaise–Mortain pocket, the better operation would be in the Pas de Calais area and for a double purpose: to suppress the robot activity[40] and to establish our people well in the rear of the German right.

In surveying the matter here, particularly the present disposition of German troops, so far as known, and having in mind the tremendous psychological impact, it appeared that a landing in the rear of Dunkirk was the ideal point and that the Dunkirk beach defenses could probably be stupefied by continuous air bombardment, to permit the airborne troops to take the port from the rear without heavy losses or delays. This would give you a harbor for the buildup of a sizable force in the rear of the German right, and would greatly facilitate the deployment of the divisions arriving in England.[41] However, you have your more accurate knowledge of the German dispositions and your own deployments on which to base a decision. Our G-2 people do not feel that the Paris–Orleans German assembly has the capability for a counterattack.[42]

---

37 The Allies crossed the Seine without the need for airborne troops.

38 Using airborne troops to take the Pas-de-Calais area would destabilize the German front and capture the V-1 rocket sites threatening London. The seizure of Calais and Boulogne would allow them to be used to supply 21st Army Group.

39 Field Marshal Walther Model (1891–1945) took temporary command of OB West on 17 August, following Kluge's suicide, and persuaded Hitler that he had to withdraw. At long last Hitler had been convinced that the threat of a landing on the Pas-de-Calais coast was a fake one. Operation FORTITUDE had kept large numbers of German troops in this area for over two months, preventing them from reinforcing the real threat in Normandy.

40 V-1 Flying Bombs.

41 The rapid withdrawal of OB West towards the German and the Dutch borders meant that, once again, an airborne operation had to be cancelled.

42 The Battle of the Falaise Pocket was coming to an end and Seventh Army and Fifth Panzer Army were looking to escape. Although the two armies were badly mauled, more units escaped than Eisenhower had hoped for. They then headed east and the final troops had crossed the Seine north of Paris by 30 August. As G-2 reported, they were in no position to stage a counterattack south of the French capital.

The Relief of Two Division Commanders

Eisenhower to Marshall   *17 August*   *Ref: CPA-90227*

Two division commanders have been relieved for failure to provide efficient leadership for their divisions. They are Major-General Leroy Watson[43] commanding 3rd Armored Division and Major-General Lloyd Brown[44] commanding the 28th Infantry Division.

I have had long personal talks with these officers subsequent to their relief. In the case of Watson, the Corps and Army commanders recommended that because of his value as a trainer of troops, he should be sent back to the United States in grade, but Bradley and I agree that if a man cannot successfully lead his division in combat he should not hold a grade of Major-General. I retained General Watson here for some days subsequent to his relief in an effort to place him with another division, but his services are not desired by any of the Corps or Army Commanders where a vacancy exists. He produced a good division and his relief seems to be more the result of an accumulation of minor mistakes, and a deficiency in drive rather than a complete lack of leadership qualities. Bradley and I both believe that he is a good type but not quite of the caliber to command a division. Consequently, it is my opinion that he should be reduced to his regular grade of Colonel.

In the case of Brown, both Bradley and I are completely convinced that he should be reduced. He has no inspirational qualities; while unquestionably a man of outstanding personal bravery, he has definitely failed as a division commander.

I request the authority of the President to reduce these officers to their regular grades and to return Brown and possibly Watson to the United States.

Eisenhower to Marshall   *19 August*   *Ref: CPA-90233*

Colonel Watson, formerly Major General commanding the 3rd Armored Division, is being assigned as assistant division commander of the 29th Division. Both Bradley and I do believe he will make good.

Eisenhower to Marshall   *22 September*   *Ref: FWD-15465*

I do not consider Colonel Lloyd Brown to be a good commander. In my opinion he is a Staff type who lacks the magnetic personality to keep an organization doing its best when the going is tough. Consequently, I would recommend against his being assigned to an Assistant Division Commander's job, because it is my experience that an officer occupying this position is frequently called upon to command troops in a semi-independent role.

He is extremely gallant and courageous and well grounded in Staff work and organizational and training requirements. My unfavorable opinion of him for command positions is based exclusively upon my belief that he does not exhibit, in times of stress, that magnetism and driving energy which are often the most important attributes of a commander.

A Corps Commander Falls Ill

Eisenhower to Marshall   *18 August*   *Ref: CPA-90229*

Major General Gilbert Cook,[45] who has performed brilliantly as Commander of XII Corps, has been relieved because of physical disability. His difficulty seems to result from an extraor-

---

43 Major-General Leroy H. Watson (1893–1975) stayed in Europe and was appointed assistant commander of 29th Infantry Division and remained so until May 1945.

44 Major-General Lloyd D. Brown (1892–1950) was reduced to colonel, his permanent rank, and returned to the US.

45 Major-General Gilbert R. Cook (1889–1963) and XII Corps had only been in France since 1 August. He was hospitalized due to circulation problems in his legs.

dinarily high blood pressure and he will be out of action indefinitely. Because of the good work of this officer, General Patton, with General Bradley concurring, has recommended him strongly for the Distinguished Service Medal. I request that you give me the authority to award the Distinguished Service Medal, with the understanding that the appropriate citation will be prepared here and forwarded to the War Department when practicable. All of us feel as badly about losing Cook as he does about losing his corps, and we are anxious to do this as quickly as possible.

Major General Eddy, heretofore commanding the 9th Division, has been given the XII Corps. Major General Craig, here for the moment as supernumerary, is being given command of the 9th Division. This is a splendid command for Craig as the 9th Division is one of our very best.

Thank you very much for your offer of Harmon.[46] I took it up with Bradley today but we have no immediate vacancy in an Armored Division. However, we're glad to know of his possible availability and if a vacancy occurs in an Armored Division command we will cable you at once.

Clarifying Who Commands

Marshall to Eisenhower   *17 August*   *Ref: W-82265*

Tremendous publicity was given throughout the United States, press and radio, and particularly editorial, to the creation of an American Army Group under Bradley, your movement to France, and your assumption of direct command of the American Group. The recent statement from your headquarters that Montgomery continues in command of all ground forces has produced a severe reaction in the *New York Times* and many other papers and I feel it is to be deplored. Just what lay behind this confusion in announcements I do not know, but the Secretary and I, and apparently all America, are strongly of the opinion that the time has come for you to assume direct exercise of command of the American contingent. I think you will have to consider this matter very carefully because the reaction here is serious and will be, I am afraid, injected into the debate in Congress within the next 24 hours. The astonishing success of the campaign up to the present moment has evoked emphatic expressions of confidence in you and in Bradley. The late announcement I just referred to has cast a damper on the public enthusiasm.[47]

Eisenhower to Marshall   *19 August*   *Ref: CPA-90230*

I received your W-82265 today while I was spending several hours with Bradley at its headquarters and discussed it with him. Like myself, he is somewhat taken aback that our plans for initial, transitional and the ultimate command systems are apparently not understood by the War Department, so it is apparent that these have not been clearly or at least officially explained. I will probably submit a short report to the Combined Chiefs of Staff. It seems that so far as the press and the public are concerned a resounding victory is not sufficient; the question of 'how' is equally important. The following is a personal and confidential report to you.

My first reaction is that it would be a great pity if Bradley failed to get the full credit due to him for his brilliant performance, merely because the general instructions and policies he has pursued have been channeled through Montgomery. The development of command

---

46 Major-General Ernest N. Harmon (1894–1979), nicknamed 'Old Gravel Voice', veteran of the North African and Italian campaigns; he would take command of 2nd Armored Division in France in September 1944.

47 President Roosevelt and General Marshall reacted to this political pressure and instructed Eisenhower to assume operational control of the Allied ground forces as soon as possible.

1 General Marshall in his
Pentagon office in 1943.
(NARA-111-SC-165909)

2 A formal portrait of
General Eisenhower.
(NARA-111-SC-198150)

3 A stern looking General Marshall. (NARA-111-SC-197543)

4 Eisenhower visits paratroopers of the 101st Airborne Division a few hours before their planes took off for Normandy. (NARA-111-SC-189996)

5 A concerned Eisenhower off the coast of Normandy on D-Day waiting for news from the beaches. (NARA-111-SC-190642)

6 General Bradley points out a strategic point to Generals Arnold, Eisenhower and Marshall, and Admiral King. (NARA-111-SC-190610)

7 Marshall stops to talk to a GI during his visit to the Normandy beachhead. (NARA-111-SC-190281)

8 A thoughtful Field Marshal Montgomery. (NARA-111-SC-190425)

9 General Hodges at work in First Army's field headquarters. (NARA-111-SC-194269)

10 General Lesley McNair on 26 July, only a few hours before
he was killed while observing the bombing raids which heralded
Operation COBRA. (NARA-111-SC-191949)

11 A candid photograph of General Eisenhower taken 'somewhere in France'. (NARA-111-SC-197446)

12 General Arnold and General Marshall at the Combined Chiefs of Staff conference at Quebec, September 1944. (NARA-111-SC-194485)

13 General Devers, Sixth Army Group, and General Patch, commander of Seventh Army, receive awards from General de Gaulle. (NARA-111-SC-201033)

14 General Hodges, First US Army, and General Dempsey, Second British Army, meet on 15 September 1944, two days before Operation MARKET GARDEN was launched. (NARA-111-SC-194540)

15 It is all smiles for the camera during Montgomery and Bradley's visit to Simpson's Ninth US Army headquarters in November 1944. (NARA-111-SC-197799)

16 Eisenhower and Bradley talk to General Louis Craig during a visit to 9th Infantry Division's headquarters in the Ardennes in November 1944. (NARA-111-SC-199344)

17 Eisenhower and Montgomery discuss strategy at 21st Army Group's headquarters on 29 November 1944. (NARA-111-SC-197292)

18 General Eisenhower and General Patton pose for the camera in November 1944. (NARA-111-SC-197033)

19 A portrait photograph of General Marshall taken in January 1945; the map of the world is a reminder that the Army's Chief of Staff was also responsible for the Pacific Theater. (NARA-111-SC-198681)

20 Eisenhower during one of his many visits to divisional command posts; on this occasion he discusses 29th Division's attack on Munchen-Gladbach with Generals Gerhardt and Simpson on 3 March 1945. (NARA-111-SC-202134)

21 Army commanders together at General Bradley's 12th Army Group headquarters on 9 March 1945: Patton of Third Army, Hodges of First Army, Bradley, Simpson of Ninth Army and Gerow of Fifteenth Army. (NARA-111-SC-207342)

22 Bradley, Hodges and Patton greet Eisenhower on First Army's airfield at Euskirchen on 25 March 1945. By now 12th Army Group has crossed the Rhine in many places, including Patton's unplanned crossing between Frankfurt and Worms. (NARA-111-SC-204079)

23 General Patton and General Van Fleet get down on their knees to study III Corps' final operation of the war on 26 April 1945. (NARA-111-SC-204756)

24 Generals Bradley, Patton and Eisenhower visit the Kaiseroda salt mine to view the gold and treasures hidden there by the Nazis. (NARA-111-SC-204516)

25 The final stage of the surrender process took place at SHAEF's headquarters in Rheims, France. A somber moment in Eisenhower's war room as each party signs the papers, bringing six years of war in Europe to an end. (NARA-111-SC-205954)

26 After a monumental eleven-month campaign, General Eisenhower has achieved his final objective, the defeat of Nazi Germany's armed forces. The look on his face says it all. (NARA-111-SC-204256)

27 Part of Eisenhower's winning team. Front row: Simpson, 9th Army; Patton, 3rd Army; Spaatz, Tactical Air Force; Eisenhower; Bradley; Hodges, 1st Army; Gerow, 15th Army. Back row: Stearley, IX Tactical Air Command; Vandenberg, 9th Air Force; Smith, SHAEF Chief of Staff; Weiland, XIX Tactical Air Force; Nugent, XXIX Tactical Air Force. (NARA-111-SC-206143)

28 Prime Minister Winston Churchill welcomes Eisenhower to the London Guild Hall just before he was given the freedom of the city. (NARA-111-SC-207715)

29 Eisenhower gives thanks to the people of London from the flag-draped balcony of the Guild Hall. (NARA-111-SC-207712)

arrangements in this campaign was as carefully considered as the operation itself and events have closely followed the plan on which all were agreed. In the first place, I have always been directly responsible for approving major operational policies and principal features of all plans of every kind. As far as the ground forces were concerned the initial beachhead and area of operations were very constricted, and it was obvious that one man, who could give his entire attention to day-to-day action and who could be actually and consistently on the spot, had initially to be responsible for such details of coordination as timing of attacks, fixing local objectives and for establishing boundaries.[48]

Because I am responsible for coordination among ground, air and naval forces, as well as for a multitude of supply, civil affairs and related matters, it was also obvious that until rather extensive communications for me and my air-naval-ground headquarters could be established in France, this organization would have to remain in England, regardless of my personal whereabouts. Because of Montgomery's experience and seniority, he was therefore placed in temporary charge of the coordination of ground operations, but always under plans of campaign approved by me.

To give only one example of the detailed nature of this detailed coordinating necessity as long as our principal battle was on a very constricted front, I recite the following. Only yesterday our left Corps and the British right Corps became entangled due to rapid advances and consequent overlapping in attacks on a converging and fluid front. It was quickly straightened out, but it took immediate, authoritative action, on the spot, to prevent the matter becoming serious.

In forecasting probable developments it was clear to us months ago that about D+60 an American Army Group would be formed and soon thereafter the battle against the enemy in Normandy should be won, and diverging lines of operation would then indicate the desirability of cutting loose the Commander-in-Chief of the Army Group of the North from the Army Group of the Center.[49] Detailed, day-by-day coordination of tactical arrangements could then be in the hands of these two Group Commanders-in-Chief, with broad coordination and allocations determined by me.

However, a transition period would necessarily ensue pending the time my own headquarters could be built upon the Continent and during which time the United States Army Group would become fully operational. We calculated this period would last about 30 days. The reason that such a period of transition was inescapable was primarily that of communications; secondarily, that of congestion in the initial beachhead; and finally, the insistent need for devoting all our shipping to the fighting elements.[50]

From the beginning of this campaign everything has been sacrificed in order to send fighting troops to the Continent and provide for their maintenance in active operations. Obviously, communications from the senior fighting commanders to their divisions on the front took precedence over the establishment of communication for SHAEF Headquarters. Our woeful insufficiency in signal troops has made it impossible, as yet, to provide for me on the Continent a headquarters which would permit me to discharge of all the responsibilities devolving upon me, and at the same time take over the broad operational coordination necessary between Army Groups. Even now, with all available United States signal units

---

48 Montgomery's 21st Army Group controlled all ground forces in Normandy with Bradley in command of First US Army; 12th Army Group was formed on 25 July.

49 Montgomery's 21st Army Group was in the north and Bradley's 12th Army Group was in the center; 6th Army Group would form in September in the south.

50 For this period of 30 days Eisenhower's main headquarters would remain in England while his forward headquarters were in France. Eisenhower has to explain why problems arose during this transition period.

allocated to Bradley, his communications with Patton are ordinarily limited to radio tele-phone or laborious code, and to his rear they are no better.[51]

However, from the beginning I not only made frequent trips to the Continent but since August 7th have remained here permanently and in the closest touch with the situation. There has been no major move made of which I have not been cognizant, or which has been contrary to the general purposes I have outlined. Moreover I am forced to bear in mind that too great a personal engrossment in details of ground command would belittle and ignore the critical role played by air forces in our successful battle. This would shake the faith also of the Air Forces in my impartiality in dealing with battle requests, as opposed to CROSSBOW and strategic missions.[52]

Our ultimate stage of command was therefore to coincide with the operational stage when 21 Army Group, reinforced by whatever strength we must give it, would be free to operate to the northeast, while 12 Army Group would clean up Brittany, possibly the Biscay ports and operate eastward on both sides of Paris, thus increasing the threat implicit in DRAGOON. We will have a Commander in Chief, Northern Group of Armies and a Commander in Chief, Central Group. Finally, when DRAGOON comes farther north, we will have a Commander in Chief, Southern Group.

The report that appeared in the newspapers, to the effect that we had already reached a stage where my headquarters was on the continent and our command organization was now taking on its final phase, was written by a reporter without any consultation whatsoever with any part of the SHAEF staff. It was passed by a censor of the Ministry of Information and thereafter similar stories were passed by SHAEF censors, who assumed that the first story had passed through military censorship. While that newspaper story outlined rather well the plan that soon will be in operation, it was incorrect at the time written and consequently the denial to which you refer was issued. This is the incident that apparently caused the terrific and sudden public interest in the question.[53]

All others here, without exception, have given full attention to the requirements of the battle and are devoted to our efforts to the winning of the victory.

But I repeat that I am exceedingly sorry if Bradley's reputation should suffer in the slight-est. As for myself, I am indifferent to what the *New York Times* or any newspaper may say about my conduct of this operation, but it is a matter of deep concern that you and the Secretary of War should be disturbed because I have, as yet, been unable to put into effect an arrangement which I fully agree is now logical and is awaiting only the physical means for implementation. But the very signal units I need have had to be given to Bradley, so that he could keep in even sketchy contact with the rapidly changing situation.

Some time ago I ordered my staff to be ready to function on the Continent by September 1st. I still hope to make that date, although it is much earlier than any other technicians believed it could be done.[54] Will you please inform Surles, who has sent a personal telegram to Smith, that:

---

51 This refers to the tenuous communications link between 12th Army Group and Third Army.
52 Operation CROSSBOW was the targeting of V-1 and V-2 factories and launch sites. Other strategic tar-gets were: (a) aircraft industry (b) oil industry (c) ball bearing factories (d) vehicle production.
53 The media caused a stir by releasing incorrect or misleading information through an unsolicited channel. Whether this was deliberate or accidental is not stated.
54 On 1 September, Eisenhower assumed overall operational control of ground forces from Montgomery. Montgomery retained command of 21st Army Group.

a) No major effort takes place in this Theater by ground, sea, or air except with my approval, and that no one in this Allied Command presumed to question my supreme authority and responsibility for the whole campaign;

b) The exact time at which my headquarters can be in position to deal directly and constantly with both Army Groups, and soon with the DRAGOON Group, must be determined by physical conditions, but will be at a reasonably early date.

de Gaulle wants to Move his Government to France[55]

| *Smith to Gammell*[56] | *30 August* | *Ref: FWD-13404* |

Reference your FX-89381 about the move of French Governmental personnel. The actual facts are, in my opinion, that General de Gaulle does not, repeat not, want all of the Algiers Government in France. Immediately on receipt of your message, I got word to him and asked him to establish priorities for air movement. I expect to receive this within 24 hours and will communicate it direct to you. Pending receipt of these priorities from General de Gaulle, suggest you hold the French Government in place as far as possible, because Paris is really not yet clear and all of France is still considered in the combat zone. General de Gaulle at present is acting in his capacity as Commander-in-Chief of the French Armed forces, rather than as head of the French Government.[57] I must say that after the first flush of indignation I got a very hearty laugh about the Hegira of Jean d'Arc.[58] I have a sneaking feeling that the Pilgrims will not, repeat not, get a very cordial welcome from Charles.[59]

Countering the Me262 Fighter

| *Smith to Arnold* | *31 August* | *Ref: FWD-13440* |

I can not, repeat not, reach General Eisenhower at the moment and Spaatz has not yet returned, so I take the liberty of bringing the following to your personal attention. In spite of an attitude of optimism on the part of the Air Ministry, I have watched with some concern accumulating evidence indicating a comeback by the Luftwaffe, based on the jet propelled fighter. This morning, through sources familiar to you, we have an indication that five groups, totaling some 250 Me262s, are completing their organization and equipment and may shortly appear on our front to be used as bombers.[60]

---

55 The Liberation of Paris started with an FFI uprising on 19 August followed by the arrival of the 2nd French Armored Division and 4th US Infantry Division on the 24th; the last German garrison surrendered on 25 August.

56 Lieutenant-General Sir James Andrew Harcourt Gammell KCB, DSO, MC (1892–1975), Chief of Staff to General Wilson, the Supreme Allied Commander, Mediterranean Theatre.

57 de Gaulle moved back into the War Ministry on the Rue Saint-Dominique and then made a rousing speech to the crowd from the Hôtel de Ville. His actions prevented the planned Allied Military Government for Occupied Territories they also prevented a communist takeover.

58 A Hegira is an escape.

59 de Gaulle flew into France from Algeria a few days before the liberation of Paris and joined the liberating forces as they entered the the the city. However, as President of the Provisional Government of the French Republic he was not recognized as the legitimate representative of France until 23 October.

60 The Messerschmitt Me 262 Schwalbe 'Swallow' was the world's first operational jet-powered fighter aircraft. Allied sources discovered the existence of the plane in the spring of 1943 and the source Smith refers to is probably the British Government Code and Cypher School at Bletchley Park, England. Although 1400 Me262s were produced, only 200 flew combat missions due to a lack of fuel, pilots and airfields. They shot down around 500 Allied planes for the loss of only 100. However, their late arrival and limited numbers meant that Smith's fears were unfounded.

I may be overly pessimistic, but believe that we must not, repeat not, underestimate the damage which an increasing force of this type of extremely fast bomber may be able to do. Our anti-aircraft, at least at first, is going to be relatively ineffective and it seems to me that the answer lies in our own jet propelled fighter. The British have a few of these in operation against the flying bomb, but there seems to be no, repeat no, great drive behind production.[61] Is our own jet propelled fighter sufficiently advanced, so that we might expect a few squadrons in the event that this German potential assumes serious proportions? I suggest that this matter deserves some careful thought.[62]

---

61 Fourteen Gloster Meteors had been in action against V1 flying bombs since 27 July; they destroyed fourteen.
62 The Bell P-59 Airacomet was the first American jet fighter aircraft but the contract was cancelled due to poor performance and none flew combat missions. The American Lockheed P-80 entered service in the closing phases of the war but arrived too late to see any combat in Europe.

9

SEPTEMBER 1944

Proposed Changes to the Command of Strategic Air Forces

Eisenhower to Marshall 2 September *Ref: FWD-13605*

Spaatz believes that at a forthcoming meeting of Combined Chiefs of Staff there may suggested be a change in the current system of commanding Strategic Air Forces here.

I would regard any such change as a serious mistake because I feel it of great importance to keep all available forces under one hand in our penetration to Germany. There has never been any clash of policy, or any sharp differences of opinion, between the British Chiefs of Staff and this headquarters, regarding the use of any Strategic Air Forces since the beginning of the campaign. But when these forces are needed in furtherance of the ground battle, the coordination must be exactly planned and this can be done only at my headquarters. Spaatz has moved over here to be near me and Air Chief Marshall Harris[1] has his representatives here. It is possible that the British Chiefs of Staff might present some reasons for separating the night bomber force and controlling it as it formerly was. But I would urgently oppose any change in the U.S. Strategic Air Force control and I know Spaatz would do the same. Consequently if Bomber Command should be separated, coordination between it and the U.S. Strategic Air Forces would be more difficult.

Eisenhower to Arnold[2] 3 September *Ref: FWD-13657*

Yesterday I sent a radio to General Marshall expressing the positive view that control of Strategic Air Forces here, now vested in my headquarters, should not, repeat not, be changed, certainly, at least, so far as U.S. Strategic Air Forces are concerned.

In order that you may have some of my reasons, in addition to those given in that telegram, I cite the following: The basic conception underlying this campaign was that the possession of an overpowering air force made feasible an invasion that would otherwise be completely impossible. Control of all available air forces therefore had to be in the hands of the authority responsible for the conduct of the campaign. The air has done everything we asked. It has practically destroyed the German Air Force. It disrupted communications, it neutralized beach defenses and it has been vitally helpful in accomplishing certain breakthroughs by ground forces. While all this was being done, the Strategic Air Forces have been committed to the greatest extent possible on strategic targets and have succeeded in preventing substantial rehabilitation of German industry and oil production.

We are now stretched to the limit in maintenance of Ground Air Forces on the continent. Our front lines are almost beyond the limit of medium range from England and of the limit

---

1 Air Chief Marshal Sir Arthur T. Harris, 1st Baronet GCB, OBE, AFC (1892–1984), nicknamed 'Bomber' or 'Butcher', Air Officer Commanding-in-Chief of RAF Bomber Command.
2 Henry Arnold, Commanding General of the US Army Air Forces.

of fighter bombers based in rear continental areas. Yet our needs for keeping up the ground attacks are so great that we cannot quickly displace forward our mediums and fighters. To help in this we will have to use, over and above all other means, some of the heavies. Moreover, during this period the heavies may have to take over some of the missions ordinarily falling to mediums. In preparation for such tasks Spaatz is now ready to use 200 bombers in transportation of troops and supplies and soon his whole force will be able to do so.

I repeat that all of us are striving to keep the heavies on normal tasks but emergency use in the battle must be assured by continuation of the command system. All this applies particularly to U.S. Strategic Air Forces. Spaatz agrees with me completely and has asked me to send this radio to you.[3]

Keeping the Pressure on in Italy

Marshall to Eisenhower (info to Devers) 3 September   *Ref: SACF 76/03*

Prime Minister sent a message to the President giving the scheme for the present offensive in Italy, and stating that Alexander had received a message from SHAEF asking that something be done to prevent transfer of more German divisions from Italy.[4] The Prime Minister expressed hope that the offensive in Italy will prevent any more harm to you due to withdrawal of German divisions, and went on to mention his talks with the President at Tehran about Istria and his confidence that the arrival of an Army in the Istria area in a few weeks would give results far outside military values.[5]

The President replied expressing confidence in the outcome of Italian operations, which should have as their objective the destruction of enemy forces. He was sure you would now be satisfied with the assistance being given you in Italy. The President stated that the decision to further use Italian Armies should wait until we know more about German intentions and results of present campaigns.

The Prime Minister came back with a message stating that since the enemy in Italy has now been reduced by the withdrawal of four Divisions, no other American Division will be requested. The Prime Minister took for granted that no more United States Divisions will be withdrawn from Italy and so expressed himself. For future plans the Prime Minister thinks employment of forces in Italy can only be in a movement to Istria and Trieste and finally on Vienna.

I am recommending that the President's reply to the Prime Minister's last message include the following: Further employment of forces in Italy can be discussed at OCTAGON.[6] It seems that United States Forces ought to be used to the best. This matter depends on the progress of the battle in Italy and in France. We must not stint the forces which Eisenhower needs to break quickly through the German fortifications and get into the enemy homeland. End of President's and Prime Minister's messages.

It appears from the foregoing that the British are going to come to OCTAGON intending to insist on commitment of the Fifth Army for operations in Northern Italy and into the Balkans towards Vienna. Will you let me have your views on this whole matter?

---

3 Eisenhower's argument is that he, as head of SHAEF, should be able to deploy Strategic Air Forces as he sees fit to meet his objectives. At this point in the campaign the front is moving forward so fast that he needs to use bombers to move troops and supplies as well as cover missions while new airfields are established.
4 Operation OLIVE was launched to break the Gothic Line; while the British Eighth Army began its advance up the Adriatic coast on 25 August, Fifth US Army's attack in the Apennines followed on 12 September.
5 Churchill's hope was that if a breakthrough could be made, Allied troops could advance northeast through the Ljubljana Gap to Vienna and Hungary, preventing the Russian advance into Eastern Europe.
6 The second Anglo-American Quebec conference, 11–16 September 1944.

Eisenhower to Marshall   *4 September*   *Ref: FWD-13792*

It is obvious from an overall viewpoint we must now, as never before, keep the enemy stretched everywhere. One of these areas is Italy. The forces there should, if possible, be strong enough to keep on attacking relentlessly. A further consideration is that, if that front should disintegrate, and we could thrust into Austria, we might do much to prevent a later assumption of guerilla warfare by fanatical Nazis.[7] But under no considerations should the force turn south from Trieste into the Balkans.[8] It should strike northeast towards Vienna. If the British deem themselves too weak in Italy, without United States help, to keep up a continuous attack I feel we should let Clark stay there for the present. In fact, with the offensive now opening in Italy, I do not see how he could be released during the next six or seven weeks, which I regard as the critical ones. Our accelerated flow of divisions should meet foreseeable needs, unless the enemy produces unexpected strength on the Siegfried Line or on the Rhine. The Italian battle will help eat him up if Alexander can keep on the offensive. Soon we should produce conditions there similar to those now existing here.

Marshall to Eisenhower   *6 September*   *Ref: W-26119*

As to the matter of United States forces in Italy, I agree that we cannot make a decision now. If the campaign in Italy should move with the speed of Patch's campaign,[9] or the one in Northern France, we can better determine then on the future employment of the Fifth Army.[10]

Allocating Limited Air Resources

Eisenhower to Marshall   *2 September*   *Ref: FWD-13605*

All reports show that the enemy is routed and running on our entire front.[11] A gale has sprung up that automatically postpones the airborne operation planned for tomorrow[12] and in any event the hostile resistance has weakened so rapidly that the Lille area, where the airborne forces were to land, will probably be overrun by ground troops tomorrow. It begins to look as if Brereton's command will make its first unified effort east of the Siegfried Line.

Marshall to Eisenhower   *3 September*   *Ref: W-24853*

The British Chiefs of Staff have requested approval of the United States Chiefs of Staff, to the issue of instructions by the Combined Chiefs of Staff to SHAEF, to dispatch 100 British transport aircraft temporarily to the Mediterranean immediately it can spare them.

In view of the urgent need for transport aircraft in your Theater, as stated by Spaatz in U-66761 and the recent dispatch of 100 C-47's from the United States, your views on this request are desired, to include the estimated period of time during which the aircraft can be spared if sent to the Mediterranean.

---

7 There was a fear that fanatical German troops would head for the Alps if the German High Command prepared to surrender. From there they could conduct a costly guerrilla campaign.
8 The US Chiefs of Staff felt that British post-war interests in the region did not meet the Allied war priorities.
9 General Alexander McC. Patch (1889–1945), nicknamed 'Sandy', commander of Seventh US Army.
10 Both Eighth Army and Fifth Army penetrated the Gothic Line but there was no decisive breakthrough.
11 After the liberation of Paris in late August 1944, the Western Allies paused to re-group before continuing their advance towards the German border. The rapid advance through France caused a considerable logistical strain on the Allies and the lack of ports made it worse. Only Cherbourg was available and it had only just opened.
12 Operation COMET would have used the 1st Airborne Division and the Polish 1st Independent Parachute Brigade, to secure bridges at Arnhem, Nijmegen and Grave to give free passage over the river Rhine. It was cancelled due to bad weather and Montgomery's concerns about the buildup of German troops.

Eisenhower to Marshall   4 September   *Ref: FWD-13784*

Our immediate need for transport aircraft is not so intense as formerly, because of the cancellation of the airborne operation in Pas-de-Calais. From the long-term view, we have a continuous need for all the transport aircraft we can get to assist in supply, and to be constantly prepared for a massive airborne operation, which will sooner or later be necessary. Already two of these large operations have been cancelled due to unexpectedly swift collapse of enemy resistance and consequent overrunning of the dropping zones by advancing ground troops.[13] There is no question, however, that in the final breaching of the line on which the Germans may choose to defend their homeland, the Airborne Army will be required and every transport plane we can get our hands on will be necessary.[14]

As put up to me, the British Chiefs of Staff would like to have 100 aircraft for a most important operation in Greece for a period of about one week.[15] While this will reduce our supply of ground troops by a certain amount, we can spare the planes for that period in view of what are stated to me to be most urgent considerations in throwing some forces and the Greek government back into Greece.[16]

General Cannon[17] who is now here has stated that due to the improvement in the supply situation for DRAGOON, he could in an emergency put on the intended operation into Greece without help from this Theater. This would manifestly be a more economical method, since the planes would be absent from station a minimum of time. General Cannon states that the whole operation will be required not to exceed three days if done with his forces. It is entirely probable that the British Chiefs of Staff are not aware of this changed condition within the Mediterranean.

Since Great Britain has reserved in England no planes under its immediate control and has placed them all under SHAEF, I feel that we should do what we can to meet their urgent requirements in such a situation. If therefore, the 100 planes from this Theater are needed for a period not to exceed a week or ten days, we will make them available.

Eisenhower to Marshall   4 September   *Ref: FWD-13792*

Recently I sent you a letter that partially expresses my personal views has subject raised in your WX-24198. The enemy forces immediately facing us are on the run. Our greatest difficulty at the moment, except for the hard battle at Brest, is maintenance. We have advanced so rapidly that further movement in large parts of the front, even against very weak opposition, is almost impossible.[18] We are now concentrating on complete

---

13 Operation BOXER was to capture Boulogne and Operation LINNET was to have captured Tournai and create a bridgehead over the river Escaut.

14 Operation MARKET GARDEN – the attempt to cross the Rhine in Holland with the help of three airborne divisions – was less than two weeks away.

15 As German and Bulgarian troops withdrew from Greece, plans were afoot for an invasion of Greece to help restore control. The government-in-exile, led by George Papandreou, moved to Caserta in Italy and under the Caserta agreement of September 1944, all Greek resistance forces were placed under the command of a British officer, General Ronald Scobie. Allied troops started landing in October to find that most of the country had been secured by Greek partisans.

16 Mainland Greece was occupied in April 1941 and was eventually liberated in October 1944 following the German withdrawal as the Red Army approached. Churchill was trying to secure the country to prevent it falling into Soviet hands.

17 General John K. Cannon (1892–1955) was responsible for all air operations during the invasion of southern France in August 1944.

18 Ports and railways in northern France had been destroyed or badly damaged and everything had to be moved forward by a fleet of up to 5,950 trucks – the Red Ball Express – carrying 12,500 tons a day to keep the Allies moving. It was never enough and the bureaucratic nature of the Communications Zone, commanded by General J.C.H. Lee, only added to the problems.

destruction of the enemy in Belgium, while pushing the siege of Brest and thrusting out our flanks to the Moselle. The closer we get to the Siegfried Line the more we will be stretched administratively and eventually a period of relative inaction will be imposed upon us. The potential danger is that while we are temporarily stalled, the enemy will be able to pick up bits and pieces of forces everywhere and reorganize them swiftly for defending the Siegfried Line or the Rhine. It is obvious from an overall viewpoint we must now, as never before, keep the enemy stretched everywhere.[19]

Until we get into Havre and Brest and Antwerp, we cannot be certain that Marseilles may not be needed to help in accepting some of the divisions coming on the accelerated schedule. Devers and Larkin[20] assure me they can take two or three divisions from the United States and process them rapidly to the front lines.[21]

Marshall to Eisenhower　　　　　*5 September*　　　　　*Ref: W-25528*
In your FWD-13792 you state that your greatest difficulty is maintenance and that the closer you get the Siegfried line, the greater you will be stretched administratively and eventually a period of relative inaction will be imposed upon you. In your FWD-13794, you state that you are disposed to release 100 transport aircraft for an operation in Greece, although this will reduce your supply to ground troops by a definite amount.

I suppose you are under heavy pressure from the Prime Minister in the matter and are embarrassed by the fact that all British transport planes have been placed under your control. About two weeks ago, we scraped everything available in the United States to give you 100 more planes. There are no more that we can give you, and yet the push on the West Wall is of major importance in the conduct of global war at the moment. Can you not handle this matter through Cannon? I should be much more disposed to bring pressure from here on the Mediterranean than to see you weaken your supply capabilities at such a vital moment in the great European battle.

In view of the provisions of your directive, I suggest that you send the Combined Chiefs of Staff at once a brief recommendation on your assumption of command of forces which have entered through Southern France. Details should, of course, be left to arrangements between you, Devers and Wilson.

Smith to Marshall　　　　　*6 September*　　　　　*Ref: FWB-13960*
General Eisenhower is away at the moment, and I am answering your Eyes Only message W-25528. The one point which was not, repeat not, brought out in his FWD-13792, is that at the moment we have more air supply lift than our loading fields, and particularly our landing fields in the forward areas, will accommodate. Consequently, at this time, and for about a week to come, it would be possible for us, without embarrassment, to release the 100 British transport aircraft for the operation in Greece. However, advance landing fields and loading fields are being developed and repaired very rapidly, and within a week to ten days we will be able to employ every transport plane aircraft available, plus a considerable number of bombers if necessary, for supplying our advancing armies. Cannon left this

---

19 The race across France would end as Eisenhower predicted. The Allies' lines of communications could not keep up with the rapid advance. First Army was close to the German border and the Siegfried Line while Third Army only reached the Moselle river and Seventh Army was moving up on the south flank. In the north, 21st Army Group had just taken Antwerp and was close to the Dutch border.
20 Lieutenant-General Thomas Bernard Larkin (1890–1968), commander of the Southern Line of Communications supporting General Devers' advance across France.
21 In the south the ports of Toulon and Marseille had been captured while the local railway system was still relatively intact.

morning, prepared and willing to take on the Greek operation, for which he has volunteered if the Combined Chiefs of Staff decision is that he should do so, and it will be much better for us if he did the job.

I can assure you that the Greek project has not, repeat not, been pressed on us by the Prime Minister, or any other member of the British Government, and the question of the temporary release of these 100 British transport aircraft for a strictly limited period has been handled entirely through channels.

Montgomery's Plans for a Single Thrust to Berlin[22]

Montgomery to Eisenhower   *4 September*   *Ref: M-160*

I would like to put before you certain aspects of future operations and give you my views:

1) I consider we have now reached a stage where one really powerful and full-blooded thrust towards Berlin is likely to get there and thus end the war.
2) We have <u>not</u> enough maintenance resources for two full-blooded thrusts.
3) The selected thrust must have all the maintenance resources it needs without any qualifications and any other operations must do the best it can with what is left over.
4) There are only two possible thrusts; one by the Ruhr and the other via Metz and the Saar.
5) In my opinion the thrust likely to give the best and quickest results is the northern one by the Ruhr.
6) Time is vital and the decision regarding the selected thrust must be made at once and paragraph 3 above will then apply.
7) If we attempt a compromise solution and split our maintenance resources, so that neither thrust is full-blooded, we will prolong the war.

I consider the problem viewed as above as very simple and clear cut. The matter is of such vital importance that I feel sure you will agree that a decision on the above lines is required at once.[23] If you are coming this way perhaps you would look in and discuss it. If so, delighted to see you at lunch tomorrow. Do <u>not</u> feel I can leave this battle just a present.

Eisenhower to Montgomery   *5 September*   *Ref: FWD-13889*

Referring to your M-160 of 4 September. While agreeing with your conception of a powerful and full blooded thrust towards Berlin, I do not, repeat not, agree that it should be initiated at this moment to the exclusion of all other maneuver.

The bulk of the German Army that was in the West has now been destroyed. We must immediately exploit our success by promptly breaching the Siegfried Line, crossing the Rhine on a wide front and seizing the Saar and the Ruhr.[24] This I intend to do with all possible

---

22 21st Army Group liberated Antwerp on 4 September 1944 before German engineers could destroy it. However, the Germans still held both banks of the river Scheldt, preventing ships from reaching the port.

23 Montgomery wanted to keep advancing on a single narrow front towards Berlin, denying the Germans time to regroup behind the Siegfried Line or the Rhine. The limitations on supply meant that the rest of the Allied armies would have to stop where they were. He wanted to make the thrust north of the Ruhr, in 21st Army Group's sector, while the two US Army Groups halted. This shows that the claim that Montgomery was always very cautious is untrue. The question of Eisenhower allowing the British Army Group to forge ahead, while the two US Army Groups stopped, did not arise; it would have caused an outcry among American generals, politicians and newspaper editors.

24 This is a brief resumé of Eisenhower's broad front strategy. His key objectives are the Ruhr in the north and the Saar on the Alsace–Lorraine border; Germany's two key industrial areas. Without them Germany could not wage war.

speed. This will give us a stranglehold on two of Germany's main industrial areas and largely destroy her capacity to wage war, whatever course events may take. It will assist in cutting off forces now retreating from Southwest France. Moreover, it will give us a freedom of action to strike in any direction and will force the enemy to disperse over a wide area such forces as he may be able to assemble for the defense of the West.

While we are advancing, we will be opening the ports of Havre and Antwerp, which are essential to sustain a powerful thrust deep into Germany. No reallocation of our present resources will be adequate to sustain the thrust of Berlin.[25]

Accordingly my intention is initially to occupy the Saar and the Ruhr, and by the time we have done this, Havre and Antwerp should be available to maintain one or part of the thrusts you mention.[26] In this connection, I have always given, and still give, priority to the Ruhr and the northern route of advance, as indicated in my directive of yesterday which crossed your telegram. Locomotives and rolling stock are today being allocated on the basis of this priority, to maintain the momentum of the advance of your forces, and those of Bradley northwest of the Ardennes. Please let me know at once your further maintenance requirements for the advance to, and occupation of, the Ruhr.[27]

Establishing Sixth Army Group

Marshall to Eisenhower   6 September   *Ref: W-26119*

This morning's reports indicate that the progress of the forces from the Southern Mediterranean has been more rapid than envisaged in Wilson's MEDCOS 181, and even faster than appears to have been anticipated in your FWD-13853. Your proposal for assuming command of ground forces advancing from the Mediterranean appears satisfactory. I think you should get Devers into Group control as quickly as possible for several reasons related to French ambitions and Mediterranean complications. I doubt if you are proposing sufficient tactical air support for Devers' command.

The DRAGOON forces have already merged into the main effort of OVERLORD and are now the right wing of the great attack on Germany.[28] There should be no improvisation in their support so long as needed resources are available. You may consider that you have adequate air support in the Ninth Air Force to supplement the one fighter-bomber group you propose be furnished from the Mediterranean. If not, there should be no hesitation in drawing more United States fighter-bombers from the Mediterranean, where there are approximately twenty United States groups with some 1,200 Royal Air Force planes of this type with the Tactical Air Forces. Arnold agrees.[29]

---

25 Poor winter weather was only a few weeks away and the need for the port of Antwerp increased by the day. Although the port has been taken, the Germans still held both banks of the river Scheldt and the estuary was mined.

26 Events did not turn out as well as Eisenhower expected. While Antwerp was liberated on 4 September, the Germans held on to the banks of the Scheldt estuary and it was late November before the port was in use. A devastated Le Havre was liberated on 12 September; it too would not be in use for a long time. The Saar–Moselle Triangle would not be cleared until 1 March 1945 while the Ruhr would not be cleared until 21 April.

27 The extra logistics for Montgomery were provided at the expense of Patton's Third Army, which had to halt due to lack of fuel and supplies short of the river Moselle. 21st Army Group did continue its advance into Holland and there were plans afoot to use the Allied Airborne Army to get across the Rhine; the plan was Operation MARKET GARDEN.

28 Following a rapid advance up the Rhône valley, Seventh Army met Patton's Third Army near Dijon on 9 September. It had advanced over 300 miles from the south coast in only 25 days.

29 The success of Operation DRAGOON and the speed of the advance through southern France had taken everyone by surprise. This cable illustrates that Marshall knew it was time to reassess the support given to General Devers' new 6th Army Group as it headed east towards the German border.

Somervell is examining as a matter of urgency, your problem concerning the diversion of divisions through Marseilles to strengthen the right wing of your effort. I think this very important, if only for the purpose of giving Patch a United States Army to match the French.

Eisenhower to Marshall   9 September   *Ref: FWD-14277*
Pursuant to your suggestion I am transmitting to the Combined Chiefs of Staff my recommendations relative to assuming command of the DRAGOON forces. These recommendations are substantially a condensed version of my FWD-13853.

I fully agree as to the advantage of getting Devers into group control as quickly as possible. My recommendations to the Combined Chiefs of Staff are designed to effect Devers initial control through an Advanced Army Group Headquarters on September 15th.

Especially careful consideration is being given to the matter of air support for Devers' command. To augment the one fighter bomber group of the 12th Tactical Air Command, the Ninth Air Force will furnish three additional groups and necessary service units so that General Devers will have air support appropriate to his mission and his command. It is possible that we may later need an additional fighter bomber group for the Twelfth Air Force but Spaatz does not believe so.

The logistical implications of diverting United States divisions through Marseilles are being studied closely here pending receipt of the results of Somervell's examination of this problem.[30]

No Further Need for Leigh Mallory

Eisenhower to Marshall   14 September   *Ref: FWD-14819*
This is my first chance to answer your letter of 6 September with respect to Leigh Mallory. I agree that under present circumstances we can get along without Leigh Mallory's headquarters, but the fact is that through every day of this campaign, Leigh Mallory has proved his intense desire to cooperate and has a very admirable grasp of the whole situation. Our plans for reorganization, when and if he is detached, will eliminate that headquarters and all the functions it has been performing will be centered right here at SHAEF. But you should not be under any misapprehension as to Leigh Mallory's qualifications and attitude. Admitting that upon first glance he seems to be a bit difficult, he is one of the type that never ceases to develop and above all, he is a real fighter, which I like. He is an experienced and valuable officer.

There is no need to manufacture a job merely to get rid of Leigh Mallory but on the other hand, as explained above, if he is taken out of here for any reason I will not assign another man to his present title.[31]

Eisenhower to Marshall   27 September   *Ref: FWD-16011*
As you know, when Leigh Mallory leaves here I do not intend to perpetuate his present position and title. The coordination of all Air Forces serving under this headquarters will be achieved here under the direction of a Deputy Chief of Staff for Air. For this position I need an experienced officer and one fully acceptable to all concerned. Could you please spare

30 The routing of divisions directly from the US to the port of Marseilles and then on to French railways would alleviate the pressure on the logistics situation in northern France.
31 Leigh-Mallory had as many critics as supporters, but this commendation from Eisenhower is an excellent character assessment of the Commander-in-Chief of the Allied Expeditionary Air Force.

General Kuter for this purpose?[32] If you could spare him I would want him to come over here soon, since the new arrangement will begin operating by the middle of October.

Eisenhower to Marshall   *16 October*   *Ref: S-62507*
One matter which I intended to take up with you when you were here, and which I completely forgot, is the question of a decoration for Air Chief Marshal Leigh Mallory, who has now been relieved as Air Commander in Chief, and who is on a short leave in England. If possible I should like to present him with an American decoration for his outstanding services before he leaves for his new post. At the same time, it also occurred to me that we should recognize the services of Air Chief Marshal Harris, who is also no longer under my command. Both of these officers should, I believe, be awarded the Legion of Merit in the grade of Chief Commander. Under the circumstances, would it be possible for you to obtain authority for awarding these decorations, the citations to be prepared and forwarded later. You are, of course, aware of the services which these two officers have performed.

Marshall to Eisenhower   *17 October*   *Ref: W-47969*
Approval granted to present Legion of Merit, Degree Chief Commander, to Air Chief Marshals Mallory and Harris. Request you clear awards with the British government prior to presentation and inform us of citation used, in order that we can publish it in War Department orders and furnish you the proper authenticated citation and certification.

Moving V-1 Rockets to the US

Smith to Bundy[33]   *16 September*   *Ref: FWD-14989*
I have received a message from Major Furman. The commodity in question, which I understand is desired to be shipped to the United States, is in the British area of operations. I do not, repeat not, think there is any question at all about our ability to secure it by a seizure or otherwise, but since both Nations are equally involved, the matter should be coordinated with the British on a high level, and we should really have a secret directive from the Combined Chiefs of Staff. Can this not, repeat not, be done during the conference at Quebec. I will take the necessary preliminary steps, and I believe the simplest solution is to ship the stuff to England, if you can handle the question of its final destination, so that there will be no, repeat no, misunderstanding, particularly since we must deal with a British Army Group commander and operate in his area. Request reply is a matter of most urgency.[34]

Personal: Was most disappointed that I did not, repeat not, get to see you while the Secretary was here. Can you not, repeat not, slip away, possibly on the pretext of concluding the important matter referred to in the previous paragraph, and get over here to spend a week or so with us during the very critical and interesting stages of operations now approaching. Sincere personal regards.

---

32 General Laurence S. Kuter (1905–1979) remained as Arnold's Assistant Chief of the Air Staff for Plans and Combat Operations, Headquarters US Army Air Forces, Washington DC.
33 Harvey H. Bundy (1888–1963), Special Assistant on Atomic Matters to Secretary of War, Henry L. Stimson.
34 Republic Aviation had built working prototypes from parts salvaged in England for some time. Plans to use American-built 'flying bombs' against Japan were shelved after the dropping of the two atomic bombs on Hiroshima and Nagasaki and the Japanese surrender in August 1945.

Radio Delays over Rerouting of Divisions

Marshall to Eisenhower   19 September   *Ref: W-32886*

There has been a back and forth exchange of radios regarding our failures here to receive word that you desired three divisions rerouted into Marseilles. A careful check would seem to prove that the message from your Headquarters, which you have been notified must be received here by September 10th, was not received until September 17th.

I have commented adversely on the fact that the O.P.D. people[35] here did not telephone on the 10th to follow up this matter. I know you were involved in a change of Headquarters with subsequent communication difficulties. However, it seems to me that someone on your side failed to follow up, and this business of follow up is vital in war. Ordinary routine will never suffice.

Possibly you will already familiar with this affair, but if not I suggest that you bore into the individual who did not follow up, despite the mess of communications.[36]

Eisenhower to Marshall   20 September   *Ref: FWD-15299*

I have checked upon the delay in the radio regarding the three divisions to be rerouted to Marseilles and I find that this was due entirely to a failure in my own Headquarters. The message left the Forward Headquarters on September 10, and I am particular concerned because I personally checked its departure. The delay occurred in the Rear Echelon in England. I have taken steps which will, I hope, prevent any recurrence of such a failure.

Smith to Handy   29 September   *Ref: FWD-16198*

We have been thoroughly investigating the delays and difficulties in communications which have caused so much embarrassment recently, and I believe things will be much better now. For your private information the whole fault lies in a premature move of Headquarters Communications Zone from Valognes to Paris, before it was possible to extend reliable long range communications from the rear. As a result, there was for several days an almost complete breakdown in traffic and since this headquarters has depended on Communications Zone communications to Washington, we have also suffered.[37]

Incidentally, we have some failures of our own to account for. All of the unanswered messages referred to in your WX-36997 have been answered within the last 24 hours, except three service messages which are now being worked on. A direct radio circuit was inaugurated between Paris and the War Department on the 27th. We are going to kick Communications Zone out of Paris, where they have no business to be, but are delaying this action until we can be assured of rapid and certain communications with Washington.

---

35 Marshall had been using a smaller, efficient Operations Division, since March 1942. It operated by delegating most decision making and using monitoring and following up to decide when to step in. It only had 550 officers and men to administer an army of nine million men.

36 Marshall needed high standards to be maintained and he expected action to be taken if anyone failed to meet them, as this example shows. A simple error or misunderstanding in communications could have serious consequences for the war effort.

37 During the first two weeks in September, at the height of the pursuit, Communications Zone moved its entire 11,000-man headquarters from Valognes to Paris. It created a major problem in communications, transportation and supply. While the move was required to improve better communications facilities, Eisenhower and Bradley disapproved of the 'stampede to Paris'.

The Desire to Maintain Naval Presence in SHAEF
Eisenhower to Marshall   *22 September*   Ref: FWD-15461

Will you please deliver the following message to Admiral King. With respect to your directions to Admiral Stark to reduce U.S. Naval representation of my Staff to total of three, I should like to ask you to defer execution until final defeat of the enemy is more definitely in sight. I have been most anxious to have all phases of U.S. military activity represented on my Staff in a healthy and balanced away, and I would exceedingly regret reducing the U.S. Naval contingent to liaison strength. We have some hard fighting still in front of us, and U.S. interests in various ports are growing instead of diminishing. If we could keep our present total strength of 14 U.S. Naval officers until active fighting is over, it would be helpful to me. [Signed] Eisenhower

Support for Operation MARKET GARDEN[38]
Eisenhower to Montgomery   *22 September*   Ref: FWD-15407

Dear Monty: Your messages of yesterday and last evening did much to clarify the situation. Until their receipt I assumed that you were basing your recommendations on the views expressed in your message to me of the 4th, in which you stated that we had reached the stage where we could make one single thrust all the way to Berlin, with all other troops practically immobile on a narrow front. With that statement I did not, repeat not, agree, but I do agree emphatically with what you have to say about retaining our immediate objective, the Ruhr.[39]

After the conference this afternoon, full particulars, including timing, of all measures I will take to meet the requirements of the Ruhr battle, will be sent to you. No one is more anxious than I to get the Ruhr quickly. It is for the campaign from there onwards deep into the heart of Germany for which I insist all other troops must be in position to support the main drive. The main drive must logically go by the north. It is because I am anxious to organize that final drive quickly upon the capture of the Ruhr that I insist upon the importance of Antwerp. As I have told you, I am prepared to give up everything for the capture of the approaches to Antwerp, including all the air forces and anything else that you can support. Warm regards, Ike.[40]

Smith to Montgomery   *22 September*   Ref: ER/3

Excellent conference; Ike supported your plan 100 per cent. Your thrust is main effort and gets full support. Army Group of South to take over corps frontage from Bradley, and will continue offensive operations, because their maintenance and L.O.C. does not, repeat not, conflict with any other Army Group requirement.[41] Patton's Army and Hodges' Army, less

38 Operation MARKET GARDEN was 21st Army Group's attempt to seize bridges across the Maas, the Waal and the Lower Rhine using three airborne divisions (1st British, 82nd and 101st American), allowing XXX Britsh Corps to establish a bridgehead on the north bank of the Rhine. While the airborne troops captured several bridges, the ground troops were delayed and did not cross the Waal at Nijmegen until 20 September. It was too late for the British garrison at Arnhem Bridge; it was overrun on 21 September and the rest of the division had to be evacuated across the Rhine on 25 September.
39 Operation MARKET GARDEN comes to an end with over 16,000 Allied casualties (German losses are hard to define accurately). Montgomery now has to plan for his next objective and it will not be Berlin; it will be the elimination of the Ruhr and all that it takes to reach it. The single thrust concept and hopes for ending the war in 1944 are over.
40 This is the first time Eisenhower has pressed Montgomery about the need for clearing the Scheldt Estuary of German troops so that Antwerp docks can be opened. It is in preparation for a broad front strategy of pushing towards the Rhine over the winter.
41 Referring to 6th Army Group which was being supplied through the ports on the south coast of France.

divisions required to cooperate with your thrust, to adopt a defensive policy. New boundary agreed to and steps being taken for two divisions to be brought up and so relieve VIII
Corps. This will take a few days before they are ready to advance northwards. Command
arrangements still being discussed but hope they will be satisfactory.[42]

No, repeat no, further airborne operations now contemplated in the future. This will
help air supply. Methods for speeding up railways discussed. Importance of early capture
of Walcheren appreciated by all and air will help all they can, and hope it may yet be possible to stage small airborne operation.[43] Provisional agreement for use of Venlo airfield by
Second T.A.F. Everyone most helpful and sympathetic. Will give you full details tomorrow.

Two Generals, Two Sons

Eisenhower to Handy   *22 September*   *Ref: FWD-13571*
This is to ask you a personal favor. Could you have someone communicate with my son John,
now on duty at Fort Benning, to determine whether he would have any objection to assignment to a division destined for transfer to this Theater? I do not know his contemplated
assignment and would want matters handled in a routine way, since I know the last thing he
would want would be preferential treatment. So my idea is that Colonel Gailey, or some other
personal friend of my son, could find out about the matter on a purely personal and friendly
basis. If John has no objection to assignment to a division allotted to a Theater commanded
by his father, I would be able to keep track of him without his knowledge, which would mean
a lot to me, to say nothing of his mother. Whether or not you can do anything, I thank you
for the trouble I cause you.[44]

Eisenhower to Marshall   *22 September*   *Ref: FWD-15459*
Stroh was here today but left before I could deliver his wife's message. However, Stroh now
knows his son has been killed and presumably will inform Mrs. Stroh. Will report your message to him.[45]

Simpson in Command of Ninth Army

Marshall to Eisenhower   *23 September*   *Ref: W-35417*
Simpson has retained nominal command of the Fourth Army and is vested with the rank
of Lieutenant General by virtue of this assignment. Since he is now commanding the Ninth
Army in France, it is proposed to submit his nomination for Lieutenant General on the next
regular list. Before proceeding further in this matter, requested is your frank opinion.

Eisenhower to Marshall   *1 October*   *Ref: FWD-16473*
Under present plans we have every intention of keeping Simpson in command of Ninth
Army. While if I had been able to foresee two or three months ago the actual developments

---

42 2nd British Army was left in an awkward salient and while it had to secure the west bank of the Maas to
its left and right, First Canadian Army had to secure the Scheldt Estuary to the west.
43 Walcheren Island was at the mouth of the Scheldt, on the north side of the river, and still held by
German troops. Mine sweepers could not start work in the river until it was taken and the coastal batteries
silenced. Operation INFATUATE I and INFATUATE II would eventually take place on 1 November, after the
RAF had breached Walcheren's dikes with bombs, flooding the island.
44 John S.D. Eisenhower (1922–), known as 'Icky', graduated from the US Military Academy, West Point on
6 June 1944, D-Day. His military career was thwarted by fears that he could be killed, wounded or captured,
causing a major distraction for his father.
45 8th Infantry Division was attacking Brest when Stroh's son, a pilot, was killed in action flying a mission
to support his father's troops. This hit Stroh hard and after a month's rest and an assignment in Washington,
he commanded the 106th Infantry Division, on occupational and prisoner of war guarding duties.

in command arrangements, I would probably have advanced a corps commander to take over this Army, but arrangements have gone so far that I think it best to follow through. Therefore I suggest that you have Simpson's commission as Lieutenant General regularized by nominating him to the Senate.[46]

A Psychological Warfare Unit Scores an Unexpected Success

Eisenhower to Marshall   23 September   *Ref: FWD-15513*
I have been waiting for months for definite proof of the actual effectiveness of psychological warfare activities, and my patience has at last been rewarded by conclusive proof, as witnessed by the following report from Seventh Army Psychological Warfare. An Air Force unit dropped four tons of proclamations prepared by Psychological Warfare and signed by General Wilson into the Bay of Marseilles, sinking a small German lighter. I am sure the above is important enough to warrant a cable to you.[47]

First Plans for a Post War Military Government in Germany

Smith to McCloy   27 September   *Ref: FWD-16012*
Murphy[48] has given me a copy of the proposed interim directive to SCAEF, regarding the military government of Germany in the post defeat period. This is the most encouraging and helpful document that we have seen in a long time, and will enormously strengthen our hand if the United States Chiefs of Staff support it and see it through.[49] I will explain to Hilldring, when he arrives, some of the difficulties we have been encountering, and he will report to you. In the meantime, I wanted you to know the pleasure it has given everyone in this Headquarters who is concerned in the problem, to realize that the United States is taking a practical view of the situation that is likely to exist as we see it now.

Marshall Plans a Visit to France

Marshall to Eisenhower   29 September   *Ref: W-38777*
I plan to leave here Wednesday next for France, to fly into France if possible without landing in England. I shall probably have with me Handy,[50] General Craig, Air Forces,[51] possibly General Clay, A.S.F.,[52] although he doesn't know it yet, and Justice Byrnes,[53] present coordinating head of all civilian war agencies. Byrnes is going at my suggestion and invitation purely to see, learn and relax with a change of scene. I hope to land at an airport near Versailles.

---

46 Ninth US Army had just captured the port of Brest and moved east across France, joining 12th Army Group. General Simpson remained in command of Ninth US Army until the end of the war.
47 An excellent example of Eisenhower's sense of humor even if it had to be sent Top Secret, Eyes Only to Marshall to stop the joke getting into the public domain.
48 Robert D. Murphy (1894–1978), an American diplomat.
49 US Secretary of the Treasury, Henry Morgenthau, Jr. submitted a memorandum proposing how to demilitarize and partition Germany, weaken the Ruhr industries and arrange restitution and reparation. It had just been used as a basis for discussion at the Second Quebec Conference but Roosevelt had to shelve it after a negative response. Although it was not used, it did influence subsequent American and Allied planning for Germany.
50 General Thomas Handy, Marshall's deputy chief of staff.
51 General Howard A. Craig (1897–1977), Chief of the Theater Group, Operations Division, War Department General Staff.
52 General Lucius D. Clay (1897–1978), Director of Material, Army Service Forces.
53 James F. Byrnes (1882–1972) left the Supreme Court to head President Roosevelt's Economic Stabilization Office and later the Office of War Mobilization. Many in Congress and the press referred to Byrnes as the 'Assistant President' due to his close relationship with Roosevelt.

After talking to you, if you happen to be there at the time, then to visit most informally Bradley, Hodges, Devers, Patton, Patch and some divisions. But all this can be arranged for me at the time in accordance with the weather, operations, convenience of your command, etc. I should visit Montgomery I suppose.

Please keep all of this confidential and do not make any positive arrangements or notify officers concerned.

Also please do not make the slightest change in your own plans. Officers with me may all go their own way and it may prove desirable to send Byrnes on his own way. We shall see.

Eisenhower to Marshall   *1 October*   *Ref: FWD-16474*
Delighted to know that you and your party will arrive soon. We can locate your temporary headquarters here in such a way that you can be largely independent of weather in your ability to visit important areas of the front, particularly of the 12 Army Group. I am keeping your intentions confidential.

10

OCTOBER 1944

Montgomery's Problems and the Need for Antwerp

Montgomery to Eisenhower   6 October   *Ref: M-260*

Dempsey[1] went to see Hodges[2] today and brought back a dismal picture. First U.S. Army is apparently unable to develop its operations properly because it has not got the necessary ammunition. This does <u>not</u> promise well for the success of our plans. Hodges' own view is that if he had the ammunition and the troops he could go right through to the Rhine easily. I considered I had better report these matters to you.[3]

Montgomery to Eisenhower   7 October   *Ref: M-264*

The overall battle situation in my area is such that I am forced to postpone the attack of Second Army towards Krefeld.[4] The main reasons are firstly, the need to strengthen with infantry divisions the bridgehead north of Nijmegen[5] and secondly, the need to be secure from enemy interference west of the Meuse and south of the line Maashees–Deurne.[6] I cannot carry both these commitments. I could carry one but not both. I had hoped the First U.S. Army would clear the country west of the Meuse but it appears to be too much for 7th Armored Division. I must therefore, do it myself. I have asked Bradley and Hodges to come and see me tomorrow. The operations of Second Army and First U.S. Army are very intimately related and it is my opinion that the present system of command is most unsatisfactory. Tedder is coming to see me tomorrow and I will explain the whole problem to him.

I am not happy about the overall battle situation in the northern part of the Allied front. The enemy has reacted very violently to our threat to the Ruhr and has concentrated strong forces again Second Army. I have three commitments which could become very awkward and unbalance the whole business in the north.

1.a. <u>The Opening of Antwerp</u>: We must get the place going and I must have reserves of ammunition ready to throw in; I may need fresh divisions.

---

1 General Dempsey, commander of Second British Army.
2 General Hodges, commander of First US Army.
3 First US Army had an extended line through the Ardennes and would continue to do so until the German attack on 16 December. The Rhine between Cologne and Koblenz was 50 miles to the east and it would take until March before it reached the river, and troops first crossed it at Remagen on 7 March 1945.
4 Northwest of Düsseldorf, on Second Army's right flank.
5 On Second Army's left flank.
6 In Second Army's center.

1.b. The Bridgehead North of Nijmegen:[7] This is daily threatened by the enemy and is none too strong. The U.S. Airborne divisions alone cannot hold it; I must reinforce them by two infantry divisions.

1.c. The Enemy Situation West of the Meuse: There is considerable enemy strength south of the line Maashees – Deurne. It was thought that 7th U.S. Armored Division could clean it up; but it cannot. First U.S. Army is very involved about Aachen. Therefore I must use VIII Corps to clean up this area and push the enemy back over the Meuse.

2. I could possibly carried Antwerp, plus b). But I definitely cannot carry all three, and also launch Second Army towards Krefeld.

3. If I carry on as we are now, and launch Second Army towards Krefeld on 10 October, that army will have two hostile flanks – as well as strong frontal opposition. A German threat north of Nijmegen, with possibly danger of some enemy success, would unbalance me completely and my thrust towards Krefeld would cease. I would then find myself very stretched, and possibly unable to hold all my gains. I might then find that the Canadian Army wanted more help to open up Antwerp; and I would not be able to supply this help.

4. I therefore consider that I cannot launch Second Army towards the Ruhr until I have eliminated the following commitments:
    Paragraph 1 a) Finish the operations for opening Antwerp.
    Paragraph 1 c) Pushed the enemy back over the Meuse.

5. I have decided to act as in paragraph 4.

I have ordered that the attack of Second Army towards Krefeld and the Ruhr are postponed.[8]
B.L. Montgomery, Field Marshal

Montgomery to Eisenhower   *8 October*   *Ref: M-266*
Bradley and Hodges came here today, and we have agreed on a plan for the immediate future. Bradley will inform you fully. I had a talk also with Marshall and with Tedder, and they will inform you of our talks. I sent you a paper by Tedder giving my situation. I told Tedder that I view with considerable alarm the fact that there is now no, repeat no, Air Commander-in-Chief.[9]

Eisenhower to Bradley copy to Montgomery   *8 October*   *Ref: ER/7*
Basic difficulty on northern flank appears to be lack of strength in view of enemy reinforcement. Consequently, plan for coordinated attack to Rhine must be postponed until strength can be gotten up, which must come from U.S. divisions still on beach. Nevertheless, plans of both Army Groups must retain as first mission, the gaining of the line of the Rhine north of Bonn as quickly as humanly possible. Moreover, there must be

---

7 Along the south bank of the Rhine, facing Arnhem, the blunted salient resulting from Operation MARKET GARDEN.
8 This situation had arisen after the failure to cross the Rhine at Arnhem, leaving 21st Army Group unable to advance east simultaneously and capture the approaches to Antwerp.
9 Tedder had been SHAEF's Air Commander-in-Chief; further explanation follows.

consistent support of Hodges' present attacks to gain his immediate objective at Duren.[10] Agreed that under changed conditions, commitments of 21 Army Group are too heavy, but since these conditions were not reported to me sufficiently early to permit my attendance at today's conference, I am sending you suggested solution by this means.[11] It appears to me that northern boundary should now be changed to the line Maasshees – Wesel.[12] The date in the change of the boundary should be when you can take the responsibility. Since coordinated attack is now postponed, I suggest to you the possibility of shifting a division from V Corps to the north and replacing it in V Corps by the 95th or 9th Armored. Suggest also that you form an ad-hoc corps out of these two divisions with Brooks as commander, and to obtain administrative help on your left flank you shift Ninth Army Headquarters and Army troops into that area as soon as you can. This will further be a development of the final plan. In any event, you will have to retain administrative responsibility for these U.S. divisions.

As an expedient, and in order to save time, the following alternative can be considered, and, if agreed upon by you and Field Marshal Montgomery; turn over the 7th Armored Division to Field Marshal Montgomery, reinforcing it by another division obtained as suggested above. These two divisions would be under operational command of 21 Army Group and your northern boundary therefore, would take a straight line from Hasselt to Sittard.[13] You would necessarily have to support administratively, and, in spite of some promise of improving logistics, you may have to reduce still further the maintenance of Third Army.

If Sylvester is not satisfactory, relieve him instantly, and assign any other officer you desire including divisional commanders still at Cherbourg.

Communicate to me as quickly as possible arrangements made and if no satisfactory agreement is reached today, please arrange for a meeting at my headquarters at Reims tomorrow noon, reaching the field you and I used last week by 12:30pm.

Eisenhower to Montgomery 9 October *Ref: S-61466*

The recent gale has reduced materially the intake at Cherbourg and Arromanches, which was counted on to assist materially the supply of the U.S. forces, has sustained severe damage.[14] This reemphasizes the supreme importance of Antwerp. It is reported to me this morning by the Navy that the Canadian Army will not, repeat not, be able to attack until November 1 unless immediately supplied with adequate ammunition. You know best where the emphasis lies within your Army Group, but I must repeat that we are now squarely up against a situation which has been anticipated for months and our intake into the Continent will not, repeat not, support our battle. Unless we have Antwerp producing by the middle of November our entire operations will come to a standstill. I must emphasize that, of all our operations on our entire front from Switzerland to the Channel, I consider Antwerp of first importance, and I believe that the operations designed to clear up the entrance require your personal attention.[15]

---

10 Northeast of the Hürtgen Forest.
11 Eisenhower only learnt of Montgomery's difficulties on 7 October, leaving him no time to attend the conference; instead he had to revise plans down to division level via this cable.
12 Now Boxmeer, south of Nijmegen east to Wesel on the Rhine.
13 Running north of Maastricht.
14 The Mulberry Harbor at Arromanches was only supposed to be a temporary measure and supplies had been expected to be delivered by ports along the French north coast by this stage. With winter storms imminent, it would soon be impossible to use it.
15 This cable had been sent following a meeting between Eisenhower and Admiral Ramsey, during which the difficulties that the Navy faced getting supplies into Antwerp were discussed.

Montgomery to Eisenhower   9 October   *Ref: M-268*
Dear Ike: Have received your S-61466 dated 9 October. Request you will ask Ramsey from me, by what authority he makes wild statements to you concerning my operations about which he can know nothing, repeat nothing. True facts are that the Canadian Army attack began two days ago and tonight is reported to be going much better than the first.[16]

There is no, repeat no, shortage of ammunition and present stocks in Canadian Army are a total over 12,000 tons. The operations are receiving my personal attention. In the minutes of the conference held at SHAEF on 22 September, it is laid down that the main effort of the present phase of the operations is the attack against the Ruhr.

In your telegram sent here yesterday for Bradley, it is again laid down that the first mission of both Army Groups is to gain the line of the Rhine north of Bonn. Actually on 7 October I stopped my operations against the Rhine for various reasons, one of which was the need to get Antwerp, and possibly Tedder has given you my notes headed 7 October. You can rely on me to do every single thing possible to get Antwerp opened for shipping as early as possible.[17] Yours always, Monty.

Eisenhower to Montgomery   10 October   *Ref: S-61621*
Dear Monty: I have seen your M-268 and notes brought to me by Tedder. Thank you for both.

As stated in my message to you and Bradley on the 8th, I realize the strength of 21 Army Group is not, repeat not, sufficient to undertake all three commitments at once, particularly because of persistent enemy reaction on your north flank. In everything that we try to do or to plan, our intake of supplies into the Continent looms up as a limiting factor, and it is for this reason that no matter how we adjust missions and objectives for both groups, and their offensive action towards the east, the possession of the approaches to Antwerp remains with us an objective of vital importance. Let me assure you that nothing I may say or write, with respect to future plans in our advance eastward, is meant to indicate any lessening of the need for Antwerp, which I have always held as a vital, and which has grown more pressing as we enter the bad weather period.

With respect to the telegram I sent you yesterday, it was not, repeat not, Admiral Ramsay who gave the report in question, which came from a joint planning conference between the Navy and the Canadian Army, and I was careful to state in my telegram that I hoped the report was not, repeat not, correct. I am glad that my concern was not, repeat not, justified and regret taking your time for something you already have in hand. In the meantime, if there is anything within the realm of feasibility that I can do in providing you temporarily with extra strength, I remain constantly ready to do my utmost.[18]

In addition to his other duties, Tedder is being made personally responsible for all air operations in the Theater and will always be constantly available for conference when your air needs transcend those immediately available to you.[19] As ever; Ike.

---

16 Montgomery's anger because he believes Ramsey has reported on 21st Army Group's situation is apparent.
17 Montgomery points out the three different objectives he has been given over the past two weeks: the Ruhr, the Rhine and finally Antwerp.
18 Eisenhower quickly points out that he did not hear about 21st Army Group's situation from Ramsey but from the First Canadian Army during a conference with the navy. General Henry D.G. Crerar CH, CB, DSO, KStJ, CD, PC (1888–1965), commanding general of the Canadian Army, had recently been taken sick and was temporarily replaced by Lieutenant-General Guy G. Simonds, CC, CB, CBE, DSO, CD (1903–1974).
19 Tedder was temporarily in command because AEAF disbanded on 15 October and SHAEF was to form a new air command organization.

Montgomery to Eisenhower 14 October *Ref: M-177*

All my information suggests that it will <u>not</u> be possible for the First Army to reach the Rhine at present, as it has <u>not</u> the necessary reserves of ammunition for continuous and prolonged heavy fighting.[20] Second Army is at present operating as in paragraph 710 of M-530.[21] The next important thing seems to me to pull Second Army in to help Canadian Army, and so speed up the opening of Antwerp. When the enemy has been pushed back to the east of the Meuse, it is my intention to move Second Army westwards with its right flank on the Rhine and clean up the country up to about the north and south line through Tilburg. This will enable Canadian Army to transfer its weight more to the west. There seems <u>no</u> point in my going off alone towards the Ruhr and to do so would <u>not</u> be good. When Bradley is ready in all respects for a dog fight battle for at least two weeks, then we can all go together.[22]

Eisenhower to Montgomery 15 October *No Reference*

Received your latest operational message at Bradley's headquarters. I completely agree with the moves you are making. In the meantime, Bradley's First Army will continue its attacks on present scale, to gain advantageous positions and to draw toward it the bulk of resistance in the north. Bradley is now making final check up on maintenance prospects, prior to capture of approaches to Antwerp, and will shortly visit you, in order that you both may make rough estimates as to timing of concerted attack. I should like very much to have a meeting with you and Bradley at a date and time convenient to us all. Because we can no longer plan with any certainty on air travel, I suggest we might need to meet at your main headquarters at Brussels, which would allow us all time to drive if necessary. If you agree, suggest a date during latter part of week. Hour should be around middle of day to allow us all time to drive.

Bad News from Italy

Prime Minister via Eisenhower for Marshall 10 October *Ref: AMSSO 5928*

I have sent the following to the President.

On the way to Moscow we had four hours at Naples with Generals Wilson and Alexander. I was much distressed by their tale. The fighting has been very hard. The losses since the battle opened have been around 30,000, of which at least 4/5 have been British or under British control.[23] The enemy is estimated to have lost 42,000, including 10,000 prisoners in our hands. Our men are tired and there are no fresh divisions to put in. It seems so much was taken away from our Italian front against the Germans just to deny a complete victory in this Theater. Alexander and also Clark tried their best with what was left to them but as I told you, I could not guarantee results[24]. Thus Kesselring may bring us to a standstill in the Apennines until they are wrapped in snow.[25] He could then withdraw five

---

20 First US Army was heavily engaged in the Hürtgen Forest (the longest single battle in the US Army's history). It started on 14 September and would not end until 10 February 1945 at a cost of 33,000 US casualties.
21 Improving its situation around Nijmegen, south of the Rhine, where it held the salient left after Operation MARKET GARDEN.
22 Montgomery wanted Second Army to clear the south bank of the Rhine rather than advancing east, moving away from First Canadian Army, which was engaged along the Scheldt. He believed there was no point advancing east towards the Ruhr until First Army had cleared the Hürtgen Forest.
23 Eighth Army broke through the Gothic line on the Adriatic coast but was unable to advance into the Po valley before the onset of winter.
24 Fifth Army's attack in the center towards Bologna ground to a halt in the mountains.
25 By early October the weather was worsening and it was clear to General Alexander there would be no breakthrough before the spring.

or six divisions to resist Eisenhower on the Rhine. The German fighting here has been of utmost tenacity, and the troops he could withdraw would be high class.

The pressure in the Dutch salient seems to me to be growing very severe and our advances are slow and costly.[26] In these circumstances we have, with much sorrow, had to recommend that we should put off DRACULA[27] from March to November and leave the British 3rd Division in France as well as sending there the 52nd Division, one of our best, about 22,000 strong in fighting troops, and the 6th Airborne Division to the Netherlands. Eisenhower is counting on these for impending operations on the Rhine and of course, this was much the quickest way to bring additional troops into France.

Could you not deflect two, better still, three American divisions to the Italian ports which would enable them to join Mark Clark's Fifth Army and add the necessary strength to Alexander? They would have to be there in four to five weeks. I consider the fact that we shall be sending Eisenhower these extra two divisions gives me a case for your generous consideration.

With regard to Istria, Trieste, etc., General Wilson is forwarding his plan to Combined Chiefs of Staff. This plan will be in accord with the overall strategic objective, namely, the expulsion from, or destruction in, Italy of Kesselring's army.[28]

McNarney to Marshall   *11 October*   *Ref: W-45048*
For your information, the substance of Wilson's estimate concerning the Italian operations, as given in his MEDCOS 201 of 9th October, follows:

Primary strategic objective of the Mediterranean Theater has been to destroy and contain Germans not committed against Eisenhower's front. Its mission has being carried out by launching DRAGOON, continuing the Italian offensive, which has retained 28 divisions in the Italian Theater, and harassing and threatening invasion in the Balkans, which has retained 21 divisions and 450,000 Germans in the area.

Wilson considers the Russian advance may have more effect on the enemy opposing him than the action of Allied forces in Italy.[29] Lacking exact information and Russian intentions, Wilson assumes that the Russian advance in the Balkans will cause German withdrawal before the end of the winter to the Alps–Adige River–Fiume–Maribor–Austrian frontier line. The Russian advance may result in the withdrawal of German Forces from all northeast Italy, including Istria.[30]

The present situation in Italy does not permit any substantial reduction in forces now attacking into the Valley of the Po. The nature of the Lombardy Plain and the weather make it impossible to take advantage of superiority in armor, artillery and air.

Alexander only has one fresh division and Wilson does not expect more than an advance to the Adige before the end of November. After reaching the Adige a pause of at least three months will be required to prepare for a spring offensive.

---

26 21st Army Group held a salient around Nijmegen, formed by Operation MARKET GARDEN.
27 Operation DRACULA was an airborne and amphibious attack on Rangoon by British and Indian forces, part of the Burma Campaign. It was eventually delayed until the end of April 1945.
28 These plans are for an advance northeast through the Ljubljana Gap, between Venice and Vienna, to Vienna and Hungary. The US Chiefs of Staff disagreed with Churchill's plans to meet the Russians as far east as possible.
29 King Michael of Romania had announced a ceasefire, proclaimed Romania's loyalty to the Allies and acceptance of an armistice to be signed with the Allies. The coup accelerated the Soviet advance through Romania but 130,000 Romanian soldiers were transported to Soviet prison camps before the armistice was signed on 12 September and Romania declared war on Germany.
30 Roughly along the Yugoslavian border, running northeast past Ljubljana.

Now that the rapid destruction of Kesselring's armies cannot be expected, Wilson states that fresh forces must be given to him, if major operations are to be undertaken outside Italy before next year. His plan for Trieste in December contemplated use of an airborne division and three seaborne divisions. The airborne assault is the most important part of the plan. Without this airborne assault, it would probably require an additional two divisions to reach a decision.[31]

Wilson raises for consideration an operation against Trieste in February or March, even though the weather and increased enemy defenses of the ports are handicaps. The same forces would be required as for those originally planned for the December operation, less the airborne division. Wilson also mentions the possibility of taking Trieste by overland advance, following up the German withdrawal, in conjunction with landings south of Fiume, to operate with the Partisans.[32]

Wilson states all the schemes of the campaign he mentions are dependent on the Russian advance and, in case of a general enemy withdrawal from Italy, it might be possible to divert the Fifth Army into France.

If Wilson can be assured of three fresh divisions before January, it would be possible to take Trieste in February or March, and to undertake a pincer movement in the spring against Kesselring's armies in Northern Italy.

On the basis of the foregoing estimate, Wilson concludes that:

a) He cannot prevent Kesselring's premature withdrawal and at the same time prepare for a Trieste operation this year.
b) A Trieste operation early next year requires three fresh divisions before January.
c) If three divisions are furnished, the plan would be to take Trieste, either by seaborne and airborne assault (requiring use of an airborne division) or by overland advance, coordinated with a landing below Fiume. The exact plan cannot now be determined. Under either plan all resources must remain in the Theater except the AKAs, APA's and AP's.

In his message to the President, the Prime Minister states a copy of his proposal on the three divisions have been furnished you. The Prime Minister's message has been referred to the Joint Staff Planners.

Alexander to Eisenhower and Clark   15 October   *Ref: MA-1723*
I know you realize and appreciate what we have done, and are doing, here to keep German divisions from being transferred to the Western Front, but the time has now arrived when my Armies will not be able to continue the offensive much longer. This is mostly due to the fact that all divisions are very tired and completely lack fresh replacements, especially in the case of the American Fifth Army. I have done everything through official channels to get replacements, but I have not succeeded. My last chance is to appeal to you personally. Anything you can do to help Clark will be to our mutual advantage. Lemnitzer has left today by air for General Dever's headquarters with full details of Clark's requirements.

---

31 The plan was to seize the Istrian Peninsula at the northeast end of the Adriatic Sea between Trieste and Rijeka, bypassing the Gothic Line.
32 A landing south of the Istrian Peninsula.

Alexander to Eisenhower   15 October   *Ref: MA-1724*

Further to my MA-1723 earlier today, I have received the following from Clark, giving the latest reinforcement situation.

My four infantry divisions were reduced to slightly below strength in infantry on 13 October. Approximately 500 usable infantry replacements are expected within the next three days. Shipment of 2,200 scheduled to arrive in Naples from the States on 28th October, with 1,300 more on 4 November. Believe the October 28 group can be placed in line about 2 November. By that date I estimate my four divisions will be short of 8,000 infantry men, which means a shortage of 75 men per rifle company.[33] This reduced strength during the critical period facing Fifth Army will seriously lower the operational efficiency of my divisions. Even when 2,200 replacements arrive in early November, they will have to be absorbed by divisions which are already well diluted by new men. For example, 91st Division has received 3,200 replacements since September 13, the bulk of which have gone to infantry rifle companies.[34]

In my message 8937, dated 9 October, to General Devers, I urgently recommended that shipments of replacements from Naples for Seventh Army be diverted to Fifth Army, but my request was not favorably considered. I feel that if General Eisenhower realized the urgency of this matter, and the influence it may have on the battle, he might be able to furnish immediately the 3,000 infantry replacements which I requested in my 8937 from SHAEF sources. I recommend that you present such a request to him.

Marshall to Eisenhower   17 October   *W-47746*

This is for your information.

The President has replied to the Prime Minister concerning the request for diversion of two or three divisions to Italy. The reply states that the President and his Chiefs of Staff are agreed that none of your divisions should be diverted to Italy. The President gave as reason for this action that the provision of additional United States forces will not affect the Italian campaign this year; the opinion of the United States Chiefs of Staff is,

> ... that the Germans are free to transfer five or six divisions from Italy to your front, whenever the enemy considers such action more profitable than containing our forces south of the Po;

> ... your need for quick provision of fresh troops, both as additional divisions and to enable you to give our front-line forces some rest;

> ... and that diversion of divisions to Italy would withhold needed fresh troops from you, while committing these forces to the high attrition of an indecisive winter campaign in Italy.[35]

---

33 A full strength rifle company had six officers and 187 other ranks, making these companies 40 per cent below strength.
34 A division had 5211 officers and other ranks organized into 27 rifle companies.
35 In summary, two or three extra divisions would make no difference to the battle of attrition being fought in the wintry Italian mountains. They too would be worn out by the spring. Two or three extra divisions would make an immediate difference on the Western Front.

The King Visits France

Montgomery to Eisenhower 12 October *Ref: M-273*

The King has arrived, and the program remains unchanged. I'm expecting a senior officer from Hodges' Department to come to my T.A.C. H.Q. tomorrow evening, Friday, to stay the night here and take the King to First U.S. Army HQ on Saturday morning in my car. He is leaving here at 09:00 hours; would be most grateful if you would check up that this will be OK. The King would very much like to meet General Marshall at lunch on Saturday if he is still in the country.

Eisenhower to Montgomery 12 October *Ref: S-61820*

Thank you for your M-273. The arrangements you suggest for Saturday will be entirely satisfactory and I will check with Hodges to make sure there is a complete understanding. I will be at Hodges headquarters to meet the King. Unfortunately General Marshall must start his homeward journey tomorrow, but he hopes you will express to His Majesty his appreciation of the suggestion and his deep regret that he will not be able to be at Hodges' headquarters on Saturday.

SHAEF's New Air Organization

Tedder for Air Ministry and A.E.A.F. 12 October *Ref: S-61867*

Eisenhower has agreed that A.E.A.F. be dissolved with effect from 15 October, 1944, and a directive to this effect is being issued today. An air staff is being formed at SHAEF to undertake the control and coordination of the air forces previously exercised by the A.E.A.F. The air staff will be in two echelons, Main and Rear, the latter being at Stanmore.[36] Establishments to implement our R.A.F. part of the above have been prepared and are with D.G.O. Would like early approval of the following proposals for filling the air ranks of the air staff.[37]

Deputy Chief of Staff (Main) Air Vice Marshal Robb[38]

Deputy Chief of Staff (Rear) Air Vice Marshal Wigglesworth[39]

SHAEF to Chief of Air Staff Air Ministry, Whitehall 13 October *Ref: S-62048*

With reference to a conversation regarding announcement of changes of air command:

1. SHAEF view is that announcement of new arrangements for control of air forces in SHAEF should be made by Air Ministry and SHAEF simultaneously. I suggest wording used is that used in the SHAEF order, which runs as follows: With effect from 00:01 hours, 15 October, 1944, headquarters, Allied Expeditionary Air Force is dissolved. Pursuant to existing policy governing responsibility for the direction of their operations, the Supreme Commander will exercise command of all the Air Forces now, or later, placed under his command, through authority delegated by him to the Deputy Supreme Commander. The Deputy Supreme Commander, in addition to his other duties, is directly responsible for the coordination of air operations in support of the Allied Expeditionary Forces.

---

36 RAF Stanmore Park, Middlesex, now north London.

37 The detailed organization and appointments followed.

38 Air Marshal Sir James M. Robb GCB, KBE, DSO, DFC, AFC, RAF (1895–1968), Deputy Chief of Staff (Air) at SHAEF headquarters since January 1944.

39 Air Marshal Sir Philip Wigglesworth KBE, CB, DSC 1896–1975), Deputy Chief of Staff (Air) at SHAEF in 1944.

2. We also feel that if possible, announcement of these changes, coupled with that which you will issue regarding Leigh-Mallory's new appointment, should not be made until after his press conference.[40] We feel that despite ban on discussion of the new arrangements here, skilful questioning by expert cross examiners will almost certainly lead to discussion around the subject, if not directly about it. We feel that would be most undesirable.

3. If you agree, I suggest direct contact between Air Ministry and the Public Relations Division of this headquarters in London, to coordinate publication.

A Corps' Commander's Health Finally Gives Way

Eisenhower to Marshall   *20 October*   *Ref: S-63258*

I am sending General Corlett home for a physical check up and rest. I am placing him on detached service for sixty days, so I do not lose my hold on him. He has performed most effectively throughout the campaign but I agree with Hodges and Bradley that he very obviously needs a rest. After he has been checked up by Walter Reed thoroughly, and provided that he has nothing seriously wrong, I should like for him to get the chance for real recreation and then return here sometime within the allotted period. I regard him as an outstanding corps commander.[41]

An Artillery Ammunition Shortage

Eisenhower to Marshall   *20 October*   *Ref: S-63259*

During my latest trip to both groups and lower formations, I found that the one thing that is worrying everybody is the shortage of artillery ammunition. Upon investigation I find further that the supply of artillery ammunition is not merely one of port capacity and distributional facilities; it likewise involves limitations in production.[42] I am having all of our statistics studied, so as to give you a completely accurate picture but in the meantime, if there is anything you can possibly do to step up shipments over the next 90 days it will have a definite effect upon the campaign.[43]

From the beginning of the invasion we have always been on a rationed basis in the consumption of artillery ammunition, but preliminary examination of records seems to indicate that whenever a division is in an active sector, whether or not it is actually in an assault, the War Department allowances do not meet minimum requirements.[44]

Marshall to Eisenhower   *22 October*   *Ref: W-50677*

Artillery ammunition. Everyone here is cognizant of your ammunition problem.

---

40 Although Leigh-Mallory was appointed Air Commander-in-Chief of South East Asia Command (SEAC), he died along with his wife when his plane crashed in the French Alps en route to Burma.

41 Corlett had health problems following his service in the Pacific early in the war and had been ill during the Normandy campaign. Although Eisenhower makes it clear that he would welcome him back he did not return to Europe. Corlett's autobiography makes it clear that he was aggrieved by his treatment, believing that he had never fitted in and that his relief was related to two angry exchanges with General Hodges during the battle for Aachen.

42 The manufacturing of shells, the delivery to European ports and the distribution to the front line were all limiting factors.

43 Ammunition problems were again threatening the success of the campaign. All supplies were still being hauled from Normandy across northern France.

44 Actual requirements in the field exceeded estimated requirements by the War Department, meaning that production and shipping were never going to be enough.

Handy[45] has already dispatched to personal radios to Crawford[46] on this subject. Ammunition is being shipped as fast as it is produced and at the present time there is no prospect of increasing October and early November loadings of the critical calibers: 8-inch gun and howitzer, 240mm howitzer, 155mm gun and howitzer, 105mm howitzer, 81 mm mortar.[47]

I believe we are meeting your requirements for the types of ammunition. However if this is not the case, your additional requirements will receive immediate consideration here. Production of critical types is going up and I hope that increased production will soon ease slightly the world wide situation.

Current allocations of critical types of ammunition provide for maximum shipments to you from present production capabilities, withholding only minimum operational requirements for other Theaters.

Two aspects of ammunition supply within your Theater are causing concern in the War Department. The first is ammunition ships awaiting discharge. By personal message to Handy, General Crawford indicated that he would have the present nineteen ships in this category containing 1,000,000 rounds of 105mm and 600,000 rounds of 81mm unloaded in 20 to 30 days. By that time nearly 2,000,000 rounds of 105mm howitzer and 600,000 rounds of 81mm mortar, which are now on route or shortly to be loaded, will have reached the Theater.

The other aspect is there is still divided responsibility for supply of the Armies in France. The War Department is receiving urgent radios from Commanding General, North African Theater of Operations, for increased ammunition shipments to meet operational requirements in the South of France, as well as in Italy. The divided responsibility makes duplication possible. Duplication of critical items means corresponding deficiencies elsewhere. Single supply responsibility is suggested at the earliest date. Meanwhile, operational supply requirements submitted by Devers or Commanding General, North African Theater of Operations, for the Southern Armies should be cleared and approved by your Headquarters before being submitted to the War Department.[48]

Infantry Reinforcements

Marshall to Eisenhower   *22 October*   *Ref: W-50676*

As you know, I have considered carefully and advocated strongly the speed up of the flow of infantry regiments to you. It is still my opinion that it is extremely important to relieve infantry regiments that have been long in the fight by fresh ones. Reference your S-63216, dated 20 October, to Handy.[49]

The Combined Chiefs of Staff are now considering the issuance, at an early date, of a directive for an all out effort to end the war in Europe before 1945, accepting by this decision, the extraordinary measures which would be required. Such measures would include the use of the Strategic Air Forces to get the maximum immediate tactical advantage

---

45 General Thomas T. Handy, Deputy Chief of Staff.
46 Major-General Robert W. Crawford, SHAEF G-4, Logistics, Assistant Chief of Staff.
47 These are the larger caliber artillery pieces and mortars.
48 It appears that two requests for ammunition are being submitted for 6th Army Group, which has been fighting alongside 12th Army Group since early September. The duplication of requests means too many shells are being delivered to the south of France while too few are being shipped to the north.
49 A similar scheme was implemented during the First World War when it was clear that while shipping could move infantry regiments quickly across the Atlantic to France, it could not carry all the artillery, equipment and horses as well. The decision was taken to ship only infantry across while the French provided heavy and bulky items, allowing US divisions to get into battle sooner. Marshall probably had this decision in mind.

from the use of our air power, expedited movement and employment of units, and the use of the proximity fuze.[50] This directive would not consider what should be done six months from now, but would indicate that every effort is desired to close out the war in Europe before the heavy winter weather sets in. It would be based on the assumption that Germany can be defeated this year by the utmost use of all our resources. Fresh infantry regiments are a vital element in this undertaking.[51]

It is estimated here that the remaining parts of the divisions (that part of the divisions less infantry regiments) can sail to you as follows; 87th, 106th, 75th, in mid-November; 63rd, 66th, 69th, and 76th in early December; 70th, 42nd, 65th, 89th, and 71st in mid-December. There will be some minor equipment shortages for these sailing dates.

Based on the above, I believe you should give further consideration to the maintaining of the expedited flow of infantry units and that you let me have your reactions. I presume you have considered the use of southern French ports. In the meantime, because time is so short that the above dates for the movement of divisions cannot be met unless all possible pressure is applied here without interruption, I am not canceling the expedited flow of infantry regiments, and am preparing the remaining parts of the divisions for movement on the earliest possible days.

I have just read your S-63358 of 21 October expressing Bradley's views, but will take no action to halt the expedited flow of the infantry units until I hear further from you, particularly in view of the Combined Chiefs of Staff action referred to above, which is now under consideration. Be frank with me. I will accept your decision.

Acknowledge, please.

Eisenhower to Marshall   *23 October*   *Ref: S-63616*

On the ground, we have never failed to apply the full power that could be launched against the vital sections of the enemy front, even frequently at considerable risk. Some of these attacks have been on almost a shoestring basis, so far as maintenance and supply are concerned. Our logistical problem has become so acute, for all our plans have made Antwerp 'a sine qua non'[52] to the waging of our final all-out battle and our effort has been to have ready for action, at the moment that Antwerp becomes operative, all of the complete divisions that we could get. However, I admit that with the divisions now here and those already afloat, there is a possibility that by keeping the infantry constantly fresh we may produce the desired break and thus wind up the war more quickly. This to my mind is another of those gambles that we are forever faced with in war, and it may be a very good one.[53]

The problem therefore resolves itself as follows: We want infantry under an accelerated flow so that we can keep up the maximum possible pressure, with the maintenance facilities now in our possession or definitely in sight. But at the moment when we become able

---

50 The proximity fuse, or Variable Time fuse (VT), exploded when the shell was in proximity to the ground rather than on contact with it, maximizing the damage it caused. The gun crew could set a pre-set burst height and a micro-transmitter used the shell casing as an antenna during flight. The continuous signal was altered when the shell approached the ground and the interference triggered detonation. It was first used to devastating effect during the Battle of the Bulge in December.

51 Marshall is suggesting waging a battle of attrition against strategic points in the German line, believing that German reserves have been exhausted and in the hope of breaking through and making rapid advances before the winter sets in.

52 This translates from Latin as 'without which there is nothing'.

53 The Allies were engaged in several fierce battles in October: First Canadian Army along the banks of the Scheldt; Ninth Army at Aachen, the first German city to fall on 22 October; First Army in the Hürtgen Forest; Third Army at Metz; and Seventh Army in the Vosges mountains.

to sustain a greater number of divisions in the actual line, then we will want complete divisions available. The task is to meet both of these objectives.[54]

Preliminary studies indicate that we could not, repeat not, accept the heavy elements of the divisions on the schedule shown in your telegram. Equipment alone would involve about 480,000 tons, and we simply could not absorb it in the space of time indicated, and some will have to be phased back. We are finding out today what proportion could be handled in Marseilles without damaging maintenance, and I should be able to give you a final decision tomorrow morning. I believe that the answer will be to send in the infantry on the accelerated program and we will give the schedule under which we can accept heavy elements, including maximum use of Marseilles.

Eisenhower to Marshall   *24 October*   *Ref: S-63876*

In furtherance of my S-63616 of 23 October, in reply to your W-50676 of 22 October, a study of the acceleration of the infantry regiments has been completed, and I feel that the following proposed plan will meet our requirements. It is based on the conception of making the maximum sustained effort during the remaining weeks of this year, in the hope of cracking the enemy by continuous pressure of fresh infantry.

This plan is based also upon our calculations as to the feasibility of pushing infantry forward over our congested lines, as well as the desirability of avoiding the breaking up of divisions prematurely, unless the infantry can be actually employed at an early date in combat, as reliefs for tired infantry divisions. For this reason the plan presents something of a compromise, particularly as it affects the last three divisions specifically allocated to this theater, and the phasing back of the heavy equipment of all divisions following the 87th, 106th, and 75th Infantry Divisions. However, if arrangements in the U.S. for accelerating the flow of infantry are so far advanced as to make awkward any modification of those arrangements, then all the infantry should come right ahead. We will have to take them directly into France because of congestion in England, and some of the regiments may have to remain near ports for a period. In any event, it is particularly important that our capacity for intake of heavy equipment of divisions be not exceeded as hereinafter explained. The following should be read in the light of those considerations.[55]

On 1 November there will be 18 infantry and eight armored U.S. divisions operational in northern France and five U.S. Infantry Divisions operational in the Southern Group of Armies. In addition, there will be three infantry and two armored divisions (U.S.) in the U.K. not yet operationally available to the 12th Army Group, and one armored and two infantry divisions staging in the Marseilles area.

There will also be the nine infantry regiments of the 87th, 106th, and 75th infantry divisions which will close into the U.K. by 2 November. These nine regiments can provide immediately one relief regiment for half of the infantry divisions now in northern France. The regiments of the three infantry divisions remaining in the UK can be utilized, if necessary, to provide a similar infantry reinforcement for the remaining nine divisions in northern France. However, the regiments of three of the last nine infantry divisions should be advanced to sail during the latter half of November in order to ensure that three reserve

---

54 Eisenhower wants only infantry replacements, and as fast as possible, with the intention of maintaining a war of attrition at key points along the front. He too hoped that a breakthrough could be made, forcing the Germans to abandon the Siegfried Line.

55 Infantry was what Eisenhower needed and infantry regiments could be shipped across the Atlantic and moved across France far quicker than entire divisions could be. At the current rate of attrition, he was facing having to curtail attacks or break up divisions if replacements did not arrive soon.

infantry divisions remain available in the theater. In view of the congested port facilities on the continent, which will exist until Antwerp is operating (estimated about 1 January), and the limited accommodations in the U.K., the shipment of additional divisional personnel for 12th Army Group should not exceed the divisional residues of 87th, 106th and 75th Divisions already scheduled for mid November.

In order to provide similar relief for infantry divisions in Devers' Group, the regiments of three additional infantry divisions should be shipped direct to Marseilles during late November.

This plan will provide a relief regiment for all of the 25 U.S. infantry divisions in France with two additional. It will also provide a strategic reserve of three or more divisions which will be in U.K. There will be nine armored divisions in France and two in the U.K.

Further details concerning the shipment of the regiments to Marseilles, and of residues to the U.K., will be submitted by 1 November. Moreover, our estimates concerning possibilities of receiving remaining three divisions still in U.S. after this program is completed will be submitted at an early date. So much still depends upon speed in the capture of Antwerp approaches that it is considered best, at this time, to defer final decisions on those three divisions as well as on heavy equipment of divisions of which the infantry will be accelerated.

Few Opportunities for Tactical Support by Strategic Air Forces

Eisenhower to Marshal   23 October   Ref: S-63616

I am quite sure that the Combined Chiefs of Staff are no more anxious to wind this thing up quicker than we are. With respect to Strategic Air Forces, we have not, repeat not, used them recently in direct tactical support on the battle line. For this there are two reasons:

> First, practically all of our heavy bomber work has had to be done through overcast weather with special technique and this technique is not, repeat not, suitable for tactical work. [56]

> Second, we know that in these conditions our best bet has been to keep hammering constantly at the enemy's oil. There is ample evidence that this is hurting his battle line operations constantly and seriously. [57]

I have every confidence that the instant we can use the heavy bomber force in closer relationship to the battle lines, particularly in supporting decisive attacks, both night and day bomber forces will be instantly available.

Will Antwerp Port Be a Target?

Marshall to Eisenhower   25 October   Ref: W-51862

1. Several cables from your Headquarters give the impression that possibly you have been forced by circumstances to put "all or most of your eggs in one basket," the Antwerp basket.

---

56 The overcast autumn weather made it difficult to use strategic bombing close to the front line. Accidents, such as the one at the start of Operation COBRA in July, were still fresh in Eisenhower's mind. Evidence of the Germans relying more and more on horse drawn transport as it became more difficult to keep motor transport on the road would have been gathered from many sources.

57 Oil targets had been given the highest priority on 3 September 1944 using air reconnaissance to ascertain the best times to carry out repeat bombing raids.

2. The area of Antwerp, according to information here, has already received several rocket attacks. This may be "ranging in" now, in order to get bigger game later. If the Germans only knew it, the biggest game they could get would be our ships filled with our most critical supply item – ammunition, including VT ammunition. The destruction of ammunition ships probably would do more to prolong the war than almost any other single item. In addition to possible rocket attacks on the port of Antwerp, great difficulties may be encountered in clearing and maintaining the Antwerp channel. Tremendous damage could be done to our entire war effort by a heavy rocket attack on that port when its harbor is filled with shipping, and when a whole offensive depends on that one vital and vulnerable area.[58]

3. It appears that another port, or ports, should be considered as, and used as, an alternative unloading point for the major portion of the U.S. supplies, which includes most of the ammunition. Railroads from Marseilles, Cherbourg, and Le Havre, although long, do run into Devers', Patton's, Hodges' and Simpson's backyards. These ports are now in operation. Antwerp may not be for some time. In other words, for safety some port in addition to Antwerp should be developed as an alternative main U.S. port.

4. The logistical bottleneck obviously now dictates strategy. Could you give me your views on this matter: what alternative plans exist for use, in case you are unable to operate Antwerp as soon as planned?

---

58 1610 V-2 rockets were fired at Antwerp (around half of all V-2 rockets fired, the rest were aimed at London) between November 1944 and March 1945, on average of thirteen a day. They caused significant damage to the city, including the vital docks that Marshall was concerned about.

NOVEMBER 1944

The Relief of an Armored Division Commander

Eisenhower to Marshall   *1 November*   *Ref: S-64984*

Major General Sylvester has just been relieved from command of the 7th Armored Division because of a failure to produce a highly efficient combat division. I have offered him to each of the Army commanders and have yet to hear from Devers, but I suspect that no one will want him. I am not yet requesting authority for his reduction, but I am simply sending you this telegram to find out whether Ground Forces might particularly desire him in his present grade for training purposes. He has had considerable combat experience but his leadership has not been of the high order that we need in combat.

Marshall to Eisenhower   *3 November*   *Ref: W-56784*

With reference to Sylvester, General Lear states that he has no place to use Sylvester in his present grade and does not particularly desire him for training purposes.

Eisenhower to Marshall   *13 November*   *Ref: B-62993*

Reference my telephone conversation regarding Major General Lindsay Donald Sylvester. Request authority of the President to reduce General Sylvester to regular rank and return him to United States. General Sylvester failed to produce a good division and since his relief no commander in this Theater, either in the Army Groups or in the Communications Zone desires Sylvester's services.[1]

Lines of Communication

Marshall to Eisenhower   *1 November*   *Ref: W-55663*

I have just had a conversation with General Hilldring, in which he makes a proposal that supply matters, and combat troops reactions to supply services, will be greatly improved if some general officers rode the line of supply, boat, rail and motor, more frequently instead of, as is the usual time saving practice of flying from point to point. He cited a number of instances of the reactions of regimental combat team commanders and others to conditions on the ground, under control of colonels as a rule, on the lines of communication.

I take this up with you first, on the basis that you will not even mention it to Smith and others, and second, because he is stating what I personally stated to General McAndrew in 1919.[2] I fought a heavy fight against the S.O.S. treatment of the soldiers and conditions

---

1 Or Lindsay McDonald Silvester (1889–1963). Montgomery had complained to Eisenhower that 7th Armored Division was unable to clear the west bank of the Meuse on 7 October. Although Sylvester had served with Patton's Third US Army during the advance across France without a problem, he did not impress Simpson when he served with Ninth US Army. Sylvester reverted to his permanent rank of colonel and returned to the US.
2 General James W. McAndrew (1862–1922), Chief of Staff of the US Army Expeditionary Forces.

on the lines of communications, and made particularly the point that general officers were unaware of the conditions because the star on their car freed them from any complications of movement, and the outrageous conditions that existed with R.T.O. officers, and the various points in France, continued without their knowledge. Both of them would have been settled in the day by a man with authority.[3] Hilldring's comments so exactly parallel my reactions in France in the old days that I am quite certain his suggestion is of some importance. I don't think you can get your cure by a single officer like Bonesteel, but I like to think that your G-4 generals and some others should be required to travel on the ground as a colonel does with sufficient frequency to know what is happening.

Please do not be irritated by the views of a visiting fireman and also please do not explain to me that you are not irritated. Just don't answer this message.[4]

A New Man to Sort out the Rear Areas
Marshall to Eisenhower　　　　　　*2 November*　　　　　　*Ref: W-56145*
Answering your S-64987, regarding an officer to work the rear areas for you: Handy and I think the best man available, that is, one who enjoys sufficient prestige and has had a great deal of experience in this particular business, is General Gasser.[5] However, he is performing a vital function here which requires a great deal of backbone, as he heads the War Department Manpower Board,[6] which means that he takes from everybody, and therefore is constantly on the spot and forcing reductions of personnel within the War Department and all over Continental America.

We do not feel we can lose Gasser permanently as things stand at the present moment, but we are willing to lend him to you for two months, and during that time we can look for a replacement or several of them if you so desire. A number of names are being considered but almost none of them, in my opinion and Handy's, meet your requirements. J.W. Anderson,[7] now commanding a corps and former commander of the 3rd Division when it arrived in Casablanca, is available. If I don't think he would irritate, but whether or not he would inspire the necessary respect for his opinions in representing them to your staff I don't know. I find some difficulty in doing it myself. This seems to amuse Handy.[8]

The Scheldt Estuary is Free
Montgomery to Eisenhower　　　　　*3 November*　　　　　*Ref: M-316*
I have to report to you to that the approaches to Antwerp and the Scheldt Estuary are now completely free from any interference. Our troops on Walcheren are now in possession of the coast from Domburg to Westkapelle and round to the east of Flushing, the whole of which town is in our hands, and we have captured all enemy coastal position guns. Our minesweepers are now at work in the Estuary and some have reached Terneuzen. We own the whole of North Beveland and South Beveland. There are still some enemy remaining on

---

3 Marshall had seen these problems at first hand during the First World War. He served with First Army headquarters during the Battle of St Mihiel operation in September 1918 and witnessed the problems of transferring 500,000 troops and 2700 guns to the Meuse-Argonne front in October.
4 It is interesting to see how Marshall anticipates Eisenhower's reaction to this problem. He understands that the necessary outside interference will annoy him and does not wish to get into a discussion.
5 Major-General Lorenzo D. Gasser (1876–1955), another officer with staff experience during the First World War.
6 The Board surveyed the War Department's employment of military and civilian manpower in the US, making recommendations on how to improve it.
7 Major-General Jonathan W. Anderson (1890–1967).
8 Marshall's sense of humor comes through as he explains one of his weaknesses: asking others to do what he finds difficult to do himself.

the northern and north-eastern parts of Walcheren Islands but these cannot interfere with shipping on the estuary, and they are being mopped up. Enemy resistance on the mainland south of Walcheren, and in the Knocke area, has now ceased and we have captured 14,000 prisoners in this area since crossing the Leopold Canal. The full and free use of the port of Antwerp is now entirely a naval matter.[9]

Eisenhower to Montgomery 3 November *Ref: S-65219*
Dear Monty: Answering your note it is, of course, quite all right for you to make the trip you suggest. I think the arrangements are now going forward for me to appear formerly in Brussels on the 9th and, as I've told you, I am personally anxious to have you with me at the ceremony.[10] I have to get this matter out of the way before First Army gets started, otherwise I could put it off for a few days. The ceremony is not of sufficient importance for you to postpone your trip, but if you are back by that time I hope you will attend. That will, of course, give us also a chance to talk over our own business.

If you do not find it possible to be back, I will still have adequate British representation at the ceremony.

I hope you can dig up some reinforcements and wish there was some way in which I could help. As ever. [Signed] Ike.

Montgomery to Eisenhower 4 November *Ref: M-322*
Dear Ike: I propose to leave for United Kingdom on 6 November and to return on 10 November so will miss you in Brussels. I have told Erskine[11] that I shall not be able to attend the ceremony on 9 November but have not told him the reason, as my trip to England is being kept very secret.

Thank you very much for your message of appreciation about Antwerp. I have passed your congratulations to Canadian Army.[12] Yours ever, Monty.

A New Commander for Fifth Army in Italy
Marshall to Eisenhower 21 November *Ref: W-66146*
In a message to the President, the Prime Minister proposed sending Wilson to Washington as Dill's successor,[13] moving up Alexander to become SACMED[14] and giving Clark the Army Group in Italy. The President answered this, giving his approval to the proposed changes. Final action has not been taken but I presume the changes will take place very shortly.

This brings up the question of Clark's successor in command of the Fifth Army[15] and before making a final decision in that matter I would like your views as to the desirability of sending Simpson, Truscott or possibly another of your present Army Commanders to the Fifth Army. Truscott's Fifteenth Army Headquarters is due to arrive in France within a day or two. I do not know how you contemplate using the Fifteenth Army, but I wonder whether

9 Operations INFATUATE I and INFATUATE II – two amphibious landings on Walcheren on the north side of the Scheldt estuary – began on 1 November. The first supply ships docked in Antwerp on 28 November.
10 A ceremony at the Belgium Tomb of the Unknown Soldier with Prince Charles, Count of Flanders, Regent of the Kingdom of Belgium.
11 General Sir George W.E.J. Erskine GCB, KBE, DSO (1899–1965), Head of the SHAEF Mission to Belgium.
12 The Canadian Army had cleared the south bank of the Scheldt Estuary and most of the north bank, an area known as South Beveland, after a costly month long battle.
13 Field Marshal Dill was Senior British Representative on the Combined Chiefs of Staff when he died of aplastic anaemia on 4 November.
14 Supreme Allied Commander, Mediterranean.
15 General Clark was about to be promoted to command 15th Army Group.

you have a real need for it. I presume you plan to keep initially in the rear areas, administering divisions recently arrived and until they are ready to assign to one of the Armies in the forward area. This may not be correct and you may contemplate putting the Fifteenth in line as soon as it is shaken down and ready to operate. If, however, you are contemplating using it in rear areas, it occurred to me that possibly a Corps Headquarters could do that job and the Fifteenth Army headquarters would not be needed.

Truscott is leaving tomorrow to return to France and when I asked him whether he would like to return to Italy, he indicated a preference to remain in France. He is considerably junior in Regular Army rank to the two Corps Commanders in Italy, Crittenberger and Keyes, but I am sure that would not affect their service in any way.

If the new commander of the Fifth Army is other than one of the present Army Commanders in France, it would probably be better to give it to Crittenberger or Keyes. I will consult McNarney on this if you do not desire to release an Army Commander.

Will you please send me your views with any recommendations as to the assignment to command of the Fifth Army that you desire to make.

Eisenhower to Marshall 22 November *Ref: S-67806*
I will be glad to make one Army Commander available to go to Italy. I still want Fifteenth Army Headquarters because of anticipated administrative and occupational tasks that can best be planned and executed by a separate army headquarters. However, I will arrange here for an acting commander of that army.[16]

I will give you the exact name of the officer I prefer to send to Italy after speaking to Bradley sometime today.

Eisenhower to Marshall 22 November *Ref: S-67869*
I have discussed the matter with Bradley. We both believe that in view of Truscott's familiarity with the Italian theater, and because Simpson, Hodges, Patton and Patch are so intimately the engaged in the battle now raging on this front[17], Truscott should be the man to go to Italy. As you know, he has always stood so high in my estimation that I hate to part with him, but I believe that under the circumstances he should be named to command that army. He has not yet arrived, but I am quite convinced that his personal preference for duty in France, and the fact that Keyes and Crittenberger[18] are senior to him in the Regular Army will not, repeat not, in any way reduce his effectiveness as commander of the Fifth Army. An additional reason for sending Truscott is that any alternative plan would compel two instead of one army commander to become acquainted with new staffs and the new subordinates.[19]

A Message for the German People

Marshall to Eisenhower 22 November *Ref: W-66936*
The President directed the following message to be sent to you. The President has this date put the following to Prime Minister Churchill:

---

16 Major-General Leonard T. Gerow was promoted to command Fifteenth Army in January 1945 and it was charged with rehabilitating units after the Battle of the Bulge, processing divisions arriving in Europe and occupational duties; it also reduced the Ruhr pocket.

17 With Ninth Army, First Army, Third Army and Seventh Army respectively.

18 General Geoffrey Keyes and General Willis D. Crittenberger.

19 General Lucian Truscott was appointed to command Fifth Army in Clark's place on 16 December 1944; he would command it until the end of the war.

1. Apparently the Chiefs of Staff would like something done by top level to help break down German morale.
2. I can think of nothing except a joint statement from you and me, and therefore suggest something along the line of the following:

"We have viewed the overall iron discipline of the Wehrmacht and the stranglehold of the Nazi party over the individuals of the German nation, and we have considered the problem of getting the truth to the people of Germany, for they have been flooded with Nazi propaganda that the Allies seek the destruction of the German people and the devastation of Germany.

Once more we wish to make it clear to German people that this war does not seek to devastate Germany or eliminate the German people.

Once more we want to make it clear to the people of Germany that we see the elimination of Nazi control and the return of the German people to the civilization of the rest of the world. We are winning. There is no question of that. But we want to save lives and to save humanity.

We hope that this slaughter of Germans can be brought to an end, but we are going to bring this war to a conclusion which will satisfy civilization and seek to prevent future wars. The answer lies in the hands of the German people. They are being pressed the whole length of their boundaries along the Rhine. They are being pressed by overwhelming numbers and inexhaustible resources in Poland and Czechoslovakia and Hungary. German towns are daily being destroyed and your enemies draw closer in the closing of an inexorable ring.[20] The simple fact remains that the Allies are united in demanding a complete military victory.

The choice lies with the German people and the German Army. Do not prolong the days of death and suffering and destruction. Join all the other people in Europe and Africa and America and Asia in this great effort for decency and peace among human beings."

President to Eisenhower   *25 November*   *Ref: White House No. 127*
Paraphrase of Top Secret and Personal message from Prime Minister Churchill to President Roosevelt:

With reference to your message concerning a joint statement from you and me, in an attempt to help break down German morale, I consulted the Cabinet and the Chiefs of Staff separately. We all seriously doubt whether it would be advisable to make any such statement. It seems unlikely to me that the Germans have very much fear of the treatment they will receive from the Armies and Governments of Britain and the United States. They are afraid of an occupation by the Russians and a sizeable proportion of their population being transported to Russia (or as they put it Siberia) to toil to death. There does not seem to be anything we can say to eradicate this fear, which is deeply rooted in them.[21]

It seems certain, moreover, that Stalin considers demanding several million Nazi youth, Gestapo men and so forth, for prolonged work of reparation, and it is difficult to say that his attitude is incorrect. Therefore, you and I could not give any assurances to the Germans without consultations with him on the matter.

---

20 Or closing of a relentless ring.
21 This prediction would come true on all levels during the final stages of the war, as civilians tried to escape the Soviet Army and German soldiers of all ranks tried to surrender to the Allies.

If I was a German soldier or General, it seems to me that I should look upon any such statement at this time, when the battle for Cologne is at its peak, as a sign of weakness on our part and as positive proof of the advantages of continued desperate opposition. The Chiefs of Staff and the Ministry of Information, both independently, are in agreement with my view that this might well be the result of any such statement now. The General Grant attitude 'to fight it out on this line, if it takes all summer'[22] appears one to which I see no alternative. Therefore, we are opposed to any reassurances being voluntarily offered by us at this time.

The brilliant success of the French in the south, the capture of Metz by your forces and the breakthrough of the American Seventh Army at Strasbourg, now also captured, are important facts which must be added to the increased pressure of the First and Ninth American Armies, and our own British efforts, in the direction of Venlo. Even if we are not successful in conquering at the strongest point towards Cologne, we have already gained enough to make the battle a notable step towards our ultimate objective. I am sure that words would play no part now and it seems to me that we cannot speak any words to which the Soviets are not parties. They are still holding on their front double the number of divisions which oppose us.

Therefore, it is my earnest hope for we shall fight the battle out until winter arrives around the middle of December and hurl extra weight into points at which we have penetrated. I am positive it would hurt our prestige, and possibly our initiative, if we appeared to attempt high level appeals to the Germans at this time. It is possible to throw all kinds of propaganda across battle lines locally, as they did to us, and the Staffs are working on a plan which is being drawn up to meet the desire of Eisenhower to reach, through underground methods, the morale of the Germans. A separate telegram will be sent on this. But to make the Great Governments responsible for anything which could have the appearance of appeasement at this stage of the game would lessen our chances, be a confession of our errors, and make the enemy resistance stiffen. If you think my attitude is wrong do not hesitate to correct me. In the meantime, I shall remain set on an unconditional surrender, which is where you put me.

[Handwritten note] General McClure informed – General Eisenhower agrees in principle with P.M. as regards this message. 27/11/44

Eisenhower to Marshall   *27 November*   *Ref: CPA-90359*

I have read the exchange of telegrams between the highest levels on the subject of Joint Proclamations to Germany. I consider that the present moment is not the best for any statement. I believe it should follow up on some operation that would be universally recognized as a definite and material success. The enemy knows we are now having difficulty, particularly with weather, and that our advances are laborious and slow, consequently, I think that a statement at this time would probably be interpreted as a sign of weakness rather than of an honest statement of intention. The conditions which would establish perfect timing in my opinion could occur either on this front or on the Eastern front, but I am quite sure that the best opportunity would be when we are moving forward rapidly in some important sector. These are personal views expressed without consultation with the Staff.[23]

22 General Ulysses S. Grant (1822–1885), commander of the Union Army, made this statement in May 1864 during the Battle of Spotsylvania House in his Overland Campaign.
23 Stiff German resistance, bad weather and a shortage of ammunition all conspired to bring the Allied advance to virtually a standstill. In fact OKW was planning its own counterattack and the timing of the proclamation would have backfired; it was never made.

12

DECEMBER 1944

Clearing up Rocket Damage in London

Churchill to Eisenhower   .   2 December   Ref: 7066

I am trying very hard to keep a good lead on the rocket bomb damage on London. We have 120,000 additional civilians working there and about 2,500 British Forces. It would be very welcome gesture on your part if you could allow any spare United States Engineers acquainted with the building arts, who are at present waiting in England en route for the front, to give us a helping hand meanwhile. I do not know what you have available but 2,000 or 3,000 would be very welcome, even if they only stayed a little while. It is thought here by my advisers on labor matters that this would be a stimulus and make the rest feel they were in the line with the troops on war work. I am sure you will look into this and see what, if anything can be done. I would like to have an answer before the debate on housing takes place probably on Thursday week. I shall quite understand of you find it impossible.[1]

Eisenhower to Churchill   3 December   Ref: S-69300

You may be sure that, to the limit of our ability, we will follow the suggestions made in your personal telegram to me concerning the use of our engineers in England. Our base commander in England is General Vaughan. He is receiving immediate instructions to contact General Ismay by telephone to find out the nature of the problem and to cooperate in every way possible. United States troops will consider it an honor to participate in this work and the only question will be the availability of the proper type of troops. I am delighted that you brought this to my personal attention.

Extra Manpower

Eisenhower to Handy   14 December   Ref: S-70772

We are doing every possible thing to help strengthen our position in manpower. We are searching rear areas, including the Air Force bases. You may be perfectly certain that we understand the seriousness of the problem at home. Yet our replacement situation is exceedingly dark.[2]

---

1 The first V-1 hit London on 13 June 1944 and before long over 100 V-1s a day were being fired at southeast England. Rocket launches ended when 21st Army Group overran all the launch sites in range in October; 9521 rockets were fired and there were 22,892 casualties, most of them civilians.

2 High casualties in the battles of 'Bloody' Aachen and the Hürtgen Forest had hit many divisions hard, and while no divisions were disbanded, it was becoming increasingly difficult to keep front line units up to strength. The rear areas were not suffering and healthy, trained men had to be found as extra replacements. Germany started doing this in the autumn, creating an 'operational reserve' by late November for the offensive which started two days after this cable: Operation WACHT AM RHEIN, the battle which would become known as the Battle of the Bulge.

The German Ardennes Offensive

Eisenhower to Montgomery   *17 December*   *Ref: S-71591*

Have just returned from conference with Bradley, Patton and Devers:[3]

The whole front south of Moselle passes to strict defense immediately, giving up all penetrations across the Saar River. Devers takes over most of present Third Army front. Patton moves north with six divisions and taking over VIII Corps temporarily, to organize major counter blow with target date of 23d or 24th. Our weakest spot is in the direction of Namur. Enemy is expected to attack with armor near Monschau to broaden his penetration and may attack with lesser strength from the Trier region.[4] He may also try to attack on north of Ninth Army, but you have reserves capable of dealing with him there. The general plan is to plug the holes in the north and launch coordinated attack from the south.[5] The contents of this telegram should be communicated to fewest possible persons. Warm personal thanks for your prompt action.

Eisenhower to Bradley and Devers   *18 December*   *Ref: S-71400*

Subject to modifications which may result from our discussions, I intend to issue the following directive after the meeting tomorrow:[6]

1. The enemy is making a major thrust through the Ardennes. He still has reserves uncommitted. He may therefore use these reserves to increase the strength of this attack or use them to launch a second attack north of Aachen. Sufficient information is not yet available to determine his action but it is unlikely that he will undertake major offensive operations south of the Moselle. It appears that he will be prepared to employ the whole of his armored reserve to achieve success.

2. Intention: My intention is to take immediate action to check the enemy advance: to launch a counter-offensive without delay with all forces north of the Moselle.

3. 6th Army Group Missions
   (a) To abandon present major offensive operations and relieve 12 Army Group westward to the Moselle.
   (b) By aggressive local action, to contain enemy forces opposing them.
   (c) To eliminate the Colmar Pocket.

4. 12th Army Group Missions
   (a) To check the enemy advances and to insure, as of vital importance, the security of the line of communications Namur-Liège-Aachen.

---

3 Early on 16 December, Army Group B attacked First US Army's line. By the end of 17 December, deep penetrations had been made in VIII Corps' line and while Sixth Panzer Army and Fifth Panzer Army were advancing northeast towards the Meuse river, Seventh Army was covering their southern flank.
4 These anticipated attacks would extend the northern and southern flanks of Army Group's front; neither were carried out.
5 Eisenhower has declared his strategy on day two of the battle. Hodges' First Army had to hold the northern shoulder and prevent Army Group B crossing the river Meuse. At the same time Patton's Third Army would move north and attack the southern shoulder.
6 This simple 350-word cable outlines Eisenhower's strategy for the Battle of the Bulge. Each Army Group commander knew what his objective was, what his new boundaries were and what changes had been made to his Order of Battle.

(b) When (a) above has been accomplished, to relieve 21 Army Group west of the Meuse in accordance with present suspended directive (S-71246)

(c) To launch a counter-offensive north of the Moselle. Attacks comprising this counter-offensive will converge on the general area Bonn-Cologne.

5. 21st Army Group Mission

When relieved east of the Meuse by 12th Army Group, and on completion of regrouping, to attack southeast from the Nijmegen area between the Rhine and Meuse.

6. Forces Assigned

In order to enable 6th Army Group to relieve 12th Army Group east of the Moselle, 12th Army Group will nominate one corps of one armored and three infantry divisions to pass to command of 6th Army Group on dates to be agreed between commanders concerned.

7. Boundaries

(a) Between 6th and 12th Army Groups inclusive 6th Army Group, St Dizier, Thionville, and thence along the Moselle River.

(b) Between 12th and 21st Army Groups, unchanged.

Eisenhower to Bradley, Lee and Montgomery   *19 December*   *Ref: S-71592*

This is just to remind you of the vital importance of insuring that no, repeat no bridges, fall in enemy hands intact. If necessary service units should be organized at once to protect them.[7]

Montgomery and the Northern Sector

Eisenhower to Montgomery   *20 December*   *Ref: S-71608*

Please let me have your personal appreciation of the situation on the North flank of the penetration, particularly with reference to the possibility of giving up, if necessary, some ground on the front of the First Army and to the north there of, in order to shorten our line and collect a strong reserve for the purpose of destroying the enemy in Belgium.[8]

Montgomery to Eisenhower   *21 December*   *Ref: M-384*

On receiving your instructions to take over command of the Northern Front, I held a conference at 14:00 hours today with Hodges and Simpson, at Headquarters First Army, and examined the battle situation. The front was in need of reorganization and I issued orders on this subject.

I have ordered Ninth Army to take over the present VII Corps sector with the divisions now in it, and to use XII Corps Headquarters for the purpose. I have ordered that Headquarters VII Corps shall take command of a reserve corps consisting of 75th Division, 84th Division, 3rd Armored Division, and this corps is to assemble in the general area about Durbuy and Marche, and is not to be used offensively until it is all assembled and ready for battle.[9]

---

7 The bridges across the river Meuse at Liège, Huy, Namur, Dinant and Givet.

8 Eisenhower's decision on 20 December to split command of the Ardennes battlefield in two was a strategically sound one but controversial. By now the bulge in the line had grown to such an extent that it was impossible for Bradley to control it all. Handing over control of the northern shoulder and First US Army to Montgomery proved to be unpopular.

9 VII Corps would extend First Army's line southwest to delay and then stop Fifth Panzer Army.

Elements of 7th Armored Division, with some other troops, are still holding out in the general area about St. Vith and there is no doubt that the brave work of these troops is slowing up enemy movement into the penetration area and westwards.[10]

I have arranged with Bradley that the boundary between us shall be the line Givet–Prüm, both places inclusive to me, and I would be glad if you would confirm this with him as the line was not very good when I spoke. I have every hope that we shall be able to restore the situation and I see no need at present to give up any of the ground that has been gained in the last few weeks by such hard fighting.

I am meeting the Army Commanders again at First Army Headquarters tomorrow and will send you another report tomorrow night.

Montgomery to Eisenhower   *21 December*   *Ref: M-385*
Had a meeting today with Hodges and Simpson. Considerable enemy pressure on front of XVIII Corps. Have pulled 3rd Armored Division into XVIII Corps and have replaced it in VII Corps by 2nd Armored Division from Ninth Army. Have transferred 51st Highland Division and 6th Guards Tank Brigade to Ninth Army to replace 2nd Armored Division. VII Corps, under Collins, will now have 75th Division, 84th Division, 2nd Armored Division, and will be assembled complete by Saturday night with Corps Headquarters at Maffe, about five miles due west of Durbuy. All going well. Met Lee at First Army Headquarters.

Montgomery to Eisenhower   *22 December*   *Ref: M-389*
Hodges was a bit shaken early on and needed moral support and was very tired. He is doing better now and I see him and Simpson every day. Ninth Army has been ordered to get two divisions into reserve from XIX Corps. 5th Armored Division I have given to First Army and the other division will be in Ninth Army reserve. Have put 3rd Armored Division back into VII Corps, so Collins now has four divisions. From information available here, I am not optimistic that the attack of Third Army will be strong enough to do what is needed and I suggest Seventh German Army will possibly hold off Patton from interfering with progress westwards of Fifth Panzer Army. In this case, I will have to deal unaided with both Fifth and Sixth Panzer Armies. Consider it vital that all bridges over the Meuse south of Givet should be well and truly held, and would be interested to hear about this. From Givet inclusive northwards, all bridges are very strongly held. First Army is now reorganized and in good trim and we will fight a good battle up here.[11]

Eisenhower to Hodges and Simpson   *22 December*   *Ref: S-71980/71981*
In the recent battling, you and your army have performed in your usual magnificent style and your good work is helping create a situation from which we may profit materially. It is especially important now that everyone be kept on his toes and that all of us look and plan ahead with calm determination, and with optimism, to take advantage of all opportunities. Now that you have been placed under the Field Marshal's operational command, I know that you will respond cheerfully and efficiently to every instruction he gives. The slogan is "Chins up." Please make sure that all your subordinate commanders exert the maximum

---

10 Over 15,000 US soldiers would escape from the St Vith salient after delaying Fifth Panzer Army's advance for a week.
11 Montgomery was moving XXX British Corps and its five divisions to guard the bridges. By 23 December a thin screen of engineers, artillery and anti-tank units were dug in along the river while French troops from the Metz garrison manned a string of checkpoints.

of leadership and example in sustaining morale, and convincing every man that he is in better condition than the enemy. Good luck and let us seek a real victory. [Signed] Ike Eisenhower.[12]

Eisenhower to Montgomery   *22 December*   *Ref: S-71982*
Dear Monty: I have just dispatched messages of encouragement and appreciation to both Hodges and Simpson. I know you realize that Hodges is the quiet, reticent type and does not appear as aggressive as he really is. Unless he becomes exhausted, he will always wage a good fight. However, you will of course keep in touch with your important subordinates and inform me instantly if any change needs to be made on United States side.

I have told both Simpson and Hodges that high morale, cheerful response to your instructions and optimistic planning ahead are the slogans we must keep before us. Good luck! [Signed] Ike Eisenhower.[13]

Montgomery to Eisenhower   *23 December*   *Ref: M-390*
It now seems quite clear that Fifth Panzer Army is swinging northwestwards and two of its divisions are already tapping in against VII Corps and trying to overlap that Corps area to the west. Sixth Panzer Army seems to have given up its attempts to break the front of V Corps and to have sheared off to the westwards.[14]

I am disturbed at the weak local arrangements, particularly in the infantry of most of the divisions in First and Ninth Armies. The divisions of V Corps are together 7,000 under strength, mostly infantry. 29th Division is 2,000 below strength. Can anything be done to get replacements for this serious discrepancy?[15]

The Promotion of Eisenhower

Eisenhower to Marshall   *20 December*   *Ref: S-71697*
Although I understand that Senate confirmation has not yet been given, I have been notified by the Adjutant General of my nomination to increased rank. Will you please pass the following message to the President:

"Permit me to express to you, my grateful appreciation of your kindness in nominating me for increased rank. I sincerely thank you for the continued confidence in me and in this command, which is implied in this promotion. With sincere wishes for your continued good health, and with respectful regard [Signed] Dwight D. Eisenhower."[16]

Eisenhower to Marshall   *20 December*   *Ref: S-71698*
I have just dispatched to you for delivery to the President a message of thanks for nominating me for increased rank. I want you personally to know that the greatest value to me in

12 This message of encouragement was sent to Hodges and Simpson after hearing from Montgomery about Hodges' weariness.
13 This explanation of Hodges' character was sent to ease Montgomery's concerns over First Army's commander.
14 Sixth Panzer Army had come to a halt around Elsenborn Ridge and in the Amblève valley and was looking to breakthrough at Manhay to the west. Fifth Panzer Army was looking to breakthrough at Marche and Rochefort.
15 The lifeblood of an American infantry division was the 5211 officers and men of its 27 rifle companies. Montgomery's figures indicate that the front line units are 30 percent below strength.
16 Eisenhower was promoted to temporary five star General of the Army; this was converted to a permanent rank on 11 April 1946.

this promotion is the knowledge that your confidence in this command has never wavered. As a personal favor, would you please thank the Secretary of War for me since I assume that he must have also been involved in this appointment.

Going Over to the Offensive in the Ardennes

Montgomery to Eisenhower　　　　26 December　　　　　　　　Ref: M-398
I will meet you 13:00 hours tomorrow, 27 December, at Brussels Evere airfield. All going well here and I am now planning to pass to the offensive.

Eisenhower to Smith　　　　28 December　　　　　　　　Ref: MA-74
Have had discussions with Montgomery and consider situation such that there is little risk of an enemy thrust westwards across the Meuse in the Givet sector. Moreover, there are great possibilities in the Bastogne to Houffalize thrust, which should be reinforced promptly and in strength. I am prepared therefore to release 11th Armored Division or 87th Division, or both, to Bradley at once, as desired by him. With the area Bastogne to Houffalize firmly in our possession, profitable operations can later be developed. Make this clear to Bradley.

Montgomery to Eisenhower　　　　31 December　　　　　　　　Ref: M-423
After consultation with Hodges, I am putting forward the attack of VII Corps towards Houffalize forward by one day and it will now be launched at first light on 3 January. Second British Army takes over the front as far east as Hotton by 2 January.

Montgomery to Eisenhower　　　　31 December　　　　　　　　Ref: M-406
I have seen Freddie[17] and understand you are greatly worried by many considerations in these very difficult days. I have given you my frank views because I have felt you like this. I am sure there are many factors which have a bearing quite beyond anything I realize. Whatever your decision may be, you can rely on me 100 per cent to make it work and I know Brad will be the same. Very distressed that my letter may have upset you and I would ask you to tear it up.
　Your very devoted subordinate, Monty.

Eisenhower to Montgomery　　　　1 January　　　　　　　　Ref: S-78249
Dear Monty. After sending you a very personal letter last evening I received your very fine telegram this morning. I truly appreciate the understanding attitude it indicates. I am delighted you have found it possible to speed up your regrouping arrangements. I am sure you will score a great success...
　With the earnest hope that the year 1945 will be the most successful for you of your entire career, as ever [Signed] Ike.

Suggestion for Promoting Bradley and Spaatz

Eisenhower to Marshall　　　　21 December　　　　　　　　Ref: S-71794
Could you consider promotion to four star rank of General Bradley and General Spaatz? I do not need to enlarge upon former, verbal reports to you concerning the heavy responsibilities these two men carry their great abilities, but I should like to point out that this will be

---

17 Major-General Sir Francis W. de Guingand KBE, CB, DSO (1900–1979), nicknamed 'Freddie', 21st Army Group's Chief of Staff, formed a close relationship with Smith, and often had to smooth over relations between SHAEF and Montgomery.

the most opportune time to promote Bradley. Spaatz, of course, should be advanced at the same time. While there was undoubtedly a failure in the current operation, to evaluate correctly the power that the enemy could trust through the Ardennes, it must be remembered that weather has restricted the effectiveness of TAC-R[18] and all of us, without exception, were astonished at the abilities of the abilities of the Volkstürm division to act offensively.[19] Nevertheless, Bradley has kept his head magnificently and has proceeded methodically and energetically to meet the situation. In no quarter is there any tendency to place any blame upon Bradley. I retain all my former confidence in him and believe that his promotion now would be interpreted by all American forces as evidence that their calm determination and courage in the face of trials and difficulties, is thoroughly appreciated here and at home. It would have had a fine effect generally.

Marshall to Eisenhower   *22 December*   *Ref: W-81088*

I received your proposal to promote Bradley and Spaatz and am sorry that it does not appear feasible to do this at the moment. Congress has adjourned and with it some measure of success. I doubt if the President would hazard a recess appointment regarding which he has already been reluctant to take action. I was glad to get your comment on Bradley but it was exactly what I anticipated his leadership would be in crisis.

Eisenhower to Marshall   *23 December*   *Ref: S-72108*

I understand the difficulty about Bradley and Spaatz. I regret that I did not make this suggestion to you prior to the adjournment of Congress, but I had simply forgotten the adjournment was so imminent.

With regard to the officers you mention, I will go over the matter today and will give you some indication very quickly.

Staff Instructed Not to Bother Eisenhower

Marshall to Eisenhower   *22 December*   *Ref: W-81088*

I gave instructions to the Staff that you were not to be bothered with any questions regarding the operations without my express approval, though one slipped through yesterday with reference to the Germans shooting prisoners.[20] I did this because I want you left entirely free from such irritations during a period that demands your complete concentration. I shall merely say now that you have our complete confidence.

Finding Replacements

Eisenhower to Marshall   *23 December*   *Ref: S-72107*

You have probably noted over the radio, or in the press, the decision of the British Government to comb out another quarter of a million men to make available for the battle line. They are doing this by transfer from the Navy and the R.A.F., by further combing out and retraining

---

18 Tactical reconnaissance was limited by poor weather. 12th Army Group failed to notice the enormous build up in German armor and infantry in the Ardennes, and Army Group B's attack took it completely by surprise.

19 Volkstürm divisions had been formed from older and younger men and recovering wounded soldiers. On the whole, they were inadequately trained, poorly equipped and had little artillery support. Army Group B used its Volkstürm divisions to break through First Army's line in the Ardennes, clearing the way for the armored divisions. In some cases this arrangement worked; in others it delayed the advance.

20 Kampfgruppe Peiper, Sixth Panzer Army's leading column, executed 84 prisoners of war at Baugnez, near Malmédy on 17 December. There were other massacres and although sources vary, the total killed was around 362 prisoners of war and 111 civilians.

of individuals in the Army and by additional levels of drafts. While I do not quite understand how the British can find this number of men, it is most encouraging news.[21]

After the Ardennes?

Marshall to Eisenhower and Deane[22]   *25 December*   *Ref: WX-82070*
On the 23rd the President sent a message to Stalin substantially as follows:

> "I wish to tell Eisenhower to send a fully qualified staff officer to discuss with you the situation in the West and its relation to the Russian front, in order that information essential to our efforts may be available to all others. The Belgian situation is not bad, but it is now time to discuss what comes next. I hope you will see Eisenhower's representative and arrange the exchange with him of information of mutual value. Complete secrecy will be maintained. An early reply is requested in view of the emergency."[23]

This ends President's message.

Deane, on 24 December, points out that at the Churchill meetings in Moscow in October, Stalin suggested the possibility of outflanking the West Wall by passing through Switzerland[24] and also the withdrawal of some of our forces from Italy and their transfer to the Balkans, with a view to joining up with the Red Armies near Vienna.[25] In recent talks with Harriman, Stalin repeated the suggestion about transferring up to eight divisions from Italy to Dalmatia, for an advance to Zagreb to join up with the Russians in Southeast Austria. Deane states Stalin also suggested the possibility of our south group of European armies breaking through enemy lines and joining Soviet left flank by advancing east. Is not clear from Deane's message whether Stalin, in speaking of the 'Southern Group', meant Clark's armies or your southern group. It may be tied to Stalin's idea of Switzerland.

We are preparing instructions for the guidance of your representative on these points, in case they are raised, to be cleared through Combined Chiefs of Staff.

Deane to Marshall and Eisenhower   *25 December*   *Ref: MX-22154*
The 'Southern Group of European Armies' to which I stated Stalin referred to, is the group of armies commanded by General Devers in France.[26] Stalin only mentioned the possibility very casually of this group of armies advancing eastward and joining up with the Red Army's left flank. I included mention of it in my cable to emphasize that Stalin's thinking is apparently pointed towards joint action between the Anglo-American Forces and the Red Army in Southern Europe.[27]

---

21 Carrying out a similar combing of other services and changing of draft rules similar to what the Germans had done the previous autumn. The strength of the British Army was 1.65 million in the summer of 1940; by May 1945 over 3.5 million men had served.
22 Brigadier-General John R. Deane (1896–1952).
23 General John R. Deane was the head of the US Military Mission, Moscow.
24 In doing so ignoring Switzerland's neutrality.
25 An amphibious landing on the Balkan coast, so they could advance to meet Soviet troops which were already east of Budapest, only 100 miles west of Vienna.
26 6th Army Group.
27 By the end of 1944, Soviet troops were in eastern Austria but the Soviet offensives of January 1945 were directed through Poland and East Prussia with the intention of reaching the river Oder and entering Germany as soon as possible.

Marshall to Eisenhower   *26 December*   *Ref: W-82104*
Reply received from Stalin, reference my WX-82070, agrees with President's proposal and
agrees to meet the officer you send and to arrange with him the exchange of information.
We are initiating formal instructions from the Combined Chiefs of Staff to you on the dispatch of an offer to Moscow.

Combined Chiefs of Staff to Eisenhower 26 December   *Ref: WX-82144*
For Info: British Chiefs of Staff and to Deane and Archer, Military Mission to Moscow[28]
Marshal Stalin has agreed to the proposal of the President and Prime Minister that you
should send to Moscow, a staff officer to meet Stalin and to discuss the Western Front situation and its relationship to the Russian Front, and to arrange an exchange of information
essential to the coordination of our effort. You should send a fully qualified Staff Officer at
once. Acknowledging at once with name of Staff Officer.

[Handwritten note] No reply has been received to General Eisenhower's message to General
Marshall.

Dispelling Talk of a British Ground Forces Deputy Commander
Marshall to Eisenhower   *30 December*   *Ref: W-84337*
I am violating somewhat my own orders to the staff here, in bringing up some questions
with you while you are still in the turmoil of this German offensive. However, as you seem to
be succeeding and my guess is that you will, without much delay, seize the offensive yourself,
I feel free to make these comments:
    They may, or may not, have brought to your attention articles in certain London papers
proposing a British Deputy Commander for all your ground forces and implying that you
have undertaken too much of a task yourself.[29] My feeling is this:
    Under no circumstances make any concessions of any kind whatsoever. You not only have
our complete confidence but there would be a terrific resentment in this country following
such action. I am not assuming that you had in mind such a concession. I just wish you to be
certain of our attitude on this side. You are doing a grand job and go on and give them hell.

Eisenhower to Marshall   *1 January*   *Ref: S-73275*
You need have no fear as to my contemplating the establishment of a ground deputy. Since
receipt of your telegram I have looked up the articles in the British papers to which you refer.
Our present difficulties are being used by a certain group of papers and their correspondents to advocate something that they have always wanted but which is not, repeat not, in
fact a sound organization. In the present case the German attack did not involve an Army
Group boundary but came exactly in the center of a single group command. The emergency
change in command arrangements, that is, the placing of one man in charge of each flank,
was brought about by the situation, since the penetration was of such a depth that Bradley
could no longer command both flanks, while the only reserves that could be gathered on the

---

28 General John R. Deane and Rear Admiral Ernest R. Archer.
29 This appears to be the British press stirring up talk of making Montgomery SHAEF's ground deputy. It
follows from Eisenhower's decision to split the Ardennes battlefront between Montgomery and Bradley, a decision based on the temporary strategic situation.

north flank had to be largely British. Consequently, single control had to be exercised on the north and on the south.[30]

Birthday Wishes

Eisenhower to Marshall   *30 December*   *Ref: S-72993*

All good wishes for your birthday.[31] I know that every member of this Theater joins me in congratulations and in thanks for the confidence and unfailing support you have given us.

---

30 Eisenhower's explanation for the temporary split in command of 12th Army Group's front to meet Army Group B's attack.
31 Marshall would turn 64 on 31 December.

13

JANUARY 1945

Summary Report on the Ardennes

Eisenhower to Marshall   *1 January*   *Ref: S-73275*

While Bradley has been making only slow and laborious progress from the south, he has held on to the key center of Bastogne and the strength he is establishing there is a definite threat to the rear of the German, who several days ago certainly intended to continue his attacks against First Army, probably directly toward Liège. The enemy has moved certain formations from the north face of the salient to the south to deal with the Bastogne problem. In the north we have at last succeeded in accumulating enough strength to start an attack of our own. This should begin Wednesday.[1]

Collecting the reserves to meet this problem has, of course, stripped the rest of our front very seriously, but I have given strict orders to give up ground to avoid useless involvement of troops in areas that are relatively unimportant to us. This applies particularly to Alsace. This morning the enemy is making attacks southward to the west of the Vosges. There is enough U.S. strength in the region to deal with this matter successfully.

The enemy is using all types of terroristic methods to create confusion in the rear. Spies work in Allied uniforms and it appears that there was a definite assassination plot.[2] Paratroopers have been dropped behind our lines and attacking troops have in many instances used our uniforms.[3] His day and night air forces have been making small raids on widespread targets and this morning he made a heavy attack on our tactical fields. He caused considerable damage but lost much himself.[4]

1 101st Airborne Division held on to Bastogne until Third Army reached the southern side of the perimeter on 26 December. In doing so the paratroopers had delayed Fifth Panzer Army's advance and tied up a large number of troops. Third Army used the Bastogne position to launch its counterattack north towards Houffalize, starting on 30 December. The main attack on 2 January ran into Fifth Army's own counterattack.

2 This refers to Operation GREIF, an operation conceived by Hitler and led by Otto Skorzeny. The plan was for German soldiers dressed in captured US Army uniforms and using US vehicles to push through First Army's lines and capture bridges over the Meuse, causing confusion along the way. A lack of vehicles, uniforms and equipment limited the operation and the commandos never reached the river. The raids did cause a great deal of confusion and a tightening of security. One rumor was that Eisenhower was to be captured or assassinated and he had to spend the Christmas period under close guard.

3 The second part of Operation GREIF was an attack by Panzerbrigade 150 using captured and converted tanks and vehicles. The attack on Malmédy was delayed until 21 December, by which time Sixth Panzer Army's advance had been stopped. Operation KONDOR was a planned night time parachute drop behind American lines. It was ordered at the last minute and problems meant that only 250 out of 1000 paratroopers were dropped across a wide area. Colonel Freiherr von der Heydte's men were soon captured.

4 Operation BODENPLATTE (Baseplate) was the Luftwaffe's surprise attack launched on 1 January, having been delayed since the Battle of the Bulge began due to bad weather. Over 1000 planes attacked 17 Allied airfields, destroying 305 planes and damaging 190. The Luftwaffe lost over 200 pilots and never recovered.

A Looming Disaster in the Netherlands

Smith to the Dutch Prime Minister[5]   *31 December*   *Ref: S-73128*

I sincerely appreciate the unprejudiced and calm presentation of the vital problem raised by your message, RR-14844. The staff is examining all possibilities, particularly those involved in handling and transporting such a very large number of refugees, as well as the possible military implications, and we will give you our views within 24 hours, as they are being prepared as a matter of urgency. Needless to say, these poor people have our complete sympathy.[6]

Smith to the Dutch Prime Minister   *1 January*   *Ref: S-73253*

Further to my S-73128 of 31 December, on the subject of the evacuation of Dutch Nationals from Venlo and Roermond. This matter has continued to receive our closest attention, and I know that you realize General Eisenhower's earnest desire to do everything in his power to help the Dutch people in German hands. The proposal seems to me to be one actuated by the Germans in their own interests, and against our military interests. I am sure you will agree that mass evacuation of civilians through our lines can only be justified where the population is isolated and there being no, repeat no, other means of safeguarding the welfare of the people.

In beleaguered towns, such as Calais, we were in full agreement with the evacuation of the civil population through our lines to avoid hardship and starvation, but in the Venlo area the situation is entirely different. We feel that we must maintain that it is a German responsibility to look after the civil populations in accordance with the usages of war, and in this case they have the whole of the resources of Germany at their disposal to ensure the welfare of the Dutch nationals.[7]

If we were to accept mass evacuation from this section of the front there is no, repeat no, reason why the Germans should not, repeat not, make similar proposals on all sections of the front on which there are Allied nationals in their hands. Were we to accept this proposal it will be difficult to refuse similar proposals elsewhere, for example, along the entire boundary between liberated and occupied Holland. You will appreciate on the grounds of security alone an influx of a large number of civilians would produce a very difficult problem for us. I therefore feel that for operational reasons this proposal should not, repeat not, be accepted. But I consider it would be unwise to return a blunt refusal to the proposal to the international Red Cross, and for political reasons the question should be kept open. I suggest the international Red Cross should be informed that the Germans are held responsible and that further information and explanation is required as to why the Germans are unable to carry out their obligations to the Dutch population. I have discussed this question at length with Prince Bernhard who, I understand, will be seeing you in the near future and will be explaining our views to you.[8]

I hope you will be coming here on Saturday next, when we will have an opportunity of discussing this problem more fully.

---

5 Professor Pieter S. Gerbrandy (1885–1961), Prime Minister of the Dutch government in exile.
6 The Dutch famine during the winter of 1944–45 was known as the '*Hongerwinter*', the Hunger winter. Food supplies were scarce and the Germans placed an embargo on food stuffs in retaliation for a railway strike in September 1944, organized to hinder the German war effort. Although the embargo was lifted in November, an early start to a harsh winter froze the canals, resulting in severe shortages.
7 4.5 million people were affected by the famine and people had to resort to eating tulip bulbs and sugar beet to supplement their meager rations. After the gas and electricity was turned off, furniture and houses were dismantled to provide fuel for heating. Around 18,000 people died.
8 Prince Bernhard of the Netherlands (1911–2004), was prince consort of Queen Juliana of the Netherlands and Commander of the Dutch armed forces.

Situation Report on 21st Army Group

Montgomery to Eisenhower   *2 January*   *Ref: M-414*

The situation report: Thank you for your outline dated 31 December and letter.

I suggest tactical victory within the salient is going to take some little time to achieve and there will be heavy fighting. Also it is all bound to get somewhat untidy in that area and I think we want to be careful to ensure that the moment for changes in command is wisely chosen.[9] I also feel after we have achieved tactical victory in the salient there may be a considerable interval before the offensive movements begin developing, though I think it is important to try and stage Operation VERITABLE at the earliest possible date.[10] Apart from these few ideas which occurred to me I have no comment on the outline plan and details can be worked out later on. You can rely on me and all under my command to go all out 100% to implement your plans.

[Handwritten note] Operation VERITABLE; Canadian Army operation to strike southeast from Nijmegen area.

A Withdrawal from Alsace – Lorraine Threatens to Stir up the French People

Marshall to Eisenhower   *5 January*   *Ref: W-87149*

President has received a message from de Gaulle, transmitted by Caffery, which states that the French Government cannot accept a retreat in Alsace and part of Lorraine without fighting, since the retreat does not seem justified strategically and would be deplorable from the French national point of view. de Gaulle confidentially requests the President to intervene in this affair.[11]

Caffery states that he communicated with you and Smith and that de Gaulle had a conference with you and came to an agreement on operational measures involved.

The President may ask the Joint Chiefs of Staff for advice in handling de Gaulle's request. If you have anything you want us to use to use in connection with this problem, I expect you will send it to me.

Eisenhower to Marshall   *6 January*   *Ref: S-73871*

In his position as head of the State, de Gaulle appealed to the President because of his objection to certain moves I had planned to make in Alsace-Lorraine, reference your W-87149. Devers' initial operations in Alsace-Lorraine during November were undertaken in order to get us an easily defended flank and one on which minimum troops would assure us of safety. That flank was the Rhine River. After Devers broke through the Vosges Mountains it appeared to him that the remaining German forces around the Colmar Pocket could and would be quickly mopped up by the French Army.[12] Consequently he turned north with the bulk of its forces to assist Patton who had fundamentally the same role, namely, the securing of an easily defended line so as to permit the constant movement towards the north of the

---

9 The methodical clearing of enemy defenses in the Roer Triangle, codename Operation BLACKCOCK, took place between 14 and 27 January 1945.
10 Operation VERITABLE started on 8 February and by 11 March had cleared the area between the Rhine and Maas rivers.
11 Operation NORDWIND was launched against Seventh US Army on 1 January 1945 in Alsace and Lorraine. By 5 January First Army was threatening VI Corps flanks and pushing into a difficult salient.
12 The Vosges Mountains run parallel to and west of the Rhine between Strasbourg and Basel. The Germans still held part of the west bank around Colmar, facing First French Army, and threatening 6th Army Group's southern flank.

bulk of all our forces. It was expected that as quickly as the Colmar Pocket had been reduced, the French Army would be capable of holding all of Alsace-Lorraine and the entire Seventh Army could be employed on and west of the Vosges Mountains sector.

As time went on, the French First Army allowed the Colmar Pocket to stabilize and it was reinforced, at least in personal and equipment, by the Germans. Consequently, when the German thrust came through the Ardennes in great strength and mobility we had on our extreme right flank, instead of the strong, easily defended line we expected, a situation that was inherently weak from a defensive standpoint. Our entire VI Corps was lying to the east of the Vosges Mountains facing north, while the 3rd U.S. Division had to be retained with the First French Army even to sustain the integrity of our lines in the Colmar Pocket. Our danger in that whole region, clearly recognized by all of us from the start, was that the enemy would attempt to drive southwards along the west of the Vosges and at the same time possibly tried to erupt with a secondary attack from the Colmar Pocket. If this happened our VI Corps would not only be unable to provide us any reserves for the rest of the front, but would actually have to turn and fight its way out of an awkward situation.[13]

If view of this satisfactory situation, and since local reserves of Devers should manifestly be stationed west of the Vosges Mountains, I ordered a general withdrawal of the VI Corps line to the Vosges, retaining in the area north of Strasbourg only light reconnaissance elements that would have to withdraw under any sizeable advance and would have the function only of reconnaissance and of preventing marauding by light bands of Germans. This move would, of course, expose Strasbourg to occupation by enemy forces of appreciable size and would force the left flank of the French Army to swing back into the mountains. Through this move I expected that Devers would have the strongest possible defensive line along his eastern flank, since we had failed to gain the Rhine, and would be enabled to collect into his own reserves at least two armored divisions in the region south of the Siegfried Line and west of the Vosges. This would have given me the opportunity to employ two U.S. divisions as a SHAEF reserve further to the north, leaving Bradley free to devote his entire power to the offensive.

Devers planned to execute this movement by stages, and until it could be completed I obviously had to leave the two divisions scheduled for the SHAEF reserves under his control. Throughout the planning of the movement the French were kept informed and they finally became convinced that it would have the most terrific repercussions in France. They became so agitated, that we here became convinced that the actual fear of de Gaulle and his administration was that they would lose control of the entire French situation and that we would have a state bordering upon anarchy in the whole country. We studied the entire matter earnestly and decided that the original plan had to be modified to the extent of merely swinging the VI Corps back from its sharp salient, with its left resting in the Vosges, and its right extending southwards generally toward Strasbourg. In the meantime, preparation of the defensive positions in the Vosges went on under service troops.[14]

de Gaulle agreed that any really strong enemy threat in the region would, under present circumstances, necessitate a withdrawal, but he was certain that voluntary withdrawal on

---

13 Eisenhower is blaming his plan to evacuate French territory on the First French Army's inability to clear the Colmar Pocket, resulting in Sixth Army Group's unstable situation.

14 In summary, the tactical situation called for an early withdrawal of VI Corps to a shorter line, leaving Strasbourg open to occupation by German troops. However, de Gaulle was concerned that the French people would react badly to any withdrawal, possibly resulting in strikes or rioting. The Allied armies depended heavily on French help along their lines of communications, particularly the rail system. Eisenhower had to concede that the best short term military scenario could result in the worst long term military scenario.

the basis originally planned would be so fatal to French public opinion that he would have to attempt to hold the region with what <u>French</u> troops he could scrape up. These troops, other than those already in the battle, was so miserably equipped and unready for fighting that they could have accomplished nothing.[15]

When de Gaulle came to see me, we had already put into effect the revised plan described above and had to forgo all, a least for the moment, the taking of any additional units from that region.

It was mere coincidence that de Gaulle's visit to me was scheduled at an hour when the Prime Minister happened also to be in my office. When shown the revised plan, de Gaulle was satisfied and left immediately. For this reason I did not report the full details to the Combined Chiefs of Staff and I understood that Caffery's telegram contained a statement that the matter had been composed, although it is true that at the moment of sending his telegram de Gaulle did not know this.

To sum up, I originally looked at the matter merely as a conflict between military and political considerations and felt completely justified in handling the matter on a purely military basis. However, when I found that the execution of the original plan would have such grave consequences in France that all my lines of communication for my vast rear areas might become badly involved through loss of service troops and through unrest, it was clearly the military necessity to prevent this.

Marshall to Eisenhower   7 January   *Ref: W-88421*

I suppose you have seen so much of the text of the President's report on the State of the Union to Congress yesterday, as refers to you and your battle. Lest you may not have seen this, I am having had sent to you by teletype. Might it not be a good thing to get the sense of the President's message down to your U.S. Armies, at least to the leaders? Maybe they already have this.

I received your statement regarding the situation in Alsace and de Gaulle's message to the President. For your confidential information, the President declined to see the French Ambassador and notified our State Department that this was none of their business. He regarded the matter is purely strategical and tactical and had the Ambassador informed that de Gaulle should take these questions up with you and not with him.[16]

Summary of Situation on the Western Front

Eisenhower to Marshall   7 January   *Ref: S-74003*

Today the overall picture is about as follows: Due to comparatively low scale of effort that the enemy is compelled to make on other fronts, an extremely high proportion of his personal and material replacements is pouring into the Western Front. Enemy units that have been badly cut up in the salient and at other places are persistently and quickly built up. Replacements in tanks and men reach the front in a matter of days from the interior of Germany. There is a noticeable and fanatical zeal on the part of nearly all his fighting men, as well as the whole nation of 85 million people, successfully unified by terror from

---

15 de Gaulle was prepared to use any French troops he could lay his hands on to keep hold of the Strasbourg area, no matter how poorly armed they were, to prove to the French people that he was prepared to stand and fight.

16 By 13 January Eisenhower was concerned enough about Seventh Army's situation that he moved divisions south from the Ardennes. Unfortunately, they were delayed en route and by 21 January VI Corps had to withdraw across the Moder river. The German offensive ended on 25 January by which time VI Corps had suffered around 17,000 casualties. In February 1945, XXI Corps helped French First Army clear the Colmar Pocket and the west bank of the Rhine south of Strasbourg.

within and fear of consequences from without. The Germans are convinced they are fighting for their very existence and their battle action reflects this spirit. Several things could help us:

(a) Certainty that the Russians are going quickly to begin a sustained major offensive, requiring German resources to reverse their flow.

(b) Sufficiently great strength here, so that I could keep some few divisions in SHAEF reserve to meet emergencies, and giving me a small pool through which to rotate tired divisions for refitting. In this connection I think the Italian front should be studied to determine conditions under which additional divisions should be brought here, and to have them ready for implementation of any plans adopted. Any unallocated divisions at home, any that could be obtained if permitted by overall strategic plans, by postponing action elsewhere.

(c) Immediate and drastic comb out here of able bodied men.

(d) If possible increase the Army ceiling, at least to extent of subtracting detachments of patients from the total allowed, so as to provide a greater flow of replacements. (Maybe the Marines would like to turn over 100,000 to us)[17]

(e) Continuous effort to expedite flow of critical ammunition types and tires.

(f) Speed up development of French divisions.

I am convinced that we cannot resort to cannibalization of U.S. divisions because of the strength needed on this long front. The enemy enjoys the advantage of short communications, fortified defense zones and total mobilization, and the only answer is sufficient divisional strength, fully maintained.

I believe that Gasser's work will do much toward getting us right down to bedrock in reaching definite and accurate conclusions.[18]

In the matter of combing out all able bodied men, there remains the fact that much of the work on docks, in depots and on roads is back-breaking manual work. We have more than 100,000 Negroes in the Communications Zone and they will have to be distributed to do as much of this heavy work as possible. On the other hand, I feel that in existing circumstances, I cannot deny the Negro volunteer a chance to serve in battle. If volunteers are received in numbers greater than needed by existing Negro combat units, I will organize them into separate battalions for temporary attachment to divisions and rotation through frontline positions. This will preserve the principle for which I understand the War Department stands and will still have a beneficial effect in meeting our infantry needs.[19]

Marshall to Eisenhower   *8 January*   *Ref: W-88482*

All here are pressing every effort to get you what you need at the earliest possible date. The best guidance for our efforts comes from messages such as your S-74003.

---

17 The Army ceiling was the maximum number of soldiers the Army could have; here Eisenhower is wanting recuperating patients (a small number in peacetime but a large number in wartime) to be removed from the totals.

18 Gasser's audit teams had found 100,000 combat-fit soldiers during their investigation of units stationed in the US. Now it was the turn of service units in Europe to turn over their spare men. General Lee had done his combing, but it was not enough and he demanded a hospitalized veteran for every man he released for the combat-training camps.

19 The US Army followed the nation's stance on segregation. Over half a million African American soldiers were working in supply and construction units in the communications zone. On 26 December Eisenhower appealed for volunteers but only 4500 had joined the training units when the offer was cancelled in early February.

If Bull and Tedder are unable to obtain a satisfactory answer in Moscow as to Russian action, I will make certain that the matter is pressed at the forthcoming conference. It may be possible to do something between now and then. It would appear that unseasonable thaws have been at least in part responsible for the delay.[20]

Marshall to Eisenhower   *8 January*   *Ref: W-88482*

With regard to the Army ceiling, this is being increased to take care of the patient factor and some other ineffectives. It seems, however, that this action would not help the flow of replacements for nearly six months. The Defense Commands, other installations in the U.S., the Panama Canal and Alaska garrisons are being combed for men for infantry replacements.[21]

Somervell will tell you personally the full story of the drastic efforts we are making to speed up the flow of critical ammunition and other types of supplies. Our efforts along this line are continuous.

As we see it here, getting new French divisions quickly into the fight is going to be dependent primarily on the ability of the French, the British and ourselves to provide the minimum essential equipment. Much can be done in providing essential equipment for these divisions by using obsolete, obsolescent and renovated equipment, and by a drastic review of the percentage of reserves held by both the British and ourselves behind critical items of equipment. Somervell's people are pressing this whole matter hard at our end. We will give you definite information very soon.[22]

On the matter of additional divisions from Italy, it appears at first glance exceedingly doubtful that we can get a real assistance for you from there in the near future. I intend to take up with the U.S. Chiefs at once the necessity of implementing to the maximum degree our agreed basic strategy that the main effort is in Europe and specifically on the Western Front.

I have given strict orders that no one here will add to the great load you carry by asking you questions. It may be, however, that we now face a situation requiring major decisions in order to prevent this war from dragging on for some time. Your personal estimates are the best guidance to crystallize ideas on actions which need to be taken. Can you some time in the next week set down and send to me, for my personal use in discussions with the other Chiefs of Staff, your broad personal estimate of the resources required and the steps which need to be taken to bring this war in Europe to a quick conclusion.

Eisenhower to McNarney   *8 January*   *Ref: S-74105*

I have just this instant seen your message of 5th January, addressed to Smith and Handy. Your voluntary action in this matter touches me deeply. The instant shipment of 3,000 replacements to Marseilles will be a godsend.

Thank you again, and come to see us whenever most convenient to yourself. Please notify Devers or the Base Commander at Marseilles of date of arrival.[23]

---

20 Tedder had been sent to Moscow to seek assistance from the Soviet Army, in the hope that they would launch early attacks to ease the pressure on the Western Front brought about by the Battle of the Bulge. The Vistula–Oder Offensive began on 12 January and by 2 February Soviet troops were less than 50 miles from Berlin. The East Prussian Offensive towards Königsberg started on 13 January.

21 In other words, combing all home units for combat effective men who could be shipped immediately to Europe.

22 By reducing the minimum limits on reserves of equipment, new French units could be mobilized.

23 Over 40,000 American soldiers were killed or wounded stopping the German advance in the Ardennes; there were a similar number of casualties during the fighting to erase the Bulge. Another 17,000 men were listed as killed, missing or injured during the Alsace-Lorraine battle.

Moving Divisions across the Atlantic

Marshall to Eisenhower   *8 January*   *Ref: W-88482*

The only divisions now in the United States not already allocated to you are the 86th and 97th Infantry Divisions, which are set up for another Theater. Action is being initiated in the Joint Chiefs to have these two divisions allocated to you at once. They are fully trained and should be able to arrive in your Theater about the middle of March. [24] Of the divisions allocated to you which are still in the United States, the 65th and 89th Infantry Divisions sail this week, the 13th Armored and the 71st Infantry Division in late January, the 13th Airborne and 16th and 20th Armored in early February. We are investigating the possibility of accelerating the sailings of the airborne and armored divisions if you will accept a delay in the movement of service units mentioned in my W-82742 of 7 December. I presume you are moving to the Continent in the near future the two divisions now in the U.K.

Marshall to Eisenhower   *9 January*   *Ref: W-88705*

The Joint Chiefs of Staff have just approved the allocation of the 86th Infantry Division and the 97th Infantry Division to your Theater.

We have restudied the shipping and supply implications of all of your divisions remaining in this country and can accelerate their shipment to you as follows: there is no change in the sailing dates, convoys and destinations of the 65th and 89th Infantry Divisions, the 13th Armored Division and the 71st Infantry Division. The 13th Airborne Division departure date can be advanced to 26th January from 3rd February for Northern French ports. The 16th Armored Division could be advanced to depart 3rd February instead of 11th February, to Northern or Southern French ports. The 20th Armored Division can be expedited to embark on 3rd February instead of 11th February to Northern or Southern French ports. The 86th and 97th Infantry Divisions can sail on 19th February to Northern French ports. Either or both of these last two Infantry Divisions could be diverted to South France provided sufficient Naval escorts can be found and it is desired by you. This matter of escorts is being investigated while we await your wishes in this matter.

These divisions have already been alerted to the new embarkation dates in anticipation that you will accept them with the acceleration indicated herein. If you do not accept them with the new departure dates, please notify us within 24 hours in order that rail lines and ports of embarkation will not be needlessly bogged down with troops and equipment.

This movement will not interfere with the flow replacements to you. Only about 20,500 troop units will be displaced from January to February, but all of these will be cleared up by mid-February. In addition all troops and troop units scheduled for February will be shipped that month, including the divisions indicated herein.

Complete equipment, less general purpose vehicles, will arrive ahead of, or at the same time, as the divisions. General purpose vehicles for these divisions can be expedited, provided an accelerated priority for their shipment to their destination is furnished by you.

Eisenhower to Marshall   *9 January*   *Ref: S-74327*

Your decision to meet our request for two additional divisions for this theater is greatly appreciated.

Reference your W-88785 of 8th January. We have restudied the implications of accelerating the flow of the divisions as indicated in your cable and can accept the acceleration

---

24 86th Division entered combat in Germany on 29 March, 97th Division three days later.

that you suggested. In confirmation, desire that all divisions be shipped to ports in Northern France as follows: 13th Airborne on 26 January; 16th and 20th Armored on 3 February; and 86th and 97th Infantry Divisions on 19 February.

There is to be no change in sailing dates and destinations of the 65th and 89th Infantry Divisions, the 13th Armored Division and the 71st Infantry Division.

Marshall to Eisenhower   *9 January*   *Ref: W-89128*
During McNarney's visit you will undoubtedly talk over with him those aspects of the problems discussed in your S-74003 which pertain to his Theater. Please ask him to send me his views on the Mediterranean situation with regard to the feasibility of transferring forces from Mediterranean Theater of Operations to European Theater of Operations and on future operations in the Mediterranean, including the various proposals for operations across the Adriatic. His thoughts on our future action in the Mediterranean are needed to assist in any discussions with the British and the Russians.

General Lear as Deputy US Theater Commander

Eisenhower to Marshall   *8 January*   *Ref: S-74291*
Please send Lear on at once. While I know him only slightly, his rank, experience and the qualities you describe would be useful to us.[25] I will make him Deputy U.S. Theater Commander, with functions chiefly those involving matters that are currently giving us so much trouble. While he will use existing staffs, rather than to establish a new and larger headquarters, his detached position directly under me will give him ample authority with respect to all senior subdivisions of the U.S. Theater.

Marshall to Eisenhower   *10 January*   *Ref: W-89267*
Lear will leave shortly. He is very much pleased to come. You will be informed of his time of departure as soon as it is definitely fixed.

Review of the European Campaign

Marshall to Eisenhower   *9 January*   *Ref: W-88777*
Brought to me by General MacReady of the British Mission this morning is a formal proposal from the British Chiefs of Staff for the Combined Chiefs of Staff action, calling on you for a report as to your proposed plan of campaign following the suppression of the present German offensive, and for the conquest of Germany. With this, for my Eyes Only, was a discussion by the British Chiefs of Staff and their arguments regarding these matters. The fact, as they put it, that the original instructions of the Combined Chiefs of Staff for primary pressure to be exerted against the Germans in the north towards Berlin had not been effectively carried out and on the contrary, judging by the number of divisions employed, etc., a major offensive effort had been launched from the Saar basin south.[26] They discussed the advisability of a single commander for the ground troops and proposed that at least the front be divided into two groups of armies only instead of three as at

---

25 Lear had taken command of Army Ground Forces following the death of McNair. He was appointed Deputy Commander of European Theater of Operations, US Army, responsible for Theater Manpower.
26 General Patton planned to attack the Saar Basin on 19 December 1944 when the German offensive began on the 16th. Third Army was ordered to immediately send divisions north to counterattack the southern shoulder of the Bulge, with Bastogne as its main objective. It then fought to clear Army Group B from the southern half of the Bulge. Army Group G responded with Operation NORDWIND on 1 January, attacking Seventh Army's line between the Saar Basin and the Rhine.

present. They feel that you have too many other pressing duties of supply, of political complexity, etc.; therefore a more concentrated direction of ground operations is required.[27]

MacReady, after discussing the matter with me, stated that he would only present a brief of the British Chiefs of Staff discussions and would omit any reference to a single commander of ground troops and anything that possibly might be construed as a criticism.

In a radio yesterday, we asked you to give us your views at the end of the week on the general situation. Under the circumstances I now think that we should have those here by Thursday night, so that there could be some discussion by the United States Joint Chiefs of Staff before the combined meeting Friday afternoon.

I am assuming, I think quite correctly, that this British paper stems from the Prime Minister's visit to France and Montgomery's evident pressure to get what he wants in the way of a larger command. I am familiar with his past efforts and I fully expected him to seize the present temporary assignment as a means to that end.[28]

I see one weak point in our position which I should like you to think over, and that refers to the command of the rear areas. Whether or not Lee is the right man does not answer the question. The trouble is, he is involved in both supplying the Front and supplying himself. While the troops on the Front suffer heavily and work with reduced numbers, he has continued apparently to operate with plenty of fat meat. This awakens an inevitable suspicion in the minds of front line commanders as to the adequacy of the support they are receiving.[29] We had exactly the same thing here, still have, though to a very mild degree at present, the continued suspicion by the Air Corps and the Ground Forces of Somervell's people, because the Army Service Forces is performing two functions, one for the army at large and an overlapping one, both in men and material, for itself. We have fairly well eliminated the most critical features of this, but only in the past ten days there was a proposal from the Army Service Forces to do away with the G-4 Division of the General Staff, which happens to be the bulwark of reassurance for the remainder of the army that their interests are impartially considered.

Somervell will talk to you about supply matters after he has had a brief chance to look over the ground and I told him to speak to you about Lear. The more I think of this, the more it impresses me, and Handy is of the same opinion, that Lear, who is loyal, stern and drastic, and very soldierly, be made a deputy of yours for command of the rear areas with the head of the supply service subordinate to him.[30]

Eisenhower to Marshall   *10 January*   *Ref: S-74437*

I consider it completely inappropriate and even desirable that the Combined Chiefs of Staff should review the strategy in this Theater, reference your W-89338. The issues at stake are so great, and the consequences of victory or defeat so vital to our cause, that there should be achieved the greatest possible degree of conviction among all responsible parties as to the line or lines of action for should now be pursued. We have just completed a rather long draft of a telegram, which will be dispatched today, which gives you a comprehensive picture of what we have done and the reasons therefore, what we propose to do,

---

27 The Western Front had Montgomery's 21st Army Group in the north, Bradley's 12th Army Group in the center and Devers 6th Army Group in the south.
28 The temporary assignment put in place at the height of the Battle of the Bulge.
29 While front line units suffered heavy casualties, and had to carry on fighting even when they were below strength, rear area units continued to operate at full strength.
30 The state of the rear areas would be addressed by General Ben Lear in his role as Deputy Commander of European Theater of Operations, US Army, responsible for Theater Manpower.

and the command system that will be employed. Frankly, there are certain features about continuous insistence upon particular points in the arguments I have seen presented leave me somewhat puzzled.[31]

There has never been any question about our intentions of making the attack north of the Ruhr as strong as it possibly could be built up and placing it under the command of one man. In fact, the staff of the 21st Army Group informed us some time ago that not more than 25 divisions could be sustained in an invasion through that area, yet I and my staff have insisted that they find ways and means of supporting at least 35 divisions. As a result of almost arbitrary action on our part, they are now preparing to do this. All concerned know that I have constantly struggled towards the conditions and the time that that particular invasion could be undertaken on the strongest possible basis.[32]

Another point on which all have agreed is that the Ruhr itself cannot be attacked frontally and that in fact we should stay out of the area as long as we possibly can. The Ruhr, therefore, marks a definite dividing line between practicable channels of approach in our advance into Germany. Consequently, it is a natural division of <u>battle command responsibility</u>. I have repeatedly told my associates and people like the Prime Minister that my intentions were to make the attack north of the Ruhr the main attack, and in the greatest possible strength, and that its operational direction would be under Field Marshal Montgomery. Since the main attacks could eventually involve a considerable greater number of American divisions than are in his entire army group, I think it demonstrates the extent to which I was really to take on my own shoulders responsibility for organizing command under my own conceptions of military requirements and I know that it involves all that one man can handle as a <u>battle</u> commander.[33]

There are two questions upon which there has been definite difference of opinion. Apparently the C.I.G.S. and Montgomery consider that it is perfectly logical to make an attack into Germany on the front from Bonn northward and with the rest of the lines south of Bonn remaining substantially as at present.

The recent German offensive should again prove that if we do not have an easily defended line, we will have to hold in strictly defensive positions a larger number of our own divisions than we are willing to spare from the assaulting forces.

Another point of argument has been the point on the Rhine from which should be initiated the principal <u>supporting</u> task for the main operation. The area Bonn–Cologne has the disadvantage of confronting the attacking force with the most difficult kind of country, immediately it has crossed the river.[34] Assuming that a supporting attack would make any progress whatsoever, Bradley and many others believe that in point of <u>time</u> the attack from Bonn – Cologne alone would be further from junction with the main attack, east of the Ruhr, than would one launched from Frankfurt.[35] This point may eventually prove

31 As far as Eisenhower is concerned he had always pursued a north thrust strategy and the only variations or delays had been introduced to counter situations caused by the Germans.
32 This is 21st Army Group's advance across the Rhine and north of the Ruhr. The number of divisions that could take part was dictated by the terrain and logistics network, in particular the bottleneck at the bridges over the Rhine.
33 The Ruhr is a huge built up area which was easy to defend. It was an area that Eisenhower wanted to capture, to deny Germany its industries, but it was an area he did not want to attack. It was the sensible geographical border between army groups and the attack north of the area was more than enough for one ground commander to control.
34 There is the wooded Bergisches Land east of the two cities and the Westerwald's wooded hills southeast of Bonn. After the experiences in the Hürtgen Forest, Eisenhower wanted to avoid them both.
35 From Frankfurt north there is open country all the way north to Kassel and Paderborn, both east of the Ruhr.

to be completely academic, since under present conditions it may well prove impossible for us to attain the resources and the time to accomplish our first and vitally important winter task, which is the closing of the Rhine from Bonn northward and still be able, without upsetting preparations, later to clean up the Saar basin and threaten the crossing at Frankfurt.

In any event, the whole purpose of any supporting task is to force the enemy to disperse his strength and to permit us the use of all possible crossings and lines of communication, in order to place in Western Germany a concentrated force of sufficient size to complete the conquest.

In every conversation with the C.I.G.S. and others that I have had on this subject, I have emphasized, therefore, the intent (1) to concentrate north of the Ruhr and (2) to launch a supporting attack with troops that were available, after the complete satisfaction of the requirements of the main attack, from such locality as study and continuous examination would indicate to be the best. Conditions of flooding on the river, location of enemy forces, and the developments during the remaining part of the winter, will all have some influence on this particular point.

If the Combined Chiefs of Staff should themselves choose to decide the location from which the supporting attack should preferably be launched, I can accept such a decision loyally and, as always, do my utmost to carry it out. But regardless of such decision I must point out that unless our long defensive flank is situated firmly on an easily defended line, we are going to have immobilized more troops than we can afford.

My ideas on command are included in greater detail in the other telegram dispatched today. But again I point out that the Ruhr is the logical dividing line, and in reaching this obvious conclusion I have submerged my own nationalistic tendencies just as I have ignored the personal ambitions of any individual.

Eisenhower to Marshall   *10 January*   *Ref: S-74461*
This is a personal review of the campaign to date and outline of future plans in answer to your W-88777. Without exception, all of us have agreed from the beginning that the main invasion into Germany, when it becomes possible, should be by the north flank. Terrain, length of our own lines of communications and location of important geographical objectives in Germany, all confirm the necessity of making the principal invasion along the northern line.

Long before D-Day this general concept of operations was outlined by my staff and approved by me.

In the initial rush across France, following the breakthrough at Avranches, several things made it impossible to thrust forward all the troops we then had north of the line Paris – Bonn. The first of these were the difficulty of maintenance. Although we were then driving against a demoralized enemy and had some hope of gaining a bridgehead over the Rhine and the Siegfried Line above Arnhem before he could reorganize and recover himself, this finally proved to be impossible. The enemy succeeded in getting troops into Holland that were capable of making a desperate stand in the Arnhem region, and although I placed the Airborne Army at the disposal of 21st Army Group, the hope of a quick breaching of his final defenses was defeated.[36] During this period, in order to provide for maintenance of the 21st Army Group, I went to the extent of immobilizing three divisions then in Normandy and turned over all of their motor transport to hauling supplies to Montgomery. This provided 500 tons

---

36 Operation MARKET GARDEN, which was launched on 17 September.

a day at Brussels but the attempt failed and it was then obvious that we had to revert to the original pre D-Day plan of opening Antwerp before we could deploy in adequate strength in the north. Verbal and written instructions to 21st Army Group constantly emphasized the need for that port.[37]

A second problem following the breakthrough was that of establishing a firm flank on our right. In southern and southwest France there were still a large number of enemy troops and if these were given the opportunity to drawback, concentrate, and undertake harassing operations against the right flank of our forces, it was manifest that we would have to immobilize a considerable number of divisions for static protective purposes.[38] The cheapest way to protect our own right flank, as well as Devers' left flank as he came up the Rhône Valley, was to join hands with him, thus eliminating the danger to our rear and, moreover, reducing the total German strength by the amount that we could capture behind the two forces. Another factor was to utilize the surplus import capacity through Marseilles to reinforce our main forces in the north. Although joining hands with Devers was obviously a most desirable thing to do, the need for all maintenance resources on the northern flank in exploitation immobilized for a considerable period the bulk of Patton's forces.[39] Throughout that period all priorities in supplies went to 21st Army Group and to the northern flank of Bradley's forces.[40]

The next stage of the operation found us, therefore, with Devers stretched along the Vosges Mountains, with the bulk of 12th Army Group facing the Siegfried line and the 21st Army Group engaged in capturing Antwerp, with its forward troops lying along the Maas River.

It was my own conviction, and it still is, that in order to concentrate north of the Ruhr all the forces needed for a successful invasion of Germany, we must have throughout the rest of the front a very firm defensive line which can be held with minimum forces. The experience of recent weeks has shown the importance of this matter. This line is preferably the Rhine. If we do not, repeat do not, have the Rhine substantially throughout its length, we have always to face up to the proposition that the enemy, protected by his very strong Siegfried fortifications can concentrate swiftly for counter thrusts against our lines of communications.[41] To counter this we will have to station all along the line more troops than we can afford. Moreover, the attainment of the line of the Rhine River would present to us opportunites for threatening the enemy at a number of points, forcing him to disperse his defending forces and thus make easier the invasion to the north of the Ruhr.[42]

In late October and early November, Bradley's directive called for him to make his principal effort towards Bonn – Cologne, while his attacks in the south directed into the Saar valley were to be definitely secondary to the northern attack, with the object of drawing off

---

37 Although Antwerp port was captured on 4 September, it took until the first week of November to clear both banks of the Scheldt estuary, allowing minesweeping to start.

38 This open flank followed the breakthrough at Avranches and the subsequent Battle of the Falaise Pocket in August. While 21st and 12th Army Groups crushed German opposition in the north of France, General Devers' troops were moving quickly up from the south of France.

39 Third Army's advance across France halted on 31 August near the Moselle river, in front of Metz, due to a lack of fuel and supplies, rather than German activity.

40 The allocation of supplies to the northern flank was made to support Eisenhower's original strategy to make the 'principal invasion along the northern line'.

41 The Siegfried Line ran along the German border from Holland to Switzerland and it followed the Rhine along the Alsace sector in the south; there were double lines of fortifications at vulnerable points.

42 If the Allies held the Rhine, the situation was reversed; the Germans had to spread their reserves to cover many danger points while the Allies could concentrate theirs.

enemy forces.[43] Because of the nature of the ground in the north, Bradley could use only a limited number of divisions at a time. Simultaneously with the effort he could make there, he could, with the aid of Devers, exert an effective threat to the enemy in the Saar valley, possibly even pushing him back across the Rhine.

However, it must be emphasized again that all these moves were principally <u>to permit the greatest possible eventual concentration in the north</u>. As early as the 1st of November the possibility began to be considered of a hostile counter offensive, including his capability of driving westward through the Ardennes region. I personally discussed this matter with Bradley, but his attitude was that it would be an unprofitable region for the enemy to use and if he made such an attack, it would subsequently lead to our advantage. At the worst it was a reasonable sector in which to take a risk and risks had to be taken somewhere.[44] With respect to this one point, Bradley and I, and so far as I know, everyone else with whom I have ever discussed the matter, felt about as follows: We do not, repeat not, believe that the hastily trained Volkssturm divisions could be used effectively in an offensive.[45] We did not, repeat not, consider that in winter time the enemy could supply a major thrust permanently through the Ardennes. In view of the strength we could finally bring to bear, we did not, repeat not, consider that the enemy could capture, through the tortuous communication lines of the Ardennes, any really vital targets, which were manifestly Liège, Namur and/or Verdun. Therefore we thought the Ardennes attack would be a strategic mistake for him.[46]

However, desirable as it was to throw back or destroy the enemy in the south, we were constantly developing the build up in the north and the First and Ninth Armies continued to have priority in ammunition, replacements and the newly arriving units. Moreover, Bradley definitely limited the time available to Patton for making one more effort to achieve a victory in the Saar valley. Regardless of results he was then to begin the transfer of his divisions to the north. The date fixed for Patton's final attack was December 19th. In the meantime the 21st Army Group, with only a total of 14 divisions, was limited to the defensive on the whole northern flank. Terrain and flooding conditions in that area permitted no, repeat no, chance of an offensive except for one under frost conditions in January or February between the Meuse and the Rhine, to clean out that area in preparation for a crossing of the Rhine.

This was the situation when the German counter offensive began and you are acquainted with all the moves made since that date in order to defeat the attempt.

Our ultimate plan is to cross the Rhine north of the Ruhr in great force. From this we have never varied and the only differences in concepts of which I am aware, involve the preliminary tasks that must be accomplished and the possible location of supporting attacks. Future operations divide themselves into three distinct phases:

---

43 Bradley had to capture the two cities to give access to the southern route around the Ruhr. However, Aachen had taken all October to clear while the Hürtgen Forest would take until mid February to clear (operations were scaled down during the Battle of the Ardennes in December and January). Third Army also had to call off its attacks in the Saar area to reinforce the Ardennes.
44 Although intelligence did not notice Army Group B's build up of units opposite the Ardennes front Eisenhower and Bradley had considered the possibility of a German counterattack there.
45 The Volkstürm divisions had been raised in the autumn by lowering conscription standards and giving them fewer heavy weapons. The Volkstürm had opened the attack, to clear the roads for the armored divisions; in many cases they took too long to take their objectives, delaying Army Group B's tight schedule.
46 Eisenhower and Bradley felt they could hold the Ardennes with the minimum of troops because the rough terrain, poor road network, lack of vital targets and bad winter weather would limit the German advance. Eisenhower's retrospective view of the Ardennes offensive was that it was a 'strategic mistake' because of the amount of men and material that the Germans had lost and could not replace in time to defend the Rhine.

a)   Defeat the enemy west of the Rhine and close the Rhine north of the Moselle
b)   To force the passage of the Rhine
c)   To advance east of the Rhine

To accomplish phase (a), I intend to go on the defensive south of the Moselle and to develop two main thrusts north of the Moselle. Firstly by 12th Army Group on the axis Prum – Bonn[47] and secondly by 21st Army Group south east from Nijmegen between the Rhine and the Meuse.[48] These operations will bring us on to the Rhine at the essential crossing places between Nijmegen and Wesel.

To accomplish phase (b) I will have to take the following factors into account:

1.   The risks involved in crossing the Rhine on the narrow front Nijmegen – Wesel.
2.   The conditions of the river itself and of the flooded areas on each side during the spring. These vary in different sectors through the spring until June.
3.   The extent to which subsidiary attacks can be relied upon to divert enemy forces from the sector of our main attack.

It will be evident to you that my plan for crossing the Rhine can not, repeat not, be fully crystallized now but must await the development of the situation in Europe as a whole and on this front in particular.

Phase (c) is still more indefinable but my plan is predicted on deploying 25 divisions north of the Ruhr, which represent the maximum which can be maintained in the area. The best location for subsidiary supporting attacks is under constant study, but there will not, repeat not, be two main attacks.

To sum up the foregoing, there is no, repeat no, difference among any of us about the necessity for having a concentrated force in the north when the crossing of the Rhine is attempted. My plans call for the availability of all the forces that can possibly be sustained. The point that we must consider is, what must our own general situation be when we are ready to undertake this great operation, without fear of our flanks and without expending, for purely defensive purposes, more strength than we can afford. Again, I must say that the thing that has guided us all the way through these operations has been the great hope of retaining defensive flanks that were strong, and then to commit to the invasion of Germany the strongest possible forces with the main effort north of the Ruhr.

With respect to command; as will be seen from the above plans for driving up to the Rhine, and for subsequent operations into Germany, there are three main areas of effort. The first is in the north, were hostile forces are to be defeated west of the Rhine and preparations made for crossing north of the Ruhr. The next is in the center, where the forces are to drive along the line Prum–Bonn, and prepare in that region to make a crossing in support of the northern thrust. At the back of these attacks will be a reserve groupment ready to reinforce success. South of the Moselle the whole task is defensive unless opportunities (which now seem rather remote) later should open into the Frankfurt area.

---

47 12th Army Group planned Operation LUMBERJACK, a pincer movement with First Army advancing southeast to the confluence of the Ahr and Rhine rivers before turning south to meet Third Army's advance northeast through the Eifel. It would bring 12th Army Group to the Rhine between Cologne and Koblenz. However, it would not be able to start until 1 March.
48 21st Army Group planned Operations VERITABLE and GRENADE to secure the west bank of the Rhine between Nijmegen and Düsseldorf. VERITABLE had been known as VALEDICTION and was supposed to start in January; it was cancelled due to bad weather. GRENADE was also delayed when the Germans flooded the area by opening the Roer dams.

In this event, Devers supporting threats and moves across the Rhine would be much more effective, as before pointed out.

These, then, on the three general tasks, each of which is to be given to a senior ground commander on the spot.

As you know, I have constantly in this war tried to eliminate purely nationalistic considerations when these conflict with the military requirements of given situations. So far as possible, however, troops and battle commanders should be of the same nationality and we should depart from this method only when it is necessary.

I do not, repeat not, see how a Commander in Chief of Ground Forces would help to secure any better coordination or better direction of the battle than is possible at present.

If we should set up a separate commander for ground operation, we would have great duplication in personnel and communications. Moreover, such an officer would necessarily have to determine priorities in allocation of divisions, of supplies, of development of communication, and decide upon broad ground strategy, all of which are functions of my own headquarters. This ground commander in chief would have to exercise command through army group commanders, and these latter officers are already in such high positions, that for their respective sections at the front they are, each, the ground commander in chief.[49]

The proposition of setting up two ground commanders would contemplate a division of the front probably along the Moselle River.[50] This would put eventually some 45 to 50 American divisions and 14 British and British satellite divisions, under one commander for offensive purposes and give the other one principally a defensive job. In view of the composition of this Allied Force, and the personalities involved, I do not, repeat not, believe this would work well.[51] Moreover, I do not, repeat not, consider it as logical a division of battle command responsibilities as that described above in my current plan.

I repeat that I do not, repeat not, believe any single individual could, or should, exercise a greater measure of control over this extensive front than is now being exercised. The organization for command is, of course, not, repeat not, ideal, but it is the most practicable one, considering the questions of nationality involved and the personalities available within the theater.

Because of the great size of the land forces now engaged on this front, it would be more convenient for me if my Deputy Supreme Commander was an experienced ground officer rather than air. In spite of my personal official admiration for Tedder he is not, repeat not, in a position to help me by visits and conferences with troop commanders. If I could have a man of fine personality, respected by all and willing to serve my deputy and not, repeat not, under independent charter from my superiors, it would be most helpful. As a corollary to such a scheme, I would want Spaatz named Air Commander-in-Chief. I am afraid it would be impossible to find such a deputy as I describe. The only one I can think of myself would be Alexander and manifestly he is not, repeat not, available.[52]

---

49 The strategy and geography of the campaign suits the existing organization of three Army Group commanders. Only Ninth US Army would serve under a commander of a different nationality (excluding the French Army in 6th Army Group). The addition of a deputy would also add an extra unwanted layer to the chain of command.
50 At Trier, southeast of Luxembourg; splitting 12th Army's sector.
51 In other words it would not be wise to give Montgomery command of the northern offensive sector and the majority of US divisions, while Bradley held the southern defensive sector.
52 While Eisenhower does not want a deputy ground commander, he does want a Theater deputy to carry out tasks delegated by his own Deputy.

Marshall to Eisenhower   *10 January*   *Ref: W-89338*

For your information, the British Chiefs of Staff submitted to the Combined Chiefs of Staff today a memorandum on strategy in Northwest Europe, the gist of which follows:

The British Chiefs feel the strategy in Northwest Europe should be reviewed by the Combined Chiefs of Staff and the opportunity at the next conference should be taken to discuss it. They cite SCAF 78, in which Eisenhower considered that the best opportunity of defeating the enemy lies in striking at the Ruhr and the Saar, and that the main effort will be on the left. They mention FACS 78, in which the Combined Chiefs of Staff direct attention to advantages of the northern line of approach into Germany and SCAF 82, in which you state measures have been instituted to give full support to the advance on the northern line of approach. The British Chiefs then review the situation in the opening of the enemy counterstroke when fifteen Allied divisions opposed ten enemy divisions in the Geilenkirchen – Monschau area[53] while in the Merzig–Strasbourg area,[54] sixteen Allied divisions opposed five German equivalent divisions, thus indicating major concentration in the north had not yet been achieved.

The British Chiefs mentioned the informal meeting with you before the British offensive in which you stated your plans to be; to keep up pressure on the enemy during the winter, to clear him back to the Rhine, and to launch (probably not before May, 1945) strong converging attacks; one attack to be carried out north of the Ruhr by 21st Army Group, with a United States Army of ten divisions, and the other on the line Frankfurt – Kassel by 12th Army Group, with the possibility of an additional subsidiary attack in the Bonn area.[55]

The British Chiefs consider that of the 80 to 85 divisions you will have next spring, from 15 to 20 will have to hold the defensive part of the line and that the remainder are not sufficient for two main attacks. Hence, it is important to decide on one major thrust, and to allocate overwhelming strength to this thrust to keep up the momentum. Only forces which cannot be employed in the main thrust should be used in subsidiary operations. Operations this winter should bear direct relation to the main front in the spring.

One man should be directly responsible to the ground forces employed in the main thrust and the British suggest one ground commander for the front north of the northern boundary of Luxembourg. The British recognize your plan will be influenced by the present fighting and by the results of Tedder's mission. They recommend dispatch of a message to you, asking you submit by 28th January an account of the progress of your operations, the effect of the German counteroffensive, and your detailed appreciation and plan of operation for this winter and next spring. They also proposed to include in the message paragraphs for your guidance, to the effect that all available resources should be concentrated in the spring on one main thrust, which should be made in the north if tactical considerations allow. They further propose to point out to you that the best results would be achieved if one man were given operational control and coordination of all ground forces for the main thrust, thus necessitating one ground commander north of Luxembourg. This ends substance of British proposal.

---

53 This was the Aachen sector; including the Hürtgen Forest sector where First Army had been fighting since mid September and would continue to do so until 10 February.

54 Third and Seventh Army sectors stretching from Luxembourg, through Saarbrücken to Strasbourg.

55 The clearing of the west bank of the Rhine was achieved two months earlier than the estimate of May 1945.

Marshall to Eisenhower   *10 January*   *Ref: W-89604*

The U.S. Chiefs presented to the Combined Chiefs of Staff this morning a memorandum stating that they consider that only that portion of the proposed British message, which requests a report and appreciation and plan be dispatched to you, and a further decision on matters raised in the British paper should await your reply.[56]

Marshall to Eisenhower   *11 January*   *Ref: W-90175*

Our first reaction to your S-74461 is agreement in the soundness of your estimate and intentions. General Handy and I have been discussing the advisability of showing the message to Admiral Leahy[57] and the President because of your last paragraph,[58] which may be taken as indicating by weakening on your part under the heavy pressure of the press and British officialdom to get some higher British military official into your general management of the Ground Forces. Frankly, Alexander's appointment as a deputy would mean two things I think. First, that the British had won the major point in getting control of the ground operations in which their divisions of necessity will play such a minor part and, for the same reason, we are bound to suffer very heavy casualties; and second, the man being who he is and our experience being what it has been, you would have great difficulty in offsetting that direct influence of the Prime Minister.[59]

I have thought all the time that you have lacked qualified individuals to offset your tremendous involvements and have tried to assist you with overcoming this deficiency in your setup. Bradley was my first offer, Bull the second, Bonesteel the third, but in each case we ended with no one to be your eyes and ears and legs for a continuous observation and discussion with top commanders along the front. Have you a suitable individual you can use for this? Is there anyone here you would want? Would it not be wise to also have a British officer on this same job?

Eisenhower to Marshall   *12 January*   *Ref: S-74687*

I am glad to get your reactions as stated in your W-90175. The two disadvantages mentioned by you to my use of Alexander's name had not, repeat not, occurred to me. I would seriously object to any officer been named as 'Deputy for Ground Operations'. My present deputy, or any other one that I might have, would have to function exclusively without portfolio and in the activities there would be delegated to him by me.[60] I was trying to illustrate the kind of man that would be acceptable to me personally because of the fine relationships I have had with Alexander him in the past and because, that so far as I know, he was never in that association in any slightest way violated the requirements of personal and official loyalty. My present deputy is equally a splendid man. The only difficulty being that experienced senior ground officers, particularly on the British side,

---

56 Leaving out suggestions for changing the command structure.

57 Fleet Admiral William D. Leahy, Roosevelt's Chief of Staff.

58 Eisenhower stated that the only man he would want as deputy ground commander was General Alexander and he was not available, to illustrate the caliber of man he desired.

59 Marshall is referring to Montgomery who they did not want as deputy ground commander because of the political and media backlash in the US. They were also both aware of Churchill's influence over Montgomery.

60 Eisenhower wants a deputy, but not to take command over the three army group commanders. He wants a deputy to deal with a host of other problems that take up his time: manpower, logistics, lines of communications, all of which have a huge impact on the efficiency of the Allied forces.

assume that he is incapable of discussing intelligently any important matter pertaining to the ground accepting the single field of air–ground operation.[61]

In view of what you have said, I think it is probably wise to make no shift in our present arrangements, except I will bring Rooks into my own headquarters. This will give me a team of Rooks[62] and Whiteley,[63] who is respected by the British, to stay on the road constantly as my eyes and ears. Smith is, of course, highly respected in all echelons and he always helps out in critical times in this way, to supplement my own efforts. Bull is also out a great deal of the time.

The only time Alexander was ever mentioned to me by the British was most secretly and personally when I was told, I think by the Prime Minister, that there was some chance that the Air Ministry wanted to get Tedder as number two under Portal.[64] They asked if that request should be made, and in addition, <u>if the Combined Chiefs of Staff should decide at any time to strip the Mediterranean to such an extent that there was no real job there for Alexander</u>, whether I would be content with Alexander as a deputy. Feeling as I do toward him, I naturally answered in the affirmative, although I did point out that my deputy was assigned by the Combined Chiefs of Staff and that I was merely expressing a personal agreement if all these eventualities should ever come about.[65]

Since the eventualities that the Prime Minister mentioned seem to be rather remote, I gave no further thought to his question. Thinking only that he wanted to know that Alexander's association with me, in the position of 'Deputy without Portfolio', which is made clear, would be acceptable to me.

It may be that after I have discussed the matter thoroughly with Tedder, I would ask the Combined Chiefs of Staff to assign Spaatz as my Air Commander, in addition to his other duties. This will take some more thought on my part.

The Sinking of the Leopoldville

Eisenhower to Marshall   12 January   *Ref: S-74859*

Surles has recommended that as soon as security permits, the War Department issue a brief statement of loss of life and survivors of the *Leopoldville*. We realize that early release is desirable from a public relations viewpoint. However, ANCXF objects and has passed proposed release to British Admiralty who oppose release and express specified desire to maintain strict silence in accordance with existing policy. In addition, our own G-2 opposes the release of information, which will be of considerable value to the enemy in his efforts to confirm information of movements of troop convoys from the Channel ports.

For your private information, I am informed by Kirk that the great loss of life on the *Leopoldville*, which remained afloat for more than an hour and sank within four miles of shore, was due to <u>at least</u> to poor seamanship and leadership on the part of the Royal Navy commodore commanding the convoy. This may get out, and we would then be exposed again to the charge of concealing weakness, since, as you know, another transport was torpedoed a few days later in mid-channel under much worse conditions with the loss of only six men.

---

61 So while Eisenhower is happy with how Tedder conducts himself as his deputy, it is the British Army commanders who have difficulties working with him. In return, Tedder criticized Montgomery and had in the past advocated Montgomery's removal from command.
62 Major-General Lowell W. Rooks (1893–1973) became Deputy Chief of Staff, G-3, Plans and Operations, SHAEF Headquarters working for General Bull.
63 General Bull's British deputy in G-3 Operations.
64 Air Chief Marshal Charles F.A. Portal, 1st Viscount Portal of Hungerford, KG, GCB, OM, DSO and Bar, MC, RAF (1893–1971), Chief of the Air Staff.
65 It appears that Churchill had already sounded out Eisenhower's off the record thoughts on Alexander.

Matter has been passed to British Admiralty delegation in Washington, and I suggest that Surles get in touch with them with a view to agreeing on earliest possible date for brief release. He should advise Public Relations Division here 48 hours in advance, so that announcement can be coordinated.[66]

General Promotions[67]

Marshall to Eisenhower   *12 January*   *Ref: W-90769*

I am now assembling the names for proposal to the President for the next General Officer promotions, which I hope to submit within the next few days. Is there any reason why Simpson's name should not go in for a temporary Lieutenant General? He holds that rank now by virtue of commanding the Fourth Army on the West Coast.[68]

I have a difficult problem to solve regarding advancements to the grade of General both as to timing and as to various Theaters. Bradley, of course, should be advanced, but having in mind the following factors, what is your personal view: the operation in the Ardennes is not completed, the fighting on the Seventh Army front continues critical near Strasbourg. What about Patton and Devers? The tremendous air effort must be recognized and Spaatz's promotion appears to be in order. The command situation in Italy seems to involve two generals, if any are made, that is Clark and McNarney.

In the southwest Pacific, the battle in the central valley of Luzon is now over.[69] Whether or not it will be a successful operation, though I certainly anticipate it will, remains to be seen. Krueger conquered Leyte, killing almost 65,000 Japs on the island. He has already made a successful landing on Lingayen.[70] He reaches 64 in a few days. Kenney has done a perfectly remarkable job from southern New Guinea and Port Moresby, north to Luzon.[71] It was his urgent leadership that guaranteed the foothold on the north side of New Guinea, Buna and Gona, to which he transported a division, tanks and heavy guns and bombers without airfields. Somervell, with a colossal job, continues as a Lieutenant General. Also Handy as Deputy Chief of Staff.

---

66 The torpedo trapped 300 men on the lower decks but the damage did not seem to be bad. When HMS *Brilliant* pulled alongside, Captain Limbor ordered all but essential crew to take to the lifeboats. Men started to jump the gap, in difficult conditions, and although some drowned, the *Brilliant* took around 500 men on board before it was full. The Convoy Commander, John Pringle, had ordered his ships to search for the U-Boat but the Cherbourg rescue craft were delayed and communication problems increased due to the Christmas holidays. After two explosions the ship began to sink rapidly and Limbor gave the order to abandon ship; with no crew to organize the life rafts, men jumped into the water. Many drowned quickly because their life jackets were over their winter coats; others succumbed to the freezing waters before the rescue ships arrived.

67 This cable sums up the magnitude of the problem facing General Marshall when he considered promotions: he had to balance the European and Mediterranean Theaters; what responsibility each man had and how long for; how successful each man had been; the balance between front line commanders and staff officers; and age and reputation. Here Marshall presents his dilemma as he looks for assistance from Eisenhower.

68 Fourth Army was dealing with the reception of divisions arriving from the US. It would be renamed Ninth US Army when it went into combat under Simpson (continuing the US tradition of using odd numbers for its armies).

69 Luzon is the largest island in the Philippines. General Walter Krueger's (1881–1967) Sixth Army had just landed on 9 January and surrounded the capital, Manila, by 11 February. By the end of the campaign over 200,000 Japanese soldiers had been killed; US casualties were fewer than 38,000.

70 Leyte is one of the larger Philippine islands. Krueger's Sixth Army began landing on 17 October 1944 and formal resistance ended on 22 December, reducing the Japanese hold on the islands; US casualties were over 15,500 while Japanese were 49,000. Lingayen Gulf is on the coast of Luzon where Sixth Army landed on 9 January.

71 General George C. Kenney (1889–1977), commander of the Allied air forces in the Southwest Pacific Area (SWPA).

Naturally he would be much easier in dealing with Congress to submit a few names at a time, but what about the hard feeling developing in various Theaters because of seemingly invidious comparisons? The Navy has a much simpler situation. They are submitting, I think, but four names, two in the Department and two in the field. The equivalent of our Group Commanders, that is, Halsey and Spruance, are already full Admirals.[72]

Let me have your confidential, personal views regarding the foregoing.

I notice in this morning's cables that McAuliffe of the 101st Airborne Division is being given divisional commander of the 103rd.[73] Should his name be added to the current list, as he has already proven himself in battle? Are there any men who have conspicuously distinguished themselves in the desperate fighting of the past few weeks who should probably be put ahead of other men on your list on which I am working? I wish to be certain that the fighter in the field, not realizing the time-consuming procedure leading up to each list, will not feel that his sacrifices and the efforts of being discounted in favor of some other fellow who has not been a party to the present desperate battle. Don't delay too long in order to be very accurate, because I cannot wait here.

Eisenhower to Marshall   *14 January*   *Ref: S-74971*
This is in reply to your W-90769 regarding promotions. The first paragraph deals with the subject of four star generals. I believe that the first consideration should be to accord this rank to relatively few officers and to preserve its traditional prestige in our army. I understand that the authorization for five star rank automatically terminates at the end of the war. Only those persons occupying positions of very great responsibility, and who have established a long record of good solid accomplishment there in should be given four star rank. I think your first list should be relatively small, covering the men whose selection would be universally approved. Thereafter, at intervals, you could make a promotion occasionally as a special recognition for services along the line indicated above. You now have only Stilwell in four star grade.[74] I believe the Navy already has Stark, Ingersoll, Halsey, Spruance and possibly others,[75] and is now nominating four. In these circumstances you could make six or seven on your first list and be well on the conservative side, considering the size of the army.

Specifically I think that both Somervell and Handy should be promoted.

In this theater I think that only Spaatz and Bradley should be promoted on the first list, but I believe that the omission of either of these names would be a mistake. I consider Spaatz to be the best all-round air commander that I know. While true that the battle of the Ardennes is not over, I should like to point out the fine record of solid accomplishment that is behind Bradley all the way from the time you sent him to me in February 1943. Moreover, the battle of the Ardennes is one of those incidents that is to be anticipated

---

72 Fleet Admiral William F. Halsey, Jr, USN (1882–1959), commander of the Third US Fleet, and Admiral Raymond A. Spruance, USN (1886–1969), Deputy Commander in Chief, Pacific Fleet.
73 General Anthony McAuliffe (1898–1975) had commanded the 101st Airborne Division during the defence of Bastogne in the Ardennes battle. He is attributed with replying with the word 'Nuts' when asked to surrender. General Charles C. Haffner Jr (1895–?) had been relieved due to ill health.
74 General Joseph W. Stilwell (1883–1946), nicknamed 'Uncle Joe' or 'Vinegar Joe', until recently Commander in Chief US India-Burma Theater of Operations, now Commander in Chief, Army Ground Forces.
75 Admiral Harold R. Stark (1880–1972) had been Commander of US Naval Forces in Europe until his relief following the Pearl Harbor enquiry, when his role as Chief of Naval Operations during the lead up to the Japanese attack was severely criticized. Admiral Royal E. Ingersoll (1883–1976), recently Commander in Chief, US Atlantic Fleet and now Commander, Western Sea Frontier and Deputy Commander in Chief, US Fleet/Deputy Chief of Naval Operations.

along a great line where contending forces are locked up in battle with varying fortunes in particular sections on the front. The real answer is the leadership exhibited by the commander in meeting his problems. I consider that throughout this affair Bradley has handled himself admirably.[76]

With respect to Devers, although he is an army group commander I am not yet ready to make a recommendation for his promotion. At a later date I will give you a more detailed evaluation of him. Patton has done a remarkable job but his promotion would simply involve you in argument and I do not believe it necessary. I probably will recommend Patton at a later date, possibly even ahead of Devers. Patton was, I think, the _first_ man to lead an American army into battle in this war and he has done a fine job throughout. But I repeat that he should wait for a little time.

If you promoted anyone at all in the Mediterranean on your first list, it should be McNarney in recognition of the great work he did as your deputy. That theater has diminished in importance from a U.S. viewpoint but you might consider that your senior officer there should be raised one notch. So far as my personal conviction about McNarney is concerned, I consider him one of our very finest officers. Moreover, Clark has been a group commander only two months or so.

In the Pacific it seems to me that Kruger was a special case. You do not have an army group commander there and moreover his age makes it impossible for him to be an embarrassment to you when you have to reorganize after the shooting is over. This is an important factor. I do not believe that any of my army commanders would be resentful if Kruger were named. I realize also that Kenny has done a remarkable job and I assume the size of his forces considerable. Therefore I see no reason why he should not be named, theoretically I suppose Eaker would have equal claim with Kenny but after all, Eaker works strategically under Spaatz and should at least wait until after Spaatz has held the rank for a period. I think it is a nicely balanced decision as to whether to make Kenny now or after waiting a little while.

New subject: With respect to Simpson, he should by all means been made a temporary Lieutenant General. He is excellent in every respect.

I think you would like to know that three of our corps commanders, Gerow, Collins and Ridgeway, have added in this battle to their former higher reputations. Without exception they are universally regarded as three of the finest officers we have and if any vacancies ever occur here in army command, these three men would be selected in the order named above. With respect to them Montgomery said as follows: "It must be most exceptional to find such a good lot of corps commanders gathered together in one army."

What to do with the 106th Division?

Eisenhower to Marshall 15 January *Ref: S-75091*

The problem for rehabilitating 106th Division is a serious one because of the loss of entire units. To attempt this rehabilitation here would be most expensive and slow.[77] I believe that the Staff has already made certain proposals to you, but I am sending this personal telegram to find out whether it would be possible for you to send us a couple of separate

---

76 It was during combat rather than training that a general showed his true leadership qualities.

77 Two regiments of the 106th Division were surrounded on the Schnee Eifel and had to surrender during the opening days of the Battle of the Bulge.

infantry regiments, preferably with their supporting artillery battalion, if this were possible. While, in the south, we have the separate Japanese unit that could be used if available, the fact is that it will not be free for some months in the future.[78] I will appreciate any help you can give is in the matter.[79]

Review of the European Situation and SHAEF's Needs

Eisenhower to Marshall   15 January   *Ref: S-75090*

In prior telegrams to you I have reviewed operations to date, including the basic purposes of the past operations in the south and the center. I have also outlined future plans, including the command system I expect to employ. The only thing to be added about plans is that they must be flexible. If we jam our head against a concentrated defense at a selected spot, we must be able to go forward elsewhere. Flexibility requires reserves.[80]

The only parts of your W-88482 that are still answered are your requests for a review of the general European situation and my estimate of strength needed to force a quick decision. The two subjects are, of course, closely related.

The worst of conditions in Europe for us would be:

a) A weak and ineffectual Russian offensive. (I do not even mention the lack of Russian offensive, for without this a quick decision cannot be obtained. We would have to mobilize much French manpower and additional U.S. divisions.)
b) A partial enemy withdrawal from Italy without compensatory reinforcement here.
c) Continued enemy withdrawal from Norway to reinforce here.

The opposite of these three conditions would represent our best case.[81]

Under the worst conditions described the Germans could keep on the Western Front about 100 divisions and maintain them in personnel and material. On the other hand, for the above factors to be in our favor then we figure that we would maintain here about 80 under strength divisions. If the Russian offensive really gets to rolling, then there should be a gradual decline in the enemy strength.

I am personally optimistic concerning the enemy difficulties in other theaters and if our Air Forces get in a few more good blows against his synthetic oil, he is really going to be stretched.

We have at present 71 divisions, with many of the U.S. divisions seriously under strength in infantry: the French divisions have at present, except for one, a low combat value. By spring we will have 85 divisions (including six airborne) with five to eight new French divisions training and equipping. By that time I hope the present five French divisions will have their combat value largely restored. The French divisions are always a questionable asset.

Our biggest problems are the enemy frontier defenses, artificial and natural. They are extremely formidable, and entirely aside from the cost of piercing them on a selected front, their greatest effect is to enable the enemy to concentrate safely for a counterattack at our

---

78 A regiment of Japanese nationals who had emigrated to the US had been formed and was heading for the Italian front.
79 106th Division was rebuilt in March and it ran prisoner of war camps along the Rhine until the end of the war. It received, screened, processed and discharged over one million German PoWs.
80 Eisenhower had to be decisive in planning and flexible in execution.
81 These three actions would require Hitler to withdraw his troops from outlying fronts to defend the Fatherland. In all three cases the Führer refused, working in SHAEF's favor.

lines of communication. <u>Unless we get a good natural line for the defensive portions of our long front, we will use up a lot of divisions in defense.</u> The line ought to be, substantially, the Rhine, although here and there it might not be worth the cost to eliminate extremely strongly constructed bridgeheads.

Should the Russian offensives be strong and sustained, I estimate that with the forces we will have, when the good weather starts, it may well be possible to defeat the enemy on our front, but we would be justified in expecting quick success only after we have closed the Rhine throughout its length, concentrated heavily in the north, and staged a definite supporting secondary attack somewhere to the south of the Ruhr. Naturally this expectancy would be greater if our divisional strength were greater. The reason for this is that for a quick decision, I should not be confined by the adoption of single course of action. North of the Ruhr is the invasion route of first importance. But this is equally obvious to the Germans, and if he concentrates in its immediate defense, I may not have the necessary overwhelming superiority to force a satisfactory breakthrough. In the interests of a speedy decision I should, therefore, have behind me the ability to maneuver. For example, the ability to advance also on Frankfurt and Kassel, rather than to rely on one thrust in the north. If success on the secondary front were to be achieved and exploited, additional divisional strength would be necessary.

I consider that of the 85 divisions available in the early summer, we will need in the defense and in the reserve:

a) 25 if we have the Rhine.
b) 35 with the line as at present south of Bonn but with the Colmar Pocket eliminated.
c) 45 if the line is substantially as at present.[82]

Omitting the six airborne divisions, I should be left with some 54, 44, 34 divisions for offensive purposes under these three cases respectively. In any case, 35 divisions must be set aside ultimately for a full scale offensive in the north. In order to be able to put in subsidiary offences at Frankfurt or elsewhere, I should need probably none under the first case, 10 under the second and at least 20 under the third. These 10 or 20 are not in sight except by intensification of the French rearmament program and possibly by transfer of two or three from other theaters. This fact brings up again the great desirability of destroying German forces west of the Rhine, and closing up to the river throughout our front. It also shows how definitely the success and direction of the Russian offensive affects us.

If the Russian attack approves ineffectual, we may be restricted by the enemy's strength to limited operations in the meanwhile. With our present forces, and the prospective build-up outlined above, I do not consider we shall meet with any serious reverse. However, in these circumstances we may be faced, initially at least, with some 100 divisions, although later the resumed Russian offensive may develop great power and draw back some forces over to that front. Moreover, the Germans will have obtained a respite during the intervening period of restricted operations to regroup their losses, rehabilitate their forces and strengthen their divisions. Our own defensive problems would be greater. In this event, <u>to insure quick success</u>, I should have to have the additional 20 divisions and definitely close the Rhine throughout as a preliminary to the great invasion. The alternative would be time and attrition.

---

82 Clearly the more of the west bank of the Rhine that the Allies held, the more reserves could be moved to support 21st Army Group's attack north of the Ruhr.

Throughout this discussion I am assuming that our divisions will be kept have to be kept up to strength in men and material.

I consider that airborne operations may play a large part in the forcing of the Rhine. Our present resources allow for a simultaneous lift of two out of our six airborne divisions. To maintain this present level in troop carrier aircraft, it will be necessary to increase the present planned inflow in this Theater.[83]

Tactical Air Forces: I consider that the British tactical air forces are adequate. But to provide sufficient force for tactical employment for the U.S. front, I shall require additional strength under the plan somewhat as follows or its equivalent:

1) Transfer of the Twelfth Air Force from the Italian Theater to 6th Army Group front, less medium and light bomber units, and less those units essential in the Italian Theater for defensive fighting and less the Spitfire squadrons at present in the Twelfth Air Force.
2) Sufficient fighter/bomber aircraft to raise the total number of aircraft in each group, including the Twelfth Air Force groups transferred as above, up to 100 aircraft.
3) One group of reconnaissance aircraft in addition to that group within the Twelfth Air Force.

Note: I shall require no additional medium or light bomber groups provided the present planned inflow is maintained.

Strategic Air Forces: The strategical bomber forces that will be available as of April 1st are considered adequate for the implementation of the strategical air plan. This plan is mainly directed against the production of the German jet propelled aircraft,[84] his oil supplies, armament factories, naval targets and communications, with an overriding priority of coordination with the ground attacks. I am, however, concerned about the development of the German jet propelled aircraft and the production of our own counterpart must receive as much consideration as does the reduction of German jet production.

The additions I require, in fighters for tactical air forces, may cause some delay in the resupply of the P-47s to the French Air Force. If so, every effort should be made to alleviate this shortage.

Naval: I have at present available balanced amphibian lift for one reinforced division with gunfire support ships, which should be adequate to ensure the reduction of the Dutch and German islands as the Army's seaward flank advances up the coast. The ships and craft are now employed in the cross channel service vital to the support of the army.[85]

In addition to the forces already available to me for the protection of ports and sweeping of channels, the Admiralty have made available further light forces to counter the present attacks by E-Boats, midget submarines and other similar types of craft. It is appreciated that this attack will be maintained, probably on an increasing scale, and it is desirable that the Combined Chiefs of Staff should not press for the transfer of coastal, minesweeping

83 Two airborne divisions 6th British and 17th American, would be used for Operation VARSITY, 21st Army Group's crossing of the Rhine either side of Wesel.
84 The Me262 jet propelled aircraft.
85 Royal Navy landing craft of Rhine Force U ferried Second British and Ninth US Army cross the Rhine during Operation VARSITY; more landing craft were needed for other Rhine crossings farther south.

and escort forces to other theaters until the full requirement to meet both this attack and the renewed U-Boat offensive are clear.

Norway and Denmark: Seaborne entries into Norway and Denmark before Operation APOSTLE have been studied as a means of shortening the war, but are considered impractical as the diversion of the shipping and military forces necessary to ensure success would militate seriously against the main effort to cross the Rhine.[86]

Sweden: I have considered the effect on the enemy should Sweden enter the war, and conclude that if she should do, and was able to hold their own without Allied support other than by air, it would be to our advantage. But in no circumstances do we wish to accumulate further commitments which would divert effort from the main front.[87]

Administration: I am not sending you detailed requirements in this cable of the various administrative requirements that we have. But you will realize that we shall want additional service and supporting troops for any additional combat forces you can make available, and we have at present critical deficiencies in certain service troops and items of ordnance equipment, which require adjustment. Moreover, large increases will be required for certain types of supply, particularly ammunition, if the increased forces are to be effective.

To Summarize: Requirements here necessarily depend on the action undertaken on the Russian front.[88] Our major requirements to ensure a quick conclusion are:

If a markedly successful Russian offensive is maintained and if the Rhine can be substantially closed, our planned strength should be sufficient, if fully maintained and supported. If these conditions are not met, we will have greater needs in strength as above indicated and more time will be required.

Provision of existing critical shortages in equipment and ammunition and provision of additional supporting and service troops for any additional divisions are located.

Additional air forces as listed above and with emphasis on jet propelled the aircraft.

This telegram should be read in conjunction with recent ones I have sent you on related subjects. Acknowledge.

Montgomery Hands Back Command of his Ardennes Sector
Eisenhower to Bradley and Montgomery 15 January   *Ref: S-75036*
It seems to me that operations are so developing that VII and VIII Corps may join hands

---

86 Operation APOSTLE was a plan to invade Norway using Force 134, a force of Norwegian, British and American troops stationed in Scotland. 12,000 Norwegian police troops based in neutral Sweden would move in to take control. SHAEF would also consider deploying troops from the Western Front in case of emergency. Two scenarios were considered: RANKIN C assumed that the German garrison in Norway would surrender after a general unconditional surrender; RANKIN B assumed that part of the Norway garrison redeployed into Germany, leaving it vulnerable to attack.

87 SHAEF was having enough difficulties maintaining its own logistics.

88 The huge Vistula–Oder and East Prussian Offensives started on 12 and 13 January respectively; by the end of the month Soviet troops were only 50 miles from Berlin.

firmly tomorrow or the next day, thus squeezing out XXX Corps.[89] I intend, therefore, to direct that First Army revert to Bradley's command, midnight 16th/17th January[90] in accordance with my outline plan of 31 December. Should the situation not develop as I anticipate and should an emergency develop calling for the new reversion of command on an earlier or later date, I want you to establish direct contact without delay and fix an alternative time and day.

Montgomery to Eisenhower   *16 January*   *Ref: M-444*

I have great pleasure in reporting to you that the task you gave me in the Ardennes is now concluded. First and Third Armies have joined hands at Houffalize and are advancing eastwards. It can therefore be said we have now achieved tactical victory within the salient. I am returning First Army to Bradley tomorrow as ordered by you. I would like to say what a great pleasure it has being to have such a splendid Army under my command and how well it has done.[91]

Montgomery to Eisenhower   *18 January*   *Ref: M-449*

Dear Ike. I am regrouping my forces and am going ahead with all preparations for VERITABLE. I have fixed 10th February as a tentative target date for VERITABLE and will get it off by then if I can be given six American divisions and one corps headquarters by 1 February. The target date for GRENADE cannot be settled just at present but I think an interval between VERITABLE and GRENADE will not matter and will, in fact, be for the best. Brad is, I hope, coming to see me tomorrow. The last few weeks have been somewhat strenuous and I would like to go to my home in England for a few days rest once all our preparations are well in hand. I thought I might get away about 24 January. Would this be O.K. by you? No chance of a rest until the war is over once we have launched VERITABLE and GRENADE. Yours ever. Monty.

Montgomery to Eisenhower   *21 January*   *Ref: M-455*

Have received your letter of today's date, for which many thanks. Have dispatched to you today my orders for future operations, M-548. You will see in paragraph 25 that I have fixed the target date for VERITABLE as 8 February and I have done this so as to be certain I can be ready for 10 February. I would like to get GRENADE launched on 15 February. I go over to my home in England on Thursday next, 25th January, and have a scrambler there if you should want to talk to me at any time.

Considering the Promotion of Corps Commanders

Marshall to Eisenhower   *18 January*   *Ref: W-22784*

I am preparing to submit a promotion list tomorrow. No full generals to be included.

Tentatively I have listed Gerow and Collins to be Lieutenant Generals.[92] Handy and I omitted Ridgway because of his short tenure in corps command and the resentment that might be aroused elsewhere under the circumstances, Keyes, Eddy, etc. How about Collins at this time? What are your comments re Ridgway? Rush reply.

---

89 The two corps met at Houffalize, reducing Army Group B's salient to a manageable size after a month of hard fighting in harsh weather conditions.
90 Immediately changed to 17/18 January in S-75943.
91 Praise indeed after the political and press repercussions after Eisenhower split the Ardennes between Bradley and Montgomery.
92 Gerow of V Corps and Collins of VII Corps had been in action since D-Day.

Eisenhower to Marshall   19 *January*   *Ref: S-75626*

Earnestly recommend immediate advancement of Gerow, who has already been assigned to command Fifteenth Army and who is available for rotation with any army commander in the battle who may need a rest. This promotion is therefore logical and will cause no resentment.

Reference your W-22794. Collins has a brilliant record and is a great leader but frankly I am afraid of the overall effects of promotion of corps commanders to three star rank until the time comes that army group commanders can be advanced, which will make it logical to begin recommending outstanding corps commanders. I repeat that Collins is a star but not far behind, and in the opinion of many, not behind at all, are Walker, Eddy, Ridgeway, Middleton and Brooks.

When I begin recommending corps commanders based on accomplishment and length of service, Collins will be my first choice.

For reasons given above, as well as that mentioned in your cable, Ridgeway should not repeat not be promoted yet.

Promoting Younger Men

Eisenhower to Marshall   19 *January*   *Ref: S-75742*

As time goes on there is an accumulation of evidence that we should constantly seek younger men in relatively high positions. Thinking of the problems that the War Department will have to solve after the war, I believe, moreover that this tendency toward giving younger men battle command experience is a good thing for the future, even where older men are at least temporarily doing very good jobs. I am thinking particularly of corps and division commanders. Any attempt to go steadily towards younger men in these positions would tend to create a wartime surplus in the major general's grade, which surplus would be comprised of officers who have done very good work and for whom any reduction in rank during time of war would be a gross injustice.[93]

The question arises as to whether it would be possible for you to absorb any significant number of individuals in this category. I doubt that it would and therefore the proposition may be largely academic, but I do think that both present and future effectiveness might be promoted in this way. For example, I now have such division commanders as Baade, Wyche, Oliver, Craig, Twaddle, Morris, Maloney and Robertson. There will not have long to serve after the war is over and the valuable experience they are getting might better be invested in younger men. As corps commanders my youngest are Collins, Ridgeway, Brooks and Eddy. They are about right for age. The others are Milliken, Middleton, Haislip, Walker and men of their age group. From the standpoint of both present and future effectiveness, my own conviction is that a corps commander should be in the late forties, division commanders should be in the early forties, with an occasional man even in his thirties. In all cases, at this stage of the war, assignments to these positions should be by demonstrated their merit in battle.

This telegram, of course, requires no immediate answer because I know that you could not adopt an inflexible policy in any case. But I am furnishing my thoughts in the matter to you so that we may talk it over when I see you later in the month.

---

93 The dilemma was how to give the younger men combat experience at a higher level of command without relieving a general who was performing well. There was no answer to the problem and by the end of the war many of Eisenhower's corps commanders were too old for active commands and were appointed to senior staff positions.

Preparing for the Malta and Yalta Conferences

Marshall to Eisenhower   *17 January*   *Ref: W-22163*

I have your radio January 15th, S-7500 and your fine letter of January 12th. Handy and Hull suggest that I stopped to see you en route to ARGONAUT.[94] I doubt if it is advisable for me to appear at SHAEF at that time. Would it be awkward for you to meet me in the south of France, say the Toulon area, about the 26th for a one day conference? Hull and others would be with me.

We sent congratulations to Stalin. In future I suggest that you approach them in simple Main Street Abilene style.[95] They are rather cynically disposed towards the diplomatic phrasing of our compliments and seem almost to appreciate downright rough talk of which I give them a full measure.

Marshall to Eisenhower   *20 January*   *Ref: W-24160*

It has been proposed that Combined Chiefs of Staff address to you and SACMED a message stating there will be a Combined Chiefs of Staff conference beginning at Malta on the forenoon of January 30. It will last three days. Proposed message states that your presence is desirable but that if you feel you cannot attend in person, you should send responsible representative. Malta conference to be followed by a Tripartite conference in the Crimea,[96] probably beginning February 2, and proposed message requests that you send a responsible representative there or attend in person if you consider that such action fits in with current military situation.

Eisenhower to Marshall   *21 January*   *Ref: S-75960*

Due to uncertainties of air transportation in winter I do not, repeat not, think it advisable for me to go beyond the limits of motor rail transport. My belief is therefore that I should send Smith and Bull[97] to the Mediterranean meeting and let Bull all go along to second meeting. Aside from this program it would be advisable, I think, for you and me to meet in south France. Because of your planned meeting in the Mediterranean I assume that day or night of 28th would be the logical time for you to be in south France. I am having confidential investigations made to determine the most convenient place. Request that future messages regarding our private meeting in the area refer to it by codeword SNOWBALL.

Marshall to Eisenhower and Alexander *22 January*   *Ref: WX-24878*

The Combined Chiefs of Staff will be holding a conference at CRICKET, beginning forenoon 30 January. Your presence is very desirable and arrangements for your accommodation have been made. If, owing to battle exigencies, you cannot attend in person you should send a responsible representative. The Combined Chiefs conference at CRICKET will be followed immediately by a Tripartite conference at MAGNETO, beginning 2 February. It is requested that you send a responsible representative to this conference or attend in person, if you consider such action fits in with the current military situation.

---

94 ARGONAUT was a conference held from 30 January to 3 February 1945 between Roosevelt and Churchill on the island of Malta.
95 Abilene, Kansas, Eisenhower's home since 1892. The Dwight D. Eisenhower Presidential Library and Museum is located in the town and President Eisenhower, his wife, Mamie, and their first born son Doud Dwight are buried there.
96 The Yalta Conference, codenamed ARGONAUT, between Roosevelt, Churchill and Stalin was held to discuss Europe's post-war reorganization.
97 General Bull, Eisenhower's G-3 staff officer responsible for planning.

Marshall to Eisenhower and Alexander 22 January   *Ref: WX-24903*
Significance of code words in FACS 130 and FAN 479 in chronological order are:

(1) MALTA, (2) YALTA in the CRIMEA

Marshall to Somervell   *22 January*   *Ref: W-24893*
Eisenhower and I are planning to meet at a point selected by him on Saturday January 27 or Sunday January 28. I shall lay over there and fly to Malta, arriving late Monday for Combined conferences beginning Tuesday morning. If convenient to your plans, arrange to meet me at rendezvous with Eisenhower and continue to Malta and beyond in my plane. I assume there will be nobody with you except your aide, but I can bring Wood in my plane if you especially wish it. Please let me know about these things.

Marshall to Eisenhower   *22 January*   *Ref: W-24894*
Your decision reference SNOWBALL is of course understood. Along with the party mentioned in my W-24610, I leave here Thursday January 25 and fly by way of Bermuda and the Azores to Casablanca, arriving there Friday January 26 and spending the night. On Saturday we move from Casablanca to the SNOWBALL location recommended in your S-76127, probably arriving there for lunch. Any arrangements you make for our conference and for accommodation of my party and me will be satisfactory. I plan to lay over at the SNOWBALL location Sunday and go to Malta Monday afternoon, January 29. The reason for the layover is to provide insurance against bad weather, and yet not reach Malta before Monday evening.

Although I am looking forward to seeing you in SNOWBALL, I do not plan to be there any longer than necessary to complete our talks, which can be on Saturday or Sunday as you elect and as weather favors. It might be more certainly economical with your time if you waited until certain I had landed in the SNOWBALL location before flying down, weather prospects of course being somewhat determining for you. If the weather is good throughout, I shall merely be marking time there after our conversations. I am sending Somervell a separate radio suggesting that he plans to meet me in SNOWBALL and fly over to Malta with me.

Eisenhower to Marshall   *23 January*   *Ref: S-76219*
Assuming Smith and Hull go to the meeting in the Mediterranean in the plane provided from here, would you have room in your plane to take Bull on next leg of journey, dropping him off on return trip somewhere in the Mediterranean where we can pick him up? With Somervell and a couple of my own staff officers, I will be at SNOWBALL in time to permit us a full discussion while you are there. Accommodations for you and party will be fully ready with all arrangements for transportation and security.

Marshall to Eisenhower   *23 January*   *Ref: W-25284*
I shall be glad to have Bull go in my plane from CRICKET to MAGNETO and also to insure his return to the Mediterranean, although this latter flight would not necessarily be in my own ship since I have not yet determined my return itinerary. I shall keep you posted on my movements and let you know my exact time of arrival at SNOWBALL as soon as possible. Messages I may address to you up to the time of my arrival at SNOWBALL will be sent through SHAEF.

Eisenhower to Combined Chiefs and British Chiefs of Staff   24 January   S-76422
In view of the present battle situation and because of uncertain weather conditions that
limit the certainty of travel, I am sending General Smith, my Chief of Staff, and General Bull,
the Supreme Headquarters G-3, to CRICKET. They may be accompanied by the other two
staff officers. Their arrival at CRICKET will be cabled direct to that point. General Hull will
proceed on to the MAGNETO meeting.

Harry Hopkins to President   27 January   S-76770
The Prime Minister told me that he was asking you to have Eisenhower meet with you and
him. There are extremely important decisions to be made here in the immediate future
which only Eisenhower can make and I hope before you agree to calling him away from the
battle that you will consult Eisenhower and Marshall.

Questions Raised Over Eisenhower's Plans

Smith to Eisenhower   30 January   Cricket-18
We have just completed the first discussion with the Combined Chiefs of Staff.

The only important question raised was by the British Chiefs of Staff who took exception to that part of your plan as given in SCAF 180 as follows: "After closing the Rhine in
the north, to direct our main effort to destroying any enemy remaining west of the Rhine,
both in the north and south."

The British Chiefs of Staff interpret this as an intention on your part to do nothing toward
forcing a crossing of the Rhine even in the north, until all the area west of the Rhine has
been swept clear of the Germans. It is obvious that they will not accept any such plan.

I have explained that while you consider it desirable to close the entire length of the
Rhine, you are not going to stop everything until this is done and, on the contrary, will
seize a bridgehead and push a crossing whenever you can, particularly in the present
favorable circumstances. I have also explained the relative weight you give to the main
and secondary efforts.

These explanations are apparently considered satisfactory, as is your plan of operations
interpreted by Bull and myself, but the British Chiefs of Staff will insist on something in writing to clinch the fact that the main effort in the north is to be pushed and that you are not to
delay other operations until you have eliminated every German west of the Rhine.

This may involve a change in your directive, which otherwise will not be tampered with,
and General Marshall suggests that you take the initiative by modifying the paragraph in
question. We suggest the following wording for subparagraphs A and B of paragraph 21 of
SCAF 180.

"My plan is as follows:

a)   To carry out immediately a series of operations north of the Moselle with a view
        to destroying the enemy and closing the Rhine north of Düsseldorf.

b)   To direct our efforts to eliminating other enemy forces west of the Rhine which
        still constitute an obstacle or a potential threat to our subsequent Rhine crossing
        operations."

If you agree to the above changes please inform me most urgent as we think this will settle
the whole matter.

Eisenhower to Smith   *31 January*   *S-77211*

I agree with the rewording of the directive as suggested in your Cricket-18 and will issue the necessary amendment. You may assure the Combined Chiefs of Staff in my name that I will seize Rhine crossings in the north just as soon as this is a feasible operation and without failing to close the Rhine throughout its length. Further, I will advance across the Rhine in the north with maximum strength and complete determination immediately the situation in the south allows me to collect necessary forces and do this without incurring reasonable risks.

New Subject: Please acknowledge time of receipt of this message by General Smith.

Montgomery Takes a Break Before 21st Army Group Attacks

Montgomery to Eisenhower   *28 January*   *63499 DMO*

Dear Ike. I am enjoying a short holiday at my home in England. I have a telephone and scrambler in my house and am in daily touch with my headquarters and with Whiteley.[98] I propose to return on Saturday next, 3 February, but if you would like me back earlier I am always at your command. Please give my best wishes to Bradley for the success of his operation that begins today. Yours always. Monty.

---

98 General Sir John F. M. Whiteley, General Bull's deputy.

14

FEBRUARY 1945

GRENADE and VERITABLE

Eisenhower to Smith   1 February   *Ref: S-77374*

For your information I am launching GRENADE very quickly after VERITABLE. Moreover, as soon as necessary divisions can be brought from the south, First Army will attack dams. GRENADE will go through without waiting for the last details of strength requested by Field Marshal. This means that everywhere south of the dam area we will be temporarily on the defensive as soon as Colmar Pocket is cleared up.[1]

Smith to Eisenhower   2 February   *Ref: Cricket-48*

Our business is satisfactorily concluded, your plans as indicated in SCAF 180, and as modified by you, are approved by the Combined Chiefs of Staff. However, General Marshall says I should remain here until Saturday as there is a person arriving on Friday who may want to ask some questions. Will return Saturday.[2]

Thanks very much for your message concerning GRENADE. Its arrival was most timely.

A Starving Population

Montgomery to Eisenhower   3 February   *Ref: M-464*

I consider that the level of subsistence of Belgium and Dutch civil population is too low and that there are signs of disintegration of morale. There have already been sporadic strikes amongst Antwerp dockers and coal miners. A strike of railway operatives would be most serious. The present ration for civilians amounts to about 1,600 calories, as compared to some 4,500 for military personnel. It is obvious that this cannot be sufficient for labor doing hard physical work.[3]

I feel that the seriousness of the position may not be fully realized and would be grateful if you would personally intervene. I suggest that at least part of the heavy stocks already accumulated for a problematical B-2 area would be more suitably employed in relief of the distressed, which is actual both in Holland and Belgium. Also should we not get authority for an increased import program of food supplies. Finally, if we do this should we not insist that Belgium Government take energetic measures to deal with the black market and so

---

1 21st Army Group planned to launch Canadian First Army's attack from the Nijmegen area, Operation VERITABLE, on 8 February, only for the Germans to destroy the dams upstream. This delayed Ninth US Army's crossing of the Roer river, Operation GRENADE, until 23 February.
2 He was returning from the ARGONAUT conference in Malta. Although the conference had started on 30 January, President Roosevelt, Smith's mystery visitor, did not arrive until the final day of the conference on 2 February.
3 While the food shortages in Nazi-occupied Holland were well known, Montgomery is making the point that his soldiers are on far better rations than civilians, yet 21st Army Group is reliant on civilian labor to keep its rear areas functioning.

ensure the extra food we provide does in fact get to people who need it. I consider the matter is really urgent.[4]

Eisenhower to Montgomery   *7 February*   *Ref: S-78134*
This is the first chance I have had to answer you M-464. In my absence General Smith has conducted a lengthy investigation, including obtaining the advice of both British and American ambassadors. General Smith is coming to Belgium as soon as a new Government is formed, in order to get this affair on an even keel and to prevent difficulties arising in the future. In the meantime, I am assured that you can go ahead and fight your battle without any concern about your rear. All parties earnestly advise that no immediate crisis is impending.

The President Hopes to Meet Eisenhower
President to Eisenhower   *11 February*   *Ref: White House 187*
I shall be passing through Alexandria sometime within the next few days. I shall let you know the exact date later. If you have anything you particularly wish to see me about and the military situation permits, I will of course be glad to see you but it is entirely up to you.[5]

Eisenhower to Marshall for President   *12 February*   *Ref: S-78731*
Although I deeply regret my inability to meet you at point suggested, I am sure that my absence from here at this time would be most unfortunate. Floods have held up an important plan and some changes will probably have to be made that no one except myself can authorize.[6] I truly appreciate the courtesy of your invitation. Request acknowledgement of message.

President to Eisenhower   *13 February*   *Ref: White House 191*
Much as I would like to see you, I of course do not wish to interfere with your duties at the front. I am following your ground offensive with greatest attention and I want you to know how constantly the battle and the Armies which you command are in my mind.

21st Army Group's Progress Report
Montgomery to Eisenhower   *12 February*   *Ref: M-555*
For your approval Ike:

VERITABLE is drawing most of the immediately available German reserves up north and we now have quite a good party up there.

That is excellent and is exactly what we want. I shall engage the whole lot in battle and will put everything into it. Intention is to give Canadian Army two more British divisions at once and this will make nine divisions available for the further offensive operations to the southeast. With these numbers we shall be able to keep up the tempo of the operations at a high level.

---

4 While food stocks were being accumulated to feed refugees, Montgomery wanted to use them to feed the civilian workers behind his lines, undermining the emerging black market.
5 President Roosevelt was returning from the Yalta Conference in the Crimea, where he had discussed the post-war plans for Europe with Churchill and Stalin.
6 The Germans destroyed the Roer dams as soon as Operation VERITABLE was launched on 8 February, delaying the start of Operation GRENADE; it was launched on 23 February.

I visited all the divisions of the Ninth Army on the Roer front today. The conditions in the river valley are appalling and GRENADE is impossible at the present and I would say we may have to wait one week, or possibly more before we can launch it.

Ninth Army is all set for GRENADE and I do not want to upset that. But, intention is to take 95th Division, which is in Ninth Army reserve, west of the Meuse and am putting it to hold a defensive sector on the Meuse north of Venlo under Second Army. This will set free the British division, which will go to strengthen VERITABLE. Apart from this, I shall leave Ninth Army as it is and which is ready to launch GRENADE the moment conditions allow. I think this is important, as it is VERITABLE plus GRENADE's counterattack which gives us the quick success we need.

VERITABLE by itself is bound to be slow. The only way to making it go quicker is to make it fresh, so that there need be no pauses. Could you by any chance lend me two more American infantry divisions? If you can do this I could get 7th British Armored Division out from Ninth Army and make it available for VERITABLE. I should also take out 6th Airborne Division and return it to United Kingdom, to get ready for the Rhine operation for which I have fixed a very tentative target date, 15 March.

The division fighting up in the Reichswald Forest sector in the north has done a magnificent job of work under the most appalling conditions. The first four days fighting has yielded 5,000 prisoners, which is not too bad, and the numbers of German dead lying about is very great.

Yours ever: Monty. Acknowledge.[7]

Eisenhower to Montgomery   *13 February*   *Ref: S-18896*
Thank you for your M-555 of 12 February. I would like to discuss it further with you and would be glad if you would meet me tomorrow, 14 February, at E.T.A.C. at 11:00 hours or as soon thereafter as possible.[8]

Montgomery to Eisenhower   *18 February*   *Ref: M-487*
Dear Ike: We have fixed GRENADE for Friday, 23 February. VERITABLE is going well and the enemy is going to find it increasingly difficult to stand up to our pressure. I shall keep it going with heavy blows all along the front every day and it will, I hope, draw in by 23 February, all the available enemy reserves, so that GRENADE may have an easier task and go all the quicker. Yours ever, Monty.[9]

Montgomery to Eisenhower   *18 February*   *Ref: M-489*
Dear Ike: I understand you would like to see me on Thursday, 22 February. Would you come and lunch with me at my T.A.C. Headquarters and I would get the three army commanders to meet you. I would fetch you in my car from your train at Hasselt or wherever he will be. Do come. Yours ever, Monty.

---

7 This message illustrates the level of detail that Montgomery provided for SHAEF headquarters, and the relaxed way that operations are reported, plans are presented and reinforcements are requested.
8 Tactical Command Post, the forward headquarters used during a battle, a temporary setup which could be easily moved.
9 Ninth US Army crossed the Roer on 23 February and, as Montgomery hoped, quickly reached the Rhine between Düsseldorf to Moers, advancing 50 miles in ten days.

Eisenhower to Montgomery 18 February

Dear Monty: Thanks for cordial invitation. I am forced to cancel my trip for this week, but will plan on seeing you early next week, at which time I would like to confer American decorations on Army commanders. I will inform you as far in advance as possible. As ever. [Signed] Ike.

Countering Press Reports on the Ardennes Battle

Eisenhower to Marshall 27 February *Ref: FWD-17402*

I have seen press reports emanating from Washington and purporting to quote the War Department official to the effect that the Ardennes battle was the costliest in American history. I also suggest that it was also one of the most profitable.

Simpson's advance has been today at the approximate rate of one mile per hour.

[Handwritten note] The casualties over the Ardennes month averaged no more than for the two months before. The cost of material was actually very light. The main effect was a major catastrophe for the Germans.[10]

---

10 US casualties were 40,000 during the German attacks and a similar number during the counterattack to erase the Bulge. The Wehrmacht suffered similar losses. Both sides lost a large amount of armor, transport and material, but while the Allies could replace their losses, Germany could not. Army Group B had not taken its objectives and the offensive had weakened its position in the West.

15

MARCH 1945

Three and Four Star Promotions

Marshall to Eisenhower   *1 March*   *Ref: W-45148*

Although you have recommended Bradley and Spaatz for promotion and have spoke of the possibility of 'two or three' promotions to full Generalcy in your Theater, I am not clear as to whom, if anyone, you recommend as the third candidate. You have spoken of both Devers and Patton. Please let me have your final view. If it should be Patton would you not have to relieve Devers? Otherwise he would be discredited.[1]

Eisenhower to Marshall   *2 March*   *Ref: FWD-17505*

Reference your cable concerning my present recommendations for promotions to four star rank.

Viewed from the standpoint of this theater only, I would prefer on the initial list to have only Bradley and Spaatz promoted in order to give special recognition to their past accomplishments and present positions. If you are contemplating for your initial list a very small number, say about a total of six outside Continental United States, I recommend that only these two be made at this time in this Theater. If you intend on nominating a greater number, then by force of circumstances and present organization Devers will have to be the third nomination. In my opinion, his contributions have not been so great as in the case of Patton, but I have no plausible reasons for changing my organization and as you point out, if Patton were made at this time in lieu of Devers, I should have to be transfer Patton to command the Sixth Army Group and Devers would have to leave the Theater. I would not be justified in such a move.

My opinion is that eventually we should give all our Army Group, and at least our most experienced Army Commanders, the four star grade. I would contemplate also recommending the outstanding Corps Commanders at a later date for three star rank. I have in mind particularly Collins.

To sum up, if you make a very small list at this time, I recommend only Bradley and Spaatz for the first list with the understanding that later I will recommend both Devers and Patton. If you have a larger list at this time, then Bradley, Spaatz and Devers are my selections, with Patton next in line, to be followed eventually by Hodges and Simpson.

I apologize for the length of this cable but since I cannot know how you are approaching the problem, I thought it best to give you my idea in some detail.[2]

---

1 As commander of 6th Army Group, Devers was senior to Patton, commander of Third Army.
2 General Devers was promoted to temporary general on 8 March 1945.

Eisenhower to Marshall 12 March *Ref: FWD-17802*

I trust that the Secretary of War will wait for my recommendation before putting in Patton's name for promotion. There is no one better acquainted than I with Patton's good qualities and likewise with his limitations.[3] In the past I have demonstrated my high opinion of him when it was not easy to do so. In certain situations both Bradley and I would select Patton to command above any other general we have, but in other situations we would prefer Hodges. If I had not absorbed Devers the problem would be simpler, because that would be a logical position for Patton, but as it is I think he should wait to be considered by the War Department with his own appropriate group.

Eisenhower to Marshall 14 March *Ref: FWD-17845*

I saw your list of four-star appointments in the paper this morning. I think that as an initial list it is absolutely logical and could not be improved upon.

New subject: I suppose you know that the Prime Minister has withdrawn his suggestion of making any change in my deputy.

Apologies Required for Bombing Switzerland

Marshall to Eisenhower 5 March *Ref: W-47851*

You will be interested in the following as it relates to Spaatz, who commands units which are responding to your battle directions. I have just dispatched it to Spaatz personally:

> "The successive bombings of Swiss territory now demand more that expressions of regret. It is desired that you personally leave immediately for Geneva or such other place as may be necessary and present to appropriate Swiss officials first hand information as to the cause of these incidents, the corrective action undertaken, and a formal apology. State Department is arranging through Ambassador Harrison for your entry into Switzerland and your prompt return. Harrison will advise you through Ambassador Caffery when these arrangements have been concluded. It is further desired that, upon arrival in Switzerland, you report to Ambassador Harrison and explain the purpose of your visit. No publicity and maximum secrecy."[4]

The Possible Surrender of the Italian Front

Alexander to Marshall, to Eisenhower for info 11 March *Ref: FX-41441*

1. O.S.S. in this Theater on 8 March made information available that Waffen S.S. Karl Wolff[5], top S.S. officer in North Italy, together with O.K.W. representative, presumably from Kesselring's staff, plus Dollmann[6] and Zimmer[7], were expected to arrive at

---

3 Eisenhower sums up the paradox of General Patton: on the one hand a great battle commander, on the other hand, prone to do or say the wrong thing at the wrong time, undermining his reputation.

4 The most serious incident had been the daylight bombing of Schaffhausen in April 1944 when 50 B-24 Liberators mistook the town for Ludwigshafen am Rhein; a smaller accident occurred on 22 February. The incident which resulted in this cable took place on 4 March 1945. Bombers hit Zurich and Basel, thinking they were hitting Aschaffenburg, 300km to the north. In both cases damages were paid.

5 SS-Obergruppenführer Karl F.O. Wolff (1900–1984), Supreme SS and Police Leader and acting military commander of the Italian area. With Himmler's agreement, Wolff had taken steps to make contact with OSS in February 1945 as part of Operation SUNRISE. Wolff had met OSS representative Allen W. Dulles on 8 March 1945. He went onto negotiate the surrender of all German forces in Italy, ending the war in Italy on 2 May 1945, six days before the end in Germany.

6 Eugen Dollmann (1900–1985), German diplomat and member of the SS, serving at Wolff's aide.

7 Guido Zimmer, SS officer working for the Reich Security Main Office (RSHA) in Italy.

Lugjo,[8] Switzerland, prepared to discuss capitulation of German forces in North Italy. Subsequent information on 9 March confirms that Wolff has in fact arrived and has indicated willingness to try to develop a program to take North Italy out of conflict. He considers mere military surrender difficult and prefers capitulation be preceded by statement to German people from German leaders in North Italy that struggle is hopeless and is merely causing needless German bloodshed. He states Kesselring not yet won over and his adherence is considered essential to plan. Wolff however stated that Rahn,[9] who is German ambassador to Fascist Italian Government, is in accord with him. Wolff is proceeding immediately to Kesselring[10] to endeavor to sell plan to him and will keep in touch with O.S.S. representative.

2. Prior to meeting in Switzerland, Dollmann promised to produce recently captured Conai (?) leader Parri,[11] as evidence as their good faith and ability to act. Information now received that Parri was in fact delivered unconditionally in Switzerland 9 March and is in good health.

3. Further discussions being held by O.S.S. with Wolff but results not yet available here. In view of these discussions, O.S.S. suggests representatives of my Headquarters be prepared to go to Switzerland to deal with situation in case of favorable developments.

4. Six further negotiations between O.S.S. and Wolff developed to extent that German representatives appear genuine and have specific proposals to discuss. I propose to act on following lines.

a) The German representative must come to Berne with signed authority from Marshal Kesselring that they have authority to speak.
b) O.S.S. to arrange a meeting place either at American or British Embassies at night. If Embassies are too difficult, another meeting place can be considered.
c) I will send General Lyman L. Lemnitzer, my American Deputy Chief of Staff, and General T. S. Airey, my British Chief Intelligence Staff, to Berne.[12]
d) They will be instructed to tell the Germans:
    1) That they must come to AFHQ for detailed military discussions.
    2) That they must arrange a method of communication with Kesselring.
    3) That the discussions will only deal with the method of surrender on a purely military and not a governmental or political basis.

---

8 The meeting was held with OSS official Paul Blum in Lugano, Switzerland.
9 Rudolf Rahn (1900–1975).
10 Generalfeldmarschall Kesselring was appointed commander of OB West on 11 March 1945, following Generalfeldmarschall von Rundstedt's dismissal.
11 Actually CLN, *Comitato di Liberazione Nazionale* or National Liberation Committee, the political group of the Italian Partisans headed by Ferruccio Parri (1890–1981), nicknamed 'Maurizio'. Parri had been arrested in Milan in January 1945 and was released in March 1945 in Lugano (Switzerland) as part of Operation CROSSWORD (or Operation SUNRISE), after secret negotiations between Allen Dulles, head of the US Office of Strategic Services (OSS) and representatives of the German Wehrmacht command in Northern Italy. Parri's release was requested as evidence of good faith and the ability to act and he was freed in time to take part in the final phase of the resistance and in the April uprising. When the Soviets found out about the meeting, the US and Britain were accused of going behind their allies' backs. The negotiations would eventually lead to the unconditional surrender of the German forces in northern Italy and western Austria on 2 May 1945.
12 General Lyman L. Lemnitzer (1889–1988) and Major-General Sir Terence S. Airey, KCMG, CB, CBE (1900–1983).

5. Please note that two of the leading figures are SS, and Himmler men, which makes me very suspicious. Nevertheless, it is all well to be prepared.

6. Request your agreement with above proposed procedure. I shall not send representatives to Berne as proposed in paragraph 3 (c) above until I receive your authorization. You will be kept fully informed of future development.

British Chiefs of Staff to Joint Chiefs of Staff   13 March   *Ref: 1603*
Following for the Chiefs of Staff: Reference Moscow telegram No. 7692 Foreign Office repeated Washington.

Request you arrange for Combined Chiefs of Staff to:

Inform Alexander of Soviet views and request him to arrange immediate transport for General Susloparov[13] to Berne, and to inform his representatives of developments and instruct them that they may contact German Emissaries when Soviet representatives have arrived.

Inform General Eisenhower of the position and request him to arrange immediate transport for General Dragun[14] to Berne.

AFHQ to Alexander   13 March   *Ref: 76083 CIGS*
For info: Joint Chiefs of Staff, Eisenhower and Wilson
Please telegraph urgently following information required by the Foreign Office. What arrangements are being made and by whom to introduce your representatives into Switzerland? Is it being done clandestinely and without the knowledge of Swiss Government? Can similar arrangements be made for Russian generals without risk of incident, even though Swiss and Soviet Governments are not in diplomatic relations? If difficulty of introducing Russians into Switzerland is insuperable, could the meeting perhaps take place not at Berne but on French territory near Franco-Swiss frontier?

Has there been any further contact between the O.S.S. and Wolff?

Alexander to AFHQ   13 March   *Ref: FWD-43235*
For info: Joint Chiefs of Staff and Eisenhower
Arrangements been made by O.S.S. to introduce my representatives into Switzerland. Colonel Glavin Asad of O.S.S., this Theater, travelled with my representatives to France this afternoon, from where they will enter Swiss territory. Detail arrangements unknown. To best of our knowledge arrangements not known to Swiss government, although Swiss intelligence agents have been used as intermediaries. Party will enter Swiss territory in civilian clothes with no military identifications. Am confident that arrangements can be made for Soviet representatives to enter Switzerland in similar manner through same O.S.S. channels, but am verifying.

No further contact between O.S.S. and Wolff was reported.

---

13 General Ivan A. Susloparov (1897–1974), chief of the Soviet liaison mission with SHAEF and the French Government, based in Paris.
14 Major-General Vasilii M. Dragun (1898–1961), Deputy Chief of 5th Section, Main Intelligence Directorate GRU.

The Russians Locate the German General Staff Bunker

Military Mission Moscow to Marshall 11 March   *Ref: MX-23173*
Info to: Combined Chiefs of Staff, British Chiefs of Staff, Eisenhower
Deane has just received the following letter from Marshall Khudyakov[15] which is quoted in full:

"Dear General Deane: According to information which we have, the General Staff of the German Army is situated 38 kilometers south of Berlin in a specially fortified underground shelter called by the Germans the 'Citadel'. It is located on the territory of Stammlawer at a distance of 5½ to 6 kilometers south to southeast from the town of Xossen and from 1 to 1½ kilometers east of a wide super highway which runs parallel to the railroad from Berlin to Dresden.

The area occupied by the underground fortifications of the Citadel covers from about 5 to 6 square kilometers. The whole territory is surrounded by wired entanglements several rows in depth, and is very strongly guarded by an SS guard regiment.

According to the same source, the construction of the underground fortifications for the German General Staff started in 1936. In 1938 and 1939 the strength of the fortification was tested by the Germans against bombing from the air and against artillery fire.

I ask you, dear General, not to refuse the kindness as soon as possible to give directions to the Allied Air Forces to bomb the Citadel with heavy bombs.

I am sure that as a result of the action of the Allied air forces, the German General Staff, if still located there, will receive damage and losses which will stop its normal work and the installation shall have to be moved elsewhere. Thus the Germans will lose a well-organized communication center and headquarters.[16]

Enclosed is a map with exact location of the German general staff.

On the British map 1:500,000 Europe (air), the area located is on the right side, about ½ to ¾ of a mile east, of the road between Xossen and Neuhof with the southwestern corner of the area at 52 degrees, 11 minutes north and 13 degrees, 28 minutes east.

Request that we be informed of the action taken in connection with Marshal Khudyakov's request."

Future Plans for an Airborne Operation

Eisenhower to Marshall   *12 March*   *Ref: FWD-17807*
On the most highly secret basis we are considering, as a feature of our whole campaign, an airborne operation on a scale of seven to ten divisions.[17] Our tentative target date is May 1 but this looks rather optimistic from viewpoint of weather and unit readiness. We feel certain that with our troop carrier and bomber forces we can assure adequacy of supply. To do the thing on this scale I will be hard put to it to find the necessary divisions.

---

15 Air Marshal Sergei A. Khudyakov (1902–1950), Chief of Staff of the Soviet Air Force.
16 Work had started in 1934 on the underground command center, codenamed MAYBACH I, and it was nearly ready for the invasion of Poland in September 1939. A second complex, codenamed MAYBACH II, was added during the war to serve as a Führer bunker, but he never visited it. The Allies first learned of the 60,000-acre complex from a prisoner taken in Italy in July 1944 but took no action, probably because they did not know its significance. 675 heavy bombers attacked it three days after this report was received; they only did superficial damage. The Germans evacuated the complex on 20 April and it fell intact into Soviet hands.
17 The plan was to seize the Kassel area, to stop German troops making a last stand. It would also facilitate the junction of 21st and 12th Army Groups 50 miles east of the Ruhr.

I am asking the British War Office to speed up the readiness date of the 1st Airborne Division, now scheduled June 1, but I cannot count with certainty on the use of more than three American Airborne Divisions. This leaves me with at least four or five infantry divisions to find and naturally I do not want to weaken materially the offensive thrusts planned for the ground campaign.[18]

What would you think of my taking up with SACMED and McNarney the possibility of their sparing one American division from that front, to be sent as quickly as possible? Under present schedules the first British division transferred from the Mediterranean will close here before the end of this month and two more will arrive by the middle of April. Quite a gap then ensues before later ones arrive. I prefer getting your opinion on the possible feasibility of such a move before I even suggest it to the Mediterranean command, because I feel you are well acquainted with their present prospects and with the probable attitude of Combined Chiefs of Staff and I do not want to upset or bother Alexander or McNarney if the matter is a hopeless one.

Marshall to Eisenhower   *14 March*   *Ref: W-52767*
It would be asking a good deal to take one of Clark's[19] six dependable American divisions at this particular moment, especially when he knows you have nearly ninety already available and that you have now closed to the Rhine over a good deal of its length, making it relatively easy for you to rest your divisions. Before expressing my own views I would like to know the whereabouts of the proposed operation, etc. The date you give seems quite distant considering your present prospects. If it comes to transferring a United States division from Italy, would the 10th Mountain Division be of any use to you? (You might get Bull's view on this).[20]

[Handwritten note] Supreme Commander instructed that <u>no</u> distribution be given the outgoing cable.

Eisenhower to Marshall   *15 March*   *Ref: FWD-17878*
I withdraw my suggestion. So long as plans and the current situation in Italy make undesirable any further weakening of our forces there, it would be unwise to transfer the division here to prepare for an operation that, of course, may never eventuate. My feeler was put out in the faint hope that the division could easily be spared there and thus allow me to plan for greater strength in the project. Because this is presumably a vital front, I was merely seeking every possible soldier to apply at what might be a decisive moment, so as to give us the greatest possible certainty of complete victory.

Marshall to Eisenhower, for info to McNarney   *26 March 1945*   *Ref: WX-58795*
British Chiefs of Staff now say they are seriously concerned as to the necessity for concentrating all available strength without delay on the Western Front and propose to withdraw a British infantry division in Italy at once to make it operational on the Western Front by

---

18 The last airborne offensive had been Operation MARKET GARDEN in September, involving 1st British Airborne, the 82nd Airborne and 101st Airborne Divisions. The 6th British and 17th US were preparing for Operation VARSITY, 21st Army Group's crossing of the Rhine on 24 March.
19 General Mark Clark, commander of 15th Army Group comprising Fifth US Army and Eighth British Army.
20 The 10th Mountain Division had been raised and trained for combat in mountainous regions and had recently deployed to Italy where it would be engaged until the end of the war.

early May rather than wait to move the 46th Division now in Greece, which would not become operational in the West until June.

According to McNarney, a British division taken from Italy would be the one which Alexander now has set up for a flanking movement across Lake Conacchio.[21] McNarney feels that Alexander's present plan has far-reaching possibilities and that to emasculate it in order to permit a minor reinforcement on your front would be unsound. Your personal belief expressed in SCAF 244, that the enemy strength on the Western Front is now so stretched that your successes will soon be limited only by the logistical capabilities, combined with McNarney's thoughts on the matter raises a serious question as to the soundness of moving this British division from Italy. It seems that if the Germans persist in continuing opposition, even though all hope to avoid a complete defeat is lost, we must face a possible necessity for forcing the surrender of each group of his forces, including those in Italy, by offensive military action on our part.

In light of the foregoing, of McNarney's opinion and your SCAF 244, is seems we should not further weaken Alexander in order to add one more division to your already considerable forces unless you have a specific foreseeable need for this particular division.

Eisenhower to Marshall	*27 March*	*Ref: FWD-18212*

General Gruenther passed through here the day before yesterday, en route to see Field Marshal Brooke concerning the British division mentioned in your WX-58795. The opinion I expressed to General Gruenther was the same as that set forth in your message. I am emphatic in my belief that we should not, repeat not, take away a division from Italy at this time if such a move means the difference been an active and passive front. It was upon learning of this consequence that I withdrew my recent request that you study the possibility of moving here another American division.

The only thing we must guard against is the possibility that the German may still find enough strength to oppose our penetrations along some line fairly deep in his own country, where our stretched maintenance might allow him to stalemate us for a length of time. When I requested you some time ago to give me the possibilities of moving another division here, I was looking forward to an airborne operation in the Kassel area which would have made it impossible for the German to do this. Now we are going so rapidly on the ground that I will have to use all my air transport command for the supply of armored columns and an airborne operation, except on a reduced scale, will be out of the question.[22]

To sum up, it is my opinion that under the conditions we have here, and under the situation you describe in Italy, the British division should not, repeat not, be transferred.

Publicity

Eisenhower to Marshall	*12 March*	*Ref: FWD-17802*

I shall try to get some publicity for the work of Collins, Gillem and McLain[23] in recent advances. One of our difficulties in publicity for particular persons or units is making

---

21 Lake Conacchio is on the east coast of Italy, north of Ravenna. Eighth Army planned to cross it on 23 April and advance north to the river Po.

22 Rapid advances on the ground stretched the lines of communications beyond their limits, as they had done during the advance across France. SHAEF had decided that the planes which would have transported paratroopers and glider troops behind enemy lines were more useful for supplying the armored divisions on the ground. It took too long to plan and prepare a large scale airborne operation during the sort of breakthrough battle the Allies were engaged in at this stage of the war.

23 General J. Lawton Collins, VII Corps, General Alvan C. Gillem Jr, XIII Corps, and General Raymond S. McLain, XIX Corps.

distinctions on such a big front where all have done extremely well. For example, in the recent battles seven of the nine Corps in the Ninth, First and Third Armies have been very active and all commanders have done well. Collins stands out because of his continuous record of brilliant work since D-Day. The same difficulty arises with respect to divisions. In spite of the long-run splendid records of the 1st, 3rd, 36th, 45th and 2nd Armored Divisions, we have newer ones, including the 104th, 90th, 4th, 30th, and the 3rd Armored, which are ranked by all our commanders as equally capable as top flight assault divisions. However, I have gotten a few people working on the job of trying to establish personalities for the various units and their commanders and to present their stories in a more colorful way to the public. I hope some results will come out of it.

Countering Criticism in the Press

Eisenhower to Marshall 12 March *Ref: FWD-17802*

It is pure bosh to say that 75% of our equipment is inferior to the German material. Speaking generally the reverse is true although, of course, if you take the present Sherman and the Panther and put them in a slugging match, the latter will win. One trouble is that even many of our professionals do not understand that a compromise in tank characteristics is necessary if we are to meet our own complex requirements in this type of equipment.[24] It is my opinion that when we have the new M-26 in sufficient numbers, and especially when we get the even newer model which has the souped up 90mm gun, our tank force will be superior in slugging power as well as in maneuverability and in numbers.[25] Our artillery, rifles, machine guns, airplanes (except for the jet airplane)[26] and in general, our clothing and equipage all outclass the enemy's. The jeep, the large trucks and the Ducks[27] are far ahead of him. The German 88 is a great all round gun and as a separate anti-tank weapon has caused us lots of trouble. But his artillery as a whole is far behind and the 90mm will match the 88.

Marshall to Eisenhower 15 March *Ref: W-53508*

Statement by you in your FWD-17802 is reassuring in view of widely disseminated, misleading information by radio and press, on the effectiveness of our equipment including adverse comparisons of certain items with the enemy's equipment. Such stories as follows, alleged to have been related to Miss Ann Stringer, United Press Staff Correspondent with the 3rd Armored Division, have been given circulation here:

By Staff Sergeant Robert Earley, "Tell them our tanks are not worth a drop of water on a hot stove;"

By Sergeant Sylvester Vila, "We pushed into this town in our old M4 tank, which the Nazis had been knocking around all through France."[28]

---

24 While the US Army had stuck with the M4 Sherman as its main battle tank, standardizing production and maintenance, the German Army pursued larger panzer designs like the Panther, Tiger I and King Tiger II. Although the German tanks had larger caliber guns and thicker armor, production was limited and it was harder to maintain a variety of tanks.

25 Production of the Heavy Tank M-26 Pershing was delayed by several factors, the most important being opposition from Army Ground Forces. Only the initial delivery of 20 tanks deployed to Europe in January 1945 saw combat during the Second World War.

26 The Me262 jet fighter.

27 DUKWs.

28 This are just two examples of comments circulating about the poor standard of American armor and equipment compared to the German equivalent, disseminated by the press. Marshall and Eisenhower are making the point that a reporter can easily obtain statements and circulate them, undermining morale. This cable makes it clear that they want to undermine the perceived value of press stories.

In order to counteract statements made by those who are not fully informed of our material and techniques, suggest you issue a strong statement, substantially as made in your cable, as to the adequacy of our material, including tanks, to be released to the press personally by you and that you take the opportunity, where appropriate, to substantiate this from time to time, over the next twenty days, by similar strong and positive releases personally by our senior commanders.

Praise for First and Third Armies

Marshall to Eisenhower   *23 March*   *Ref: WX-57751*
Please pass the following from me to General Bradley:

> "I am filled with admiration over your handling of the operations involved in the development of the Remagen bridgehead[29] and the clearing of the Saar basin.[30] I want General Hodges and General Patton and their Corps and Division Commanders to know that their great military successes of the past few weeks have registered a high point in American military achievement. Incidentally I am profoundly impressed with the remarkable logistical support of the Remagen bridgehead and the supply of Patton's forces which made possible the rapidity of their bold advances."[31]

If you think it is wise, that is, without offense to Devers Group or Simpson's Army, and as a possible antidote for an overdose of Montgomery which is now coming into the country, you have my permission to release this in Paris.

[Handwritten note bracketing the message] Must be paraphrased prior to publication.

Eisenhower to Marshall   *23 March*   *No Reference*
Many thanks for your fine message which I have passed onto Patton. I am going to Ninth Army today to witness jump off.[32] Bradley will now push his established bridgehead vigorously.

---

29 First Army crossed the Rhine at Remagen on 7 March after demolitions failed to destroy the Ludendorff Railway Bridge. Over the week that followed, temporary bridges were installed and Hodges' troops expanded the bridgehead despite German efforts to eliminate it.

30 Third Army advanced along both banks of the Moselle river and while the northern pincer reached the Rhine on 10 March, the southern pincer advanced to the Saar Basin, which Hitler had ordered to be held at all costs. On 15 March Seventh Army attacked from the south while Third Army attack from the north, taking the Germans by surprise. The Saar Basin was secured on 23 March, virtually ending German resistance on the west bank of the Rhine.

31 Third Army crossed the Rhine south of Frankfurt using what equipment it had to hand and without pausing to stop and build up supplies. Patton had taken a risk but his troops found only scattered German resistance on the far bank, and they quickly advanced east. When Patton was being driven across the river, he asked his driver to stop so he could urinate in it; it was his symbolic statement about the defensive capabilities of the river.

32 Simpson's Ninth Army was about to cross the Rhine upstream of Wesel as part of 21st Army Group's Operation PLUNDER.

Plans for Attacks East of the Rhine

Morgan[33] *to Eisenhower*   *23 March*   *FWD-18113*

Recommend a cable substantially as follows be dispatched to Combined Chiefs of Staff forthwith. Do you approve?[34]

"With the conclusions of operations west of the Rhine, a review has been undertaken of the appreciation and plan for future operations as outlined in SCAF 189 (amended by SCAF 194). In doing so the original directive from the Combined Chiefs of Staff has been borne in mind, namely that the object is to undertake operations aimed at the heart of Germany and the destruction of her armed forces. Note has also been taken of the importance assigned by the Combined Chiefs of Staff to the advantages of the northern line of approach into Germany as opposed to the southern.

Since SCAF 180 was dispatched, the situation has improved to the extent that we have reached the Rhine throughout its length before launching major operations east of the river. This will result in an economy in defensive forces and will make more forces immediately available than originally anticipated.

I am still convinced that it is essential to complete first the isolation of the Ruhr. The operations north of the Ruhr, however, only have limited possibilities for deployment owing to restricted routes. The maximum force which can probably be deployed in that area until railroads have been carried across the Rhine amounts to some 35 divisions. There will be available for the offensive some 40 divisions which cannot be deployed in the north for at least two months subsequent to the crossing.[35]

I shall therefore be able to widen the base of the operations to isolate the Ruhr, by advancing also in force from the south. This will greatly increase the speed of deployment of offensive forces against the enemy as it will enable them to be deployed through two bridgeheads and on a wider front.

These northern and southern thrusts would be instructed to join up in the Lippstadt – Arolsen area.[36] They would then proceed at once to the clearing up of the area enclosed by the thrusts. This would ensure the reduction of the defensive commitments of the inner flanks of the thrusts and along the Rhine. Depending on the situation it may be necessary to complete this operation before concentrating forces for a further advance into the heart of Germany. On the other hand enemy strength may be so reduced at this stage that the further advance could be undertaken concurrently.

I intend therefore to allocate initially three armies of 30 to 35 divisions to the north of the Ruhr, three armies of 30 to 35 divisions to the thrust from the Saar, to employ two armies in a defensive role along the upper and middle Rhine respectively, and to retain six divisions in SHAEF reserve (not counting the airborne divisions), with a view to exploiting either of the thrusts as proves expedient."

---

33 Lieutenant-General Sir Frederick E. Morgan KCB (1894–1967), British Army officer who served as Smith's deputy for Intelligence and Operations. He was often called upon to smooth over relations between Montgomery and senior American staff at SHAEF headquarters.
34 By 23 March the Allied armies had cleared the west bank of the Rhine. 12th Army Group had a bridgehead in the Remagen area and Third Army had just crossed south of Frankfurt and was planning further crossings near Koblenz over the next few days; 21st Army Group was about to launch Operation VARSITY to cross the Rhine in the north.
35 It is made clear that 21st Army Group's area north of the Ruhr did not have the infrastructure to support a major offensive east of the Rhine.
36 Thrusts would have to come from north and south of the Ruhr to make sure the maximum number of divisions was being deployed; they could then strike into the heart of Germany once the Ruhr was surrounded.

Eisenhower to Marshall	*30 March*	Ref: FWD-18331

I am preparing an immediate answer to your W-60507 which should be with you in a few hours. Frankly the charge that I have changed plans has no possible basis in fact. The principal effort north of the Ruhr was always adhered to with the object of isolating that valuable area. Now that I can foresee the time that my forces can be concentrated in the Kassel area, I am still adhering to my old plan of launching from there one main attack calculated to accomplish, in conjunction with the Russians, the destruction of the enemy armed forces. To disperse strong forces along the northern coast <u>before</u> the primary object is accomplished will leave me too weak to launch a powerful threat straight through the center. My plan will get the ports and all the other things on the north coast more speedily and decisively than will the dispersion now urged upon me by Wilson's message to you.

The Final Drive into Germany

Marshall to Eisenhower	*27 March*	Ref: W-59315

From the current operation reports, it looks like the German defense system in the West may break up. This would permit you to move a considerable number of your divisions rapidly eastward on a broad front. What are your views on the possibility and soundness of pushing United States forces rapidly forward on, say, the Nürnberg – Linz or Karlsruhe – Munich axis? The idea behind this is that in a situation where Germany is breaking up, rapid action might prevent the formation of any organized resistance areas. The mountainous country in the south is considered a possibility for one of these.[37]

One of the problems which arises with the disintegrating German resistance is that of meeting the Russians. What are your ideas on control and coordination to prevent unfortunate instances and to sort out the two advancing forces? One possibility is an agreed line of demarcation. The arrangements we now have with the Russians appear quite inadequate for the situation we may face and it seems that steps ought to be initiated without delay to provide for you the communication and liaison you will need with them during the period when your forces may be mopping up in close proximity or in contact with Russian Forces.[38]

Eisenhower to Marshall	*28 March*	Ref: FWD-18273

I have today dispatched a cable to Deane and Archer, transmitting a message from me to Stalin on the question of where we should aim to line up with his forces. You will have seen the copy sent to the Combined Chiefs of Staff for information. My views agree closely with your own, although I think that the Leipzig–Dresden area is of primary importance. Besides offering the shortest route to the present Russian positions, it would divide the German forces roughly in half and would overrun the one remaining industrial area in Germany to which also the High Command Headquarters and Ministries are reported to be moving.

I also agree on the importance of forestalling the possibilities of the enemy forming organized resistance areas, and will make a drive toward Linz and Munich as soon as circumstances will allow.

As regards control and coordination of our forces and the Russians, I adhere to my views expressed in SCAF 141. You will see from SCAF 252 that I am still trying to do everything possible to perfect liaison arrangements. I am conscious of present shortcomings in this

---

37 Marshall is referring to the Alps; Seventh Army would have the task of driving fast along the northern side of the area, stopping German units from withdrawing into the mountains.
38 The fear was that the air or ground troops could accidentally fire on each other, which would at best cause a diplomatic incident and at worst escalate into full blown conflict.

respect and would appreciate any help you can give me. I do not think we can tie ourselves down to a demarcation line but am approaching the Russians through Deane with the suggestion that when our forces meet, either side will withdraw to its own occupational zone at the request of the other side.

Marshall to Deane, Eisenhower for info   *30 March*   *Ref: WX-61011*
The British Chiefs of Staff presented to the Combined Chiefs in connection with their discussion of SCAF 252 a message from Archer giving substance of a message Deane sent to Eisenhower concerning his SCAF 252. We naturally assume that Deane presented to Stalin the contents of SCAF 252 as soon as received. It is represented that hereafter information copies of messages of the nature of those reported through the Combined Chiefs of Staff and Archer be furnished here.

Deane to Marshall, for info to Eisenhower   *31 March*   *Ref: MX-23558*
SCAF 252, received by me at noon 29th March, directed Admiral Archer and me to do anything we could to assist in getting a full reply to General Eisenhower's message to Marshal Stalin.

I felt, and Archer agreed, that a personal interview with Marshal Stalin, which could only be arranged through our Ambassadors, promised the best results. I cabled General Eisenhower at once for background information which we could use in discussion with Stalin. Our Ambassadors on 29th March requested a meeting with Stalin for 30th March, and yesterday we were told that the meeting would be held tonight, 31st March, at which our Ambassadors, Archer and I, and undoubtedly Antonov, will be present.[39] I informed General Eisenhower of the time set for the meeting in my M-23546 to him yesterday. In the same message I suggested to General Eisenhower that I propose to Stalin that a radio-teletype channel between Moscow and SHAEF be established at once. The equipment for such a channel is already here. I asked General Eisenhower for an urgent reply if he did not wish me to propose the radio communication channel.

I was wrong in not sending an information copy of my cables to General Eisenhower to the Combined Chiefs of Staff and the British Chiefs of Staff, and shall not make the mistake again.

Eisenhower to Marshall   *31 March*   *Ref: FWD-18393*
You may be sure that in future policy cables passing between myself and the Military Mission to Moscow will be repeated to the Combined Chiefs and the British Chiefs of Staff, reference your WX-61011 to Deane.

Deane to Eisenhower, Marshall   *1 April*   *Ref: MX-23572*
Meeting with Stalin tonight at the Kremlin. Molotov was present.[40] Stalin was given an English and Russian text of the message contained in SCAF-252. After Stalin had read Eisenhower's message, we pointed out the operations described in the message on the map.

Stalin immediately reacted and said that the plan seemed to be a good one, but that he of course, could not commit himself definitely until he had consulted his staff. He said

---

39 General Aleksei I. Antonov (1896–1962), Chief of Staff of the Soviet Army.
40 Vyacheslav M. Molotov (1890–1986), the People's Commissar for Foreign Affairs.

that he would give an answer tomorrow. He seemed to be favorably impressed with the direction of the attack in central Germany and also of the secondary attack in the south.

We emphasized the urgency of obtaining Stalin's views in order that the plans could be properly concerted. We called attention to Eisenhower's proposal that liaison officers from SHAEF be attached to Stalin's headquarters in Moscow and suggested in that connection that a radio teletype channel should be set up at once between SHAEF and Moscow.

We then said that Eisenhower would like to have Stalin's current estimate of the enemy situation. Stalin stated that he could not give his estimate then, but would do so in his answer tomorrow. He asked us if we were prepared to give Eisenhower's estimate during the present meeting. We then gave the highlights of Eisenhower's estimate of the enemy situation.

Stalin asked if Eisenhower had any knowledge of prepared positions towards the center of Germany, to which we replied in the negative. Stalin then asked if we knew of German withdrawal of troops from Norway. We stated Eisenhower had not given us any indication of this. Stalin asked whether the advance of the secondary attack in the south would come from Italy or from the Western Front. We said that we understood it would come from the Western Front.

We then went over the present German order of battle on the Western Front with Stalin as he indicated that he was interested in having us do so. Stalin asked if we could verify Soviet information that there were 60 German divisions on the Western Front. We replied that we had counted 61, but gave him the most recent changes that have been received from you. Stalin wished to know if the Germans have any additional reserves on the Western Front, but we replied that apparently they had not.

Stalin was much impressed with the number of prisoners that had been taken in the month of March and said certainly this will help finish the war very soon.

Harriman[41] asked Stalin about the weather conditions on the front in Eastern Germany. Stalin replied that it had considerably improved. Harriman then pressed him further by asking if his previous estimate that the operations might be bogged down the end of March still held good. Stalin replied that the situation was much better than he had anticipated. The floods came early this year, and now the roads are in the process of drying. He left us all with the impression that Russians are not tied down because the weather.

Stalin said that the Germans were resisting strongly in the mountains of Czechoslovakia but that the resistance was of such character that it could be overcome. He said that the Germans had concentrated armored divisions northeast of Lake Balaton,[42] but that these had been defeated. He said that the Germans are now centering their resistance in the Bratislava Gap[43] but that he felt confident in overcoming it. The Germans still had sixteen divisions in Latvia, but he thought at best that they could only move out three divisions without their artillery and that it would take a month.

Clark Kerr[44] commented on the valuable contribution by the Red Army in capturing Gdynia and Danzig.[45] Stalin said that it took about week to reduce Danzig. Evidently there was only about a third of the Germans who wanted to fight. The S.S. troops shot down in sight of the Red Army those Germans who wished to surrender.

Stalin had apparently been considering Eisenhower's message all through the discussion,

---

41 William A. Harriman, US Ambassador to the Soviet Union.
42 Lake Balaton is in western Hungary and is the largest inland lake in Central Europe.
43 Bratislava in modern day Slovakia, close to the border of Austria and Hungary.
44 Sir Archibald Clark Kerr, 1st Baron Inverchapel GCMG, PC (1882–1951), British Ambassador to the Soviet Union.
45 Two ports in Gdansk Bay, on the Baltic coast.

and at this point he reverted to it and said that the plan for Eisenhower's main effort was a good one, in that it accomplished the most important objective of dividing Germany in half. He felt that the direction of the attack would also be favorable for a juncture with the Red Army.[46] He felt that the Germans' last stand would probably be in the mountains of Western Czechoslovakia and Bavaria.

The meeting ended with Marshal Stalin assuring us that he would give a reply to Eisenhower's the message tomorrow.

Montgomery Disagrees with Eisenhower's Plans for the Advance to the Elbe

Montgomery to Eisenhower   27 March   *Ref: M562*

1. Today I issued orders to Army Commanders for the operations eastwards which are now about to begin. My general plan is as outlined in the following paragraphs.[47]

2. My intention is to drive hard for the line of the Elbe using Ninth Army and Second Army. The right of the Ninth Army will be directed on Magdeburg and the left of Second Army on Hamburg.

3. Right boundary of Ninth Army will be the general line Hamm–Paderborn–Magdeburg. Left boundary of Second Army will be the general line Hengeou–Lingen–Haselunne–Bremen–Hamburg. Inter Army boundaries will be the general line all inclusive Ninth Army Munster–Hanover–Wittenberg inclusive on the Elbe.

4. Each Army will use two corps forward and one watching its rear on the outer flank. Ninth Army will have XIX Corps right and XIII Corps left and XVI Corps watching the Ruhr and the general area about Lippstadt and Paderborn. Second Army will have XVIII Corps right and XIII Corps left and XXX Corps watching the general area about Lingen and Enschede.

5. Canadian Army will operate as ordered in paragraphs 40 to 42 of M559 dated 9th March, so as to open up the supply route through Arnhem. The Army will then operate to clear northeast Holland and west Holland and the coastal area to the north of the left boundary of Second Army. The order of batting for these tasks is not yet clear.

6. The operations will be similar in design to those when we crossed the Seine and drove hard across the rear of the Pas de Calais with the Canadian Army mopping up the coastal belt of the Pas de Calais later.

7. I have ordered Ninth and Second Armies to move their armored and mobile forces forward at once and to get through to the Elbe with the utmost speed and drive. The situation looks good and events should begin to move rapidly in a few days.

46 This agreement over the direction of SHAEF's advance into the Leipzig area of central Germany would be made by 12th Army Group.
47 Codenamed Operation PLUNDER the advance from the Rhine around Wesel, heading northeast past the north side of the Ruhr industrial area, aiming to meet 12th Army Group in the Kassel–Paderborn area.

8. My Tactical Headquarters move to an area about 1033 northeast of Bonninghardt on Thursday 29th March. Thereafter the axis on which my Tactical Headquarters move will be Wesel–Munster–Wiedenbruck–Herford–Hanover – thence via the Autobahn to Berlin. I hope.[48]

9. Please acknowledge.

Eisenhower to Montgomery　　　　*28 March*　　　　　　*Ref: FWD-18272*
Reference is made to your M-562 to T.A.C. Headquarters 21 Army Group. I agree in general with your plans up to the point of gaining contact with Bradley east of the Ruhr. However, thereafter my present plans are now being coordinated with Stalin area as outlined in following paragraphs.[49]

As soon as you have joined hands with Bradley in the Kassel–Paderborn area, Ninth U.S. Army will revert to Bradley's command. Bradley will be responsible for mopping up and occupying the Ruhr and with the minimum delay will deliver his main thrust on the axis Erfurt – Leipzig – Dresden to join hands with the Russians.

The mission of your Army group will be to protect Bradley's northern flank with an inter-army group boundary similar to your right boundary of Second Army, Munster–Hanover inclusive to Bradley, and thence Wittenberg or Stendal as decided later.[50]

When your forces reach the Elbe it may again be desirable for Ninth Army to revert to your operational control to facilitate the crossing of that obstacle. If so, necessary orders will then be issued.

Devers will protect Bradley's right flank and be prepared later when the situation permits to advance to join hands with the Russians in the Danube valley.

As you say, the situation looks good.[51]

Montgomery to Eisenhower　　　　*29 March*　　　　　　*Ref: M562/1*
I note from FWD-18272 that you intend to change the command set up. If you feel this is necessary, I pray you do not do so until we reach the Elbe as such action would not help the great movement which is now beginning to develop.

Eisenhower to Montgomery　　　　*31 March*　　　　　　*Ref: FWD-18389*
This message is in further explanation of our recent exchange of telegrams reference future plans. My plan is simple and aims at dividing and destroying the German forces and joining hands with the Red Army. Subject to any information which I may receive from Stalin, the axis Kassel–Leipzig appears to be the most direct line of advance to achieve this object. On this axis our forces would also overrun the important Leipzig industrial area and the area to which the German ministries are moving.

I therefore intend to have the bulk of my disposable strength concentrated in the center ready to move, after we have attained our Leipzig objective, first, if feasible to the north

---

48 At this stage Montgomery expects to be advancing all the way to Berlin, even though the Soviet Army have been less that 50 miles east from the city for some time.
49 Eisenhower's plan was going to be presented to Stalin on 1 April.
50 Montgomery wanted to continue advancing towards the Baltic coast and Berlin with both armies under his command. Eisenhower was going to transfer Ninth US Army to Bradley's 12th Army Group to reinforce its drive across central Germany to meet the Soviet advance from the east.
51 The general orders for the advance given in this letter were copied to General Bradley at 21st Army Group and General Devers at 6th Army Group on 29 March.

to seize the important naval, political and shipping objectives across the Elbe or to the south to destroy any effective concentration of forces which the enemy may succeed in creating. The course which I will adopt must depend upon the development of a very fluid situation.[52]

The situation in the Ruhr must be brought under control before Bradley can initiate the thrust to Leipzig. To achieve this quickly, certain forces of the Ninth and First Armies must be employed. These must be reinforced and relieved promptly by divisions of the Fifteenth Army passing over the Rhine Bridges of the Ninth and First Armies. A mopping up task of this nature, in a densely populated area, should clearly be controlled by one commander. Moreover, it is Bradley who be straining to release his thrust to the east and it is clearly very desirable that he should be in the position to judge when the situation in the Ruhr warrants it.[53]

For these reasons I must adhere to my decision about Ninth Army passing to Bradley's command when firm junction has been effected at Paderborn. Naturally I will give you warning, at least 24 hours, before withdrawing Ninth Army from your command and in selecting the date my chief concern will be to maintain the general flow of our advance. As I have already told you, it appears from this distance that an American formation will again pass you at a later stage for operations beyond the Elbe.

You will note that in none of this do I mention Berlin. That place has become, so far as I am concerned, nothing more than a geographical location, I have never been interested in these. My purpose is to destroy the enemy's forces and his powers to resist.[54]

Manifestly, when the time comes, we must do everything possible to push across the Elbe without delay, drive to the coast at Lübeck and seal off the Danish Peninsula.[55]

Praise for the 4th Armored Division

Marshall to Eisenhower   *27 March*   *Ref: W-59318*

Reports indicate the 4th Armored Division is again carrying out a particularly brilliant operation, with the same dash and power it demonstrated in the drive to the Rhine and that to the south of the Moselle. Might it not be well to cite it now on the success of these three specific actions?[56]

If a citation is believed by you, Bradley and Patton, to be merited by this division, now appears to be the time. If there is any delay in acting there may well be a number of divisions spearheading advances all along the front and serious resentment would be engendered. An immediate citation would act as a spur to all.

If you have the same view, this is your authority to act.

---

52 By concentrating the advance to Leipzig, Eisenhower would be meeting the Soviets as soon as possible, splitting the German armies in two. Then they could move either north or south, whichever was more profitable at the time.

53 Ninth and First Army would have to contain the 425,000 troops of Army Group B in the Ruhr until Fifteenth Army had crossed the Rhine and taken over the task. There were also millions of civilians trapped in the devastated area.

54 This is the first intimation that Eisenhower is not interested in capturing Berlin; rather, he is focused on bringing about the capitulation of the German armed forces.

55 Montgomery's drive would cut off the German troops in the Danish Peninsula from the rest of the German High Command.

56 This is an unusual recommendation from Marshall for an individual division. Commanded by Major-General Hugh J. Gaffey (1895–1946), previously General Patton's Chief of Staff at Third Army headquarters, it had spearheaded the advance to Bastogne during the Battle of the Bulge, advanced from Luxembourg and crossed the Moselle at Trier. Gaffey was replaced by Major-General William M. Hoge just before it crossed the Rhine on 24–25 March.

Eisenhower to Marshall   *28 March*   *Ref: FWD-18258*

Bradley, Patton and I are all in full agreement with your suggestion for citing the 4th Armored Division. This will be done immediately and the citation will include the operation for the advance on Bastogne, the penetration to the Rhine, the attack across the Mosel and the later advances across the Rhine. Copy of the citation will be forwarded to the War Department.

Praise for Bradley and Hodges to Counterbalance Reports on Patton

Eisenhower to Marshall   *30 March*   *Ref: FWD-18341*

In our latest spectacular successes which have carried advanced elements of First Army just south of Paderborn, Hodges has been the spearhead and the scintillating star. From the end of February, when he started driving southeast from the Cologne area with III and V Corps, to cut the communications of the enemy in the Eifel and succeeded also in seizing a bridgehead at Remagen,[57] his drive, clearheaded thinking and tactical skill have shone even more brightly than they did in his great pursuit across France, in which First Army's part was the most difficult given to any U.S. formation but brilliantly and speedily executed, often against much resistance.

East of the Rhine he not only boldly and rapidly built up the Remagen bridgehead but at all times was clear as to the advantages we could gain from the exploitation of that position. He attracted to himself a total of sixteen of the depleted German divisions and yet by his constant aggressiveness, prevented them from solidifying a line and so facilitated the later crossings of the Rhine by both Third and Seventh Armies.[58] As quickly as he had built the necessary number of bridges he made a spectacular breakout and was even able to thrust strong armored columns deep into Patton's zone, in order to assist the rapid advance of Third Army.[59] He had handled his forces magnificently. Now he is well up toward the Paderborn area and on his right and rear, Third and Seventh Armies are echeloned on a broad front.

I should like very much to see Hodges get credit in the United States for his great work. Locally I have the embarrassment that always applies to an Allied commander if he singles out any one part of the whole front for a particular commendation, but it occurs to me that as a purely United States proposition, Surles[60] should be able to build a story from his situation maps and by tracing progress of First Army from the day of the invasion to the present moment, with emphasis on the action during the past month. Incidentally there seems to be a mistaken notion at home that Third Army made the breakthrough at Avranches.[61] This was done by First Army under Bradley, as is evident from the fact that Third Army Headquarters was not even brought into action until August 1st.

Equally with Hodges, the part that Bradley has played in this campaign should be painted in more brilliant colors. Never once has he held back in attempting any maneuver, no matter how bold in conception, and never once has he "paused to re-group" when there was an opportunity lying in his front. His handling of his army commanders has

---

57 9th Armored Division crossed the Rhine at Remagen on 7 March after German engineers failed to destroy the Ludendorff Bridge.

58 Over the days that followed, First Army pushed everything it could across the river under difficult conditions, and kept advancing before the German reserves rushing in could stabilize the area.

59 In other words, Hodges helped Patton's advance east of the Rhine.

60 General Surles, Director of Bureau of Public Relations, War Department.

61 This was the breakout on 12th Army Group's western flank, at the culmination of Operation COBRA, opening the route south and east into central France and west into the Brittany Peninsula.

been superb and his energy, common sense, tactical skill and complete loyalty have made him a great lieutenant on whom I always rely with the greatest confidence.

I do not, repeat not, decry or deprecate the accomplishment of the other army commanders because all have performed in the finest fashion. What I am trying to say is that First Army's part in this whole campaign has been seemingly overlooked by the headline writers and others have received credit for things which Hodges and Bradley were primarily responsible. I consider Bradley the greatest battle-line commander I have met in this war. In a recent press conference I paid particular tribute to the brilliant work of Bradley in handling his forces from February 23rd to date, but I do not know whether this was picked up by newsmen.[62]

I hope that Surles will put his imagination to work to figure out some way of giving Hodges his proper credit and showing that Bradley's handling of 12 Army Group has been masterful.

---

62 Eisenhower is clarifying what often happened during the European campaign: the press attributing the deeds of another general to Patton. This exaggeration of Patton's accomplishments at the expense of other commanders has been continued by some historians.

16

APRIL 1945

Explaining SHAEF Strategy to Churchill

Churchill to Eisenhower   *31 March*   *Ref: 2072*

Following is Private, Confidential, Personal and Top Secret from Prime Minister to General of the Army, Eisenhower.

Very many thanks for your FWD-18334. It seems to me personally that if the enemy's resistance does not collapse, the shifting of the main axis of advance so much farther to the southward and the withdrawal of the Ninth U.S. Army from the 21st Army Group may stretch Montgomery's front so widely that the offensive role which was assigned to him may peter out.[1] I do not know why it would be an advantage not to cross the Elbe. If the enemy's resistance should weaken, as you evidently expect and which may well be accorded, why should we not cross the Elbe and advance as far eastward as possible? This has an important political bearing, as the Russian army of the south seems certain to enter Vienna and overrun Austria. If we deliberately leave Berlin to them, even if it should be in our grasp, the double event may strengthen their conviction, already apparent, that they have done everything.[2]

Further, I do not consider myself that Berlin has yet lost its military and certainly not its political significance. The fall of Berlin would have a profound psychological effect on German resistance in every part of the Reich. While Berlin holds out, great masses of Germans will feel it their duty to go down fighting. The idea that the capture of Dresden and junction with the Russians there would be a superior gain does not commend itself to me. The parts of the German Government Departments which have moved south can very quickly move southward again. But whilst Berlin remains under the German flag, it cannot in my opinion fail to be the most decisive point in Germany.[3]

Therefore, I should greatly prefer persistence in the plan on which we crossed the Rhine, namely that the Ninth U.S. Army should march with the 21st Army Group to the Elbe and beyond to Berlin. This would not be in any way inconsistent with the great general thrust which you are now so rightly developing as the result of the brilliant operation of the Armies south of the Ruhr. It only shifts the weight of one Army to the northernmost flank and this avoids relegation of His Majesty's Forces to an unexpected restricted sphere.

---

1 Having been made aware of Eisenhower's new strategy, Churchill wants Eisenhower to reconsider and continue with 21st Army Group leading the advance.

2 While Churchill's wish is to advance as far east as possible, Eisenhower has many difficulties to consider, including meeting the Russians safely, withdrawing to occupation zones and keeping Stalin informed of his intentions.

3 While Churchill believes that the capture of the German capital is key to ending the war, Eisenhower has to consider the risks of advancing on the capital against his objective: the defeat of the German Armed Forces for the minimum number of Allied casualties.

Of course I am treating this correspondence between as personal and private, just as if it were an unofficial talk. I may use some of my arguments again in other quarters but no with reference to anything that has passed between us.[4]

Eisenhower to Churchill   *1 April*   *Ref: FWD-18428*

After reading your 2072 dated yesterday, I think you still have some misunderstanding of what I intend to do. In the first place, I repeat that I have not changed any plan. I made certain groupings of this force in order to cross the Rhine with the main, deliberate, thrust in the north, isolate the Ruhr and disrupt, surround or destroy the Germans defending that area. This is as far as strategic objectives of this force have ever been definitely approved by me, because obviously such a victory over the German forces in the west, and such a blow to his industrial capacity, would necessarily create new situations requiring study and analysis before the next broad pattern of effort could be accurately sketched.[5]

The situation that is now developing is one that I have held before my staff for more than a year, as the one toward which we should strive, namely, that our forces should be concentrated across the Rhine through the avenues of Wesel and Frankfurt and situated roughly in a great triangle with the apex resting in the Kassel area.[6] From there onward the problem was to determine the direction of the blow that would create maximum disorganization of the remaining German forces and the German power to resist. I have never lost sight of the great importance of the drive to the northern coast, although your telegram did introduce a new idea with respect to political importance of the early attainment of particular objectives. I clearly see your point in this matter.

The only difference between your suggestions and my plan is one of timing and even this might yet be relegated to a matter of relative unimportance, depending upon the degree of resistance met. What I mean is this: in order to assure the success of each of my planned efforts, I concentrate first in the center to gain the position I need.[7] As it looks to me now, the next move thereafter should be to have Montgomery cross the Elbe, reinforced, as necessary, by American troops, and reach at least a line including Lübeck on the coast.[8] If the German resistance from now on should progressively and definitely crumble, you can see that there would be little, if any, difference in time between gaining the central position and crossing the Elbe. On the other hand, if resistance tends to stiffen at all, you can see that it is vitally necessary that I concentrate each effort, and do not allow myself to be dispersed by attempting to do all these projects at once.[9]

I am disturbed, if not hurt, that you should suggest any thought on my part to "relegate his Majesty's forces to an unexpected restricted sphere". Nothing is further from my mind and I think my record over two and a half years of commanding Allied forces should eliminate any such ideas. But further to this point, I completely fail to see how the role, actions or prestige of the Second British and the Canadian Armies are materially affected by the fact

4 Off the record Churchill wants the British Army to play a key role in the final battle for Germany, in particular the capture of Berlin.
5 Eisenhower is reminding Churchill that his objective had been to surround the Ruhr, severely limiting Germany's industrial capacity. Having done that it was time to consider the next move and Eisenhower had to include the Soviets in his plans.
6 Advancing east from Wesel and northeast from Frankfurt, meeting at Kassel to isolate the Ruhr. The advance would then head east towards Leipzig, as agreed with Stalin.
7 Meeting the Russians in the center of Germany, from where 12th Army Group could turn north or south, whichever seemed most profitable.
8 Reaching the Baltic coast, cutting off all German troops in Holland, northwest Germany and Denmark.
9 Eisenhower has to guard against a last determined stand by German forces, and concentrating his own forces in the center is the best way of countering any such resistance.

that Ninth Army, advancing in its own zone, is controlled by Bradley, until I can be assured that our rear areas are substantially cleaned out and the thrust to Leipzig is successful.[10] British and Canadian Armies will work in exactly the same zone that Montgomery planned for them and he has even been given the opportunity to change that boundary if he so desires. The maximum extent to which his plans could be affected would be a possible short delay in making a power thrust across the Elbe, but I repeat that if "power" tactics are still necessary at that time then we must concentrate for each job, and the rear must be in a satisfactory state.

Quite naturally if at any moment "eclipse" conditions should suddenly come about every-where along the front, we would rush forward and Lübeck and Berlin would be included in our important targets.[11]

Churchill to Eisenhower   *2 April*   *Ref: 2096*

Thank you again for your most kind telegram. It would be a grief to me if anything in my last message disturbs or still more pains you. I only meant that the effect of 21st Army Group arriving on the Elbe so spread out that it would be condemned to a static role, would be a good deal less than what we hoped for, namely to enter Berlin side-by-side with our American comrades. This impression arose in my mind because of what now turns out to be a misprint in your FWD-18334, paragraph 4, which reached me in the follow-ing form. "Montgomery will be responsible on patrol task and I propose to his increase forces" etc. The expression "on patrol task" disturbed me. It is now established that what you really said was "for these tasks", namely clearing the northernmost ports and forcing the Elbe. The words "on patrol tasks" were in fact substituted for "these tasks" by clerical error. The exposure of this error will, I am sure, explain my phrasing to you.[12]

Returning to the main theme, I am however all the more impressed with the impor-tance of entering Berlin, which may well be open to us by reply from Moscow to you, which in paragraph 3 states "Berlin has lost its former strategic importance". This should be read in light of what I mentioned of the political aspect. I deem it highly important that we should shake hands with the Russians as far to the east as possible.[13]

In a telegram which I sent yesterday to the President, I included the following passage: "Beginning at this point, I wish to place on record the complete confidence felt by His Majesty's Government in General Eisenhower, our pleasure that our armies are serving under his command and our admiration of great and shining quality, character and per-sonality which he has proved himself to possess in all difficulties of handling an Allied command. Moreover, I should like to express to you, Mr. President, as I have already done orally in the field to General Eisenhower, my heartfelt congratulations on the glorious victories and advances by all armies of the United States centered in the recent battle on the Rhine and over it." End.

The arrival of your additional information in SCAF-260 has largely allayed the anxieties of our Staff and they have telegraphed in this sense to their opposite number in Washington. You will, I am sure, make allowance for the fact that we heard nothing at all about this either

---

10 A sharp reminder from Eisenhower that his strategy has never been nationalistic; after all 21st Army Group had been given the leading role during the advance across France and Belgium into Holland in the autumn of 1944, and again during the crossing of the Rhine only two weeks earlier.

11 Eclipse conditions means a sudden collapse of the German armed forces.

12 This illustrates how easily tension and misunderstanding could arise by the mistyping of a couple of key words.

13 While Eisenhower was focused on the defeat of Germany's armed forces and pursuing a strategy agreed with Stalin, Churchill was concerned about the post-war situation.

officially, or from our Deputy,[14] until we saw your telegram to Stalin and this telegram made them think that very large changes were proposed.

I regard all this business as smoothing itself down quite satisfactory, though some correspondence is still proceeding between our Chiefs of Staffs Committees.

Again my congratulations on the great developments. Much may happen in the West before the date of Stalin's main offensive.[15]

Marshall to Eisenhower   6 April   *Ref: W-64244*
In a message to the President, the P.M. has stated that the changes in your main plan have turned out to be very much less than the British had at first supposed, and that his personal relations with you are of the most friendly character. Further, that he regards the matter as closed and to prove his sincerity he uses one of his very few Latin quotations "amantium irae amoris integration est", which I understand means "lovers' quarrels are part of love". The P.M. did make the statement "It was a pity that Eisenhower's telegram was sent to Stalin without anything been said to our Chiefs of Staff or to our Deputy, Air Chief Marshall Tedder, or to our Commander-in-Chief, Field Marshall Montgomery." Question, was Tedder informed or consulted in the matter?

Eisenhower to Marshall   7 April   *Ref: FWD-18707*
The message I sent to Stalin was a purely military move, taken in accordance with ample authorizations and instructions previously issued by the Combined Chiefs of Staff. Frankly, it did not cross my mind to confer in advance with the Combined Chiefs of Staff. Because I have assumed that I am held responsible for the effectiveness of military operations in this Theater, and it was a natural question to the head of the Russian forces to inquire as to the direction and timing of the next major thrust, and to outline my own intentions.[16]

We are now holding up a message to the Mission in Russia, the purpose of which is to establish some concrete arrangement for mutual identification of air and ground forces, and to suggest a procedure to be followed in the event our forces should meet the Russians in any part of Germany, each with an offensive mission. It is critically important that this question be settled quickly on a practical basis. Our respective tactical air forces will soon be meeting each other daily.[17]

I hope it will not be forgotten that some of the ablest members of my staff are from the British Army. Such men as Tedder, Morgan, Whiteley and Strong[18] possess great ability and are absolutely unimpeachable in their objective approach to every question. Tedder was freely consulted when developing the outline of our major plan and on the necessity of communicating with the Russians in the attempt to achieve coordination. Due to his absence from headquarters, he did not see the exact terminology of the message. He completely agreed in principle with the action taken.

---

14 Air Chief Marshall Tedder.
15 Stalin's main offensive on Berlin started on 16 April.
16 As far as Eisenhower is concerned he has the authority to agree strategy and make practical arrangements with the head of the Soviet armed forces now that their two armies were moving closer. Marshall is concerned about the political complications of this final stage of the war.
17 Eisenhower illustrates that while the politicians are focused on the post-war situation, the Allies still have to bring the war to a conclusion. While the Germans have been virtually defeated, there still remains the problem that two huge armies are advancing rapidly towards each other.
18 Air Chief Marshal Tedder, Deputy Supreme Commander of SHAEF, General Sir Frederick Morgan, Deputy Chief of Staff to General Smith, General Sir John Whiteley, deputy to SHAEF Assistant Chief of Staff, Operations (G-3), and Major-General Sir Kenneth W. D. Strong, (1900–1982), SHAEF Chief of Intelligence (G-2).

Montgomery to Eisenhower   9 April   *Ref: M-1070*

Have received your letter dated the 8 April. It is quite clear to me what you want. I will crack along on the Northern flank 100% and we'll do all we can to draw the enemy forces away from the main effort being made by Bradley.[19]

Death of an Armored Division Commander

Eisenhower to Marshall   1 April   *Ref: FWB-18439*

You probably know that General Maurice Rose,[20] commanding 3rd Armored Division, was killed in action two days ago. Assuming the official notification has been furnished his family, will you please see that Mrs. Rose receives the following from me:

> "My dear Mrs. Rose: Although I have not been privileged to meet you personally, my admiration, respect and affection for your late husband were so profound that I feel impelled to send you some words of sympathy in your tragic loss. He was not only one of the bravest and best, but he was a leader who inspired his men to speedy accomplishments of tasks, that to a lesser man would have appeared almost impossible. He was out in front of his division, leading it in one of its many famous actions, when he met his death. I hope that your realization of the extraordinary worth of his services to his country will help you in some small way to bear your burden of grief. The thoughts and prayers of his legion of warm friends in this Theater are with you. Most sincerely, [signed] Dwight D. Eisenhower."

Safeguarding German Industry in the Ruhr[21]

Marshall to Eisenhower   6 April   *Ref: W-64236*

Discussion here by G-2 and Mr. Stimson relates to effect of the complete destruction of Ruhr industry on the economic future of Europe, destruction that would result from further Allied offensive action. Admiral Leahy, King, Handy and Hull are opposed to asking you any question.[22]

Aside from purely military considerations concerned with advancement of campaign to destroy the German Army, there are the two schools of thought in high government circles here regarding a post war pastoral Germany and a policy of leaving some industrial capacity to benefit the related economy of other European countries lacking Ruhr resources.[23] We naturally assume that you are proceeding in the manner best adapted to the security and rapidity of your thrust into Germany.

Without thought of compromising yourself, or in effect limiting your present military intentions, will you please give me for no other eyes but Mr. Stinson's, mine, Handy's and Hull's, most confidentially, your present intentions as to the Ruhr pocket and your

---

19 After earlier expressing his concerns over the removal of Ninth US Army from 21st Army Group, Montgomery acknowledges his new objective.

20 General Maurice Rose had taken command of 3rd Armored Division, nicknamed the 'Spearhead', in August 1944. He often commanded from the front and on 30 March his jeep ran into a group of German tanks south of Paderborn; Rose was killed as he drew his pistol.

21 The Ruhr had been surrounded by Ninth US Army to the north and First US Army to the south; the two had met near Lippstadt on 1 April and they completed the encirclement by the 4th.

22 Fleet Admiral William D. Leahy, Roosevelt's Chief of Staff; Admiral Ernest J. King, Commander in Chief, US Fleet and Chief of Naval Operations; General Thomas T. Handy, Deputy Chief of Staff, US Army; General John E. Hull, Assistant Chief of Staff, Operations Division.

23 One school of thought wanted to remove Germany's industrial capacity to punish her people for waging war in Europe. The other school believed that Europe needed Germany's industrial capacity to recover from the war.

view as to desirability, or feasibility, of any procedure by which the Ruhr proper might be sealed off.

I assume your forces are already deeply committed to operations directed against the pocket.[24] This message must not in any way embarrass you, or have the slightest effect in limiting your present point of view or intentions. As yet I have no views whatsoever in this matter, except that I think the fat is probably now in the fire and whatever the political conclusions it is too late, too impractical to take any action for such reason.

Eisenhower to Marshall   7 *April*   *Ref: FWD-18697*

I regard the substantial elimination of the enemy forces in the Ruhr as a military necessity. At the very least we must compress his remaining elements into a relatively small area, where they may be contained with a few divisions and so that our problem of maintenance may be minimized. Our attacks against the pocket are coming from the east and southeast, so as to avoid built up areas as far as we can. If the enemy is finally driven into the densely built up areas, where he could be contained with four or five divisions, we would cease those attacks as no longer profitable and let him starve himself into surrender.

In our advance into Germany, we are experiencing the same thing that always happens in an invasion of enemy territory, namely, the need to drop off fighting units to protect the rear and to preserve order among the population. This task is becoming a particularly acute because of the habit of displaced persons, released by our advances, to begin rioting against their ex-master's.[25] Because of this drain on our forces, we must economize everywhere if we are to maintain the vigor and strength of our planned offensives.

In accomplishing the substantial destruction of the enemy in the Ruhr area, we have no intention of inflicting useless or unnecessary damage on existing facilities of any kind. Where step by step fighting takes place in any village or town, some destruction is of course unavoidable and in many instances the Germans themselves have partially destroyed machinery in factories. Moreover, our heavy bombers have already accomplished a tremendous destruction in cities such as Cologne, Essen, Hamm, Düsseldorf and others. Nevertheless, there will be certain assets remaining and I realize that these should be preserved, so far as possible, so that political heads of the United Nations may later dispose of them as they see fit.[26]

I repeat, however, that I cannot afford to have the German forces remain in that area in their present strength and occupying their present extensive area, which is approximately 4,000 square miles. The attacks will proceed to the point where it is cheaper to contain rather than destroy. Incidentally, the enemy in the pocket is fighting obstinately. Our air forces operating in the pocket have already ceased attacking anything, except purely military targets, by which I mean elements of the enemy's armed forces.[27]

---

24 430,000 German soldiers, or 21 divisions, of Army Group B, and millions of civilians were trapped in the Ruhr Pocket.

25 Displaced Persons (known as DPs) were released prisoners from concentration camps, slave labor camps and refugees. It needed a lot of troops to maintain law and order in occupied areas.

26 In summary, while the Ruhr had already been devastated by bombing raids, Eisenhower intended to minimize damage to Germany industry whenever possible. The politicians could decide what to do with the industrial capacity of the area after the war.

27 The last units finally surrendered on 21 April and Army Group B's commander, Field Marshal Walter Model, committed suicide in a forest south of the city of Duisburg.

Justifying Ignoring Berlin as an Objective

Eisenhower to Marshall   7 April   *Ref: FWD-18710*

For your personal information, I give you the following as background in my reluctance from the military viewpoint to lay down Berlin as a major objective of our operations.[28] In the first place, through bombing, as well as through partial transfer of German governmental offices, Berlin has lost much of its former military importance. Next: As a means of ensuring the complete practical division of the enemy on the Western Front, I believe that my central thrust should be in great strength to the area including Leipzig. You will note that in Stalin's reply to my message, he agreed that the best place for us to meet was in the Dresden – Leipzig–Erfurt area, which is deep into that part of Germany that the Russians are eventually to occupy.

The success of that thrust having been assured, it seems obvious that we should get our left flank firmly established on the coast near Lübeck, which is not only on the boundary of the British occupational zone, but the holding of it would prevent Russian occupation of any part of the Danish peninsular. To this extent I thoroughly agree that the north thrust is the most important one. Another move that seems most important is a thrust through the southern mountainous areas, as suggested in one of your telegrams.[29]

If we succeed in doing all these things, a mere glance at the map will show you what enormous areas will be in our possession and consequently how much of our force will be engaged in keeping order in the rear, and how badly our maintenance facilities will be stretched. Our front will then be a bit thin.

I have tried to emphasize that my drive into the Leipzig area is not only the proper direction for the decisive thrust, since it almost completely divides the enemy, but gives me the maximum flexibility. At any time that we could seize Berlin at little cost we should, of course do so. But I regard it as militarily unsound at this stage of the proceedings to make Berlin a major objective, particularly in view of the fact that it is only 35 miles from the Russian lines.

I am the first to admit that a war is waged in pursuance of political ends, and if the Combined Chiefs of Staff should decide that the Allied effort to take Berlin outweighs purely military considerations in the Theater, I would cheerfully readjust my plans and my thinking so as to carry out such an operation.[30] I urgently believe, however, that the capture of Berlin should be left as something that we would do if feasible and practical, as we proceed on the general plan of;

(a) dividing the German forces by a major thrust in the middle,

(b) anchoring our left firmly in the Lübeck area, and

(c) attempting to disrupt any German effort to establish a fortress in the southern mountains.[31]

---

28 Some observers at the time, including General Simpson, whose Ninth US Army was closest to Berlin, criticized Eisenhower's decision. Post-war historians have followed up these claims, some stating that it was one of Eisenhower's biggest mistakes. Here Eisenhower explains his reasoning behind not wanting to advance to Berlin so that General Marshall can present his case to the Combined Chiefs of Staff.

29 21st Army Group to the Baltic coast to protect Denmark on the north flank; 12th Army Group to meet the Soviets around Leipzig in the center, as agreed with Stalin; 6th Army Group to the Alps to stop German units waging a guerrilla war in the mountains.

30 Having stated his reasons for not wishing to advance to Berlin, Eisenhower knew that he had to leave the final decision to the Combined Chiefs of Staff and the politicians. Their final decision was to support Eisenhower's strategy.

31 Eisenhower also knew that the decision to split post-war Germany into four had been made at the Yalta meeting in February 1945. Berlin lay 200 miles inside the Soviet zone, meaning that Allied troops would withdraw to the Elbe after taking the city. He would have also anticipated that casualties fighting for the German capital would be high; it is estimated that the Red Army suffered over 300,000 casualties in the Berlin area. Finally, there was always the chance that Allied and Soviet troops could end up accidentally fighting each other, possibly triggering a conflict between the Allies.

Promoting Corps Commanders

Marshall to Eisenhower   7 April   Ref: WX-64658

I am considering additional promotions to the grade of General and the gradual commencement of advancement of Corps commanders to Lieutenant General. For the moment Handy[32] and I have in mind promoting Hodges and Patton, together with four or five Corps commanders, to Lieutenant General, one of these last in the Italian Theater and one in the Philippines Theater would leave three for you.

What is your reaction as to the entire proposition? What Corps commanders would you propose? Would this procedure stir up resentments? If three is too few, how many would you consider it necessary initially to advance and whom?

I doubt if I can go forward with more than five at this time because I have the obligation to advance three Bureau Chiefs[33] who have served out their four-year term with great distinction but who have not been given equal rank with three or four Bureau Chiefs of the Navy who were made Vice Admirals almost a year ago. The whole thing is most difficult with the constant drive against me in Congress for having overdone high rank in the Army, because we only had one Lieutenant-General in the Civil War[34] and two in the A.E.F.[35]

Eisenhower and Marshall   8 April   Ref: FWD-18815

Bradley and I have been discussing for some time the subject mentioned in your WX-64658. With respect to four star appointments, the selection of Hodges and Patton should not, repeat not, create resentment here because of the length of time these two officers have been bearing the burden of Army command and because also of their fine records.

We are in favor of beginning the promotion of Corps commanders and realize that only a few can be named initially. We consider that priority should be based primarily upon length of service as a successful Corps commander in combat, rather than to attempt to distinguish among refinements of abilities of our successful commanders. Agreement could never be reached on merit basis anyway because each Army commander is perfectly certain that the three best Corps commanders are in his particular army.

My intention had been to recommend on the first list; Collins, Walker, Haislip and Middleton. They are the four Corps commanders, aside from Gerow, who is already promoted, who entered battle prior to August 1st.[36] If the original quota is three I would remove Middleton, in spite of the fact he entered combat earlier than the other two. He was voluntarily retired for some years prior to the war and I feel that the other two, who have stuck with the job continuously, should get the call at this time. Patton and Bradley agree with this view.[37] The selections suggested do not give a promotion at this time to Ninth Army, but that Army has not been so long in combat.

I fully understand your embarrassment in promoting offices to high rank, particularly because of our traditional negative practice. I think we should start to make it clear through our Public Relations that in many respects this war differs from all others in its requirements for considerable rank:

---

32 General Thomas T. Handy, Marshall's Deputy.
33 Department heads.
34 The American Civil War, 1861–1865.
35 American Expeditionary Force which served in France in the First World War.
36 Collins with VII Corps, Walker with XX Corps, Haislip with XV Corps and Middleton with VIII Corps.
37 Colonel Middleton retired from the US Army in October 1937 and become Dean of Administration and later acting Vice President at the Louisiana State University until he was recalled to active duty in January 1941.

- We have the largest army that we have ever produced.[38]
- Hard fighting by large numbers of corps and divisions has far exceeded in duration our World War experience.[39]
- Intimate association with Allied fighting units, which are usually commanded by officers of a very high rank, make some revision of our former practices most desirable (all corps commanders in the British Army are Lieutenant-General automatically):

To men who have borne the burdens of high command in battle over many months, there is little recognition that can be given, except in the form of promotion. For example, Collins has commanded in continuous battle since last June 6, an average of about 70,000 fighting men. Only once or twice in the Civil War battles did General Lee have a larger force under his command. Hodges and Patton have each commanded Armies that have lately averaged 350,000.

It would be my suggestion that some publicity of the nature indicated above be started now, in preparation for the submission of your list. It is even possible that we might create some popular demand for this kind of recognition for individuals, so as to eliminate any embarrassment in your submission of the recommendations.

As an additional suggestion, you might consider the following: I could send you formal recommendations on the men named above, giving practically a citation in each case. Then if you so desired you could publish my full recommendations, if this would help.

Marshall to Eisenhower   *10 April*   *Ref: W-65823*
Please carry out your suggestion as to formal recommendations on the officers named in your message. While I would much prefer that the selections of corps commanders for promotion be made solely on the basis of outstanding performance, I can see your difficulties and I accept your views, and those of Hodges and Patton. However, I do not see the logic of basing the selection upon length of service as a successful Corps commander in combat and then making an exception in Middleton's case. We have consistently followed a policy of promoting on merit regardless of status, whether Regular Army, Reserve, National Guard or retired. I would like to have any further views you have on this matter.

Eisenhower to Marshall   *11 April*   *Ref: FWD-18934*
I have given further study to your W-65823, reference selection of Corps commanders. I have always held that merit should be, so far as possible, be the basis of all promotions, but just as you had the problem in your recent four star slate of distributing recognition somewhat around the world to all theaters, I have the same in distributing them among my several armies. In addition, one reason that Bradley, Patton and I give principal weight to the length of service as a successful corps commander was that the long pull gives the opportunity to test ability, so as to eliminate the probability of mistakes.

In Middleton's case, Patton's detailed opinion is that the only other corps commander he would prefer is Walker, but that if compelled to name a man for a higher echelon, he would take Middleton. This seems to make Walker the logical choice, as I have no probability of needing a new army commander. In any event, Collins will get such a post. Another type of example is that of Gillem in the Ninth Army. He has performed brilliantly and all are agreed

---

38 The US Army transported 1.6 million soldiers to the UK for the European campaign alone.
39 Although the AEF entered the trenches in April 1917, most American units only took part in the final campaigns of St Mihiel and the Meuse Argonne.

that he is worthy of any recognition we can give him, but his combat experience compared to Walker, Middleton and Haislip is still limited.[40]

In a personal conversation with Patch of the Seventh Army, he believes that Haislip is the one that should be recognized in the Seventh Army, both by reason of his sound leadership and his length of experience as a successful corps commander. However, his newest corps commander, Milburn,[41] has made such a deep impression upon Patch that he says "in some ways I consider him the best of the three".

I give you all this to show them that my initial selections, when confined to a total of three, necessarily represent something of a compromise, based on demonstrated ability as a corps commander over the long pull, a necessity to distribute the promotions among the armies but definitely coupled with the factor of merit as corps commanders, so far as I could sort out the judgments of the several army and army group commanders.

I have always ignored the differences between Regular Army, National Guard and Reserve. In the case I mentioned, I merely pointed out that all of the officers concerned had been Regulars, but my thought was that since one of them had previously retired, and would presumably get back on the retired list at the end of hostilities, this seems to us to tilt the scales in favor of someone else.[42] To show you the wide differences of opinion these matters, I have at least one army commander who would not willingly take Collins in his army, yet I am perfectly certain that he is the logical number one choice. As between Haislip, Walker, Middleton and Gillem for numbers two and three, I have been having a hard time as you can see from the length of this telegram, attempting to explain my so-called mental processes.[43]

Close if any behind this list, I have such outstanding fighters as Van Fleet, Eddy, Brooks, McLain, Milburn and Huebner. Every one of them is experienced and able, and would be a credit anywhere, either as a corps or even an army commander.[44]

In an immediately following telegram I am making mindful recommendations.

Eisenhower to Marshall   *11 April*   *Ref: FWD-18946*

The following are for recommendations for promotion to grades of general and lieutenant general.

If any part of a telegram is published it should be paraphrased.

For immediate promotion to four star rank:

Lieutenant General George S. Patton Junior:

This officer has served under me as a corps and army commander in the Mediterranean and as Third Army commander in Western Europe. In Sicily, his drive and initiative contributed markedly to the speed with which the stronghold was reduced. In this Theater he entered action shortly after the break out of our forces from the Normandy beachhead and conducted a magnificent pursuit and exploitation directly across France in the direction of Metz, and including the occupation of the Brittany Peninsula. In later operations, including the battle of the Ardennes, of the Eiffel, of the Saar and of the later thrusts into Germany, his leadership has been characterized by boldness and skillful fighting ability.

---

40 Walker's and Haislip's corps had been in action since August 1944 while Gillem's had only been since November 1944.

41 Milburn's corps had only been in action since January 1945.

42 The someone else being Middleton.

43 In summary, Eisenhower had spoke to his two army group commanders and four army commanders and had to compare their opinions while taking into account combat experience.

44 Van Fleet of III Corps, Eddy of XII Corps, Brooks of VI Corps, McLain of XIX Corps, Milburn of XXI Corps and Huebner of V Corps; all in Theater promotions.

Lieutenant General Courtney H. Hodges:

This officer served as Deputy Commander of the First Army during much of the planning stage for the invasion of Europe, and assumed personal command of the Army immediately following the breakout from the Normandy beachhead. The conduct of his pursuit and exploitation to the north-eastward was a model of boldness and daring. During this pursuit elements of his forces were constantly compelled to fight important battles, each of which, under his direction, was conducted with the greatest degree of tactical skill and resulted in the elimination of great numbers of the enemy. His tactical operations on the Roer River, in the Ardennes battle and later in his thrusts southward to cut the communications of the Germans in the Eifel, were tactical masterpieces. His early establishment of a bridgehead across the Rhine at Remagen and his later furious attacks and advances, were so conducted as to yield the maximum in results and his high order of tactical skill played an important part in minimizing our own losses.

For promotion to lieutenant general I submit the names of the following Corps commanders:

Major-General J. Lawton Collins, commanding VII Corps:

This officer was in command of one of the Corps conducting the assault on the Normandy beaches and since that time his Corps has been practically continuously in battle. He is a master of tactics and is a dynamic leader. He has been faced again and again with difficult tactical situations, but has never once failed to conduct his battles to the entire satisfaction of his Army and Army Group commanders. He is at one and the same time a real leader and a driver.

Major-General Walton H. Walker, commanding XX Corps:

General Walker brought his Corps into action about the time of the breakout in the Normandy beachhead, after he had served a period as deputy Corps commander in the XIX Corps. Since that time he has been continuously in battle and has frequently been commended for his energy, leadership and tactical skill by his Army and Army Group commanders. Both during the pursuit across France and later in the battles of the Saar and the invasion across the Rhine, he has constantly led his corps with an exemplary boldness and success. He is a fighter in every sense of the word, whether in pursuit, or in more difficult situations of attack against fortified positions.

Major-General Wade Haislip, commanding XV Corps:

General Haislip brought his corps into action just as the American forces succeeded in breaking out of the Normandy beachhead, and since that time has been continuously in battle. First taking part in the pursuit to the northeastward across France, his Corps was later transferred to the Seventh Army, in which his corps took a prominent part in the battles of Alsace-Lorraine and against the Saar Basin. He has more recently led his corps across the Rhine, as part of the general attack against the heart of Germany. He is calm and cool in action but a determined and resourceful leader. He possesses a high tactical skill and experience.

In addition to the above the following two offices should be considered for promotion to three star rank at any time that this can be accomplished:

Major General Troy Middleton, commanding VIII Corps:

General Middleton brought his corps into the battle on June 14 and took an important role in the operations leading to the breakout near St Lô. He then led his corps into the Brittany Peninsula and finally reduced the stronghold of Brest. Later, occupying a long defensive line, his corps withstood the initial shock of the German attack in the Ardennes battle, and although widely dispersed, he calmly retained control of his retiring forces and so conducted his operations as to impede and limit the extent of the German advance. In succeeding operations he has taken a prominent part in all the advances of the Third Army. General Middleton is particularly highly qualified as a tactician. He has great experience as a combat soldier both in this war and in 1918. He is noted for sound judgment and a shrewd sense of the capabilities of the troops under his command.

Major-General Alvin C. Gillem Junior, commanding XIII Corps:

General Gillem's Corps has been a part of the Ninth Army since its formation, and he has firmly established a high reputation as a fighting leader. His operations on and across the Roer River where flawlessly executed, as have been his later movements across the Rhine as part of the Ninth Army. He inspires confidence and is shrewd, calm, confident, and highly respected by superiors and subordinates alike.

The Discovery of Nazi Treasure

Marshall to Eisenhower   10 April   *Ref: W-65929*

For your information the following memorandum has been received from the State Department and has the approval of the Treasury Department:

> "It has come to the Department's attention that American Armed Forces have captured in Germany a quantity of gold, foreign currencies and art treasures. Pending final decision as to the ultimate disposition of the foregoing, which will require careful study and probable consultation with our Allies, the State Department hopes that this treasure may be moved to a place of safe keeping in the proposed American Zone of Occupation in Germany for the time being and carefully guarded. The Department feels that this temporary solution will be less likely to cause unfortunate political complications."

Please keep me advised on this subject.

[Handwritten note to Marshall] In answering we should say the treasure is being moved to Frankfurt but that we think that information should be kept <u>very secret</u>! No use telling enemy everything. Initialed DE; Eisenhower.

Eisenhower to Marshall   11 April   *Ref: FWD-18954*

Gold and art treasures uncovered south of Gotha, near Wiekers, Germany, were promptly inspected by Colonel Bernstein, formally U.S. Treasury, with two other offices of my Staff, and arrangements commenced for its removal. Major Pererra, Finance Officer Third Army, who has actually inspected the boxes, estimates the gold bullion amounts to between 225 and 250 tons, and objects of fine arts, some 2,000 boxes. Treasure is being moved to bank vaults in Frankfurt, where it will be inventoried and held under my control and carefully guarded.

Reference your W-65929, 10 April. Party consisting of Colonel Moore, Chief of Germany Currency Section G-5, Colonel Claiborne, Colonel Craig and other offices, all of Currency Section G-5, this headquarters, together with Mr. St. Germain, official of guaranty trust company, who is an expert on identification of gold bullion, proceeded to Frankfurt this morning, to assist Bernstein in the inventory and custodial work. Treasure found in an old salt mine, reported approximately 2,000 feet deep. Further details will follow as received. May I suggest that information concerning the location of this treasure be kept very secret.[45]

Thoughts on Ending SCAEF's Responsibilities

Marshall to Eisenhower   12 April   *Ref: W-66921*

The British, in making their proposal in connection with WX-66731, stated they objected, for both military and political reasons, to using inter-zonal boundaries as references during hostilities. They also propose that your message to the Russians include a proposal that respective armies will stand fast upon cessation of operations until they receive orders from their governments. In reply, the United States Chiefs proposed the message you have received, stating they would comment further on the method of control of United States and British forces after hostilities cease. Request your comments on the problem set forth above.[46]

Eisenhower to Marshall   15 April   *Ref: FWD-19256*

In my view, SCAEF must retain its present responsibility for operations until outstanding mopping up jobs have been completed, as, for example, Norway and the Southern Redoubt.[47] Until these tasks are completed we cannot say that hostilities have 'ceased'. If these jobs prove to be rather serious ones, it is obvious that our combined resources, rather than strictly nationalistic resources should be used for their completion. Moreover, I believe that SCAEF must necessarily remain in control until substantial deployment of the British and Americans into their respective national zones has been completed. To terminate SCAEF responsibility earlier would result in confusion in all areas where combined forces are situated and with no authority present to make readjustments.

Parenthetically, I should like to say that these jobs will be completed with the utmost speed of which we are capable, because ensuing tasks of redeployment and reestablishment of occupational facilities will require so much talent and time that the U.S. elements of SCAEF must be released for these jobs at the earliest possible moment.

During all this period readjustments with the Soviet forces will manifestly be required. As I interpret the latest instructions from the Combined Chiefs of Staff, as contained in their FACS-176, the Combined Chiefs of Staff themselves intend to issue general directives governing this phase of necessary readjustments. I do not understand, however, how this can work except with <u>firm prior</u> understandings with the Soviet Government, because if we should be faced by an arbitrary demand from a Soviet commander to vacate any part of

---

45 On 11 April 1945, 90th Division overran the town of Merkers in Third US Army's sector. Soldiers were given information about treasures in Kaiseroda salt mine and they discovered virtually the entire gold and currency reserves of the German Reichsbank. $238 million of gold reserves and other monetary reserves were moved there after a bombing raid badly damaged the Reichsbank on 3 February. They also discovered art treasures removed from Berlin's museums for safety and documents relating to the Holocaust.

46 Although Germany had been divided in four sectors for post-war occupation, no one knew where the respective armies would be when the Germans surrendered.

47 The Southern Redoubt was an area in the Alps where the Allies expected the Germans to head to make a last stand. Hitler's mountain retreat at Berchtesgaden, south of Salzburg, was expected to be a rallying point for those who wanted to fight on.

Germany allocated to Russia by the three governments, I do not see how I could refuse to do so without the danger of creating grave misunderstandings, if not actual clashes. Military Mission Moscow's cable, MX-23875, of 14th April, is a clear indication of Soviet suspicion on this question of zones of occupation.[48]

The Russians Renew their Attack on Berlin

Military Mission Moscow[49] *to Eisenhower, Marshall and British Chiefs of Staff*

16 April   Ref: MX-23897

At the end of a long meeting with Stalin last night on other matters, Harriman mentioned that the Germans had announced that the Russians where planning an immediate renewal of their attack directed against Berlin. The Marshal stated that they were in fact going to begin an offensive; that he did not know how successful it would be, but the main blow would be in the direction of Dresden, as he had already told Eisenhower.[50]

Difficult Days in Holland

Marshal to Eisenhower   19 April   Ref: W-70055

The Prime Minister and Eden are asking what the American view is on a proposition made by Seyss-Inquart.[51] According to the Prime Minister's information, Seyss-Inquart will not surrender so long as there is an effective Government or military authority in power in Germany, and if Montgomery's forces attempt to advance beyond the Grebbe Line,[52] the dykes will be blown, the country flooded, Holland will be ruined and the population starved. Alternatively, Seyss-Inquart offers, if the Grebbe Line is not forced, to leave the dykes intact, to allow Red Cross supplies to be flown in, and to surrender unconditionally as soon as Germany is finished. The proposition includes food for the German forces in Holland. The Prime Minister points out the need for saving the Dutch nation and proposes to place the Dutch area in a neutralized position, allowing relief to come in for a period of two or three months, or until the complete breakdown of Germany.

The Joint Chiefs of Staff are commenting informally to the State Department, pointing out that Holland is already bypassed and there is no need to press operations against the area. They point out, however, the military objections to trafficking with the enemy, the question about tampering with the "Unconditional Surrender" formula, and the Russian interest and reaction to such a proposition. The Joint Chiefs recommend nothing be done without consultation with the Russians and that you be consulted, through the Combined Chiefs, before any action is taken.

There has been a question in my mind as to how much you intend to press operations against Holland in the near future, in view of the need for a rapid advance by Montgomery

---

48 Eisenhower is urging caution of what happens after the cessation of hostilities because the Soviets are already expressed their suspicions.

49 Commodore Clarence E. Olsen, US Navy and Rear Admiral Ernest R. Archer, RN.

50 The offensive to capture central Germany and Berlin started on 16 April with an assault against the German positions along the Oder and Neisse rivers. By 24 April Berlin was surrounded.

51 Arthur Seyss-Inquart (1892–1946), head, or *Reichsstatthalter*, of Austria after the Anschluss in March 1938, when it became a province of the Reich known as the Ostmark. He was administrative chief after the invasion of southern Poland in September 1939 and *Reichskommissar* for the Netherlands after the country was occupied in May 1940.

52 The Grebbe Line was a line of defenses running from the Ijsselmeer, the large shallow lake northeast of Amsterdam, southeast along dykes and lakes to Rhenen on the Rhine river.

to the Northwest. Will you let me have your thoughts on the Prime Minister's proposition for guidance, in case this matter is pressed further.[53]

Eisenhower to Marshall   *20 April*   *Ref: FWD-19562*

This will answer both your W-69492 of 18 April and your W-70055. I am certain that the time has come where we must attempt to give some relief to the Dutch for humanitarian reasons, even though it may be at some expense to our own operations against the enemy. However, the proposals made by Seyss-Inquart would actually be of military advantage to us, in that it would allow us to hold the Grebbe Line with minimum forces and observation, plus some reserve, and would leave us relatively free in the North for other operations of more importance from a military standpoint. Certainly the Seyss-Inquart proposals are the only hope for Northwestern Holland as, if we are required to make a full scale effort to reduce this fortress area, it will probably mean the demolition of many of the larger towns and cities.

Consequently, from both the humanitarian and military viewpoints, I concur with the Prime Minister's proposal, subject always to the necessity for securing Russian concurrence, which I understand has been made the subject of a message from the Prime Minister to Eden in San Francisco.

If this concurrence is not obtained, I believe it will be necessary before very long to press operations in the Northwestern areas, with the larger part of the Canadian Army, because of the advanced state of starvation of the population in the largest cities, which will create a pressure that we will be unable to resist. Even now, if we do not send in supplies, and send them very soon, deaths by starvation will amount to truly terrible proportions. Free-dropping by aircraft may be impracticable unless we reach some agreement with the enemy, because of the necessity to fly in extremely low before dropping. Also, if it is to be maintained, I understand that the War Office must make great efforts to get enough specially packed rations ready.

The technical aspects and selection of suitable areas are under study here now, but the only alternative prior to the Seyss-Inquart proposals, seemed to lie in the possibility of sending Red Cross ships to Holland.

Accordingly, I am very hopeful that some agreement can be arrived at, which will allow us to assist the Dutch, while at the same time economizing to the fullest possible extent on our military strength in the Northwestern areas. If possible such agreement should include the cessation of offensive operations by enemy naval forces from Dutch bases, but this point should not be pressed if it would prejudice the main object, which is the speedy relief of the Dutch.

In either case, I believe that a special effort should be made to arrange for the sending of Red Cross ships to Holland. The possibility that a proportion of the supplies would fall into German hands does not seem to be sufficient reason for withholding this assistance.[54]

---

53 This cable shows one of the huge dilemmas faced by the Allies. Should they ignore the starving Dutch population and push on to complete the war as quickly as possible, resulting a huge loss of life and the devastation of northwest Holland? Alternatively, should they do a deal with the Nazis, undermining the desired surrender terms and risk upsetting the Soviets?

54 Supply ships from Sweden were the first to deliver flour. Operations MANNA (RAF, 29 April–7 May) and CHOWHOUND (USAF, 1–8 May) were 5500 sorties to deliver 11,000 tons by air drop; Operation FAUST followed. On 2 May, 200 Allied trucks began delivering food through German lines.

De Guingand[55] *to Smith*   25 April   *No Reference*

Reference our telephone conversation:

Following sent by Prince Bernard night 23/24 April:

> "To C.B.S. from Prince Bernard. Understand flooding is taking place contrary to proposed agreement. Suppose, therefore, you point out that Allied Forces have not advanced over the Grebbe Line and, therefore, flooding is unjustified in view of negotiations. Press strongly that no further action be taken until result of present discussions is clarified. In view of this please reply what German intentions are."[56]

Following paraphrase a message from C.B.S. in Holland received evening of 23 April:

> "Offer of free route to Rotterdam for relief of civil population is proof of good faith of Germans in present negotiations. Allied failure to reply to proposals causes appalling difficulties, as Germans cannot avoid taking measures necessary for defense against superior forces, such as inundations. Thus Germans have been forced to inundate Wieringemeer Z-17, to guard against parachute troops."

Negotiations to Surrender German Troops in Denmark

Eisenhower to Marshall   20 April   *Ref: FWD-19550, SCAF-290*

1. We have been informed by Special Force Headquarters that the Freedom Council in Denmark[57] has been approached by General Lindemann, German Commander-in-Chief, Denmark,[58] with an offer that the Wehrmacht in Denmark will lay down its arms, but not including the SS and Police.[59] The Freedom Council asked for guidance.

2. We accordingly had a message passed to the Freedom Council, directing it to find out further details of Lindemann's proposal, without disclosing that contact has been made with London, and without making any commitments whatsoever, and to report results to Special Force Headquarters. We have had no report to date.

3. Believe that possibility exists that information of our action in paragraph 2 may be passed to Soviet authorities by representative of Freedom Council in Moscow.

4. Recommend that we be empowered to inform Soviet High Command, through military channels, of Lindemann's offer and the action we have taken. Request you inform Soviet High Command accordingly.[60]

---

55 Major-General Sir Francis de Guingand, KBE, CB, DSO (1900–1979), nicknamed 'Freddie', Montgomery's Chief of Staff at 21st Army Group.

56 On 17 April German command ordered the Wieringermeer dike to be blown up to flood the area on the northwest side of the Zuiderzee. The population was warned to evacuate the area and a combination of high water and storms destroyed most of the infrastructure.

57 The Danish Freedom Council was established in 1943 to lead the liberation struggle.

58 Generaloberst Georg Lindemann, German Commander-in-Chief, Denmark (1884–1963).

59 The SS and the Police were controlled by Himmler, and Lindemann did not have control over them.

60 Eisenhower was determined to keep the Soviets informed of any local surrender negotiations, so as not to undermine the overall negotiations. SHAEF's FWD-19693 was a paraphrased version of this cable sent from to the Military Mission Moscow on 22 April.

Hodges Rather than Bradley to go to the Pacific

Eisenhower to Marshall   *26 April*   *Ref: FWD-19985*

I believe I can do better, with respect to Hodges and his First Army Headquarters, than suggested in your W-72734. Hodges is delighted with the prospect and a small planning group could leave here immediately on any day you may set. If desired, Hodges can accompany this advance group. The remainder of his headquarters could follow very quickly. His Army special troops could come along as now scheduled, because their movement will be determined by availability of shipping.[61]

While MacArthur's failure to form an Army Group command is of course his own business,[62] I personally recommend urgently against Bradley going to the Pacific as an Army commander for two reasons:

Bradley has been the principal battle line commander of the Allied effort in the European war. In general we have placed upon him, the ultimate in operational responsibility and the command of the greatest number of troops. The Twelfth Army Group today numbers over 1,200,000 men. To give him an army assignment in the Pacific would make it appear to all soldiers in this Theater, and to the public, that this was a rather minor league or easy affair, whereas we have been fighting the most highly prepared and skilful army that existed, until they got up against well-equipped, experienced and battle-wise American and British divisions. Such an assignment would have the further effect of diminishing Bradley's stature in the post-war army and public opinion, and it is my conviction that we should prevent any such possibility at all costs. His brains, selflessness, and outstanding ability as a battle line commander are unexcelled anywhere in the world today. His tactical skill in the handling of large forces is remarkable. I think it very important that the War Department do everything possible to preserve his reputation, so that his influence in the post war army and reorganization may be unimpaired.

In a very definite sense, troubles in this Theater are going to be multiplied by the arrival of V-E Day. Bradley's services in handling all the troops forward of the Rhine will be needed and there will be a swarm of heavy tasks in which his experience, prestige and leadership will be most useful. Moreover, in the remote eventuality that anything should happen to me, Bradley is the logical person to succeed to my position. He has the respect and admiration of everybody, including our Allies, and these things are very necessary to anyone called upon to handle the intricate problems of occupation, redeployment and coordination with other forces. I do not believe we can afford to contemplate his early departure.[63]

In Europe there are other men, who have been thoroughly tested as high combat commanders, including Simpson, Patch, Patton, Gerow, Collins, Truscott and others. Anyone of these can successfully lead an army in combat in the toughest kind of conditions.

After dictating the above, I called Bradley in person to determine his own feelings in the matter. His only answer was: "I will serve anywhere in any position that General Marshall assigns me." Nevertheless, I distinctly got the impression that he feels that to go to the Pacific as an Army commander would be belittling, in the American mind, the magnitude

---

61 Hodges never went to the Pacific; the war in Japan came to an end in August 1945, following the dropping of an atomic bomb on Hiroshima on 6 August and Nagasaki on 9 August. Emperor Hirohito announced Japan's surrender on 15 August.

62 The nature of the war in the Pacific, with less than thirty Army and Marine divisions fighting their way from island to island, did not favor an Army Group. Instead Sixth, Eighth and Tenth Armies, comprising 1.4 million troops, reported directly to MacArthur.

63 Bradley eventually returned to the US to serve as administrator of veterans' affairs (1945–47), Chief of Staff of the Army (1948–49) and then first chairman of the Joint Chiefs of Staff.

of American accomplishments here and the services of more than 3 million U.S. soldiers. However, he did not, repeat not, express any opinion as to his personal desires.

Marshall to Eisenhower   *27 April*   *Ref: W-73649*
My intention was not to move Bradley to the Pacific unless he desired to go. In view of your message he will no longer be considered for such an assignment. My purpose was an endeavor to meet Bradley's personal request to me on the OMAHA Beach, in the first twenty minutes after I landed in Normandy.[64] When MacArthur stated he did not wish to have any Army Groups, I put the proposal to you of giving Bradley an Army, if he cared for that. The matter will be dropped.

Himmler Plans to Surrender to the Allies

Marshall to Eisenhower   *26 April*   *Ref: W-73250*
Winant furnished you British report of Bernadotte's conference with Himmler. State Department received similar report from Ambassador Johnson in Stockholm, which is identical except for phrasing.[65]

Marshall to Eisenhower   *26 April*   *Ref: W-73283*
The President has received the following from Marshal Stalin, in answer to the President's message of last night, repeated to you through Winant as W-72816. See also our W-73250. Stalin replied as follows:

"I have received your message April 26. Thank you for your information of the intention of Himmler to capitulate on the Western Front. I consider your proposed reply to Himmler, along the lines of unconditional surrender on all fronts, including the Soviet front, absolutely correct. I ask you to act in the spirit of your proposal, and we Russians pledge to continue our attacks against the Germans. For your information, I wish you to know that I have given a similar reply to Premier Churchill, who communicated with me on the same question."
End of Stalin's message.

The President has dispatched to Mr. Johnson[66] at Stockholm the following:

"Replying to your NIACT April 25th, 3:00am, inform Himmler's agent that the only acceptable terms of surrender by Germany are unconditional surrender on all fronts to the Soviet Government, Great Britain and the United States. If the above stated terms of surrender are accepted, the German forces should surrender on all fronts at once to the local commanders in the field. In all theaters where resistance continues, the attack of the Allies upon them will be vigorously prosecuted until complete victory is attained."

---

64 Marshall had visited the Normandy beachhead a week after D-Day.
65 By early 1945, Himmler believed that Germany could not win the war and decided to seek peace with Britain and the US to try and preserve the Nazi regime. By this time he also believed that Hitler's decision to stay in Berlin made it impossible for the Führer to lead Germany. Himmler contacted Count Folke Bernadotte of Sweden at Lübeck as the provisional leader of Germany and told him that Hitler was likely to be dead within two days and that he wished to surrender Germany to the West, hoping the Allies and the Wehrmacht would fight side by side against the Soviets. At Bernadotte's request, Himmler put his offer in writing.
66 American minister in Stockholm, Herschel V. Johnson (1894–1966).

Eisenhower to Marshall   *27 April*   *Ref: FWD-20032*

I hope it is fitting for me to register my extreme satisfaction with the message sent to Mr. Johnson at Stockholm. Two nights ago when the Prime Minister called me up, upon his first receipt of the message from Sweden, I advised him strongly to take the attitude expressed in your message. He agreed completely that the offer looked like a last desperate attempt to create a schism between ourselves and the Russians. In every move we make these days, we are trying to be meticulously careful in this regard.[67]

The Importance of Reaching the Baltic Coast

Eisenhower to Montgomery   *27 April*   *Ref: FWD-20042*

Dear Monty: All our plans have agreed on the tremendous importance of anchoring our flank on Lübeck as quickly as possible. I know that you fully appreciate the importance of this matter in the mind of the Prime Minister. I note in this morning's briefing that the frontier on the front around Stettin is, as we anticipated, growing fluid.[68] This re-emphasizes the need for rapidity. While I realize that you are straining every nerve to move as quickly as you can, I want you to let me know instantly if any slowness on the part of the U.S. Corps assigned to your command might hold up your plans for a day, or even an hour.[69] I am informed here that additional logistical support promised your Army Group is fully forthcoming. This Headquarters will do anything at all that is possible to help you ensure the speed and the success of the operation. As ever, [Signed] Ike.

Montgomery to Eisenhower   *27 April*   *Ref: M-576*

Dear Ike: I have always realized the great importance of getting quickly up to the Elbe and crossing it without delay, and it was for that purpose that I issued my M-563 dated 28th March. That plan could not be implemented quickly, as you took the Ninth Army away from me on 3rd April and left me very weak in the north. The whole tempo of operations in the north slowed down after that and I did the best I could with what I had left. We have had some very heavy fighting against fanatical resistance.[70] It is not easy to recover lost time. You can rely on me and my troops to do everything that is possible to get Lübeck as quickly as we can. Yours ever. Monty.[71]

The Capture of German Nuclear Secrets

Eisenhower to Marshall   *27 April*   *Ref: FWD-19991*

The special ALSOS, repeat ALSOS, Mission, headed by Boris Pash,[72] working with the Tare Force of Sixth Army Group, have hit the jackpot in the Hechingen area,[73] and have secured personnel, information and material exceeding their wildest expectations. Full details will be

---

67 On 28 April, the BBC broadcast information about Himmler's negotiations and Hitler flew into a rage upon hearing the news. Hitler often called Himmler 'der treue Heinrich' ('the loyal Heinrich') and afterwards told his supporters in the Berlin bunker that it was the worst act of treachery he had ever known.
68 Szczecin, now in Poland, where Soviet forces had broken through and were moving quickly west.
69 XVIII US Airborne Corps.
70 Particularly in Bremen and Hamburg.
71 21st Army Group reached Lübeck on 29 April, only hours before Soviet troops.
72 Operation ALSOS was part of the Manhattan Project, to investigate the German nuclear energy project. Personnel looked to capture German nuclear resources and personnel to further American research, to prevent their capture by the Soviets and to discover how advanced the Germans were. Lieutenant-Colonel Boris Pash was the military commander and Samuel Goudsmit was the scientific leader. Personnel were taken to England to be interviewed and it was discovered that the German project was understaffed and underfunded.
73 Halfway between Strasbourg and Ulm.

reported later through the usual secret channels, but we now unquestionably have everything and none of this information was leaked out.

The Liberation of Czechoslovakia

Marshall to Eisenhower   *28 April*   *Ref: W-74256*

The British Chiefs of Staff state that in the opinion of His Majesty's Government there would be "remarkable political advantages derived from the liberation of Prague and as much as possible of Czechoslovakia by U.S.–U.K. forces". They therefore propose dispatch of a message to you, which recognizes that an operation into Czechoslovakia is unsound on military grounds, if it detracts from the might of your efforts against Austria and Denmark outlined in SCAF 280. British propose, however, in light of political advantages to be derived, that you be directed to take advantage of any improvement in your logistical situation, or any weakening of enemy resistance, to advance into Czechoslovakia, provided such an action does not harm or delay the final German defeat.

Request your comments on the above. Personally and aside from all logistics, tactical or strategical implications, I would be loath to hazard American lives for purely political purposes. Czechoslovakia will have to be cleared of German troops and we may have to cooperate with Russians in doing so.[74]

Eisenhower to Marshall   *1 May*   *FWD-20225*

Current operations towards Lübeck and Kiel in the north and towards Linz and the Austrian Redoubt in the south are straining our resources and I am convinced that they must have priority. When the means are available, I consider that we should continue to attack the Germans wherever they may be holding out, and I have had in mind the possibility of operations into Western Czechoslovakia, in Denmark and in Norway. The last two of these operations, if necessary, must be done by the Western Allies, whereas the Red Army is in a perfect position to clean out Czechoslovakia.

The Soviet General Staff contemplate operations into the Vltava valley,[75] which would result in the liberation of Prague. It seems that they could certainly reach this objective before we could. However, my intention as soon as my current operations will permit, is to move at once to destroy any other remaining organized German forces. If a move by us into Czechoslovakia is then indicated as desirable, and if conditions there are as our present estimate indicates, our logical move would be on Pilsen and Karlsbad and possibly Budweis initially and to effect firm junction with the Russian forces.[76] I shall <u>not</u> attempt any move I deem militarily unwise merely to gain a political prize, unless I receive specific orders from the Combined Chiefs of Staff.[77]

---

74 Here the British Chiefs of Staff are placing an extra objective on the table, recognizing that it could only be taken if the Allied situation improved remarkably. Again there were three problems for staging an advance into Czechoslovakia for post-war political gain. Firstly, insufficient Allied troops; secondly, the possibility of high casualties; thirdly, a high chance of clashing with Soviet troops.

75 The Vltava valley runs from south to north through what is now the Czech Republic, passing through Prague before meeting the Elbe.

76 Three towns in western Czechoslovakia; now western Czech Republic.

77 Again Eisenhower is focused on military objectives, not political objectives, and would only consider advancing into Czechoslovakia if German troops made a last stand there.

17

MAY 1945

Surrender of the Northern Army Group

Eisenhower to Marshall   2 May   *Ref: FWD-20402*

With respect to assignment of 82nd Division instead of 13th to Ridgway's Corps[1]. All assignments to that corps were made in the interests of speed and economy in fuel and transportation. As a result of the speed, Ridgway advanced practically without opposition and is already on his assigned objectives at Wismar and Schwerin.[2] A message has just been received by 21 Army Group Commander from the German Army Group Commander at Lübeck, by the name of Blumentripp, offering to surrender at 11:00 hours tomorrow.[3] Since this is a local military surrender, no effort has been made to contact Russians. Formal report is being made to Combined Chiefs of Staff. Request this be held very secret until further notification because something might happen in this meantime to mess things up.

The Surrender of Norway

Marshall to Eisenhower   5 May   *Ref: W-77610*

On the morning of 4 May, Kleist[4] saw a member of United States Embassy in Stockholm and stated he was certain Germans in Norway would agree to some arrangement for internment in a specified area in Norway, providing they were assured protection of their lives until the Allied authorities took over. Kleist stated he would be willing to contact Terboven on the matter.[5]

In the very early morning of 5 May, the Swedish Foreign Minister met British and United States Ministers, and were advised that Schellenberg[6] was arriving in Stockholm at 10:00am on 5 May with full powers to arrange for surrender to the Swedes of German troops in Norway.[7] The Swedish Minister thought this would mean interment in Sweden until forces could be taken over by the Allies, and the Swedish Government asked for an

---

1 13th Airborne Division to XVIII Airborne Corps.

2 In Mecklenburg-Western Pomerania, north of Berlin.

3 Günther Blumentritt (1892–1967) commanded Army Group Blumentritt from 8 April 1945, a collection of units along the Weser river between Hameln (Hamelin) and the Baltic Sea. The Group tried to keep the Baltic sea ports open as long as possible so that German refugees could escape from the Russians. After the death of Hitler he ordered his men to end resistance and acted as the first emissary to Montgomery for the surrender in northwest Germany.

4 Bruno Peter Kleist, Himmler's representative in the Baltic States.

5 Josef A.H. Terboven (1898–1945), *Reichskommissar* for occupied Norway, planned to turn the country into a Nazi stronghold until Admiral Dönitz, Hitler's successor, commanded him to follow orders. Terboven was dismissed on 7 May; he committed suicide the following day.

6 SS-Brigadeführer Walther F. Schellenberg (1910–1952), Head of Foreign Intelligence following the abolition of the Abwehr in 1944, had already persuaded Himmler to try to negotiate with the Allies.

7 On 5 May Eisenhower forwarded a message to General Franz Böhme, Commander-in-Chief of German forces in Norway, informing him how to open surrender proceedings.

expression of views of the American and British Governments. As to the Russians, the Swedes wish to inform them if they are to be told.

The British and United States Ministers are of the opinion that representatives from SHAEF should arrive at Stockholm at once, to advise them on the matters under consideration. Swedish Government has no objection to SHAEF representatives coming in uniform and with armed escort planes, providing adequate notice is given to allow instructions to be passed to Swedish anti-aircraft.

War Department suggested to State Department that Stockholm deal with you directly in any matters connected with the military surrender in Norway. As to the matter raised by the Swedish Foreign Minister, United States Chiefs have before them a recommendation that the State Department be advised there is no military objection to the Germans surrendering to the Swedes; that it appears necessary to inform the Russians of what is going on, (Swedes have requested they have the first opportunity to do this) and that the Combined Chiefs of Staff are being asked to dispatch a message to Eisenhower instructing him to make arrangements directly with British and United States authorities in Stockholm on these matters.

Marshall to Eisenhower   5 *May*   *Ref: W-77739*
Johnson now reports from Stockholm the following: Schellenberg arrived this morning with full powers from Dönitz to negotiate with the Swedes regarding Germans in Norway. Schellenberg considers he is empowered to contact SHAEF representatives for the same purpose. The Swedes now suggest that SHAEF immediately dispatch mission to Stockholm and are prepared to go along with any SHEAF proposition for temporary internment for Germans in Sweden. This ends gist of Johnson's message.

United States Chiefs of Staff believe that Russians should be informed but that Swedes should be given the opportunity to do it, since they have so requested. State Department has informed Johnson, United States is agreeable to Swedes informing Russians and has instructed him to repeat all messages hereafter to you.[8]

Anxious Times before the Surrender of Germany
Eisenhower to Marshall   8 *May*   *Ref: FWB-20911*
A group of my representatives, headed by my Deputy Supreme Commander, have just departed from Berlin to sign, in company with Marshal Zhukov,[9] the formal instrument of military surrender.[10] The meeting, completely concurred in by the Russians, finally relieves my mind of the anxiety that I have had due to the danger of misunderstandings and trouble at the last meeting. This anxiety has been intensified by very skillful German propaganda that was inspired by the German desire to surrender to us instead of the Russians. All the evidence shows that the Germans in the East are being paid back in the

---

8 On 7 May the German High Command ordered Böhme to adhere to the capitulation plans. Following a radio broadcast to his troops, the 40,000-strong underground resistance, known as the Milorg, mobilized and occupied key buildings while a new administration was set up overnight. The Allied military mission arrived in Oslo on 8 May to deliver surrender terms, calling for the internment of Nazi officials, members of the SS and around 400,000 German troops. Norwegian and Allied troops were then sent to Norway to take control.
9 Marshal Georgy K. Zhukov (1896–1974), commander of 1st Belorussian Front.
10 The German Instrument of Surrender was the legal instrument ending the Second World War in Europe. The first one was signed by representatives of OKW and SHAEF on 7 May in SHAEF's headquarters in Rheims, with French and Soviet representatives signing as witnesses. Since the ceremony had not been agreed with the Soviet High Command, this second ceremony was held in Berlin on 8 May. The head of OKW and representatives of British, American and Soviet High Command attended.

same coin that they used in their Russian campaigns in 1941 and 1942 and they are now completely terrified, collectively and individually, of Russian vengeance.

If it is true, as alleged, that the head of the A.P. Bureau[11] here broke the pledge of secrecy, under which he was permitted to witness negotiations, and in addition used commercial lines out a Paris merely to get a scoop for his company, then he was guilty of something that might have had the most unfortunate repercussions, involving additional loss of American lives. To be perfectly frank, the four days just passed have taken more out of me and my staff than the past eleven months of this campaign. However, as noted above, I am at last reasonably certain that in so far as hostilities are concerned, the Russians and ourselves are in complete understanding and the meeting today should be marked by cordiality.[12]

While I personally was very anxious to go to Berlin, I felt that inasmuch as the Russians had a designated one of their army group commanders to sign for them, I should, in the interests of Allied prestige, pursue a similar policy and refrain from going in person. The group I sent is very representative of all services involved, even including General de Lattre as representative of the French.[13]

Personal Thanks for General Marshall

Eisenhower to Marshall   *8 May*   *Ref: FWD-20926*

With the attainment of what at least appears to be the final and complete surrender of the enemy to ourselves and to the Russians, I feel a compulsion to attempt to tell you some things personally what have been very real with me during this war, but which I have left unsaid for obvious reasons.

Since the day I first went to England, indeed since I first reported to you in the War Department, the strongest weapon that I have always had in my hand was a confident feeling that you trusted my judgment, believed in the objectivity of my approach to any problem and were ready to sustain to the full limit of your resources and your tremendous morale support, anything that we found it necessary to undertake to accomplish the defeat of the enemy. This has had a tremendous effect on my staffs and principle subordinate commanders. Their conviction that you had basic faith in this headquarters and would invariably resist interference from any outside sources, has done far more to strengthen my personal position throughout the war than is realized, even by those people who were affected by this circumstance. Your unparalleled place in the respect and affections of all military and political leaders with whom I have been associated, as well as with the mass of American fighting men, is so high and so assured that I deeply regret you could not have visited here after this Army had retained its full growth and before the breakup necessarily begins. Our Army and our people have never been so deeply indebted to any other soldier.

While I personally may attempt in this way to let you know something of the depth of my gratitude, appreciation and admiration, I will always hope that you may yourself gain a sense of the extent to which these sentiments are shared by hundreds of thousands of Americans and their Allies in this Theater.

After preparing this cable your personal telegram of commendation was brought to me. It so overwhelms me that I now consider the only thing I can say is feeble anti-climax.

---

11 Associated Press Bureau.
12 Eisenhower's concerns over bringing the war to a swift and safe conclusion had been many. While German propaganda had tried to drive a wedge between the Allies and the Soviets, he was always worried that there could be friendly fire incidents, which have could have escalated.
13 Air Chief Marshal Arthur William Tedder, Eisenhower's deputy, represented Eisenhower and Britain while General Carl Spaatz, commander of the US Strategic Air Forces, represented the US.

Nevertheless, because of the sincerity of my feelings, I am dispatching it as I originally intended. I truly thank you for your message.[14]

Montgomery Takes a Break

Montgomery to Eisenhower   *8 May*   *Ref: M-1135*

If it is OK by you, I plan to go to England on Monday 14th May for a short rest.

Eisenhower to Montgomery   *8 May*   *Ref: FWD-20970*

Dear Monty. Delighted you can take a short rest in England. I hope you don't hear the word 'war' while you're gone. Best of luck. [signed] Ike.

Saving German Aircraft from Destruction

Churchill to Eisenhower   *9 May*   *Ref: 2967*

I have heard with some concern that the Germans are destroying all their aircraft in situ. I hope that this policy will not be adopted in regard to weapons and other forms of equipment. We may have great need of these someday and even now they might be of use, both in France and especially in Italy. I think we want to keep everything worth keeping. The heavy cannon I preserved from the last war fired constantly from the heights of Dover in this war.[15]

There is great joy here.

An Unstable Situation in Montgomery's Area

Montgomery to Eisenhower   *10 May*   *Ref: M-1142*

XVIII Corps' area contains 350,000 PW[16] at present. I have about one million PW elsewhere which are being sorted out. I motored today for twenty miles into the Russian area and it is a dead area with not one single German civilian about. XVIII Corps area contains about half a million civilians who have fled from the Russians. There are some awkward problems ahead and I consider that it is essential to keep a very firm front facing east on the general line Wismar–Dömitz.[17] 52nd Division and 6th Airborne Division are both to leave me.[18] I cannot possibly release the U.S. divisions or corps headquarters yet. Hope you will agree.

Note by General Eisenhower: "G-3, we must agree for present but Montgomery must be told that I expect one British Division to be on flank facing east." Above note passed to G-3.

How to Take Over Zones of Occupation

Marshall to Eisenhower   *10 May*   *Ref: WX-80015*

General cessation of hostilities in Germany and Austria will soon bring up question as to when and how U.S., British, French, and Soviet forces should take over their respective zones of occupation. At present, Combined Chiefs of Staff instructions require that you refer any major adjustment of forces to the Combined Chiefs of Staff.

In his message to the President and Stalin, the Prime Minister mentioned that our next task upon cessation of hostilities is the establishment of Allied Control Commissions in Berlin and Vienna and re-disposition of our forces into their respective occupational

---

14 A fitting tribute to General Marshall from his subordinate, acknowledging the unshakeable support that SHAEF headquarters had been given by the US Army's Chief of Staff, even during the worst situations.

15 Churchill was the British Minister of Munitions under Prime Minister David Lloyd George when the Armistice was signed on 11 November 1918.

16 Prisoners of War.

17 On the Baltic coast, east of Lübeck, 100 miles directly south to the river Elbe.

18 To occupy Denmark and northwest Holland.

zones. The Prime Minister went on to state that the Allied Control Commissions have to be entrusted with the task of making detailed arrangements for withdrawal of the forces to their agreed zones of occupation.[19]

Perhaps with forces committed in Holland and Denmark, the British will not immediately have sufficient forces to assume control of their complete zone in Germany. Inter-related is the question of the termination of combined command, which you have indicated should not occur until major readjustments are completed.

Will you give me your views to assist in formulating our thoughts on this problem, which seems bound to arise.

Eisenhower to Marshall and McNarney 15 May   *Ref: FWD-21571*
The disposition of forces into National Zones is subject.

We have assumed that paragraph 3b) of FACS-191, only applies to action involving any major withdrawal from the areas now occupied by an Allied Expeditionary Force, and does not apply to moves facilitating the final occupation by United States and British of their respective zones.[20]

Re-disposition of United States and British forces into their national zones will commence as soon as possible.[21] Instructions are being issued, stressing the necessity for the utmost speed, in order that redeployment requirements may be met. Prompt submission to this Headquarters of plans agreed by 12th and 21st Army Groups, has been directed. It is not yet possible, however, to state an estimated date when re-disposition of United States and British forces will have been effected.[22]

It is planned that prior to the United States / British withdrawal from the Russian zone, British forces should take over the area north of the present United States / British inter-zone boundary extended, thus facilitating the final redistribution of forces. It is also planned that the French Army will be left in its present operational area, and no major French adjustments effected, pending firm information regarding the French occupation zone.[23] Further, in the absence of instructions from the Combined Chiefs of Staff, we do not contemplate holding any conversations with the Russians regarding United States / British withdrawal from the Russian zone.

These, and other circumstances arising, point to the desirability of the early institution of the Allied Control Party for Germany.[24] Pending the setting up of this body, I am continuing to take all necessary steps through the medium of the cumbersome machinery of coordination now available to me.

---

19 Germany had been split into four zones of military occupation. The Russians in the east, the British in the northwest, the US in the south and the French in the southwest. US troops had advanced to the river Elbe, deep in the Russian Zone, by 8 May 1945 and would have to withdraw.

20 Allied troops would initially withdraw from the Soviet Zone, covering Magdeberg, Anhalt, Halle-Merseburg, Leipzig, Thüringen and parts of Saxony, an area held by 12th Army Group, measured 180 miles from north to south and up to 100 miles deep. 12th Army Group also had to withdraw from western Czechoslovakia while 6th Army Group had to withdraw from northern Austria.

21 Britain would hold the area north of Münster and Hanover, with shared responsibility for Bremen port on the North Sea coast. The US would hold central and southern Germany.

22 Allied forces did not withdraw until early July.

23 A strip ranging from 10–80 miles wide along the Franco-German border between Bonn and the Swiss border.

24 The Allied Control Council or Allied Control Authority was the military occupation governing body of the Allied Occupation Zones in Germany. It dealt with war criminals, disbanded Germany military and government departments, handled denazification, and handed over control to the German people. Disagreements with the Soviets started in September 1946, increasing when Britain and the US merged their zones, ready to form an independent West Germany. Cooperation with the Soviets ended in March 1948.

Should Eisenhower go to Moscow?

Eisenhower to Marshall   *12 May*   *Ref: FWD-21249*

If Combined Chiefs of Staff should consider that a courtesy call by me on the Commander-in-Chief of the Red Armies might have any desirable later effect, I am willing to attempt to arrange a short visit to Moscow. Any such visit would have to be a very short one, preferably going one day and returning the next. If approved by Combined Chiefs of Staff I would merely ask the Mission in Moscow to inquire whether Marshal Stalin, in his capacity as Commander in Chief of the Red Armies, would particularly welcome a courtesy call by the Supreme Allied commander on this front. The only good it might do, as so far as I can see, would be the possible speeding up of the organization of the Allied Control Commission. From what I have learned of the bomb damage in German cities, I suspect that the location of the commission will have to be Leipzig.[25]

I should make it clear that I have no, repeat no, particular personal desire to make such a trip and this suggestion is presented merely to determine whether the Combined Chiefs of Staff would see any advantage in doing so. Unless the Russian reply should be definitely cordial, I am certain I should not, repeat not, go. If trip were made, I would include either Air Chief Marshal Tedder or other high ranking British officer in party.

Tito Causes Problems in Yugoslavia[26]

Marshall to Eisenhower   *16 May*   *Ref: W-83021*

I have just talked to the President, who consulted me regarding the increasingly acute situation with Tito and the Yugoslavs. I saw Alexander's message to you, requesting that you take over control of certain Austrian provinces that are in his bailiwick.[27]

The President is naturally most anxious to avoid the tragedy of an open fight; at the same time he feels that the actions of the Yugoslav Government, and of Tito, have become so aggressive and contemptuous of the Allied authority and responsibility in the matter, that there is a limit to how far we can go in tolerating further adverse development of the situation. He asked me my views, I have previously urged him against committing himself to action which might, in my opinion, provoke fighting and which was being urged on him.[28] I told him that we might play another card by strongly reinforcing Alexander with armored forces and that, for example, if three or four or even five armored divisions moved into the region and if Patton's name could be connected with them, it might solve the problem without an open rupture. He was particularly enthusiastic over the psychological effect of Patton's name, and was in accord with my suggestion that I communicate with you on the basis that if you could make such a force available, he might informally discuss the matter with Alexander and if you and he were agreement, it could then be confirmed by the Chiefs of Staff.

There would be command complications because Alexander has the V British Corps in control of the situation operating in the Eighth British Army area, with our 91st Division

25 The Control Council eventually constituted itself in the Schöneberg area of Berlin on 30 August 1945.
26 Josip Broz Tito (1892–1980). On 12 September 1944, King Peter II called on all Yugoslavs to come together under Tito's leadership and on 28 September he signed an agreement with the USSR, allowing Soviet troops to fight alongside partisans and drive the Germans lines out of Yugoslavia. On 7 March 1945, Tito assembled a provisional government of the Democratic Federal Yugoslavia in Belgrade. All external forces were ordered off Yugoslav territory when the war ended.
27 US troops taking over a British area of authority.
28 Tito had announced claims to Trieste and Gorizia and the area east of the Isonzo river, which were Italian. The Yugoslav 4th Army and the Slovenian IX Corps seized Trieste on 1 May 1945 but the 7000-strong German garrison refused to surrender until New Zealand troops under Lieutenant-General Sir Bernard C. Freyberg entered the city the following day. Yugoslav forces began occupying the area east of Isonzo with Soviet backing, leading to a potential clash between Allied and Soviet troops.

as part of the Corps and the Eighth Army under Clark. However, these are details, the main issue being the desire of the President to make this sort of an effort, in the hope of reconverting the Yugoslavs to a more reasonable and tractable course. We do not know here to what extent you could free armored divisions for this work, and how long it would take them to move, speed of action being very necessary.[29]

Eisenhower to Marshall   *17 May*   *Ref: FWD-21699*

The depressing possibilities described in your W-83021 were outlined to me yesterday by the Prime Minister.[30] My Operations Division is making an immediate study with Patton along the following lines: Patton to be reinforced in armor, up to total of five divisions if possible, which will be concentrated well southward in the area where he could strike swiftly and where Tito would inescapably know of its presence. If operations should be precipitated by Tito, the force should constitute an army under Patton's command. I think we would necessarily retain administrative and maintenance responsibility in this Theater, but the force would be under operational orders of Alexander, who could delegate this to Clark if he so desired. As quickly as we can determine our possibilities, we will communicate both with Alexander and with you. The following are merely personal views and probably have already occurred to you. The aggressive attitude assumed by Tito would indicate that he feels certain of strong backing. However, I simply cannot believe, in view of the tremendous efforts made by Russia during the past four years that she would welcome any major trial of strength further to the West than the line she now occupies. If, however, she is deliberately using Tito to create a situation in which she might later intervene with her own forces, the concentration of a sizeable portion of our own formations in the Southern mountains would not, repeat not, favor our general readiness in Germany.[31]

My own belief, for what it is worth, is that Tito is being urged to act aggressively, possibly only to see how far we will go in upholding principle. But we must consider the possibility that if we should get more awkwardly placed, even than at present, all along this tremendous front, the Yugoslav attitude might grow successfully more bold and aggressive, and Russia might come into the open with even more impossible demands elsewhere. I suppose an attempt is being made to determine Russia's attitude, by requesting them to make to Tito an announcement similar to the British–American statement.[32]

A final point to consider is that of the press. To secure desired deterrent effect on Tito, we would probably have to make some announcement about Patton and troop movements. Even if we did not do so, there would quickly develop many questions as to our reasons for making these moves.

---

29 V Corps was not strong enough to face Tito's forces on its own so Marshall wanted to move Patton's Third Army, reinforced by several armored divisions, into the area to face them and hopefully make them back down.

30 Although the Allies had no objections to studying Tito's claims to the area, they did object to his plans for a military occupation. President Harry S. Truman said: 'Tito had already violated the Yalta agreement by setting up a totalitarian regime and was now trying to extend it to Venezia Giulia by force. If Tito persisted in this, we would meet him with overwhelming force, and the time had come for a decision.'

31 The Cold War was still in the future. The Allied and Soviet armies had worked together to beat Nazi Germany and it was difficult for Eisenhower to comprehend how Moscow could be working against him covertly so soon. Trieste was perceived wrongly as Stalin's exertion of pressure and influence, using Tito as the instigator, against the Allies. In fact the desire to control the city was down to local nationalism and territorial objectives.

32 Stalin would be aware that the US was still engaged in a war against Japan while both the US and Great Britain would be looking to scale down the number of troops deployed in Germany. Now would be a good time to take advantage. Churchill ordered planning for Operation UNTHINKABLE, a plan to attack the Soviet Union with US, British, Polish and German troops. The British Chiefs of Staff deemed it to be hazardous!

Eisenhower to Marshall   16 May   *Ref: FWD-21800*

As you know, we have been planning for many weeks toward of maximum speed in redeployment. The requirements of this objective are so intricate and involved that all other considerations have had to take secondary places in our plans. Movement of troops, rebuilding of lines of communication, location of depots, and utilization and transfers of personnel are all proceeding upon the assumption that operational considerations could be ignored in Europe, following the unconditional surrender of Germany. Some time ago we stopped the shipment of ammunition to this theater and have turned back some ships and reloaded others to meet needs in the Pacific.[33]

The outlook on Alexander's front, especially if there is any possibility of concrete Russian support of Tito, creates doubt as to advisability of emphasizing redeployment to the practical exclusion of all other considerations. Only today we started the movement toward the rear of the first two divisions scheduled for redeployment. One of them came from the area in which we are now trying to make the show of strength. This illustrates the direct conflict in purpose with which we will be confronted until the Tito question is disposed of.[34]

Alexander has been almost desperate in the tone of his request to me to take on the task of caring for, and feeding, several 100,000 additional prisoners in the mountainous area, but our maintenance situation there is as bad as is his, except, of course that we do not have the threat of Tito's forces on our flank. A staff officer from Alexander is visiting us today and in the meantime, I am informing him of our possibilities in concentration along his northern flank. As I pointed out yesterday, if we could be assured that the trouble in that region could be completely localized, even if it should tragically burst into open operations, we would still be able to pursue safely our present plans, although some modifications would be necessary. But if there is[35] any possibility of trouble along this entire front, we are getting into an increasingly awkward position, both through rapid redeployment of land and air forces and through the contemplative shift of a portion of our strength to the southward.

The delay in the establishment of the Allied Control Commission, and agreement as to the French zone, both add to the complexities of our problems, as do the monumental tasks of controlling and feeding millions of prisoners and displaced persons.

For the moment at least I shall continue to push redeployment. So far as other matters are concerned, I will attempt to meet them hour by hour, as they arise, in the hope that eventually some good sense may evolve out of this hazy situation.

Marshall to McNarney[36]   17 May   *Ref: WX-83709*

Yesterday, 16th May, I informed Eisenhower of the President's anxiety to avoid the tragedy over open hostilities with Tito, while at the same time feeling that the Yugoslavs have become so aggressive that there is a limit to how far we can go in accepting their actions.

The President accepted my suggestion that Eisenhower be asked, informally by me, his opinion of the proposal to reinforce Alexander with several armored divisions under Patton and that we couple this force with Patton's name to undertake a show of force, which might solve the problem. The President agreed that if Eisenhower was in accord with

---

33 All SHAEF's efforts had been devoted to preparing for withdrawal into zones of occupation. At the same time ammunition stocks had been run down so they could be moved to the Pacific.
34 Eisenhower's is concerned that the Allies are drawing down forces in Europe too quickly in the face of what he believes to be a Soviet show of strength.
35 'believed in the highest quarters to be any threat'; crossed out.
36 General Joseph T. McNarney, commanding general of the US Army Forces, Mediterranean Theater.

the suggestion, then he, Eisenhower, might informally discuss the matter with Alexander preliminary to taking the matter up with the Chiefs of Staff, if the two agreed that the course of action was a good one.

Eisenhower now informs me he is pressing forward urgent studies and, that as quickly as the possibilities can be determined, he will communicate with Alexander. He has in mind the immediate concentration under Patton of up to five armored divisions well to the southward in the area where Tito would certainly know of his presence. We had in mind its deployment as a part of Alexander's forces and in actual contact with Yugoslavs.

The foregoing is for your information and in order that you may apprise Alexander that Eisenhower may be discussing the above cause of action with him shortly.

McNarney to Marshall and Eisenhower 18 May   *Ref: FX-77552*
Greatly appreciated was URAD WX-83709. We agree action such as proposed, might well solve the problem. We had hoped for something along this line when we requested assistance from Eisenhower in the occupation of the British zone in Austria. General Eberle,[37] G-3, is now at SHAEF to discuss the matter. Field Marshal Alexander has asked me to express his appreciation for your action in this matter.

Marshall to Eisenhower and McNarney 19 May   *Ref: WX-84922*
Concerning your plans in SCAF 397, your difficulties particularly as to logistics are appreciated. However, it appears to us here that your concentration must be immediately adjacent to the disputed areas, else its effect upon very doubtful or too long delayed.

What follows is a draft of a proposed message to the Prime Minister I am making to the President through Admiral Leahy:

"I agree that we cannot leave matters in the present state. It seems our immediate action should be to reject Tito's answer as unsatisfactory and urge him to reconsider his decision. At the same time, I suggest we have Field Marshal Alexander, with assistance from General Eisenhower, immediately reinforce his front line troops to such an extent that our preponderance of force in the disputed areas, and the firmness of our intentions, will be clearly apparent to the Yugoslavs.

General Eisenhower has already communicated with Field Marshal Alexander concerning preparations for some such action. I suggest that we now direct General Eisenhower and Field Marshal Alexander to proceed with the implementation of a show of force, both air and ground, and that the presentation in Belgrade of our objection to Tito's stand be timed, if practicable, so that our commanders' troop movements will already be evident to Tito.

I agree the time has not yet arrived withdraw our Ambassadors.[38] There should be no question about our commanders taking essential precautions to prevent their forces from being placed in an untenable military position. However, I think we should make it very clear to our leaders that this should be done with maximum precautions to ensure that the overt act, if any, comes from Tito's forces.

It may be that a heavy show of force will bring Tito to his senses. I question, however, that if hostilities should break out, it could be considered as frontier incidents."

In keeping with the foregoing, I, therefore, propose that you and I issue the following instructions to Alexander and Eisenhower:

---

37 Major-General George L. Eberle (1894–1978).
38 Sentence changed to 'I must not have any avoidable interference with the redeployment of American forces to the Pacific' in WX-85442 from Marshall to Eisenhower and McNarney on 21 May.

"In connection with the problems of occupying Venezia Giulia and portions of Austria, Marshal Tito's reply to our proposals is unsatisfactory and he is being urged to reconsider his decision. Meanwhile, Field Marshal Alexander is directed, with maximum practicable assistance from General Eisenhower, immediately to reinforce his troops in the disputed areas, so that our preponderance of force in those areas, and the firmness of our intentions, will be clearly apparent to the Yugoslavs. Special precautionary measures will be taken so that an overt act if any, will be by Tito's forces and will not be based on some local display by a few turbulent individuals."

Eisenhower to Marshall   *22 May*   *Ref: FWD-22008*
Following a visit to this headquarters of Alexander's staff officers, and Alexander's telegram FX-78668, I have already ordered preliminary measures to be taken to ensure the most rapid possible move of my forces, when ordered by Combined Chiefs of Staff, to relieve Allied Force formations in the two areas selected by Alexander. These are Linz–Spittal and Tamsweg–Judenburg.[39] Alexander will then be in a position to concentrate his forces in the Austrian–Yugoslav frontier area. To carry out its probable missions, it appears our force will be composed largely of infantry divisions, with such armor as can be effectively employed.

This telegram and SCAF-403 answer paragraph 1 of your WX-84922.

Promoting Corps Commanders

Eisenhower to Marshall   *21 May*   *Ref: FWD-22096*
I am delighted that you have some prospect of promoting a few more of our corps commanders. Every army commander here is perfectly certain that each has, in his own command, the best of the lot. To give you an idea of the quality of our corps commanders, of the twelve major generals now commanding corps, all but three are battlefield promotions. One of them started out as a regimental commander.[40] Nevertheless, so far as I can possibly differentiate, the priorities given below are based upon the excellence of performance, with some preference for long service in the battle line.

Major-General Troy Middleton would be number one if he were remaining in the service.[41] However, he has already applied for immediate return to civil life, for his own convenience. This has been approved here and I believe also in the War Department.

Excluding Middleton, my number one man is Major-General Matthew B. Ridgeway.[42] He has never undertaken a job that he has not performed in a soldierly and even brilliant way. He has commanded airborne operations and a corps in a normal battle line. Everyone with whom he has served speaks of him in the highest terms. Definitely a fighting leader.

My number two choice is Major General Alvin C. Gillem Jr.[43] He started as a corps commander and his length of service is not equal to some of the others. Nevertheless, every report I have had on him, and my own impressions from the few visits I have been able to make, are of the highest. He is sound tactically, a real leader, he has fine judgment and the respect of all.

39 Lienz and Spittal an der Drau in Carinthia, southern Austria; Tamsweg and Judenburg in Salzburg, central Austria. Along what is now the Slovenian border.
40 General James van Fleet, commanding 8th Infantry Regiment on D-Day and commanding III Corps since March 1945.
41 Commanding General VIII Corps, March 1944–August 1945.
42 Commanding General XVIII Airborne Corps, August 1944–September 1945.
43 Commanding General XIII Corps, December 1943–July 1945.

The next three are so nearly equal that in their cases it is particularly difficult to distinguish among them. However, after long thought and consultation with Bradley, in whose Army Group all are serving, I give them priority as follows:

Number three is Major General James A. Van Fleet, commanding III Corps.[44] On D-Day he led a regiment against Utah Beach. Within three days thereafter his corps commander [J. Lawton Collins] recommended Van Fleet for immediate promotion to divisional commander. He succeeded McLain in command of the 90th Division, and these two officers, between them, raised the 90th Division from an unsatisfactory unit to one of the very finest reputation in this whole army. He is extraordinary courageous, a driver, and a leader. I have heard Patton and others describe him as "the greatest fighting soldier this war has produced".

Number four is Major-General Raymond S. McLain.[45] This officer is from the National Guard and started the war as a division artillery commander. His personal leadership and courage and his remarkable drive have brought him successively into divisional and corps command. Every report I have had on the services is of the highest type. He is so close to Van Fleet in brilliancy of his record that if you find it possible to make only three corps commanders, and wanted to give the National Guard this recommendation, I would agree to his selection above Van Fleet.

Number five is Major General Stafford LeRoy Irwin,[46] commanding the XII Corps. His experience as a corps commander does not cover a long period, having taken over when Eddy was physically disabled. He started the war as divisional artillery commander in Tunisia and brought the 5th Division into action in Normandy very shortly after D-Day. His fighting record has been so good that on a number of occasions his name was urged upon me for consideration for advancement to corps commander. He was held back to some extent because of an exterior appearance of slowness, which appearance is extremely false. He is a tough fighter and his division and corps have performed beautifully under him.

In naming the above as my five first choices, I know you will not consider this as any slightest reflection on the others who should be listed in roughly as follows: Huebner, Brooks, Gaffey, Milburn, Harmon, Anderson. I want to say again that even the last name man on this list is a top-flight corps commander...[47]

Arranging a Meeting of the Four Allied Commanders in Chief

Murphy to Smith   *31 May*   *Ref: S-89971*

On May 20, Winant,[48] pursuant to instructions from the Department of State, contacted Mr. Eden in order to carry through smoothly, the abandonment of procedure proposed by the United Kingdom Government on May 24, and in order to secure full United Kingdom support for United States proposal on procedure.

On May 29, Winant introduced following draft recommendation, which comprises the United States proposal into European Advisory Commission:[49]

44 Commanding General III Corps, March 1945–1946.
45 Commanding General XIX Corps, November 1944–1945.
46 Commanding General XII Corps, 21 April–September 1945.
47 Further discussion over staff officer promotions.
48 John Gilbert Winant OM (1889–1947), US Ambassador to Great Britain and US member on the European Advisory Commission.
49 The EAC had been set up in London in January 1944 to study post-war political problems across Europe. It organized the Allied Control Council, drafted the unconditional surrender terms for Germany and proposed post-war administrations. It worked out the occupation of Germany and Berlin, as well as the occupation of Austria and Vienna.

"The E.A.C. makes the following recommendations to the governments of the United States of America, the United Socialist Soviet Republic, the United Kingdom and the provisional Government of the French Republic:

The four Allied Commanders in Chief will meet in Berlin, and not later than June 1, to sign and issue a declaration on the defeat of Germany and the assumption of supreme authority with respect to Germany;

Upon signature of the declaration, the four Allied representatives will constitute the Control Council, in order to deal with matters affecting Germany as a whole and in order to begin the establishment of control machinery, as provided in the agreement on control machinery in Germany, of November 14, 1944, amended by the agreement regarding amendments to the above mentioned agreement of May 1, 1945."[50]

Although they felt that a date somewhat later than June 1, perhaps June 4, would have to be selected, the United Kingdom and French delegation generally supported this recommendation. Winant made it clear that the United States proposal is designed to expedite as much as possible issuance of the declaration and the beginning of putting into operation control machinery.

Gousev[51] maintained at one stage in the discussion that Article 6 of the September 12 protocol on zones of occupation provides for that protocol coming into force on signature of the surrender instrument, and that paragraph 2 of the report of November 14 on the control machinery agreement implied to him that establishment of control machinery would take place after completion of occupation of assigned zones. Winant pointed out that the gradual establishment of control machinery, and the movement of the Allied forces into their respective zones and into the Joint Greater Berlin Zone, requires close coordination by the Commanders in Chief which could usefully develop from their proposed meeting in Berlin. Winant also made it clear that United States proposal is merely further working out of agreed procedure and constitutes no alteration of agreed procedure.

Determination of date on which the two agreements on Zones of Occupation and control machinery are to come into force is the basic question which troubles Gousev. He feels that the four Governments must agree on a definite date and accordingly instruct their Commanders in Chief. Both Gousev and the French representative raise the question of how the four Commanders could constitute the Control Council on signing declaration, unless the agreement on control machinery has been declared in force by that date.

Winant reiterated that the easiest way to get the Allied agreements into operation is to bring the four Commanders together to sign the declaration and to constitute the Control Council; they could then consider questions arising from implementation of the agreements on control machinery and on zones. Winant believes on the basis of today's discussion that United States proposal would be acceptable to Soviet delegation if paragraph 2 were replaced by the following paragraphs 2 and 3:

2. Upon the signature of a declaration, the agreement on control machinery in Germany, of November 14, 1944, amended by the agreement regarding amendments to the above mentioned agreement, of May 1, 1945, comes into force. At the same time the

---

50 After Adolf Hitler committed suicide on 30 April 1945, Admiral Karl Dönitz (1891–1980) became president of Germany in accordance with Hitler's last political testament. He authorized the signing of the unconditional surrender of all German forces and tried to establish a government under von Krosigk. This government was not recognized by the Allies; British forces arrested Dönitz and the other members on 23 May.
51 The Soviet ambassador in London and delegate on the EAC, Feodor T Gousev.

protocol of agreement on zones of occupation in Germany and the administration of "Greater Berlin", of September 12, 1944, amended by the agreement regarding amendments to the above mentioned protocol, of November 14, 1944, an amended by the declaration of the Crimea conference of February 12, 1945, to provide for a French Zone of Occupation, likewise comes into force.

3. Upon the signature of the declaration, the four Allied representatives will constitute the Control Council in order to begin the practical implementation of the agreements on control machinery in Germany, and on zones of occupation in Germany and the administration of "Greater Berlin", and in order to deal with matters affecting Germany as a whole."

Some such provision for setting a definite date to bring into juridical force the agreements on zones and on control machinery would no doubt meet the Soviet view as expressed today. Considerable time would be required for the execution of the practical question of actually implementing these agreements. Control over the timing would require the unanimous agreement of the four Allied Commanders in Chief.

Winant requested the Department of State's reaction to this addition before discussing it with his E.A.C. colleagues at the next meeting, scheduled May 30.

18

JUNE, JULY AND AUGUST 1945

Fraternising with the Enemy

Eisenhower to Marshall   *2 June*   *Ref: FWD-23142*

Continuing surveys among our troops show that non-fraternization rules are fairly well observed except in the case of small children. Everyone must recognize that the American soldier is not going to be stern and harsh with young children, but on the contrary feels an inner compulsion constantly to make friends with them. Under existing orders all individuals of German blood are included in the non-fraternization policy and the fear of all commanders is that the breaking down of the order with respect to the child will inevitably have its effect upon the whole proposition and upon discipline in general. Ordinarily I would on my exclusive initiative take such steps here as I deem necessary to correct the situation. However, the most important thing at the moment seems to be public opinion in the United States and consequently I am forwarding herewith for your comment an order that I am considering publishing. Will you let me have your ideas as to its possible effect at home?[1]

"Orders on non-fraternization require the avoidance of contact with the German population except on matters of official business and the necessary activities, involving procurement of services and supplies. They also require all responsible officers to accord to Germans detained as suspected war criminals, including high ranking German officers, only those facilities as are absolutely essential for their proper safeguarding and prevention of disease. Pending the bringing, by proper authority, of these men to trial and punishment, all contacts with them will be on the strictly official basis and will be limited to a minimum necessary.

Published orders involving non fraternization and official deportment, with respect to German population, are obviously not expected to be applied to children below the age of possible complicity in any war crime, or conscious the support of the ex-Nazi regime. Those below twelve years of age are deemed to fall within this classification."

Suspicions Rise Due to Delays in Establishing Military Zones

Eisenhower to Joint Chiefs of Staff   *6 June*   *Ref: FWD-23724*

At the meeting of the four commanders at Berlin, 5 June, the only positive action taken

---

1 This was the first step in the delicate process of allowing soldiers to fraternize with German civilians. It is interesting to see that Eisenhower is sure what to do for the best in Europe but is conscious of the press and public reaction in the US.

was to sign a four power declaration, with the correction indicated in OURAD, 5 June.[2]
I proposed, and British and French concurred, to have the Deputies sit immediately to
develop methods and procedures for control machinery. Zhukov made it clear that he
was willing to meet periodically to discuss matters not related to governing Germany as
a whole, but that any steps to set up control machinery must await withdrawal into the
agreed zones. He stated that he would be willing to join in establishing control machinery
as soon as withdrawal starts.

You authorized this question of withdrawal to be resolved by the Control Council in URAD
W-11367, of 3 June. I suggested to Zhukov that it was a question which could be discussed
by the Control Council.[3] Montgomery concurred and stated that the Group Council could
make a recommendation for the decision of the several governments. Zhukov apparently
wanted an answer rather than a discussion.

The Russians treated us cordially. I gave Zhukov, in the name of the President, the
Legion of Merit in the grade of Chief Commander and he reciprocated by awarding me
the Order of Victory. Montgomery was likewise decorated and De Lattre was given a lesser
decoration. Zhukov is to return my visit by a visit to Frankfurt on 10 June.

Nevertheless, it is my opinion that the question of withdrawal must be considered by the
Combined Chiefs of Staff and resolved by the U.S. and U.K. governments before any further
discussion of control machinery with Zhukov will serve any useful purpose.

Also it is of utmost importance that the zone boundaries in Germany proper, and in the
Berlin district, be determined finally.[4] I do not believe this can be accomplished in Group
Council. Nevertheless, they remain as obstacles to prompt establishment of control machinery.

I stated on several occasions to Zhukov that there was much that the Group Council could
accomplish in preliminary organization, prior to withdrawal of Allied forces from the territory included in the Russian zone, pointing out that the two problems were not necessarily
so closely related that they could not be dealt with separately. Obviously there are many
steps in organizing the Group Council which could be undertaken now, however, the fact
remains that there is some justification for Zhukov's position that he is unable to discuss
administrative problems in Germany when he is still not in control, and hence not familiar
with, the problems of the zone for which he will eventually be responsible. As a result of
my discussion with Zhukov I am optimistic that the Russians will join in some form of control machinery when withdrawal is accomplished, and will agree to our forces entering into
Berlin concurrently with our withdrawal from their zone.

However, neither I nor members of my party found any evidence of Russian organization
for the Group Council government. This may have resulted from the apparent unwillingness
of the Russians to have anything considered at this meeting other than the signing of the
four power declaration. It is possible that the Control Council may become only the negotiating agency and in no sense an overall government of Germany.

---

2 The Supreme Commanders of the four occupying powers signed a common 'Declaration Regarding the
Defeat of Germany', known as the 1945 Berlin Declaration, formally abolishing any German governance
over the nation. The German Government had collapsed following the death of Hitler but this meeting
legally formalized Allied military rule.
3 The Allied Group Control Council was the military occupation governing body of the Allied Occupation
Zones in Germany set up late in 1944 and split between the US, the UK and the Soviet Union. France was
added later but it had no duties. The Council would deal with the disbandment of German army and government agencies, restoration of order into German hands, denazification, war criminals and the eradication of
militarism.
4 Berlin lay in the Soviet sector and steps had to be taken to establish a route to the city as well as how to
divide up the ruins between the four powers.

As our plans for governing our part of Germany must give cognizance[5] to this possibility, I suggest that our Government should consider now the possible alternatives to quadripartite control of Germany as a whole. We must know if our zone in Germany is to be administered as an economic unit, rather than as part of the German economy as a whole, if we are to plan soundly. As I see it, if quadripartite government does not treat Germany as a whole, we must either establish tripartite control of Western Germany, to permit its treatment as an economic unit with full realization of all the implications involved, or else be prepared to govern our zone on practically an independent basis. I realize the undesirability of either alternative and hope that the necessity for the adoption of either will not materialize.[6] Nevertheless, sound planning now does indicate that consideration should be given to this problem as many of our actions within our zone must be governed by thereby.

Eisenhower to Marshall   *8 June*   *Ref: FWD-24075*
The following is from Mr. Hopkins[7] to the President:

"Have discussed Russian situation in Germany with Eisenhower and have obtained his impressions of his conference with Zhukov in Berlin. I am convinced that present indeterminate status of date for withdrawal of Allied troops from the area assigned to the Russians is certain to be misunderstood by Russia, as well as at home.

It is manifest that Allied control machinery cannot be started until Allied troops have withdrawn from the territory included in the Russian area of occupation. Any delay in the establishment of control machinery interferes seriously with the development of governmental administrative machinery for Germany, and with the application of Allied policy in Germany. A delay of a week or two in starting the withdrawal would not be disastrous; however, this question should not remain in its present status until the 15 July meeting.[8]

As a concurrent condition to our withdrawal we should specify a simultaneous movement of our troops to Berlin under an agreement between the respective commanders, which would provide us with unrestricted access to our Berlin area from Bremen and Frankfurt by air, rail, and highway on agreed routes.

I am not sure of the British reaction to such a proposal. However, I am sure that every effort will be made there to obtain British agreement to a cable to Stalin, that you are prepared to stop the withdrawal of American troops by 21 June, subject to the respective military commanders working out an agreement with respect to the phasing of such withdrawal, the movement of our troops into Berlin, and the guarantee of routes of communication to our Berlin area. It is anticipated that the United Kingdom will take parallel action.

If you believe that the settlement of the Austrian question should be a prerequisite to withdrawal from the Russian area in Germany, I suggest that your cable advises Stalin accordingly, to include the specific conditions to be settled. However, if this

---

5 Recognition.
6 The Federal Republic of Germany (Bundesrepublik Deutschland) was established from the eleven states in the western zones of occupation in May 1949.
7 Harry L. Hopkins (1890–1946) was one of President Roosevelt's closest advisors and administrator of the Lend Lease program to the UK and the Soviet Union. He had first met Stalin in July 1941 and accompanied the President to the meetings at Cairo, Tehran, Casablanca and Yalta. He wanted to resign after Roosevelt's death but made one final visit to Moscow for President Harry S. Truman.
8 Suspicion between the US and the Soviet Union was starting to creep into the negotiations and delays to the movement of troops into their zones were hampering the administrative progress.

question is to be included as one of the requirements for our withdrawal I strongly urge that you advise Stalin that final authority to settle zone questions in Austria has been delegated to our military commander, to work out with his military commander, and that this question be withdrawn from the European Advisory Commission discussion.

As matters now stand in Germany, Eisenhower is an embarrassing position of not being able to discuss a specific date for withdrawal with the Russians. Moreover, the Russians have not been advised as to any specific requirements which we may have been viewing as a condition to such withdrawal.

I consider the decision as to the date we begin withdrawal into our own zone in Germany, to at least specify in detail to the Russians the conditions which they must fulfill before such date can be established of major import to our future relations with Russia. Delays now may make withdrawal at a later date appear to have resulted from Russian pressure. I urge the prompt action be taken to dispose of this issue.

I am prepared to remain in Paris if this question will be decided in the next several days. I would appreciate very much being advised of your wishes, to know if I may have the opportunity to discuss it further with Eisenhower prior to reporting to you on my return."

Plans for the Nordhausen V-Rocket Site[9]

Eisenhower to Marshall   *7 June*   *Ref: FWD-23939*

Though neither 21 nor 12 Army Group has been consulted relative to your proposal to include the Nordhausen Caverns area within the 21 Army Group area, this action is believed to be practicable. The four United States divisions in the bulge north and north-west of Nordhausen are scheduled as of 8 June to move south, relinquishing all territory north of the approved boundary line between the Russian and British zones of occupation. 21 Army Group are accordingly prepared to move forces into the area, which approaches to within ten miles of Nordhausen.[10]

G-2 has certain information on the Nordhausen Caverns which may have a bearing on your decision. At the present time Anglo–American intelligence agencies are preparing for firing trials of V-Weapons assembled from parts taken at Nordhausen, and are removing weapons and certain critical equipment, though their task is slowed by a lack of transportation. The United States and British intelligence agencies have nowhere near completed the project at Nordhausen and feel that the installations should not be destroyed until all possible requirements of the War Department, War Office and other interested agencies have been met.

Eventual destruction of Nordhausen for the express purpose of preventing disclosure of V-Weapon information is considered to be futile, since similar information is believed to have been uncovered by the capture of the research center at Peenemünde and of practice firing sites in Eastern Europe.

Furthermore, it is the belief of the G-2 that the British request for destruction of the Nordhausen Caverns is premature, since they too have numerous unfulfilled intelligence target requirements in the caverns.

---

9 Nordhausen KZ tunnels and the Mittlewerk/DORA concentration camp were on the southern edge of the Harz Mountains in northern Thuringia. Production of the V-2 moved to the site after a bombing raid called Operation HYDRA on Peenemünde. 5200 V-2 rockets were built using slave labor between September 1944 and February 1945.

10 The area was going to pass into Soviet control and the Soviets would eventually destroy the entrances to the huge tunnel system where the rockets were made.

Pending your reply, no further action will be taken in this matter. 21 Army Group will not be consulted nor will any change in boundary be discussed in order to determine its practicability.

Eisenhower to Marshall 9 *June* *Ref: FWD-24240*
Officers from SHAEF and 12 Army Group are going to 21 Army Group immediately to press for British takeover of area of Nordhausen Caverns. Any information on strength of British desire for destruction, obtained from 21 Army Group, will be forwarded at once. Meanwhile intelligence work is being pushed.

Eisenhower to Marshall 18 *June* *Ref: FWD-25383*
Further to our FWD-24240 and FWD-23939, conversations with 21 Army Group have developed the following information relative to the 21 Army Group viewpoint on the destruction of the Nordhausen Cavern equipment and the proposed change in boundary between 12 Army Group and 21 Army Groups.

21 Army Group agree with the G-2 information and opinion expressed in our FWD-23939, and state they have no, repeat no, interest in the destruction equipment. They express these views as their own and it is considered that such views are not, repeat not, necessarily those of the War Office.

21 Army Group also state they propose that no, repeat no, action be taken relative to shifting the boundary so as to include the caverns within the British area unless the Combined Chiefs of Staff direct such action.

Closing Down SHAEF

Eisenhower to Marshall and McNarney 15 *June* *Ref: FWD-25131*
Comment is made herewith on the questions contained in Eyes Only cable from General Marshall, WX-15563 of 12 June.

On the question of termination on 21 June of my responsibility as Supreme Commander for Military Government, I consider that this is practicable. British troops will not fully complete relieving United States troops now within the British Zone until 26 June but arrangements can be made with 21 Army Group, which will solve this problem satisfactorily.

On the question of the termination of Supreme Command itself, and the dissolution of SHAEF on 21 June, while it is possible to do this, I do not consider it essential to the purposes expressed in the reference of paragraph 1. As inferred in my FWD-24953 or 13 June, it is entirely practicable and feasible to split off the military government, or even segregate combined functions into their respective nationalistic channels, prior to the official date for the dissolution of SHAEF. While I have no objections to the prior announcement of the intention to dissolve, I hope you may be able to agree to the proposal made in my FWD-24953, that the official date be a flexible one dependent upon the date of my return to this Theater. In the meantime, all necessary organizations are being set up and all necessary actions taken to accomplish the dissolution when ordered.[11]

On the subject of command in Austria its seems to me that the question of whether or not there must be an interim period of A.F.H.Q. control of U.S. forces under Clark, must depend

---

11 SHAEF was dissolved on 14 July 1945 and US Forces, European Theater (USFET), took command of US forces, the majority stationed in Germany. USFET was in turn reorganized as EUCOM (US Forces, European Command) on 15 March 1947.

on the dissolution of 15th Army Group as an agency of combined command and it must be for McNarney to say. When the U.S. Zone in Austria, including part of Vienna, is incorporated in E.T.O., Clark and the troops under him should pass to my command for all purposes except military government and political matters, on which he should be responsible and report directly to the U.S. Joint Chiefs of Staff. Thus I would be responsible for logistical support (as I have always planned), for the administration of his troops, and for operations in Austria, and on these matters he would report to me; on military government matters he would report to you. Were I to be appointed U.S. representative for both Germany and Austria, with Clark as my deputy for the latter, he would lack authority and prestige in his dealings with other representatives and I would no doubt find myself in the unfavorable position of delaying action in Control Council meetings in Berlin and Vienna, in the event of conflict of dates for the two Control Council meetings.[12]

Moving Troops into their Zones of Occupation

Eisenhower to Marshall   *19 June*   *Ref: S-91687*

Redistribution of troops into agreed occupational zones in Germany and Austria is subject.

In respect to Germany, warning orders to the United States and British troops are being issued and only await executive orders of Combined Chiefs of Staff to begin movement on 1 July. I foresee difficulties in occupation of Berlin on quadripartite basis unless E.A.C. and governments have agreed on zones prior to move-in. To obviate,[13] suggest it be arranged on governmental level that United States and British forces will move into zones heretofore agreed on tripartite basis with the understanding that the French Group Council will be accommodated temporarily in ours and/or British zone as agreed by the three commanders concerned and with the further understanding that French troops will be brought in when the final agreement is reached by the four governments. If recommendations contained in SCAF 453 of 13 June 1945 are approved, it is our intention to arrange with the French to occupy the zone in Germany we have offered and which we understand has now been agreed by them in E.A.C.[14]

In respect to Austria, warning orders are being issued to 12th Army Group to be prepared to begin advance on 1 July to complete occupation of the United States zone coincident with Russian withdrawal from it. Lacking governmental agreement on zones, 12th Army Group is being directed to plan on the zone which we are informed is most likely to be agreed, on assumption that executive orders of Combined Chiefs of Staff for movement will prescribe the zone. It is recommended that the French stand fast in the zone in Austria now occupied pending governmental agreement, should this not have been reached prior to 1 July. It is assumed that problems of movement of British troops into British zone and movement of United States, British and French troops into Vienna is one for settlement between Combined Chiefs of Staff and Allied Force Headquarters.[15]

---

12 General Mark Clark was appointed Commanding General US Occupation Forces in Austria and US High Commissioner for Austria on 5 July 1945, posts he held until 16 May 1947.

13 Prevent.

14 Initially France did not have an occupation zone due to its minor role in the Alliance and concerns over its historical animosity with Germany. Charles de Gaulle argued until the British and the Americans ceded parts of their zones. The French zone had two areas along the Rhine and the French military government headquarters was in Baden-Baden. France would also have a zone of occupation in Berlin.

15 The Allied zones of occupation in Austria were as follows: France occupied Tyrol and Vorarlberg in the west; the US occupied Oberösterrich and Salzburg in the central north; Britain occupied Steiermark and Kärnten in the central south; Russia occupied Niederösterrich and Burgenland in the east; Vienna was also split between the four.

In respect of Czechoslovakia we plan to stand fast in line with recommendation contained in our S-91011 of 16 June 1945 unless instructed to the contrary, making only such changes in the agreed coordinating line as are necessary to tie in on the flanks with the zones in Germany and Austria.

Preparing for the Tripartite Meeting in Berlin

Eisenhower to Marshall and Military Mission   14 June   *Ref: FWD-25028*

Your W-15519 of 12 June received. Recommend you approve my sending following message to be:

> "In order to make necessary advance arrangements for the meeting in Berlin on 15 July, I wish to send to Berlin on 17 June a group, headed by Major General Floyd Parks,[16] of ten officers together with the necessary enlisted personnel to hold a preliminary conference with representatives from Marshal Zhukov. The purpose of the conference is to arrange for accommodation, signals, security and movement into Berlin of necessary U.S. troops and required supplies, simultaneously with our withdrawal from Russian Zone. General Parks' party will arrive in three transport aeroplanes at Templehof Airdrome, via Stendal.[17] E.T.A. 12:00 hours. Air escort will not be provided and none is considered necessary. Please ascertain if Marshal Zhukov will designate representatives to discuss this matter. Will appreciate his arranging transport at airport."

Eisenhower to Moscow Mission   19 June   *Ref: S-91539*

In view of brief time remaining before the meeting of President Truman with Marshal Stalin, it is imperative that the reconnaissance group proceeds to Berlin at once to survey the facilities available locally for his accommodation, and that of his party, so as to assemble and move necessary men and supplementary equipment to Berlin and complete essential preparations by mid July. This cannot be postponed until the return of Marshal Zhukov to Berlin on 28 June. Arrangements for a meeting of this magnitude cannot be made in two weeks time.

It is absolutely necessary that General Parks and a reconnaissance party of approximately 50 officers, 175 enlisted men and fifty vehicles, with necessary transport aircraft, go to Berlin tomorrow and be shown the United States sector by the Soviet commander acting in Marshal Zhukov's absence. Based on Parks reconnaissance, the necessary troops and material to install communications, messes, quarters and other facilities, must be sent to Berlin as and when determined necessary by Parks. Continuing unrestricted running rights on autobahn Dessau–Berlin for vehicles and air way Halle–Berlin for transport aircraft will be required, effective tomorrow.[18] This is a matter of urgency and agreement must be reached at once if the target date for the 'Big Three' meeting is to be met. Conference with Marshal Zhukov or his senior staff officers is not, repeat not, necessary for such administrative details and formal meeting with the Marshal can be deferred until 28th or 29th June as Antonov suggests.[19]

---

16 Major-General Floyd L. Parks (1896–1959), commander of the First Airborne Army from May 1945 and commander of the US Sector and Berlin's Military Governor from July.

17 In accordance with the Yalta agreements, Soviet troops turned over Tempelhof Airfield to the US Army 2nd Armored Division on 2 July 1945. Stendal is 60 miles west of Berlin.

18 Dessau is 60 miles southwest of Berlin. Halle is 25 miles northwest of Leipzig and 100 miles southwest of Berlin.

19 General Antonov, Chief of Staff of the Soviet Army.

Eisenhower to Marshall   19 June   *Ref:* S-91687
In respect of 'Big Three' meeting in Berlin, all efforts to secure approval to send in Party immediately to make preliminary survey to determine requirements for preparing, staffing and securing United States accommodations and facilities have so far met with no success. Latest message from Deane quotes Antonov as saying it appears likely that we will be permitted to send in such a party on 28 or 29 June. You will have seen our S-91539 of 19 June 1945 to Deane on this subject, for the success of which we are not too hopeful. We hesitate to suggest that further pressure should be applied from Washington but we are convinced that unless prompt favorable action by the Soviet High Command is forthcoming, it will be necessary to depend upon the Russians for accommodations, or, alternatively to defer the meeting.

Devers to Marshall   20 June   *Ref:* S-91755
All attempts to secure permission for General Parks and party to proceed to Berlin immediately for reconnaissance and making necessary arrangements for conference have been unsuccessful. Mission Moscow is advising that Antonov will not agree to Parks' entry prior to 28th or 29th June. It is considered highly improbable that adequate arrangement can be completed by date now scheduled for the conference if initiation of work is deferred until 28th or 29th June. Accordingly recommend that steps be taken through governmental channels to secure necessary Russian permission.

Devers to Moscow Mission, Berlin District, Marshall   22 June   *Ref:* S-92255
Five aircraft with crews of two officers and two enlisted men will proceed via Stendal–Berlin, transporting Major General Parks and party of fifteen officers and fourteen enlisted men, arriving Templehof airdrome 16:00 hours Greenwich Mean Time, 22 June. Hereafter desire use direct air route Halle–Berlin. Request motor transport to accommodate General Parks and party meet aircraft at Templehof. Request base camp facilities be established closest proximity to airdrome where radio and air communications will be set up. First serial of vehicles will proceed via Halle–Dassau–Berlin autobahn and rendezvous at junction of autobahn–Ringbahn at 08:00 hours Greenwich Mean Time, 23 June. Request Russian liaison party meet convoy and escort it to bivouac area.

Eisenhower to Military Mission Moscow   23 June   *Ref:* S-92697
Parks returned this afternoon. Crown Prince Palace, Potsdam, lends itself admirably for a neutral meeting place.[20] The residential section of Babelsberg, fronting on Griebnitzsee, has been evacuated of Germans and is being renovated by Soviets for billeting conferees.[21] Three compounds therein have been laid out in which each nation will have absolute rights and responsibility as to security, messes, etc; about 70 residences in the U.S. compound. Parks inspected the one which Colonel-General Kruglov suggests for the President. It is spacious, although old fashioned, and is believed adequate.[22] Compound will house about 500 with some expansion possible by tentage. Space for service units, press camp,

---

20 The New Palace is situated on the western side of the Sanssouci Royal Park in Potsdam.
21 Babelsberg is an eastern suburb of Potsdam adjacent to Griebnitzsee lake.
22 Colonel-General Sergei N. Kruglov (1907–1977), First Deputy People's Commissar of Internal Affairs, NKVD. Kruglov spoke reasonably good English and was awarded the Legion of Merit and made an Honorary Knight of the British Empire for organizing the security of the Yalta Conference and the Potsdam Conference during the Second World War. He was also created an Honorary Knight Commander of the Order of the British Empire during the Potsdam Conference, becoming the only Soviet intelligence officer to receive an honorary knighthood.

and overflow needed elsewhere, and can be found in Zehlendorf, a district in Berlin in U.S. sector of Tripartite division.

Parks cordially received by Colonel-General Kruglov and every facility and request granted within his power.

Following matters beyond his authority need favorable action at once:

- Authority to reconnoiter vicinity of Zehlendorf for additional camp sites and billets.
- Authority to operate supply vehicles over Halle–Berlin Autobahn without special permission in each class. This to be in addition to vehicles now in Babelsberg, for which authority to operate over that route was given by Marshal Zhukov's Chief of Staff today.
- Authority to increase the size of Parks' party now at Babelsberg as deemed advisable by this headquarters without further reference to Soviet authorities. This must be expedited as signal technicians, including Major General Stoner who was sent by the War Department especially for conference installations, should go to Babelsberg for survey not later than 25th June. Stoner considers proposed site favorable for establishing satisfactory signal communications.[23]

Eisenhower to Military Mission Moscow   25 June   *Ref: S-93051*
Parks unable to secure permission locally in Berlin to establish radio telephone and teleprinter terminal and relay points to connect with this headquarters.

Essential that immediate instructions are sent from Moscow to Berlin commander to agree to installation of very high frequency telephone terminal in Berlin area at suitable location and relay point in the vicinity of Luckenwalde (near Belzig). No physical wire telephone circuits exist at present on axis of communications westward of Berlin, into either U.S. or British occupied areas.

Imperative that action be taken to authorize local Soviet authorities to arrange these and similar details. Dealing thru Moscow on such minute points is so time consuming and cumbersome that target date cannot be met unless rectified. Introduction of air staff and airdrome control personnel now held in abeyance, awaiting reply to our S-92697, relative to increasing Parks' party.

Bradley to Parks, Berlin Commander   *unknown day in late June*   *Ref: S-93451*
Yesterday afternoon Deane again discussed with General Antonov's representative your matters respecting use of the Dessau–Berlin Autobahn, installation of a V.H.F. terminal, and freedom of entry into U.S. of Berlin; also the reconnaissance of Zehlendorf and air route Halle–Berlin. Deane anticipates early permission to send in communications personnel, whose estimated strength he informed Antonov would total ninety persons, prior to 1 July.

Securing Naval Bases for Northern Europe

COMNAVEUR[24] *to Rooks*[25]   1 July   *Ref: 011422B*
The following message has been sent to COMINCH;[26] references not held by you, nor needed.

---

23 Major-General Frank E. Stoner (1894–1966), Chief of the US Army Communication Service.
24 COMNAVEUR was Commander, US Naval Forces Europe, Admiral Harold R. Stark.
25 General Lowell R. Rooks, Deputy Chief of Staff, G-3 (Operations), at SHAEF.
26 Commander in Chief, US Fleet.

. Following after investigation and conference with Headquarters USAETO:[27] Oslo is suitable, except for fuel and the fact that Army Air considers weather and air security not as satisfactory as Copenhagen. Copenhagen is suitable except for fuel and security. Security is unsatisfactory due to lack of U.S. Ground Forces. Army states no assurance that British and Danish Governments will permit U.S. troops to enter. Further that if Copenhagen is to be used we must be immediately informed, in order that arrangements can be initiated for entry and establishment of U.S. troops. At both Oslo and Copenhagen fueling the arrangements can be made through ADMTY.[28] Both have an airfield from which C-54's can operate.

Pilots picked up as follows.[29]

For Oslo: Coastal Personal pilot off Lister. Oslo Fjord pilot off Store Faerder Island. Inner fjord pilot off Drobak. Oslo Harbor pilot off Harbor entrance.
For Copenhagen: Norwegian pilot off Lister. Swedish pilot off Paternoster light. Danish pilot off Viken.

Bremen: Bremershaven not considered suitable because of danger from mines.
Hamburg, Kiel, Rotterdam, Amsterdam, Cuxhaven, Bergen and other North Sea ports not considered suitable by Army or Navy.

Extending Fraternisation Rules

Montgomery to Eisenhower   *10 July*   *Ref: M-1195*
My government has now authorized me to relax the present rules regarding non-fraternization in the British Zone, as may seem desirable. I think it is very necessary and a similar policy should be followed in the British and American Zones and that we should act closely together in this matter.

My view is that it is difficult to re-educate a nation if you are never to speak to the people and I consider that by continuing with our present rigid rules, we are merely making our task more difficult.

I would like now to allow our troops to speak to adults as well as to little children. This would constitute a definite bound forward and I would not go any further than that yet. I consider that this bound will meet the case for the moment and I would recommend that in issuing the order about it, it is stated that troops are not allowed to enter German homes or houses. Once we allow that, the ban on fraternization must be lifted completely.

Summarizing the above, I therefore suggest to you that we relax the present rules, so as to allow the troops to speak to and mix with adults, and that we bring this into force on 15 July.

Will you let me know if you agree with paragraph 4.

Eisenhower to Montgomery   *12 July*   *Ref: S-97003*
I have your M-1195 of 10 July and concur in general with the proposal and paragraph 4, although I would propose the use of the phrase "engage in conversation with" rather than "to speak to and mix with".

I suggest that we both issue statements for release at 6:00 PM, 14 July, that orders will be placed in effect the following day relaxing present regulations on non-fraternization.

---

27 US Army, European Theater of Operations.
28 The Admiralty.
29 Instructions to guide vessels into the ports.

If you agree with this simultaneous release of statements, I would issue the following:

"In view of the rapid progress which has been made in carrying out an Allied de-Nazi-fication policies, and in removing prominent Nazis from all positions of responsibility in German life, it is believed desirable and timely to permit the personnel of my command to engage in conversation with adult Germans on the streets and in public places. Orders are being issued accordingly." [30]

Please reply.

Montgomery to Eisenhower   *13 July*   *Ref: M-1199*
I have your S-97003 of 12 July and agree entirely with your wording. I will issue and release a statement at 18:00 hours 14 July, as suggested by you. Thank you very much. Have you had a good trip home. Looking forward to seeing you soon.

Reciprocal Visits for Eisenhower and Zhukov

Eisenhower to Marshall   *31 July*   *Ref: S-14710*
At Berlin yesterday, I found that Marshal Zhukov had some information of my probable future visit to Moscow. The President instructed me that I was to accept such invitation, when and if it comes to me. In this connection, you informed me that upon receipt of such invitation you intended to issue one to Marshal Zhukov to visit the United States. I suspect that he has received some inkling of this intention, possibly from someone connected with the President's staff. He expressed a great desire to see the United States and I merely told him that someday I was sure he would find it possible to visit our country. I tell you this merely because of its possible effect in determining the timing of your invitation. [31]

I found Zhukov most friendly and feel rather hopeful that he will cooperate in making the Berlin organization an effective machine.

Marshall to Eisenhower   *31 July*   *Ref: W-41476*
While you were here, Harriman[32] was instructed to extend an invitation to Zhukov to visit the United States in the name of the President, should Marshal Stalin extend one to you to visit Moscow. As yet there's been no indication from Harriman that this is being done.

Eisenhower to Marshall   *3 August*   *Ref: S-15377*
Today Ambassador Harriman communicated to me an invitation to come to Moscow on August 11th, to be there for a big celebration on the 12th. The ambassador thought I might be expected to stay a day or so extra. In accordance with the expressed desires of the President, I authorized Ambassador Harrison to accept in my name. I shall probably take four or five staff officers.

---

30 In July troops were allowed to speak to German adults in certain circumstances and in September the non-fraternization policy was dropped in Austria and Germany.
31 Eisenhower's visit was planned for the middle of August.
32 William A. Harriman (1891–1986), a Democrat politician who served President Roosevelt as special envoy to Europe and served as the US Ambassador to the Soviet Union and US Ambassador to Britain.

Pierre Laval is brought into Custody

Eisenhower to Marshall and Clark   31 July   *Ref: S-14795*

Pierre Laval,[33] accompanied by wife, arrived by plane on Linz airfield this morning and was taken into custody by 65th Division. Arranged through Clark's headquarters to transfer them today to French custody. Since this is in Clark's territory, he no doubt will report full details. I will keep you informed.

Eisenhower to Marshall and Clark   31 July   *Ref: S-14807*

Additional information reference to Laval. Laval and wife arrived at Linz in a Ju-88 with two German pilots. Through Clark's arrangement with French headquarters, Laval and wife, in custody of General Copeland of the 65th Division, left Linz at 15:30 hours today by car for release to French custody at Innsbruck. Expected time of arrival at Innsbruck, 20:30 hours.[34]

Eisenhower's Visit to Moscow

Eisenhower to Marshall   16 August   *Ref: S-17867*

I have just returned from my Moscow trip, where I was received with every manifestation of courtesy and hospitality. Today I am writing you a letter transmitting the personal message to you from Generalissimo Stalin concerning an incident of last winter.[35]

---

33 Pierre Laval (1883–1945) served twice as head of government of the Vichy regime following the German occupation of France.
34 After his arrest Laval was tried, found guilty of high treason and executed by firing squad in October 1945.
35 By November 1945, American-Russian relations had grown cold, and Zhukov turned down Eisenhower's invitation to visit the US.

19

OCTOBER 1945

Problems with Operation CROWCASS and De-Nazification

Smith to Marshall   8 October   Ref: S-27000

I must bring to your personal attention a situation existing in CROWCASS which, from our point of view, is completely unsatisfactory.[1] Primary mission for which CROWCASS was activated by SHAEF was to furnish wanted and detention reports for war criminals and security suspects. In this it has failed completely. There are no, repeat no, current, complete or accurate wanted and detention lists in existence today, nor do the wanted or detention reports published by CROWCASS even approach completeness, currentness or accuracy.

I very much fear that the increasing pressure in the matter of war criminals, and the attention given by the press to this subject, will cause both of us serious embarrassment unless immediate and drastic steps are taken to increase the efficiency of CROWCASS ...

Would point out that while CROWCASS is a joint responsibility of USFET and BAOR,[2] the only contribution made by BAOR to this agency is the services of the two British officers now attached to CROWCASS, one of whom is the senior and officer in charge. All costs of the organization including installations, rental on buildings and equipment as well as labor are born either directly or indirectly by the United States. The salaries for French civilian employees alone amount to $600,000 per year and the total expense is quite large.

An inspection of CROWCASS has just been completed by a staff officer of this headquarters, and as a result of his reports I request your concurrence by placing Colonel George G. Elms[3] of this Headquarters immediately in charge of CROWCASS with complete authority concerning personnel, equipment and operations, Responsibility to remain as at present jointly to USFET and BAOR until taken under quadric-partite control, and to supplement the staff of CROWCASS with American enlisted men as clerical personnel, as needed to meet the present situation. Since this move would undoubtedly be embarrassing to Lieutenant Colonel Palfrey,[4] now in charge, I strongly recommend that he be replaced by another British officer, lieutenant colonel or major, with the necessary qualifications and with a fresh and vigorous viewpoint.

May I have your reply tomorrow as I must leave for London shortly after noon, and this matter may come up while I am there.

---

1 In the spring of 1945 SHAEF set up the Central Registry of War Criminals and Security Suspects (CROWCASS) to gather information on anyone suspected of committing war crimes or atrocities to help the United Nations War Crimes Commission (UNWCC). Both CROWCASS and UNWCC published lists of prisoners and wanted persons.
2 US Forces European Theater and British Army of the Rhine.
3 Colonel George G. Elms, CROWCASS officer.
4 Lieutenant-Colonel William Palfrey was assisted by 400 French women but their work was hampered by a lack of funding and support. Processing of prisoners was slow and it resulted in many senior Nazis escaping prosecution. Palfrey was eventually forced to resign and was replaced by Lieutenant-Colonel R.F. Luck.

Galloway[5] to Smith   *10 October*   *Ref: A(PS 4) 4884*
Reference your S-27000 of 8 October

Cannot agree contention that CROWCASS has failed to implement directive issued by Supreme Headquarters Allied Expeditionary Force. Complete records of sort required, inevitably require considerable preparation. Colonel Palfrey has carried out this organization under great difficulties.

First intimation the U.S. Forces European Theater considered CROWCASS inefficient was your S-26531 of 4 October.

In view of fact the control of Paris is easier by U.S. Forces European Theater than British Army of the Rhine; agree however to appoint Colonel Elms in command subject following provisos.

1) Appointment of temporary pending quadripartite agreement concerning future control of CROWCASS.
2) No important order to be issued by CROWCASS without conference with British Army of the Rhine.
3) Equal officer representation be maintained between U.S. Forces European Theater and British Army of the Rhine on CROWCASS staff.
4) Colonel Palfrey will be relieved after hand over to Colonel Elms.
   Please confirm you agree.

Galloway to Smith   *29 October*   *Ref: A(PS 4)14503*
Report has been made that Colonel Elms, commanding officer CROWCASS, has been making important changes to CROWCASS staff, by appointing extra U.S. officers, thereby upsetting balance of representation as agreed, without consultation Headquarters, British Army of the Rhine. In view of concession made to your request to appoint American Commanding Officer, I must insist that Colonel Elms be instructed to adhere strictly to the agreement. All this trouble is very regrettable and is not best settled by exchange of telegrams. If agreeable to you, General Graham will visit you for personal talk.[6]

Europe Faces a Catastrophic Epidemic

McCloy[7] to Eisenhower and Clark[8]   *10 October*   *Ref: NX-55599*
Have concluded a visit to Berlin, Frankfurt, Vienna and Budapest and it is about the same welter of problems wherever you go: food, transportation, communication, displaced persons, the oppressions of occupation, particularly the weight of Russian forces and their requisitions scarcities, with no continuing means of restoring the needs, no industry, with all metropolitan areas on a virtual relief basis, everywhere the fear of hunger, disease and Russians. The Army is heavily handicapped by the redeployment and demobilization programs, key men are leaving, or are being called back, just when the social and economic problems of the occupation are becoming most acute.

---

5 Lieutenant-General Sir Alexander Galloway KBE, CB, DSO, MC (1895–1977) was appointed Montgomery's Chief of Staff of 21st Army Group at the end of the war, replacing the exhausted Freddie de Guingand.
6 CROWCASS published a list of 600,000 names in 1947 and it became known as the 'Nazi Hunter's Bible'. It was divided into four volumes; Germans, non Germans and two supplementary lists. Not all were war criminals; some were wanted for interrogation or to act as witnesses.
7 John J. McCloy, Assistant Secretary of War and a key figure in setting US military priorities.
8 General Mark W. Clark, Commanding General US Occupation Forces in Austria and US High Commissioner for Austria since July.

Clay's[9] problems are set forth in his September report, which you should shortly get, and in his last letter to me. Incidentally, it is important to see that he continues to receive our letters while I am away. The German situation requires the best soldier we can find if Eisenhower is to leave, and he should be selected regardless of any considerations but ability, imagination and force. Clay and his staff seemed to be making slow but definite progress.

Clark's Headquarters are impressive. They are hardworking and alert. Gruenther's[10] departure at this juncture will be of great loss, however.

Key[11] at Budapest reports the same, slow, exasperating efforts to make progress with the Russians. His position there is largely bypassed, though he keeps determinedly at it and is on a friendly personal relation with the Russians.

The following are my general conclusions and recommendations:

Our policy to date has been one of cleaning up the immediate debris of active warfare. Our emphasis has been on demobilization, denazification and decentralization. All of Middle Europe needs the restoration of some industry, unless we are to establish permanent soup kitchen feeding. For all practical purposes, there is no industry in Germany or Austria and unless there is, it is a constantly losing game. The time has come to place more emphasis on the reestablishment of telephone and postal services. It is unthinkable that such a large area should continue to be without even rudimentary means of communication, which is now the case. There should be the relaxation of our travel control, so that there can be full access within and among the zones. If the Russians do not come along, we should be certain the French and British conform. We cannot afford to continue the almost medieval isolation of existing life.

There should now be a greater consultation with the native leaders on matters relating to their social, economic and political restoration. Above all we should not hesitate to encourage the reestablishment of more industry and commerce. I repeat, without it there will be collapse and progressive physical and social deterioration of the people in the area, whose influence is such that it will set the level of European living so low that we will also be demoralized by it. Moreover, unless we do, there will be little hope for the reestablishment of anything like political wisdom in the area.

I recommend that our directive be now reexamined, with the idea of moving them into a more constructive form, having the above considerations in mind.

We must have a better centralization of our policy on displaced persons. This is a problem that cuts across all our areas of occupation and influence. By displaced persons, I include the refugee population from Austria and Czechoslovakia, as well as our perennial DP's. There are calling to O.S.S. reports, which seem to reliable, horrible situations developing in Eastern Germany due to the expulsions from Poland. Behind Churchill's black curtain the reports are that we are having repeated some of the horrors that used to appall us in Asia Minor, at the time of the Armenian expulsions. The expulsion of the Austrian Germans is a great relief to Austria and General Clark, but the order terribly complicates Eisenhower's problem and only increases the U.S. taxpayers European feeding costs, for there will not be

---

9 General Lucius D. Clay, Eisenhower's Deputy.
10 General Alfred M. Gruenther, Clark's Chief of Staff.
11 Major-General William Shaffer Key (1889–1959), Head of the US Military Control Commission in Hungary.

enough food to take care of them without direct U.S. or UNRRA aid.[12] Probably it should be done, but it must be worked out in conjunction with the return of the Sudetens and the Polish Germans, and it must be done with the help of the Germans. It can only be done as a real project under the humane conditions prescribed by the Potsdam agreement. It is dangerous to set time limits. If we do not proceed on a thoroughly planned basis, we will soon have on our hands scenes and episodes which would revolt us.

As for the Jewish DP's, I have asked numbers of my party to inspect and report on the camps. (These men are not connected with the Army. They were Dr. Freeman, John Vincent and Colonel Parker U.S.M.C.).[13] None of them had seen the early camps and consequently they were not comparing them with a prior condition of the camps, or impressed by the progress which has taken place in the treatment of the enormous problems of the DP's generally. Their reports add up about as follows:

These accounts vary from good to indifferent, none scandalous or anywhere near so. Definite improvements can remain in several fields, but in many cases only with great energy and direction, due to the heavy difficulty of disciplining the inmates to the constant necessities which go with clean and pleasant camp conditions. There is no problem with the educated Jew but the bulk of the population of the camps are of a peasant, or lower living standard type. Observers uniformly report unexpectedly sound morals, adequately nourished appearance and a low sick rate in spite of cold and lack of fuel, with Trojan efforts to achieve cleanliness.

It is fantastic for anyone to say that their condition is the same as it was under Hitler, except for the extermination policy, and the Jews who seem friendly resent this statement as much as anyone. We must fix a definite policy towards these people. We must determine how far the preference is to go, for the mere movement of them into former German's or Austrian's houses does not solve the problem. Are they to receive permanently higher rations than the non-Nazis about them or preferment in business? It may well provoke a more acute anti-Semitism if an attempt is made to make a permanent any preferment. This is something which Rifkind[14] should consider both as it affects Germany and Austria. Clark will be glad to have him look over and study the Austrian situation.

There is a determined economic infiltration policy now being pushed by the Russians in Hungary. The recent elections in Budapest, which were won by the Small Holders' Party[15] rather than the Communists, may encourage the government to resist this policy more but it is apparently a definite attempt to take over control of Hungarian industry, as distinguished from the broad trade agreements being put forward in Austria. Incidentally the small holders' party celebrated their election success in front of the American Mission's Headquarters.

This movement emphasizes again the supreme importance of the economic element in the whole picture. The political is even less important, for without the former there is nothing on which to build politically. Our economic planning must be at the highest level and it

---

12 United Nations Relief and Rehabilitation Administration was an international relief agency. It was founded in 1943 to 'plan, co-ordinate, administer or arrange for the administration of measures for the relief of victims of war in any area under the control of any of the United Nations through the provision of food, fuel, clothing, shelter and other basic necessities, medical and other essential services.' It became part of the United Nations in 1945 and closed down in 1947 after distributing $4 billion of aid; its activities were taken over by the Marshall Plan.
13 Dr Freeman, John Vincent and Colonel Parker; unknown independent inspectors of the Jewish camps.
14 Simon Hirsch Rifkind (1901–1995) was a prominent US federal judge and trial lawyer. In 1945, Rifkind took a leave of absence from the bench and acted as an adviser on Jewish affairs to US Forces, European Theater (USFET), helping the US Army aid Holocaust survivors.
15 Full title the 'Independent Smallholders, Agrarian Workers and Civic Party'. Its leader, Zoltán Tildy, was appointed Prime Minister. The party was removed by a Communist Party coup in 1947.

must be strengthened. If we are to pull out our troops it becomes even more necessary.

As to how long we should keep our troops in Austria and Hungary, I have not has yet been able to arrive at a firm judgment. The greatest oppression, in spite of the many stories of loot and rape, is the mere presence of large numbers of Russian soldiers in the area. The heavy requisitions alone are sufficient to demoralize the people, apart from the looting which does not count. The greatest boon and first relief project would be to get all the troops out except small garrison forces, but for the present I would keep the divisions we have in Austria until the Russians greatly diminish their forces and I would urge that any credits or UNRRA benefits be held up pending their withdrawal, for it is incongruous to send in American financed food when the country is being reduced to poverty by the requisitions of unnecessarily large forces. Italy and Czechoslovakia present different considerations but I would go slow there as well. Any decision as to Czechoslovakia should be considered in relation to the whole problem.

At present, the presence of our troops is not burdensome, because we mainly feed ourselves and we give the population hope against the Russians fear. There is no doubt that the presence of troops during this period is a substantial aid to our policy in these areas of Middle Europe. They need not be large but they should be more than ceremonial detachments.

There is no doubt that local political opposition to Russian pressures gains encouragement in this control period by our mere presence. The presence of well disciplined, well behaved and well disposed troops affords a continuously favorable impression on both the people and indirectly on the Russians. The dislike of the Russian is creating a political condition unfavorable to him and the local Communist elements, which can only have tangible results as long as we are on the ground or until all troops are removed.

The French eat out of Clark's hands in Austria and of course can only remain here because of our help. My feeling is that the difficulties they are causing in Germany when any efforts to centralize controls arise, ought to be dealt with on a governmental level at which France's entire position in Europe is taken into account. They would then be more apt to conform. I do not know what the appropriate time to face up to the Ruhr–Rhineland problem is, but I suggest that the Army must know soon what steps he should take in the event the Quadripartite Administration breaks down. Though there is no reason to believe that it will be any worse than it is now and it may be a great deal better as we go along, for at least until recently Clay was reporting good progress. In spite of the deep inexperience and distrust of the Russians, there is still much cause for optimism but the fact remains it may break and situations may arise, beginning with this winter, so acute that time and events just will not wait on the continued slow processes of such administration. Therefore we ought to have alternative plans for coping with Western Germany and the keystone of such planning is the Ruhr Rhineland question.[16]

Coal and transportation. Every problem seems to resolve itself in terms of coal and coal also means transportation. The industry of France suffers from a lack of it as Monnet[17] comments, but France is only a part of it. This entire occupation area will never be anything but a relief area until coal can be supplied. To supply it, more transport facilities must be built. A goodly portion of the Ruhr coal must be turned back to fabricate the means to

16 The Morgenthau Plan was proposed during the Second Quebec Conference on 16 September 1944 by US Secretary of the Treasury, Henry Morgenthau, Jr. It suggested removing Germany's ability to wage war by placing centers of mining and industry (Saar, Ruhr and Upper Silesia) under the control of other countries; heavy industry would then be dismantled or destroyed. The deteriorating situation across central Europe illustrated that this would affect the whole of Europe and was likely to lead to thousands of deaths through starvation and disease.

17 French civil servant Jean Monnet proposed the Monnet Plan, giving France control over the Ruhr and Saar, using their resources to rebuild France while limiting Germany's industrial capacity.

produce more of it. Locomotives and railway wagons must be produced in large quantities of Germany to make any real impression on the industrial situation and continuously rigorous steps will have to be taken to induce and transport Silesian coal production. The manner of the urban transportation is of the greatest importance to provide means for people to go to work and food to be distributed. This requires coal. Closely connected with it is the freeing of the river traffic of Europe. The whole Danube Basin is stagnant now because of obstructions, political and physical, and the Rhine is only at the barest beginning of being freed. Coal involves much more than furnishing coal men as I have pointed out in my earlier cable. It is the first tangible thing to achieve, in order to build a floor to support our immediate, as well as long range political and economic objectives.

The next most important thing I should say was a big stockpile of medicines. Every indication is that there is a great danger of an influenza epidemic of major proportions in Europe induced by the cold, the movement and general malnutrition of the people.[18] Sulfadrugs and the other medicinal necessities to check such outbreaks must be on hand in every area, for it does not work, I am told, unless the outbreak can be checked immediately in the area in which the commences. UNRRA must supply medicines everywhere and irrespective of prior belligerency.

Gale,[19] *War Office to Morgan,*[20] *UNRRA*   10 October   *Ref: 419*
I have been trying to get you on the telephone without success. I think it important that in your discussions with Robertson,[21] you should have some background on our negotiations with the armies. It is the established policy of His Majesty's Government, as one of the member states of the UNRRA, that UNRRA should assume responsibility for the Displaced Persons[22] operation and any whittling down of UNRRA's responsibilities may well be unacceptable to this and other governments. If difficulties arise in taking over those responsibilities from the military, it is ultimately a matter between the governments concerned and its commander in the field, and not a subject for UNRRA to give way on unless in matters of detail. Any difficulties we may have for example on the British side are in consequence of great interest to the Foreign Office and, I understand, of personal interest to the Foreign Secretary.

I am doubtful therefore whether it is proper that you or I should meet the Field Marshal[23] to discuss the agreement, unless it appears from your discussions with Robertson that the amendments desired are of a minor nature and do not affect UNRRA's statutory position. I rather feel that when the matter comes to a personal discussion with the Field Marshal, they should be a matter for the Cabinet to handle and not UNRRA. We are not seeking to assume these responsibilities for the administration's own sake, but because the member governments of UNRRA have decided that we shall do so. I do not know when you are meeting Robertson, but I think it important that I should hear from you immediately the results of your discussions.

---

18 Between June 1918 and December 1920 a deadly influenza pandemic (the Spanish Flu) spread across the world. Estimates put the number of dead between 50 and 100 million (3 per cent to 6 per cent of the world's population), making it one of the deadliest natural disasters in history. With the onset of winter there was a danger that another pandemic could spread across Europe.
19 Lieutenant-General Sir Humfrey M. Gale, Representative of Director-General of UNRRA.
20 Lieutenant-General Sir Frederick E. Morgan, Chief of Operations for UNRRA.
21 Sir Brian Hubert Robertson, Baronet of Welbourn, CBE, CB, DSO, MC (1896–1974), Chief of Staff, British Zone in Germany and Deputy British Representative on the Control Council.
22 UNRRA helped many Displaced Persons or DPs (refugees, prisoners or slave laborers) return home.
23 Field Marshal Bernard Montgomery, now Commander-in-Chief, British Forces of Occupation in Germany and Member of the Allied Control Council Germany.

I shall be in London all weekend, perhaps you will let my office know if you wish to communicate during Saturday night or Sunday, as I must then arrange to be in the office.

I hope this background will assist you in maintaining UNRRA's position in your discussions, but at the same time I realize that it is up to us to strengthen our organization by posting new people or transferring certain soldiers, where such as source is indicated as likely to improve our relations with the military.

Eisenhower to Hilldring   *21 October*   *Ref: S-28804*
What can you tell me in confidence, as to the future general attitude of our government towards UNRRA? I have been watching with considerable sympathy, the efforts of General Morgan, now in charge of the European Division, to put his house in order and know some of his difficulties. It would help us in preparing our plans to know whether we can count on the continuance of a supported UNRRA, due to the job we have always contemplated would be done by this organization. Can you also give me any idea as to the source from which competent U.S. personnel can be obtained in the future? At present I am aware that Morgan, who is being obliged to secure competent people to at least enable him to get started, has been forced to turn largely to British sources as British military personnel becomes available through retirement. He is apprehensive that he will have to fill all of these positions thus, as he is unable to tap any supply of highly qualified U.S. personnel. What I am asking for you is your estimate, even if it is only a guess, as to what the future has in store for UNRRA from the U.S. point of view, and anything you can give will be appreciated.

Epilogue

Eisenhower to Smith   *5 December*   *Ref: War 86984*
Thank you very much for your letter. Please do not bother about rugs. Will try to get off a letter to you with my plane, but I must say that in four rather busy war years, the last three days have been by far the worst.

[General Eisenhower was on his way back to Washington DC to take over from General Marshall as Chief of Staff of the US Army.]

INDEX

The index is split into four sections: Codenames and Operations; Military Units; People; Places.